EMOTIONAL
INTELLIGENCE

How To Improve your Social Skills

This Book Includes:

Mental Models, Stoicism, Master Your
Emotions, Overthinking, Covert
Manipulation, Dark Psychology
(EQ Agility 2.0)

David Drive

6 Manuscripts in 1 Book:

BOOK 1) Mental Models: A Collection of Thinking Tools Helping You To Manage Productivity, Thinking In Systems, To Improve Your Day-To-Day Decision-Making, Problem-Solving and Logical Analysis Skills

BOOK 2) Stoicism: The Manual of Ancient Stoic Philosophy as a Way of Modern Life - A Beginner's Guide to Develop Mindset Through Critical Thinking and Self-Discipline, and to Increase Your Wisdom Daily

BOOK 3) Master Your Emotions: A Practical Guide to Overcome Negativity through Emotional Intelligence, Manage Your Feelings with Anger Management Techniques and Declutter Your Deceptive Tricky Mind

BOOK 4) Overthinking: The Fast Cure for Women and Men Who Think Too Much and Want to Stop Procrastinating - Proven Tips to Turn Off Relentless Negative Thoughts in Place of Optimism and Strong Focus

BOOK 5) Covert Manipulation: An Introducing Psychology Guide for Beginners – How to Perform Mind Control to Win Friends, to Analyze & Influence People Learning Persuasion Techniques & Reading Body Language

BOOK 6) Dark Psychology: How to Use the NLP Secret Methods of Manipulation for Social Influence, Emotional Persuasion, Deception and Mind Control - A Guide Based on Hypnosis and Brainwashing Techniques

Table of Content

MENTAL MODELS

A Collection of Thinking Tools Helping You To Manage Productivity, Thinking In Systems, To Improve Your Day-To-Day Decision-Making, Problem-Solving and Logical Analysis Skills

Introduction to Mental Models

The following chapters will discuss what you need to know in order to start using mental models for your own needs. There are a lot of different time management tricks and tips that you can try out, and many of them can work well, but if you want to shorten the time it takes to make decisions, ensure that you will make the best decisions, and overall just make your life a bit easier. This guidebook is going to take some time to discuss what mental models are, how these are going to work for your benefit and the different types of mental models that you can use based on what you would like to solve.

To start this guidebook, we are going to take a look at what mental models are all about. This helps us to see what these models are about and some of the benefits that come with them. We can also look at the power that is behind these mental models, and the ten top mental models that can be used with a lot of the other topics that we will discuss in this guidebook. After we have some of the basics about mental models organized and ready to go, it is time to dive into some of the practical applications for these mental models and how you can use them for a lot of different aspects and personality types as well. You will find that these mental models work well for making decisions, for entrepreneurs and others parts of running a business, for those who are researching and inquisitive, to help you improve your parenting, for critical thinkers and educators, and even for those who are trying to work on their own personal development. With these topics, we are going to explore more about what these mental models are, and see how they can be used in every part of your life.

To finish off this guidebook, we are going to take a look at some of the different case studies about these mental models. These will help us to see the mental models in works, so we are not just working with theory, we can see the exact ay that these mental models can be used! A lot of time and effort can be wasted thinking things through and making decisions, and often the longer we sit on these thoughts, the more confused we get. Mental models help us to cut through the clutter by providing us with some of the plans that we need to really get things on track. When you are ready to learn more about these mental models and how they work, make sure to check out this guidebook to help you get started.

Chapter 1: An Understanding of the Mental Models

One fact of life that we just can't deny is that our brains will be responsible for everything that the body does. This means that anything that affects our brain will then affect all of the other facets of our lives. Yes, the brainpower is going to rely a lot on its software or the mindset that you have, and the hardware, which is going to be the nerves. We know it is really hard to work with a system that is sophisticated, with lots of good hardware, and then have some bad software on it. This just ends up being a bit energy-wasting blend of silicon and metal in the computer. In order to help put these mental models into the proper perspective, it is important for us to take a look at some of the different elements that are at the core of this idea, and how we are able to use them to our advantage. First, we need to take a look at what the model means for our "mental model". A model is simply going to be a microcosmic representation of the real object. This object can be either non-physical or physical, it really doesn't matter. It is going to be like a blueprint, a diagram, a mold, or a map and it is going to depict some of the key features of the real object, without having to bear all of the costs that come with this model being around.

Modeling is something that we are going to see in a lot of technological and scientific endeavors. However, this doesn't mean that we have to leave the models confined to only those two fields. There may be a ton of different options out there that promise to work on getting things done more effectively, and a lot of promises that are going to try and help you to manage your time and more, but some of the best options out there for you to use are going to be these mental models.

You get to choose which one you use, and the more of them that you learn about, the easier it is to grab one out of your toolbox and put it to good work. This opens up a whole new world of what you are able to do, how easy it is to get tasks done, and how you will be able to succeed in any endeavor that you attempt to do. How many of the other options out there are going to be able to provide what these mental models will provide to you as well? This does not mean that you can't use some of the tools that are out there and available to those who want to enhance the mental models. And if you are working on things like time management and want to use charts or diagrams or the Pomodoro timer to help you, then this is perfectly acceptable as well. But you will find that working with these mental models can be effective, even without all of the other equipment along for the ride.

There are a lot of core reasons why you may want to take a look at modeling and see how it can work for a lot of different technological and scientific adventures. Some of the most common reasons for this include:

1.   A model is going to help you to depict a mental concept, and this makes the model concept a lot easier to understand overall compared to the main concept.

2.   The model is going to make it easier and cheaper to present the real object to others.

3.   A model is going to be a lot cheaper to make and use than the real object. This means that the cost of creatively destroying the model if needed will be low.

4.   A model is easier to adapt to the changes in the main concept than the real object.

5.   These models are going to be cost-effective methods to avoid some bigger mistakes. Mistakes, faults, and even misconceptions can be easily detected when we look at the model and appropriate corrections done to it prior to launching the real object.

While it is true that there are some models that we are able to look at in physical form, there are others that do better when we look at them in virtual form. Physical models are going to be for objects that contain some form such as planes, cars, ships, building, territories and the like. Virtual models, on the other hand, is going to be for things that are not physical, such as the thoughts, imagination, senses, and interpretations. Mental models are going to fall within the virtual nature above because the mind is not really a physical object. Some of the virtual models that you may see that relate to this could be things like strategic military models, culture models, organization models, and more.

What is a Mental Model?

With this understanding with us, it is time to take this a bit further and look closer at what a mental model is all about. A mental model is going to be a blueprint of how you can boost up the cognitive engine's capacity to make decisions that are more strategic and intelligent. A mental model is going to be just a one-dimensional view of reality. This means that if we want to make sure that we have a better view of multi-dimensional reality, you would need to work with more than one of these mental models at a time. When we are working on a real-life situation, we are going to not rely on a single model but will rely on a mental multi-model instead. This brings up the question of why these mental models are so important. Just like software is able to help direct some of the functional behavior that we see with a computer, a mental model is going to help to direct some of the functional behavior of your brain, and because of that, it directs the rest of your body as well.

Using the analogy of the computer a bit more, you will be able to more easily see and deduce some of the core reasons that makes it imperative to start using these mental models in your own life. Some of the biggest reasons why these mental

7

models are so prevalent and such a great option for you to use in your life includes:

1. They are efficient: A mental model is going to help the brain learn how to run more efficiently, especially when it comes to dealing with some tasks that may be repetitive and routine. This is going to allow the brain to be more creative and to focus on novel inputs instead.

2. Effectiveness: These mental models are going to help limit the errors that we see, and will make sure there is less wasted effort. This is going to make the brain power more effective in delivering the outcome that you are looking for.

3. Economy: This is a term that is all about the efficient and effective utilization of the resources that we have. the brain is going to need a ton of different resources to help it operate. In fact, you will find that the brain is the most resource-intensive organ in the whole body. Because of this, any increment to the effectiveness and efficiency of the brain means that you are going to use your resources more wisely.

4. Certainty: The mental model is going to help you bring about some level of certainty when it comes to common challenges in your life. Because of this, a mental model is able to coordinate the brain function of several people inside the same team or group. This means that the model is going to bring in a bit of

predictability that you need when it is time to handle challenges and more.

   5.   Productivity: With certainty and economy added to the mix, the productivity that you will see with the brain is going to go higher. In the end, the productivity of not just the individual person, but also the whole team, is going to go up.

The neat thing is that these mental models are going to be able to do a lot of different things for you. They can first step in and enable you to see the world in a more accurate manner, and then you can use this new form of accuracy to predict the future in a much better way than it would have been without them. This model can also help you to form a new mastermind kind of alliance because you will then be able to find some people who can suit your model and then the connections that are built up from this are going to be mutually beneficial. These connections are important because they will sharpen up the mental model that you have, making them more precise. And finally, the mental model is going to help you to generate some breakthrough ideas because they will have a unique angle view of the situation that is at hand. Another thing that we need to take a look at before we move on with these mental models is the origins of them, or how they got started. we are not able to tell with a great deal of certainty where these models begin with because it is believed they started at the beginning of time. while we are going to be able to create some mental models deliberately from our knowledge, it is possible to have some mental models that are created in a more instinctive manner. For example, it is possible to have one of these models etched into the genes. It is going to be these that will help an infant learn how to respond to some of the external stimuli in a certain way that we can predict from the moment they are born. For example, all infants know how to respond to heat and light, how to identify their mother, how to suck, and how to cry, even though they had no chance to learn how to do these things. Over time though, the infant is going to develop some of their own mental models so they learn the best way to communicate and interact with their mother. Because of this, it is believed that these mental models are going to be as old as humankind. We can call some of them primal mental models. But then there are the mental models that we can create for our own needs, the higher or the secondary mental models. These are the ones that we are going to consciously and deliberately generate out of our learning and some of the practice experiences that we have. Even with this in mind, some of these secondary models are going to be etched into our genes after some time if we use them in the proper manner. This is done to help future generations learn how to cope and adapt with some of the changing environment that is out there. For example, epigenetics is going to be an interesting field of study that can help us to look this over a bit more as well. In this guidebook, while we recognize that all of the mental models can be important we are going to spend our time focusing mostly on the higher or the secondary models, the ones that adults are going to purposely create to help them make things easier.

How Our Minds Work and Why the Models Help

To help us learn a bit more about these mental models, we first need to take a look at how the mind works and then how the models can come in and make a difference. The best first step that we can take to help understand how the mind works is to look at a computer model. A human-like robotic computer is going to be the closest that we can get to seeing how the mind works for now, so let's focus on that.

Using a computer model, there is going to be a part for the hardware, and a part for the software. The robotic computer is going to have what is known as the main body, which will include the torso and the head, as well as some limbs that are a part of the peripheral limbs. The thinking part of this kind of model is going to rest in the head, just like with us. Inside the head, we are going to see that there is a CPU, which is going to act as the brain of the computer. The visible part of this CPU is going to be the hardware and the parts that we are not able to see will be the software.

In the same way, the brain is going to have parts that are the software and then parts that are the hardware. The part that is the software is going to be the mind. We are able to see the mind as a type of container where our mindset will be able to reside. And the mindset is simply going to be a set of a lot of different software programs we use. Just like the software on a computer has several sets of programs that are meant to play their own role, this helps to make sure that everything functions the way that it does.

To clarify, the mind is going to be like the software. And the mindset is going to be the collection of a unique set of instructions, or programs, that will each tell the brain how to execute the specific functions that it should. When it comes to working with computer software, we do have the system software as well as the application software.

To start with the system software, this is going to be the part of the brain that will manage all of the internal functions of our mind, with regards to how it is going to properly manage any resources that it has. The application software is going to comprise of different sets of programs, and each one is going to be designed to execute specific functions when it is triggered by some kind of stimuli that is external, such as the environment. Because of this, the Application software is going to be based on the environment that is around it. This could be more specific by talking about how to interact productively with the external environment.

The software itself, which is going to be our mindsets here, is going to be crafted more like an interface that works between the external environment and the internal environment. This software is going to be crafted based on a lot of different models. First off, the "System software" in the mind is going to be based on some of the internal things that we hold inside the body. Then the "Application software" is going to be crafted based on how the external model outside of the body is behaving.

However, we will see that the actual interface that happens between the two of these needs to be both external and internal features. They have to be able to work well together in order to get the mind to work the way that we want. The external model is going to be more dynamic compared to the internal one. The reason for this is because the external environment is going to be more dynamic and fluid, and this results in us needing more dynamism, adaptability, and flexibility in our application model.

This means that we need to make sure that the Application model is going to turn out multidimensional as if in a way to obey Adam Smith's concept of the many-sided man. This is the reason why we are going to have hundreds, if not more of these Application models, which are going to come about naturally because humans have a big desire to cope with the external environment that is always changing around them.

It is going to be on the basis of this multidimensional and many-sided perspective that this book is able to establish some of the foundations that we are going to work on. Our goal is to explore, dissect, and then synthesize some of the best mental models that are established, ones that have been put together to make it easier for humans to cope with the ever-changing environment that is all around them.

It is common for a lot of us to feel lost in the modern world, trying to adapt to things that are always changing and we may not always know how to deal with these kinds of situations. But with the help of these mental models, we can better understand the world around us, become more adaptable, make better decisions, and so much more.

Mental models are going to be one of the best things that you can work on for your best health, for your creativity, and for your own efficiency. They may sound a bit more confusing right now, but as we go through this guidebook and you see a few of the examples of how they can work, it will make more sense what we are doing here, and why you would benefit so much from using some of these mental models.

The Benefits of These Mental Models

There are a number of benefits that come with using mental models. This is why so many people enjoy using them to help make decisions easier, to help them with time management, and to make things easier overall. If you are someone who struggles to manage their time or to make some of the important decisions you need and even end up making the wrong decision in a lot of situations, then it is time to use these mental models.

The first benefit that comes with these mental models is that there are so many of them to learn about. There are believed to be hundreds of these mental models that you are able to choose from. While most of these are going to be variations on some of the most common mental models, you will find that you still get a lot of different choices when it comes to the kind of mental model that you need to use in different situations. You are not stuck with one or two models that you have to work with, and if you don't want to use one, and you don't like it, you don't get any options. Mental models come in a variety of types and choices, so you can find the one that works the best for you.

You will like that they can be customizable for your needs. You can take any of the mental models that we have in this guidebook, and customize them for your needs. We will take a look at a few examples of how you are able to change this around a bit, and use the same mental model in different manners along the way. This helps you to find the right mental model,

These mental models can work for almost any kind of situation that you need in life. We are going to take some time to look at many of the situations where you are able to use these mental models and the different types of mental models that you are able to use in the process. This will help us to see that no matter what kind of situation we encounter in our lives, we can rely on these mental models to help us out.

These mental models can make decision making easier. There are a lot of different types of mental models that you can choose from, and many of them can help you to really take control of the decisions you make. indecision is going to really cause us to fall behind and miss out on some of the best opportunities out there. We also worry that we are going to make the wrong decisions along the way, which can make it harder for us to know when we should slowdown and when we can speed up when it comes to making decisions for every aspect of life.

Mental models are able to come into the scene and solve this kind of problem. They are set up so that you can eliminate the bad choices right away, or even learn how to go with one of the first options that you think about because these are often the best, and then just jump right in. We waste too much time with indecision and we make the wrong decisions because we just have too many options to choose from. With these mental models, we learn the right steps to take to get things done, and often this helps us to make better decisions than we did before.

Time management can become a breeze when you start to use these mental models for your needs. Do you struggle with being able to manage the time that you have in a day? Do you feel like you are working hard to do all of your work, but you get to the end of the day, and you are so far behind that you have no idea how you will get it all done?

Many people are going to struggle when it comes to time management. They feel like they are doing a lot of work, but then they are always behind and won't be able to get it done on time. Often it is more about taking care of the right tasks at the right time, minimizing the things that distract you, and getting your mind to stay on track.

The right mental model is going to make this happen. We will talk about a lot of different types of mental models that can work to make you more efficient, to help you get more of your work done quickly and to keep you on track. Utilizing these don't only make your work easier, you may find that you can get the work done, with a little extra time, helping you to leave work with nothing left undone, and less stress overall.

Mental models can be a great addition to your life because they can really change up your view of the world. And often this is in a positive manner. Too many times we spend our efforts concentrating on things that take too much time, debating against too many decisions, and even dealing with procrastination. These mental models are going to come into play because they help us to take control over these problem areas, and focus our attention on how to get things done, and get them done in a quick and efficient manner.

And with all of the different options that you are able to work with when it comes to these mental models, you are sure to find the one that works the best for you, no matter what kind of situation you are dealing with. Think about how much easier your life can be, and how much more you can get done on a regular basis when you are able to implement these mental models in an effective manner.

Mental Models Affect the Way that You Are Going to View the World Around You

It is important to remember that these mental models are going to be a unique way to look at the world. They are going to be a set of tools that you are able to use to help you think in a more effective manner. Each mental model is set up in a manner that is different, with a framework that helps you to look at life, or even at an individual problem that is coming your way.

While there are a lot of ways that you are able to work with mental models, you will find that they really shine when you use them to develop more than one manner to look at the same problem. For examples, let's say that you would like to make sure that you avoid procrastination and make sure that your day is more productive.

If you understand some of the different mental models that we will talk about in this guidebook, then you are going to have a range of options that you can use to determine your priorities, and actually get things done. Remember here that one mental model is not necessarily any better than one of the others. It just depends on which one you like the most, and which one seems to be the best for you. These mental models are going to work to give you a large range of options that will help you determine your priorities while getting important things done in the process. When you have a lot of different mental models available to use, it is easier to pick out the one that is going to work the best for your current situation, rather than only using the one that you have learned how to use.

The Law of the Instrument

According to Abraham Kaplan in "The Conduct of Inquiry", the Law of the Instrument is going to be important. This one is going to be based on the idea that if you give a hammer to a small boy, then the boy is going to find that everything he encounters needs pounding. We can look at this in a similar manner as if you only have one framework for thinking about the world, then you are going to try to take each problem that comes to you into that framework, and that doesn't always work. But if you have a set of mental models to work with, your potential for finding a solution is going to increase.

One thing that is also interesting with this one is that the problem you are facing is going to become more pronounced as your expertise in an area starts to grow. If you are talented in one area, you re going to have a tendency to believe that your skillset is going to be the answer to most of the different problems that you face. The more that you start to master a single mental model, then the more likely it is that this will be your downfall, simply because you will rely on it too much. This is why we need to work to have a bigger toolbox of mental models, you are going to improve your ability to solve a lot of problems. This is because you provide yourself with more options for getting the answer that is right. When your toolbox is full of lots of different mental models, you will be better set up to choose the best tool for the given situation.

Chapter 2: The Power of Mental Models

Now that we have had a bit of time to look at these mental models and get a feel for what they are all about, it is time to stop and look at some of the roles, and the powers, that these mental models are going to be able to do this. To help us to get a better understanding of this topic though, we need to first break down the mental model into its core characteristics and elements.

A mental model, when it is done in the right manner, is going to comprise itself of an indistinguishable mix of interpretations and facts. With that in mind, there are four core elements that come with this kind of model, and those four components are going to include:

1. It interprets: A good mental model is going to act as a type of context that can grant meaning to the given observation. This kind of observation can include things like relationships, people, circumstances and events. While granting some room for context, the mental model is going to give them more of an appearance of objective reality.

2. It disguises: As this model is going to grant some kind of observation an appearance of objective reality, it

is also able to help disguise our interpretations of this observation as the only Truthful reality. This interpretation is going to be achieved in a variety of manners including collective agreements, position statements, deliberations, and explanations.

3. It determines: After being able to disguise our interpretations as an objective reality, it is going to exclude all of the other possibilities because it deems these as unreasonable, impossible, or illogical. Because of this, it is going to fence off this interpretation and will block out all of the alternative interpretations that can come in.

4. It dictates. This mental model is going to eventually start to dictate some of the beliefs that we have about certain topics, our actions, our behaviors, our habits, and our attitudes in such a manner that it helps to make the interpretation we have to appear more of objective reality.

In addition to the four core principles that we just listed above, you will find that there is going to be a fundamental attribute that goes along with this idea, and that is going to be the idea of invisibility. Being invisible simply means that the fallacies of interpretation become hard to detect or notice by those who hold the interpretation as truthful reality.

While facts remain facts no matter what your interpretation is, interpretations are going to be as good as the mind of the one holding onto them. Because of this, the interpretations can't be taken without the beholder's opinions, reasons, judgments, biases, and presumptions being a big part of how they see that situation. This brings up the question of how many of these mental models actually exist? We know that there are a lot of different methods that you can use in order to come up with your interpretation of things and to see the world in a certain way. But we need to take it a bit further and explore more of what we are able to do with these mental models and why they are so different. The four primary types of mental models that you are able to work with, and that we will concentrate on in this guidebook, include:

1. The individual mental model
2. The identity mental model
3. The collective mental model
4. The fundamental mental model.

Each one of these mental model types is going to play a different role in how we are able to perceive the world, how we can actually create our own unique perception of reality, and how we can even start and enter into some of the relationships that we have with those around us. Let's dive into this a bit more and explore some of the different types of mental models and how they each work.

The Fundamental Mental Model or FMM

The first model that we are going to take a look at is the Fundamental Mental Model. The primary power and role that comes with the FMM is that they are going to determine how we think and what we can or can't think about, what is possible, and what is not possible. We will find in our study of FMM that there are two primary types to focus on and these will include:

> 1. The FMM is going to advocate for OR and EITHER. But not for AND and WITH. The keyword for this model is going to be OR.
> 2. The FMM that is able to advocate for AND and WITH, but not for EITHER and OR. The keyword that is used with this one will be AND.

The FMM OR model is only going to be able to switch between two possibilities so that is all that you can work with. For example, me OR you would show us how this model works. Whenever this FMM OR is showing up, it is going to have the power to create exclusivity, separations, and some divisions, so be ready to see some conflict show up with this one over some of the others. It is going to be pretty egocentric with power as well.

It is going to be the OR mental model that will show us more about individualism and will allow the individual to be above the nation, above society, and any other grouping form. It is going to place the personal individual identity above the crowd and it doesn't like to share the limelight. You will find that with this one, you become an abominable presupposition, especially when it comes to things like ownership, possession, privileges, and rights. The OR model is going to create a type of world view where things are always black and white, with no areas of grey to go along with it. There is true or false, right or wrong, and good or bad in this kind of world. While the OR model is going to be good in that it advances the individual, personal effort, and lots of creativity, it can also be negative because it could include things like loneliness and greed in the process.

The World of OR

Collective MM is not necessarily devoid of the FMM OR. When a group of individuals coalesces against another group, these are going to be collective actions that still have individualism, identity ego, and some of the other attributes that we could see with the FMM OR. Collective MM in the world of OR can be seen as those in collective OR entities, including regional, national, and religious, along with anything else that would promote a configuration that is US vs. THEM.

When economics claim the power of money, politics are going to claim the power of the law, science will step in to claim the power of knowledge, and religion will finish it out with some claims to the power of truth. When these groups do actions like this, they are doing manifestations of the Collective MM within the world of FMM OR. This does not mean that a collective MM is only going to exist hand in hand with the FMM OR. It just means that you can find some of the collective MM inside of this mental model as well. Not all collectives are going to see the world in the view of us vs. them, but some of them will.

As we have seen, lots of different groups can be a Collective MM within the FMM OR world. These entities are going to attain a unique identity that will help them to stand out from the rest of the world. For example, one religious entity could claim to be the one that holds onto the absolute truth while claiming that some of the other religious entities are only spreading falsehoods. As such, this kind of religious entity is going to be able to identify itself back to God, while claiming that the other religious entities around can only have 'gods' instead. Nationalities are often going to claim exclusive ownership of a given territory, and then they would issue National Identity Cards just to those whom the political system within that nationality is going to identify as citizens. Those who are seen as the non-citizens are not going to get the National IDs and they will have to get things like a passport or a visa before they can temporarily reside, pass through, or even enter that identified territory. We can seven see this happen when we work with a political system. You may have one kind of political system that claims to be the only one that has any civility, while it brands the other competitor as backward, barbaric, or primitive. As such, it is able to pass laws that will grant itself the power to do what it would like to rule over, settle, and invade while grabbing from nations that it claims are from the backward system. This is stuff that has been seen with neo-colonialism, colonialism, and slavery. You can also think of the so-called democratic world employing tools like genocide, military force, and assassination in order to bring things like liberty and freedom to other countries. Think of the "communist world" that was trying to heal up the failures that it says is in the democratic world through revolutions that usher in collectivity and equality, which then ended up with some of the most brutal dictators and genocides in our history. These are just a few of the examples of what can happen with the collective mental model. It can definitely be more than one person who steps in and takes control like this to get what they want. They may have a good message attached to it, but the basics that it comes down to will be the idea of US vs. THEM and that we are better than others. In the name of Identity MM, millions of people have ended up losing their lives, millions in Europe during the world wars, millions in the Soviet Union during the Bolshevik Revolution, and so on. The world of OR, whether it comes from individual MM, identity MM, or collective MM has the power to breed a lot of brutality, wars, and conflict if it is not used in the proper manner. This, of course, doesn't mean that the FMM OR is going to be bad or dangerous all of the time. it is going to be based on the person and on the truthful reality that they decide to focus on. Individual power is not always a bad thing, and if it is used in the proper manner, it can be a really good thing too.

There are a lot of benefits that we are able to see with this individual power. For example, individual power is going to enable someone to:

1. Be right and fight off any wrongs.
2. Avoid having other people control us all of the time.
3. Avoid looking bad, by learning how to look good
4. How to avoid being dominated while dominating ourselves.

The important thing to remember when we are working with the FMM OR mental model is that the world is not going to be just black or white. The extreme of any of the above mentioned can, of course, be dangerous, this is why this kind of mental model needs to be measured out. This is why we need to bring in some of the other mental models in order to ensure that there is always a healthy balance present to work with.

The World of AND

Now that we have had a chance to talk about the world of OR, and what can happen when that individuality and that it can become a bad thing when it is taken too far, whether by the individual or by a group, it is time to switch gears for a moment and look a bit at the world of AND. As you can imagine, learning how to shift away from the FMM OR can be a good thing. This is because some of the hallmarks that end up with the FMM AND are going to include things like mutually beneficial collaborations, peaceful unity, and genuine partnerships. It is only from this kind of context that the collective MM is going to craft a powerful and sustainable team spirit. This does not mean that you have to give up your individuality. But it does mean that you see that the world is not about you vs. them. Both parties can benefit, and live in more peace and harmony when we view the world through the lens of the FMM AND. With this kind of worldview, we are going to see that the world can provide us with a WIN-WIN outcome in each scenario.

This doesn't mean that there won't be times when it is difficult and when things are not going to always work out the way that we would like. But it does ensure that we keep an open mind during the process of communication and that both parties will be open to hearing the other side, making some compromises, and coming up with solutions that are the best for both. It is only in this kind of world where we are going to see that the ceiling for development will be removed and that the sky is no longer a big limit for us to reach with others. Instead, the sky becomes one of our milestones along the way. true education is what will open up all of the different possibilities so that we end up with a world of more FMM AND. Now, there are benefits that work with the OR and the AND world view. The best mental models that are out there will be able to hide the negatives while balancing out the benefits that come with FMM AND along with the FMM

OR. It is a mental model that is able to optimize the benefits that come with both worlds, the idea of collectivism and individualism.

This is not always going to be easy. When you do this, you will pretty much be working on a nice balancing act that can hardly stay perfect all of the time, thanks to our ever-changing world. As such, it is going to be a journey, not a final destination point, that is going to include a lot of improvement, change, discovery, and exploration along the way. Creating the best mental model for you and for those around you can be tough. You want to make sure that you are taking care of yourself and not getting others to walk all over you. And there is certainly nothing wrong with having an individual spirit and wanting to stand strong against others at times. But we can see what can happen when the OR MM goes too far. We need to be able to combine both the OR and the AND model together in order to allow us to get some of what we want in the process, while also taking care of the other person in the mix, and not causing them a lot of harm in the process. And while this may seem like such a monumental task right now, we are going to take an even closer look at the different mental models, and how you can do exactly that, as we go through this guidebook.

Chapter 3: Some of the Most Common Mental Models

The neat thing about these mental models is that there are actually quite a few of them that you are able to work with. This allows you to think and act in many different manners and can help you when it is time to make some big decisions. With this in mind, we are going to focus on the top ten mental models, even though there are at least 80 of these models that can be applicable to our modern world. The top ten mental models that we are going to focus on in this chapter will include:

The Map is Not the Territory

The rationale that we are going to follow with this model is that the way we are able to see the world isn't really itself. Rather, the worldview that we have is going to be based on our own mental construct. A map is just going to be the mental construct that we use. Territorial borders are going to change over time, and things around us can change as well.

In a greater perspective, the map is not the territory will warn us against some of the logical fallacy that occurs when we confuse the labels, semantics, and artifacts with the things that are real. Some of the other fallacies that are similar to this will include misplaced concreteness and reification. Each one of us is going to have or own mental map that helps us to view the world. Yet the world is really complex, and it is impossible for a human to totally comprehend what is going on. This means that our attitudes, beliefs, assumptions, and conclusions are not going to be the best parameters all of the time for helping us to understand the totality of the real world.

When it is time to look at our communication and interpersonal relationships, it is likely that we are going to try and impose our own mental map onto others, or we think that they should be able to read our mental map. But we have to remember that the other people we are around have their own mental maps as well, and they would like us to follow theirs instead of ours. This is where a lot of misunderstanding, confusion, and sometimes extreme conflict, is going to come into the picture.

Yes, it is possible for two people to be in the same place, and even see the same situation or circumstance, but then leave with a different experience. With these different experiences, we are going to see that there are different interpretations and different worldviews in the process. If this is the mental model that you are going with, remember that you should not try to impose your worldview on others, just try to make yourself understood, while also accepting the worldviews of others.

There are several ways that you are able to apply these mental models in your life. These include:

1. Decision making
2. Relationship management
3. Leadership

The Circle of Competence

There is no one who has all of the knowledge in the world. There are always going to be some blind spots in our competencies and the knowledge that we have. it is important that we acknowledge the things that we don't know. This is not a bad thing to not know everything, because it is just not possible. Focusing on the things that we do know, and seeing how that can move us ahead in life is so much better.

Through the circle of competencies, you are going to be able to open up your mind to some more learning. You will be able to avoid some of the common assumptions and fallacies along the way. You can work to discard the ignorant ego and become more reasonable in your understanding the extent of the competency that you have.

This is going to benefit you so much. It can help you to know where your strengths are, and your weaknesses. It is able to point you in the direction that you need to break away from the cocoon of mediocrity and will help you to connect with the right kinds of people so that you are able to learn more from them and grow your knowledge base. Some of the different applications that you can use with the circle of competence will include:

1. Career development and advancement
2. Decision making

First Principles Thinking

It is going to be a lot more about separating the underlying facts and the ideas from the assumptions that you are able to make. when you decide to apply the first principle of thinking, you will be able to decompose a problem into its constituent elements, or to the root causes that are present, and then it is easier to deal with them in the most appropriate manner, rather than running around and hoping that you make the right decisions along the way. You are able to isolate out some of the pathogens that will cause you the disease from its symptoms. And because of this, you will end up providing some healing to the disease, rather than just some relief to the symptoms that you are feeling. Reaching to the depth of the constituent elements, you will find that you can use these elements to build up to something that is brand new. Some of the applications that you are going to see with this one include:

1. Decision making
2. Problem-solving
3. Engineering
4. Chemistry

5. Medicine

The Pursuit of Knowledge That is Liquid

Solid knowledge is going to be comprised of pellets that are going to be collected into silos. For example, you could have biology silo, a physics, silo, mathematical silos and so on and solid knowledge is hardly going to be fluid, hardly dynamic at all, and hardly flows.

Great free thinkers are going to go beyond the solid knowledge that is offered in schools to the liquid knowledge that is uncondensed, unrefined, and freely flowing. This kind of thinking is going to be a knowledge gathered from your own experiences, from your own discoveries, and your own exploration. This allows you to have a nice adventure while you work on your discovery of knowledge, which can make things easier and more pleasurable along the way.

Thought Experiment

Thought experiments are going to be devices of the imagination that are then used in order to investigate the nature of the things around us. Thought experiments are going to be essential any time that you would like to break into new frontiers, especially when you are trying to go into new and unknown territory. This territory can be unknown and new to you, or they can be unknown to others as well. This kind of thought experiment is going to allow one to crack the impossible, evaluate the potential consequences, and then compare these consequences with some of the known to help them make some informed deductions.

You will find that, in a manner different than some of the empirical examinations that you can do, thought experiment is going to be conducted just in the mind, even though you are able to demonstrate it physically in order to prove it. As such, this kind of mental model is going to be known as a laboratory of the mind instead.

Galileo is actually one of the famous scientists who worked with this thought experiment to help come up with some of the scientific principles that are still seen to be true today. Albert Einstein also used this method as well. The biggest challenge that comes with this kind of mental model is that, without being able to prove it empirically, it is something that we are not able to prove as true or false. Thus, there are some philosophers who are going to consider it more of a mental modeling of the physical realm instead. Some of the applications of this mental model will include:

1. It can help you to research the formulation of your hypothesis.

2. Scenario simulation and synthesis.

3. Scientific exploration

Second-Order Thinking

The first question that we may have here is whether or not there is a First Order? Of course, there is! Before we start to take a look at this Second Order of thinking, we need to do a brief introduction to what the First Order is all about and then compare the two.

When we are working with the First Order thinking, people are going to make decisions that are hasty and quick, ones that are based on what they can see on the surface and in appearances. Because of this quick decision making, the person is not going to be able to go into the depth that they should to understand why things turn out the way that they are. They react quickly, on first impressions, without actually focusing on what is happening and whether they should react in this manner or not.

Then we have the Second Order thinking. With this one, the person is going to take their thinking and decision-maker a bit further. They are going to study some more of the fundamentals that are behind the phenomenon so that they can identify the various variables that are behind this as well.

Those who end up using the Second order thinking, rather than rushing into the decision and going into the decision too quickly, may find that they make a decision that contradicts what their First Order thinking would have done. Let's take a look at an example of how to do this. When there is an explosion that happens, the First Order thinkers are going to try to run away because they assume that the explosion was from a bomb and they want to get away from the danger as quickly as possible.

But then there are the Second Order thinkers. Even though they may want to follow their instincts and take flight, they will be more likely to pause and think about what it could be that caused the explosion, figure out if they are close to the explosion, and then figure out what they could do about it. Maybe they find out that it was just a big tire that burst by them and there was no reason to run off and be scared of it.

So, in some manners of thinking, the First Order thinkers are going to reach to the already existing mental image that is in the mind of this kind of thinker. The actual occurrence that shows up is going to just be the trigger for that action, but not the cause of the action.

Another good example of First Order to Second Order thinking is in the sphere of investment. For example, if Company A declares that there is a profit warning, most First Order thinkers are going to anticipate that the price of the share is about to fall. Because of this, they are going to rush to get rid of the shares as quickly as possible. This causes the shares to happen, but this is because the traders jump in too quickly, not because the value of the shares actually went down.

On the other hand, we can see that a Second Order thinker is going to have done the process of a fundamental analysis on the profit warning to figure out what is going to cause that profit warning. This could easily be something small, like a new investment decision that resulted in less profit, but a bigger asset base. This means that if you hold onto the shares, there may be a temporary dip thanks to the First Order thinkers, but overall, your value from the shares are going to heat back up.

There are a lot of different times when you will be able to use the idea of First Order vs. Second Order mental model to help you make decisions. Some of the best applications of this mental model are going to include:

1. Decision making of any kind
2. In a fundamental analysis
3. Investment decisions
4. Emergency response

Occam's Razor

This is a model that is going to posit that the simple explanations are the ones that are more likely to be true, rather than going for the explanations that are more complex. So, if you are using this mental model, you will find that it works the best if you can pick out a solution that has fewer assumptions in it. What this means is that when someone makes a decision, they need to be able to minimize the assumptions as much as possible, with the help of experimentation, study, and research before they implement a new decision concept that they want. In case there is not a lot of leeway in the amount of time that is available, then the concept that has the fewest assumptions is the one that is considered the most ideal for implementing.

The reason for this is that when you have more assumptions present, the risk of having some decision errors is going to be higher. Some of the applications of this mental model is going to include:

1. Personal development
2. Career choices
3. Management
4. Leadership
5. Decision making

Inversion

The next mental model that we are going to take a look at is inversion. Inversion is the idea that you will think backward. With this one, you are going to create some likely scenarios after the action or decisions and then you need to seek out how to address all of the scenarios before you decide on which course to take, or before you decide to execute it. This means that you need to be able to approach the problem from the opposite of the natural starting point.

Let's take a look at an example of this. You may be considering a separation or a divorce from your spouse. Before you jump into this and go ahead with some of the divorce proceedings, by inversion, you would stimulate some of the potential scenarios that would happen with this. It could include a strained relationship with your in-laws, loss of your home, increased costs of childcare, loss of your partner, property division and more. If possible, you can then start to mitigate some of the adverse effects of these scenarios before deciding for or against the divorce.

To make this one work a bit better, you have to make sure that you attack your decisions by going backward. This helps you to really plan things out, imagine that things are already done, and consider what decision is actually going to give you the results that you are looking for. Some of the different applications for the inversion mental model will include the following:

1. Career choice
2. Leadership

3. Decision making
4. Personal development
5. Family planning

Probabilistic Thinking

When you work with probabilistic thinking, you are going to use a variety of probability tools, including statistical tools, to help them approximate the likelihood that a certain event is going to occur. There are two major technologies that already use this including machine learning and artificial intelligence. Some of the different applications of using probabilistic thinking as a mental model will include:

1. Strategic planning
2. Actuarial science
3. Computer sciences, especially when we look at machine learning and artificial intelligence
4. Decision making
5. Investment

Hanlon's Razor

The best look at what the Hanlon mental model is all about is "never attribute malice to that which can be simply explained by stupidity". The gist of this is that you should never assume that something bad is happening because of the wicked intents of others on the situation. Sometimes it is just incompetence or stupidity on the part of the actor, rather than some malice on their part. Stupidity, in this case, can be from the other person, or from you. It is possible that your own stupidity is causing problems because you made the wrong assumption, but then it could be the stupidity of the other person as well.

Due to the egocentric view that most of us have of things, which, in our subconscious minds, assumes that everything in the world revolves around us, we end up assuming a prominent role in the story of everyone else, even though this isn't true. This means that when we are around someone who seems a bit annoyed, we assume that it has to do with us and that we have made them made. When another person is rude to us, it is because they are angry at us or just being mean to us. When we see that someone doesn't want to congratulate us, we assume that they are feeling jealous of us.

As part of the stupidity that comes with us, we are going to perceive some negative responses as malice against us, without being able to consider that it is often due to factors that have nothing to do with us. Hanlon's Razor model is going to be helpful because it can avoid paranoia, anxiety, and stress. It will eventually save us from taking a bad situation and making it worse. When we use this mental model, we have to understand that to be human is to err, and that there are times when people make mistakes, and even we are going to make some mistakes on occasion. This means that we need to find out if there are other explanations for what has occurred, rather than assuming that there is some malice that comes with this. This is why with Hanlon's razor, it is always best to assume the best intentions or some good faith before we try to prove otherwise.

Some of the applications that we are going to see with the Hanlon's razor will include:

1. Relationship management
2. Decision making
3. Diplomacy
4. Conflict resolution
5. Crisis management

As you can see, there are a lot of different mental models out there that will help you to make decisions, based on the way that you see the world and the point of view that you are looking for along the way as well. Each of these can be effective and ill help you to see some of the results that you want with making decisions that are going to be based on sound judgment, rather than on our emotions or something else that can be subjective. You can determine which of these mental models, as well as some of the others we will talk about in this guidebook that you would like to use to help you make some good decisions and to ensure you can make the best decisions for yourself.

Chapter 4: The Right Mental Model for Those Who Like to Make Decisions

In one case or another, everyone is going to have to make some decisions at one point or another. We all will have to make some decisions. However, there are going to be those who have to make a lot of decisions, and they are often leaders in some key organization. In this chapter, we are going to take a look in particular at some of the best mental models that can be used for those who have to make decisions on a regular basis that impact a company, and those who just need some help making some decisions.

Circle of Influence

The first mental model that we are going to take a look at here is going to be the circle of influence. Before you are able to make a decision, you need to understand where you excel and what your skills are in terms of expertise and knowledge. Then you need to also know some of your weaknesses when it comes to expertise, skills, and knowledge. This is going to give you a nice springboard to work from so you know where to go, what options are not the best and more. This ensures that you are able to keep your decisions towards areas where you excel while staying away from ones where you don't. from there, it is easier for you to slowly expand out the areas of competence in terms of depth and spread when it is time.

The neat thing here is that there are a few different mental models that you are able to use that fit in with this kind of idea. Some of the most common options are going to include:

1. Availability heuristics

This one is going to be based on the idea of "if something can be recalled, then it is important. If it can't be recalled, then it is not important". We can also think of this one like out of sight, out of mind. When we are on this kind of model, the things that come to our mind right away will provide us with the best solutions to the challenges that we are dealing with.

This means that you should not have to struggle as much to find the solutions that you need to the challenges that you have. you should be able to find the solution based off some of the first ones that come to your mind. You should also choose to use the tools and the concepts that you have mastered, and some of the practical methods that you are competent in, to help you out with this. This helps to keep things simple and doesn't waste time on learning new skills right away (you can learn them as you go), and on looking for an idea when you are going to pick one of the first you came up with anyway.

2. Regret minimization framework

When we are working with this kind of model, you will first need to look at your present away from some moment in the future. You can move into the future and think about how you would feel concerning that situation or that decision later on. Think in terms of "how I feel that I did this, and it happened and succeeded". If you feel that the result of doing an action will lead you to the least amount of regret in the process, then this is the one that you are going to choose to go with.

Inversion

We talked about this one a bit before, but we are going to explore how you can use this to help you make some of the decisions that you need in life. Inversion is a mental model that is all about thinking backward. When you are doing inversion, you are going to create out a few scenarios after your action and your decision, and then seek out ways that you are able to address each scenario that you pick before going with the decision or executing it. Let's pretend that we are working as a startup entrepreneur. In this role, you may have the right ambition that requires you not only to use your savings and other available funds but also to borrow some more to get it done. Some of the questions that you may be asking yourself about this kind of decision is what if I go bankrupt? What if the idea is a bad one and fails? What if I succeed beyond even my expectations?

From these questions, you would then be able to use the strategy of inversion to help you deal with each in their turn on the plan. You are going to be much better off with this than someone who is only driven by some of their blind ambitions and ho have not put into place some fail-safe options. Inversion is not meant to make you pessimistic about life, but it is more about having some assured optimism that can then be guarded by prudence. From the foregoing to visible benefits, you can see that inversion works because:

1. It is going to be the most helpful when it comes to deconstructing a problem than using the traditional forward-thinking.

2. It is going to help you to weigh the consequences of your decision or your action before you try to execute them. This helps you to stay grounded, calm, and more assured of yourself in the process.

3. It is going to safeguard your enterprise from the vagaries of primitive, raw, and unbridled ambitions.

The Contrarian Approach to Motivation

The next option of mental models that can help out a lot when you are working with making important decisions is known as the contrarian approach to motivation. Motivation is often going to have some raw emotions, unchecked ambitions, and self-ego attached to them. To someone who is a strategic thinker, the worst blunder is to be taken over by these three things. Stripping yourself of the motivation when you are thinking critically is going to help you to really make the best decision, without falling into the trap of thinking with your emotions instead of your head.

The Why Model

Every action or decision that you want to work with is going to have a 'why' attached to it, whether it is implicit or explicit, known or unknown ahead of time. because of this, whenever a certain thing does happen, the most imperative question that anyone needs to ask here, especially when they are the leader, is Why?

Why is what is going to breed the mission. A mission in this sense is going to be the grandest why. This is the main core of every venture or every endeavor that you decide to work on, whether it is in your business or otherwise. When you see a mission lacking, then you will notice that the direction is lacking as well. In the profound noise of confusion, there is always going to be a silent cry of Why that needs to be answered. Unfortunately, not until someone, usually a leader, listens to this kind of cry, and then answers it, the noise is going to persist. This is a noise that is often heard in wars, crises, conflicts and more. This one is going to ask us to look at the root cause of why things are happening when they do, the way they do, and more. When we learn the why of something, we are better able to find the right solution that is going to help us take care of the issue, and get it to work the way that we want. This is one of the best ways for you to work with making some of your decisions because it helps you to cut out some of that noise.

The Eisenhower Matrix

When we look at the principle of the Eisenhower matrix, it is simply going to state that what is important is rarely urgent, and what is urgent is rarely important. Of course, there is going to be some grey area that falls between the circle of what is important and the circle of what is the most urgent because it is possible that something is going t0 be urgent and important. This is the thing that you will have to get done and make your foremost priority. Nonetheless, according to this kind of matrix, it is going to be important to take all of your tasks and categorize them into four different groups including:

1. Urgent and important
2. Important, but not really seen as urgent.
3. Urgent but not that important
4. Neither important nor urgent

All of our tasks are going to fall within these four categories. Implementation priority needs to be ranked in the same order. If something falls into the last category, then it is best if you are able to just discard it. Most of the tasks that fall into groups three and two need to be delegated if possible, the ones that you need to do in group two have to be scheduled for a later performance, and then the tasks that fall into the first group are the ones that you need to focus on doing right away.

The Pareto Principle

The Pareto principle is going to be the idea of 80:20. This is a principle that states that 80 percent of our outcomes are going to be generated by 20 percent of our efforts. This means that if we are trying to improve our levels of productivity, then we need to identify the 20 percent of these efforts, and then put the majority of our focus on that. We also have to realize that it is worth it to sacrifice some of the 80 percent of our efforts in order to do this because all that work is only yielding the 20 percent. The Pareto principle is going to be all about focusing our energies on what is going to matter the most. If something falls inside the least productive spheres, then it is time to discard it. If it still happens to be worth pursuing, it is the best candidate for you to delegate or outsource to someone else to get it done if you don't have the time.

The Paradox of Choice

The last mental model that we are going to take a look at is the paradox of choice. This one is going to hold to the idea that the more choices there are to go from, the more confusing it can be to make a decision at all. And this often results in us making the wrong decision because of this confusion and all of the choices that come with it. We often think that it is better to have a lot of choices.

This gives us some freedom in the process and can make it easier for us to get the results that we want. But in most cases, this is just going to make the situation much worse, and it is not going to help us to make any good decisions at all. To help us avoid the paradox of choice, we need to learn how to narrow down our choices as much as possible. If we have twenty options to choose from, we need a system that quickly gets us down to five r fewer. The fewer that we are able to get ourselves down too, the easier it is to make not only a good decision but the right decision for us.

Making decisions is something that can take a lot of time. We miss out on a lot of opportunities and feel a lot of stress and anxiety about working with making decisions because we don't know the method that we should pick out or which one is going to be the best for us. The mental models that we discussed in this chapter are meant to show you some really quick methods that you can use to get those decisions made so you can pick the right one for you and move on with the rest of your day.

Chapter 5: Mental Models to Help You Become the Best Entrepreneur

The next types of mental models that we are going to take a look at are ones that work the best for business practitioners and entrepreneurs. The business field can be really wide, and this allows for a wide array of mental models to apply to this. We are going to focus mainly on some of the fields for you to use within the business fields to make this work a bit easier. Let's get started!

Mental Models for Marketers

Marketing is a very crucial function for any business to be successful. Marketers are going to play the role of getting the information about a company out to the public so that they can make good decisions about what to purchase and from whom. But which of the mental models should marketers put into their mental toolbox? There are quite a few to work with, but to help us be more effective, we are just going to take a look at some of the top options including.

Anchoring Bias

This mental model is going to talk about the phenomenon where people are going to rely heavily on the first piece of information that comes their way and will use this information to base and make future assumptions. Let's say that you have a pair of shoes in the store, and the customer asks you how much it is going to cost. You quote a price of $99, and the customer makes a counteroffer of $75. You request them to meet you a bit higher and they make a final offer of $80 when you accept the deal. The customer is going to walk away feeling that they were able to get a good deal. But the trick is that you would have been just fine if you sold it for $60. The customer made a counteroffer based on the $80. If you told them the shoes were for $60, there is no way they would have offered $80, and you would have probably had to sell them for $50 or something lower. This means that as a marketer, the first piece of information that you are able to provide to a customer is going to help lead here their subsequent assumptions are going to go with a product. This is why you want to make sure that the very first piece of information that you provide to them is the one that you want to stick in their minds.

Loss Aversion

Naturally, most people like to avoid loss. There are very few people who are going to deliberately desire to lose unless the cost of gaining is extremely high compared to the cost of losing. Psychologists have found that people are going to prefer it if they are able to avoid losses rather than acquiring an equivalent gain. For example, most people would rather not lose $100 rather than gain the $100. If they had a chance to win $100 but there was an equal chance of losing that same amount of money, then most of the time, people are going to walk away from the opportunity. Every marketer, especially when they are trying to get into a new market, is going to use loss aversion as one of their marketing strategies. The marketer is going to try to craft up their own strategy that can help eliminate that sense of loss in the mind of the customer so that the customer is more likely to choose this product over one of the others.

Product/Market Fit

A market is simply a place where the supply is going to meet with demand. The demand that we are talking about here is going to be the expression of the wants and needs of the customer. The product is simply a solution that is devised in order to satisfy the wants of the customers. This means that in a product/market fit, it is going to be the situation where a supplier's product is going to be the best fits a customer's demand. In essence, a solution that is best going to fit the given need. This kind of model is going to work because it encourages businesses to seek to gain a better understanding of the wants and needs of the consumer, before developing any products. If this doesn't happen, then the business is going to run a higher risk of the product failing to meet the market or the needs of the consumer. Traditionally, a company would try to create a product and hope that it was successful enough that the market would want it, and they could make a lot of money. This could end up being really costly though because the market may have no use for the product, and then the business is out a lot of money in the process.

Mental Models for Financiers and Accountants

Financiers and accountants are going to find that they rely quite a bit on these mental models, especially the ones that are designed by economists. Economists are probably only rivaled by the field of psychology when it comes to generating some of these mental models, which means that the people in this group are going to have a lot of different mental models that they are able to rely on to help them get work done. Even with this in mind, we will only take the time to consider a few of the mental models that are available for this group. Our goal is to focus on the mental models that are generally applicable and won't be confined to just their professional domains, even though these business individuals are going to be able to use these models in a variety of manners. Some of the different mental models that are perfect and helpful for those who are financiers and accountants are going to include:

Compounding

The first mental model that we are going to look at is known as compounding. This model is going to look at each new earning as an income stream. For example, if you have an investment of $100 and you earn 10 percent in interest, which is

$10, this is going to become $10 of a new income stream. And it keeps compounding on itself over and over again to help you make more money. This is the simplest form of compounding in the world of financing and accounting and of course, there are other, more complicated methods that you are able to use as well. But one of the most important things that you have to remember about the compounding mental model is that it is going to help a financier and an accountant of the potential worth of every new income stream.

Sunk Cost

A sunk cost is going to be any kind of cost that occurs that can't be redeemed at all. This means that the cost is going to be irreversible. The sunk cost model is going to remind people in this kind of group that they have to be more conscious of the ways they are incurring and expending their costs. Some sunk costs can't be avoided, but it is important to limit this as much as possible so that money is not wasted. Since the sunk cost is something that we are not able to recover later on, accountants are often advised that it is best to write these off. This is a much better thing to do than to laboriously keep them on the record, which is sometimes going to affect the true financial position of that company and could really negatively affect the quality of decisions that are made.

The danger that comes with not writing off these sunk costs is that it could consume more costs down the line. for example, following up on a bad debt can end up being very costly. There is going to be a point in time when the cost-benefit is not going to work out, and you spend more money on that debt that it was worth to get paid. When it becomes more expensive to try and recover the bad debt, rather than just writing it off, then this is not a good thing.

Opportunity Cost

The opportunity cost is going to be the benefit of the next best alternative that has been sacrificed to get where you are. In a real-world scenario, we are going to be confronted with a lot of choices, and we have to decide on just one choice over all the others. Let's say that you forego a job that is going to pay you $18 an hour in order to take up a job that is going to pay you $20 an hour. The opportunity cost of the chosen job is going to be $19. Thus, comparing the two jobs, you have made a net gain of $2 per hour. The $2 an hour is going to be the actual pay that you will get above the opportunity cost. Many times, we are tempted to make some decisions without taking the time to factor in the opportunity cost of that decision. Then we eventually realize that we should have factored this in, or we would have picked a different choice than the one we went with.

The Time Value of Money

Another mental model that is popular is going to be the time value of money. This is actually seen as one of the most important concepts when it comes to the fields of accounting, finance, and economics. What you have at the moment could end up being worth more than what you expect to have at some point in the future. As such, you can't equate what you have right now against a similar value in the future. The time value of money is what is going to account for things like depreciation, interest rates, and inflation rates in the accounting world. Using the idea of the compounding model that we talked about earlier, it is easier to see that $100 now can't be the same as it will be ten years from now. If this $100 is factored with a 10 percent compound interest rate per year, in 10 years' time, this is going to be quite a bit of money due to the multiple income streams that are earned with the interest compound. This means also that if you lend someone $100 and they promise to pay it back in ten years, such as with an endowment plan, retirement benefits, and pension, you have to ask yourself what it is worth now. Knowing what that money is worth right now is going to help you to avoid a new opportunity cost that is higher than the promise they are giving. Another thing that we have to keep in mind here is that we have income as a factor of time. income is just the rate of dollar flow per a given interval. This could be per second, per hour, per month and so on. When we are able to put this all together, we will see that all of this makes it easier for an accountant to calculate out a lot of things such as how much it costs when employees are absent or late, the cost of moonlighting and more. Then they can take this information and tell the business how much it is losing every second an employee is out of work and not doing what they were supposed to do.

The Pyramid Model

When we take a look at the world of accounting, the pyramid model is going to be used to group together accounts that are pretty simple. For example, there are going to often bet three main classes of accounts when we are in accounting and these include Liabilities, Capital, and Assets. Most of the money and how it is used in the company will ensure that it fits into one of those three categories along the way.

All accounts related to transfer, decrease, or increase the assets are going to just be grouped together into one class that is known as Assets to make it easier. In a similar manner, all of the accounts that are going to record the transfer, decrease, or increase of capital in any form will be grouped under the category of Capital Account. And finally, all of the accounts that are related back to a transfer, decrease, or increase of liabilities will be added to the Liabilities account. This is done in order to make things flow together a little bit easier. If we tried to put them into all of those accounts, in this case about nine different ones, the accounts, and the charts that you use to monitor all of these, are going to get full pretty quickly, and it is going to be difficult to figure out what is going on. When they are grouped together in just those three categories, it makes the job of your accountant so much easier to work with. In this case with finances and accounting, the pyramid model is going to be used in a manner to help organize all of the accounting information so that it is in a more systematic way, making it easier to interpret, analyze, and read before making decisions based on the business performance. If this information is in order, then we have a much better look at how the business is performing based on its financial transactions, and it is much easier to make the changes that are needed. Accountants and financiers have to spend a lot of time looking at numbers, transactions, and more to ensure that a business is doing well and that they are not headed for disaster. Even with this in mind, there are a lot of mental models that can come into play to help you get things done and to ensure that you will be able to get the work done effectively, and with no mistakes along the way!

Mental Models for Business Entrepreneurs

Now that we have had a chance to look at some of the mental models that can work for marketers, it is time to take a look at some of the different mental models that we are able to work with as business entrepreneurs. Entrepreneurship is one area where you will find mental models really aiding when it is time to come up with novel solutions that can change society and make a big impact. Some of the different mental models that work for business entrepreneurs well include:

The Idea Maze

This mental model is going to warn against rushing over an idea without doing the due consideration ahead of time, and without making sure that you know the exit point. There are a lot of entry points that can come with a maze. It is important that you don't just focus on these, but you also consider the exit point of all the entries before you invest money, time, and effort into that channel. If you don't, then it is possible that you will get trapped and have no exit except to head to your entry, and this can result in a huge loss. The Idea maze is going to caution one to consider that one of the ideas that you have may not be unique. Consider others who have gone through with similar ideas and how they invested their energy and time. Then consider if they were successful with their work or not. This way, you can make sure to save your business by not getting entangled into a death trap that already caught someone else earlier on. The idea that comes with this one is that it encourages a potential startup to ventilate enough of its ideas first, before using them, by simply exposing it to others so that the opinions and views of those others can be weighed into it as well. It is going to try and discourage the desire by most startups to hold onto the idea with the thought that if they try to share their ideas, then the idea will get stolen.

The Problem Hypothesis

This is going to be another example of a mental model where you are going to try and reframe your great idea around some kind of problem that you are able to test and validate. This means that your idea is going to turn into something that can solve a given problem. Some things to consider with this one include:

1. The problem has to be one that actually exists.

2. There is no better solution to solving the problem, outside of your idea.

3. That your idea can generate a Minimum Viable Product (we will talk about this in the next mental model).

The problem hypothesis is going to help you to avoid some of the pitfalls that are common that many upcoming entrepreneurs are going to face, which is that they try to create a solution to a problem that does not exist. Because of this, the solution is going to fail to gain traction in the market, as there is no real need case. This mental model is going to require that you work with the scientific approach to validate all of your ideas before you actually try to use any of them in your business.

Minimum Viable Product

Another mental model that you can work with to ensure that your business is a success is the minimum viable product. This is simply going to be a product that has just the very basic of features to satisfy early adopters and can provide the creators of the product with some feedback about the real needs of the market. this feedback can be used in such a way that it helps to guide some of the future development of that product. It is hard for a lot of potential entrepreneurs to come up with a complex final product, and spend all that time, money and effort on it, just to find out that it doesn't meet the product/market fit criteria. They may lose out with this one because the product is not really what the consumer is looking for, for a variety of reasons, and they are not able to make any money from it. Instead of letting the risk of that happen, the Minimum Viable Product is going to be a model that is going to require a lot of little changes to the product, based on the feedback that you get from the market. you start out with a product that has just the basic features and the fundamentals that make it work. From there, you wait to get some feedback before deciding which direction to take the product, what new features to add and more. This helps with decision making. You don't have to worry about making the wrong decisions any longer because the consumer is basically making them for you. And you don't have to risk things as much, or waste as much time, but the changes that you make are small, and then you can release the product again, make some money in the process, and then bring it back in for some more changes based on some of the new feedback that you hear from your customer along the way.

Mental models for CEO and Managers

The next part of the business that we need to talk about in terms of mental models is going to be the ones that work well for chief executives, managers, and even supervisors. These are the individuals who have to deal with a lot of challenges when it comes to running a company, making sure they meet the needs of the consumer, and training and leading their employees. Because of this, they are going to have a lot of things on their plates, and there are a few mental models that work well for them as well. Some of the best options for mental models that can work for CEO's and other managerial positions will include the following:

Casual Loop

The casual loop model is going to be able to help us see the cause and effect relationship that happens between the various components of a system. This is going to help us see the impact of changing one of the variables on the system as a whole. The reason that many managers like to use this is that it allows them to see how their decisions will affect what kind of outcome they are going to get. For example, they may be weighing the impact of shifting from monthly salary to hourly wage to see how it is going to influence the morale of the workers and their productivity in the process.

Reversible vs. Irreversible Decisions

This kind of decision model is going to be one that you can use to categorize decisions into those that can be undone, and the ones that you are not able to be undone. For example, if you purchase a product that has a return period, then this is something that is reversible. On the other hand, if you fire an employee, this is something that is usually not reversible because it is not very prudent and can make things difficult. Working with this kind of model will enable a manager to re-evaluate the likely impact of their decisions before they try to execute them, and this helps them to see in a clearer picture what is really at stake for each of these decisions. The reversible decisions are going to be the ones that have the lower stakes compared to the irreversible decisions. This makes it imperative that you put more of the thought energy has to be allocated to evaluating the likely impact of the irreversible decisions. And to help reduce some of the stakes that you are seeing, you want to make sure that you turn as many contracts and as many decisions into reversible ones as possible. This allows you to create some escape routes if they are needed. This is why some companies are going to hire an employee and will work with extended probation, short term contracts, freelancing, and more.

The Pyramid Model

The pyramid model is going to mainly be one for the Chief Executive or some of the top managers who are going to design the organization structure. In this kind of model, the related functions are going to be grouped together with one department or division. This means that at the top, there is only going to be one group that can break down into several groups as it goes down and each group is going to break down into more groups until you get to the smallest group possible in the end.

99/50/1

This is a model that is going to be suited the best for supervisors. The core part of this model is that you have to follow up when a task has just begun and then again when it is about 99 percent complete. This is done to ensure that the people who are assigned the responsibility of doing this task are actually working on it, and they are doing it in the right manner. Afterward, you can check again when the task is close to 50 percent complete.

This is going to be done in order to confirm that it is substantially done and that you can then anticipate when the completion time is going to happen. And then the final leg of this is going to be that the supervisor should check when the project is just about done, or when there is about 1 percent remaining. This ensures that you are there to help out and check on the finishing of the project and the wrap-up of everything. Each of these mental models are going to help you whether you are marketing for a company, trying to be the head of the company and you want to make sure you are providing a product that the consumer actually wants, and when you are one of the supervisors who want to check that you are going to get things done on time. Working with the right mental model can make it so that decision making is effective, fast, and accurate as much as possible.

Chapter 6: Writing and Inquisitive? The Best Mental Models to Help You

Investigators, inquisitors, journalists, and writers all have one thing in common with each other. They like to establish facts and then report these facts for some kind of action. In this chapter, we are going to take a look at these mental models and how they can be used to help those who are involved in establishing facts from stories, allegations, insinuations and other kinds of information to achieve their very important missions as effectively as possible.

The Socratic Questioning Technique

This is going to be a mental model that has been devised in order to inspire some critical thinking along the way. This technique is going to employ a set of questions that will enable someone to learn about their own fallacies, their unfounded assumptions, and limiting beliefs. And by this discovery, the person is going to be able to think in a more critical manner. You will continue to work with this one until you can come up with the right answer that makes the most sense of the situation.

The Why Iteration

The next mental model that we are going to take a look at is known as the Why iteration. This one is going to be where you ask the why question five times at a minimum. The point of this one is that you want to get to the root of the initial response, rather than stopping at some superficial point along the way. the assumption with the Why Iteration is that the first response is rarely the final one, and relying on this first response is not going to give you the true picture of things that you need. Here we see that the more questions we ask, the closer we can get to the root of the matter.

You are able to consider each Why in order to address a specific layer in the structure. And you also have to consider the problem as a type of root that has five layers down. The first why that you ask is going to be able to address the respective portion of the root in the first layer, but there are four other portions and four other layers that you need to spend some time on before fully understanding the problem. One thing to keep in mind with this one is that the 5 is not really empirical, but more of an encouragement. Some structures could have fewer numbers, and others are going to have more. But don't use this as an excuse to just ask why two times and give up. Work at adding in as many different layers to the problem as you can, and see what a difference it can make.

The NLP Meta Model

The NLP Meta Model is going to be similar to the Socratic model that we talked about before. It is going to help us to make some deep inquiries into information that may not be availed by word labels. What a person says is often just a small percentage of the entire information that is held by that person, basically just the tip of the iceberg. It is not always the intent of the other person to filter out the information, but they may do it to shorten up the conversation if needed or to just give you their perception of the most important information. In the process of perceiving information from a sensory organ, the brain:

1.   Deletes a bit of the sensory information to make it easier to do the processing.
2.   Distorts part of the sensory information based on what experiences you have had in the past.
3.   Generalizes the sensory information, especially if the information was really repetitive in nature.

All of these are going to be done in an endeavor to effectively utilize the limited space in the memory, to fit the existing mental models, and to prioritize the functional benefits a bit. Thus, to help us get a clear picture, we need to ask some specific questions that we can recycle or reconstruct the deleted portion of the message, to straighten out the part that is distorted, and unwrap some of the generalizations so that e can get more information out of this person. A good example of what this is going to look like when we work with the NLP model includes:

1. Distortion: I am pretty sure that he is feeling jealous, I am sure that his congratulation message is not genuine.

2. Deletion: No one likes seeing me successful. When people tell me they do, it's always a fake compliment.

3. Generalization: All women are gold-diggers.

From the statements above, you can see that there is so much information that we are missing out on and that is being withheld from this. Using the NLP meta model, you will be able to ask a specific set of questions to that other person in order to figure out what is at the root of that statement. This one is also a good option to use in therapies because it gives you the ability to understand the problems of others better, or to help them to understand their own problems in a deeper manner.

The Response Bias

Response bias is going to occur where an interviewee is going to give a response that is not really based on the facts, but it is more based on some of the other factors that are nearby. It could include some factors like the desire to please, fear, a desire to look politically or socially correct, a desire to conform, and even a desire to avoid telling the other person the truth.

Because of this bias, researchers, journalists and more need to learn how to not overly rely on a given response without putting it to strict empirical test and proof. You want to make sure that you are getting the right answers from others, rather than getting this bias that is going to distort the kind of image that you are able to get from the other person. If you can learn how to take away some of the bias, and get the other person to feel more comfortable and open around you, you may find that they will give you better answers, without the bias, and this can do some wonders in the process.

Even someone who has more of an inquisitive mind and who wants to be able to get to the root of the problem and find all of the facts will be able to use some of the mental models that we discuss in this guidebook. Learning how to use these, when to use these, and the best time to pull each one out is going to ensure that you find the results that you ant as well.

Chapter 7: Improving Your Parenting with Mental Models

Parenting can be tough. We have to work at raising small children who, even though they rely on us for a lot of things, and need us to care for them and watch out for them, have their own personalities and their own way of viewing the world. They won't share the same thoughts and feelings as us, mainly because they are children and are going to have a different way of viewing the world, and partly because they may have different personalities than us.

In addition to the basics of raising these children, we also have to focus on a lot of other topics. We have to worry about which daycare to use, which school, how to balance family time, work time, and time in activities. We worry about their friends and what they are learning along the way. There is just so much to keep track of and worry about when it comes to being a parent, whether you have one child or many.

Parenting is often seen as one of the most challenging professions in the world. Yet it is not really going to get a ton of attention when it comes to the formal schooling ideas. Because of this, it is found that very few scholars are going to bother to device an appropriate methodology for parenting and even coming up with the best mental models to help parents out.

This doesn't mean that you are stuck without any kind of mental model. We just need to be a bit creative here to find the answers that we need. Thanks to the diversity that comes with social orientations, environments, and cultures it is sometimes hard to find a uniform methodology, and therefore a universal mental model, that is going to be tailored to parenting.

Nonetheless, we can come up with some of the mental models that are already around, and use that in a customizable way to help fit the parenting role across societal orientations, environments, and cultures. We are going to take a look at some of the different mental models that you are able to follow that can help you to make parenting a little bit easier to handle.

Regret Minimization

As a parent, you may find that there are things that you regret. You may regret that you did not spend enough time with the kids during the day. You may regret that you have to run errands rather than hanging out and relaxing. You may even regret the activities that you signed your children up in. but with this mental model, we are going to embrace regret minimization as much as possible.

The first thing to like about the regret minimization mental model is that it is going to help you to reflect on how you would like to see your children being once they turn into adults. As such this can help you to raise them in a manner that will ensure they become responsible adults when they grow up. Regret minimization is also going to work from the side of the children. In what way or manner would you like your children to perceive you once they are grown u? DO you want them to see you as a great parent who went to great lengths to ensure that their childhood as well lived? Or are you fine with them seeing you as not wroth them as a result of the suffering that you inflicted on them due to abuse, neglect, and abandonment?

Of course, most of us want to go with the first option, and regret minimization will help you to learn the best method to use to minimize the regret as much as possible. You can use this to pick the course of action that is going to cause you the least amount of regret. For example, are you going to regret the dishes sitting there a bit longer, or the time you missed out playing with the kids? Yes, you do need to clean the house on occasion, but putting the dishes off until the kids go to bed rather than doing them right now may help you to minimize regret, while getting to spend more time with your kids. There are a lot of things in life that can cause you to regret. You aren't able to avoid all of them, no matter how much you may wish that you were able to do so. But when it comes to being the best parent possible to your child, learning how to limit the regret as much as you can will really make a world of difference to the results that you are able to get. When making any decision regarding your child, don't waste a lot of time thinking through a list of pros and cons. Think about how much regret you will have doing one action over another, or the regret that you will have if you decide not to do the action at all. And then make your decisions based on this in the first place.

Compounding

The next type of mental model that we are going to take a look at is the idea of compounding. Every effort that you put into the process of raising each child is going to compound. Imagine with this one that a little bit of effort spent on your children whether it is helping them with a project, taking them to an activity, making them lunch, or playing with them, is going to have a profound effect on them for the rest of their lives. It doesn't have to be a ton of effort or even a lot of time. Ten minutes spending time with them, rather than viewing your phone and social media, can really add up and compound with this mental model. Your children are going to remember you, and they are more likely to do the same things with their children, and it continues on down the line. All because of the simple actions that you were able to take with them today.

Imagine some of the simple words and terms that you try to teach your baby? Even though you start out small and don't overwhelm them with new information, these simple terms are going to build up into a language that they can use to communicate with those around them. And then they can use these terms to teach their own children and so on.

What you do to your children is going to end up with a compound effect on the entire generation. You can change up this entire generation by simply changing up the way that you bring up your own children. A child who has been raised well is going to become the foundation of a healthy new generation, so keep this in mind. You may sometimes feel that your efforts are in vain and that you are doing a lot of work that is not noticed or appreciated at all. But this is not the case. In fact, just a bit of your time, given over a consistent basis, can make a world of difference in the lives of your children. Take some time to spend with them, rather than overthinking things or worrying about all of the household things you need to get done, and you will find that it can really help you out.

Think of how amazing it is going to be when you can imagine your actions as compounding not just with your children, but with your grandchildren, your great-grandchildren and on down the line! A simple act of spending time with your children, and giving them the love and attention that they need and ant can really compound into the future.

The 10/10/10 rule

The next kind of mental model that we need to be able to focus on is going to be the 10/10/10 rule. This one is going to be based on the idea of foresight. You simply need to ask yourself the following questions below involving the interval of 10. Let's look at the questions:

1. How will I feel about it in ten minutes?
2. How will I feel about this in ten months?
3. How will I feel about this in ten years?

As you can guess, this will work with a lot of different aspects of your life, and not just with child-raising. But it is a good way to really put things in perspective in life and can help you to not sweat the little things, while also enjoying some of the little things along the way as well.

For example, when your kid spills milk on the floor, you can bring in this mental model. Think about how you will feel about this spill in ten minutes. Yes, you may still feel a bit upset about it, and that is fine. But how are you going to feel in ten months? This is probably as far as you are going to need to go with this one because by then, you won't even remember the spill because it was such a small and insignificant part of your life. If it isn't going to matter to you in ten months or ten years then it is something that you can just let go and not worry so much about.

Let's look at this another way. As a parent, you will remember all of those long and sleepless nights, holding the baby and being kept awake. You were tired, and worn out, and thought it would never end. Let's use this principle here. In ten minutes, you're still going to be tired and hoping the baby will go to sleep so you can get some sleep and not feel so tired.

But how about in ten months? Likely the baby will be out of this phase, and while there may be a few times you get up at night, you won't be sitting in the rocking chair and holding them, and you won't be sleepless as much. At this point, you may feel grateful that you get a good nights' sleep and like you are able to parent a little bit better.

But what about in ten years? With this one, the child is probably 10 or 11. They have their own friends, spend their day in school, and have the activities that they like to do on their own. They won't be your little baby anymore, just wanting to snuggle in your arms and have you hold them. At ten years, you may find that you miss the snuggles and the closeness that you once had with your child. This is a good way to keep some of the hard things in parenting in perspective. It helps you to realize that your time as a parent is going to be short. Yes, you will always love them and always be their parent, but being the one responsible for everything for your child is going to come to an end sooner than you know. Keeping these thoughts, and the 10/10/10 rule in mind can help you keep it all in order and keep yourself feeling better about the whole ordeal. This is also a good one to use on some of your own personal development as well because it helps you to put things into perspective and realize all of the good things that you have in your life. Whether you are going to use it in parenting or for your own happiness and personal development (and it can work well with both, to be honest), you will find that the 10/10/10 rule is going to be a great option to use.

The Pareto 80/20 Rule

We talked about the Pareto rule a bit before, but now we are going to look at it from the view of parenting and how we are able to use this for helping us to raise good and smart children along the way. The Pareto 80/20 rule is going to apply to parenting, as it does to a few of the other methods that we have talked about in this guidebook.

This rule is going to talk about how just 20 percent of the efforts of the parent was going to contribute to 80 percent of the lifetime gain of the child, while about 80 percent is going to contribute to only 20 percent of this same kind of gain. Educating a child, especially for a parent who is busy and working, while keeping up with all of the other things that they need to handle, can be one of the least efforts but it is going to contribute to the biggest lifetime gain of your child. Don't count education or school to do this. This can never, and will never, match that kind of education that a parent is able to impart over to their own children. While focusing on education can be important, you want to make sure that you are focusing on a few other options as well. This can include play, a good amount of healthcare (such as taking them to their doctor appointments), and a healthy and balanced diet. They are easily going to fall into the twenty percent effort that can be provided by the parent but they are really going to provide the child with a ton of great benefits.

The Pareto rule advises parents to focus as much of their energy on this 20 percent rather than on things that may seem important, but really are not. This ensures that you are not running around doing a lot of things that don't really matter in the long run, while helping you to give your children the highest lifetime heritage possible.

The Expert Generalist

The final mental model that we are going to take a look at is the expert generalist. If there is any field where being a specialist is a disability to how well you do, then parenting would be it. When it comes to the world of parenting, you have no choice other than learning how to be an expert generalist if you want to be good at everything. As one of these expert generalists, you have to be a bit of everything. Parents are a wonderful mix of a dressmaker, lab technician, psychologist, games coach, security guard, mechanic, teacher, nurse, nutritionist, daycare provider and more. Your child is going to prove to be a big challenge for you in all of these, and it is impossible for you to learn how to be an expert in all of them. This may mean that while your job will demand you to be a specialist to bring home a check being a parent demands that you become a generalist. You don't have to know everything, which can be a great relief to parents trying to do it all. But knowing enough to keep up with the rapidly changing moods, preferences, motion, tastes, and growth of your child can be enough to become a great parent to them.

Parenting is going to be a challenge. Each child is going to be different, and often they have their own minds and want things to go their way, not the way the parent wants. When we add in all of the other obligations and challenges that parents face along the way in trying to raise these children, it can become hard to get things done and make sure that you are being the good and loving parent that you want to be.

This is why mental models can be used here to help make a difference. The mental models that we have talked about in this chapter are meant to help you make the right decisions for you and your children, and to show you that you are more than likely doing a better job with parenting than you had thought!

Chapter 8: Mental Models for Educators and Critical Thinkers

Critical thinkers, psychotherapists, and educators are all going to come with one thing in common, they are going to be actively concerned when it comes to the methodology that is used for knowing, acting, and perceiving. The good news is that even this group of individuals will be able to work with some of the mental models to help them see some of the results that they want in critical thinking and decision making.

Mental Models of Perceiving, Acting, and Knowing

Often, we are going to see things, not really for what they are, but as we are. We are able to create a reality in our minds. And without the mind, we are not going to have any reality. Without the mind, there is not going to be a world, and in essence, there is no view of the world. It is common for a lot of us to confuse the world and the earth. On a larger scale, we are going to confuse the world with the universe. These are different topics, but basically, the world is just going to be a mental model of how we are able to perceive nature, the nature of beings and the nature of things. As such, the world is going to be a kind of mental model on its own.

With that in mind, it is time for us to take a look at some of the different mental models that you are able to use when it comes to working with mental models for critical thinkers and educators.

The Cognitive Bias

This mental model is going to be an error in reasoning that is able to deviate the decision-maker from making any deductions that are rational. To some extent, we will find that the cognitive bias that we have is going to be a completely natural phenomenon. It is simply the way that the brain is going to work. Often it is going to be a very complex process for the brain to work through each and every piece of information that reaches it from all of our senses, from touch, taste, sound, eyes, and more.

This is just too much energy and our mind is not able to give full attention to all of the aspects that are a part of our existence. Because of this, there is going to be some form of cognitive bias to help make sure that the brain knows which information to focus on, and which to avoid. There is just not enough energy or resources in the brain to handle everything, and it would end up driving us all insane in the process to try this, so the cognitive bias helps us to utilize, in the most effective manner possible, the limited amount of resources and energy that are available. Keep in mind here that there are going to be a few kinds of cognitive biases that are not seen as natural. These are going to be created out of a few different things, like misinformation and parental nurturing, schooling, traditional practices, and more. It is unnatural to have these kinds of cognitive biases and if you realize that these are things you are dealing with, then it is something that you do have to confront early on. It is important to note that critical thinking is something that you will not be able to use to the optimal level if you are controlled by this cognitive bias. Yet, it is through the critical thinking process that you will be able to debunk most of these biases in the first place. For this to happen, the mental models will become of primary essence as an external source of reinforcement against your cognitive bias in the first place.

The Socrative Dialogue

The next kind of mental model that we are going to look at is the Socratic dialogue. This is going to be the most commonly applied critical thinking models when you want to go through an intellectual discourse. With this method, instead of directly criticizing someone or telling them, in a blunt manner, that their statement is wrong, and thus pushing the other person to feel attacked and like they need to go on the defensive, you are able to work with the Socratic dialogue in order to ask a set of questions so that the other person, rather than yourself, is going to make the inquiry to themselves. With the help of this self-inquiry, the person will then be able, on their own, to come to their own conclusions, often to the idea that the statement they put up is not factual, and that they have some naked beliefs, assumptions, and fallacies that they need to be able to work on. Since you were able to prompt the person to go through this self-inquiry, rather than pushing them into it and making them defensive, you are assisting the person in actually thinking through things, rather than being lazy and accepting things. When this is able to continue, the person is going to gain the habit of making this kind of inquiry into themselves before they come up with any statements in the future.

Of course, you don't have to use this mental model just on other people. You can use this as a dialogue within. Before you hold onto a position, ask yourself some pertinent questions about this position, as if someone else were holding onto it. This way, you can get rid of the assertions with no basis, the baseless assumptions, the unwarranted beliefs, the cognitive biases, and even some of the matters that may be held in your concept, but which are not actually factual or adding to it. These are the main models that work for those in this kind of category. Some of the others that you can consider if these don't seem like the right ones for you to use include:

1. The Fifth Discipline
2. Abundance Mentality vs. Scarce Mentality
3. Defensive Reasoning
4. Contagion Anxiety
5. Causal Attribution

Chapter 9: Using Mental Models to Help You to Be Happy and In Personal Development

Now that we have had some time to look into some of the different mental models that you are able to work with in other aspects of your life, it is time to take a look at some of the mental models that you can use to increase your happiness and help with personal development. Americans and others throughout the world spend hundreds of dollars, if not more, each year working with personal development classes, training events books, and other options. But instead of doing that, we can simply work with a mental model and change our lives around. It is such a simple idea, and it is likely that these mental models are going to be similar, and just as easy, as the ones that we have already been able to discuss in this guidebook so far.

In the human sphere, it is all going to begin in our own individualism, before things can spread out into relationships between these individuals. Because of this, personal development is going to take a central role when it comes to first improving the individuality of a person, and then spreading out the benefits that come with that improvement to the rest of their relationships with friends and family members.

We have already been able to consider the effects of the FMM AND and the FMM OR mental models earlier in this guidebook. Each of these is important and can be beneficial, as long as they are used to balance one another out. Do not forget these as you work to reach your own personal development. If either of the FMM is out of order or one becomes stronger than the others, this can be a problem. It results in us getting out of control, taking over, using our ideas to influence others in a negative manner, or, on the other side, letting others take full advantage of us in the process.

In this chapter, we are going to take a look at a few more of the mental models that you are able to utilize in your own life to see some great results. These are going to ensure that you are able to reach the happiness that you are looking for, while also promoting your own personal development in the process. So, let's get started!

Mental Models for Personal Development

The Circle of Competence

The first mental model that we are going to take a look at when it comes to being happy and working on your own personal development is the Circle of Competence. You can't have complete knowledge of all the spheres in the world. You can't be skilled and talented in all of the fields and all of the talents out there. it is just impossible so why waste our time and our energy trying?

Because of this, it is important to learn ahead of time what we can do, and who we are! It is important to acknowledge where you are not fit and seek to develop some of the core areas where you are really at your best and where you are able to shine. The Circle of Competence is going to be important when it comes to a lot of different spheres of your life, but specifically when it comes to your career choice, and in developing your career. Choose one or a few areas where you are able to do really well, and outshine others in that field, and then focus on just doing that and showing that off in your job.

This does not mean that you are going to overlook, neglect, or ignore the areas that are on the fringes of your life and where you are not the most competent in. Over time, as you are developing more of your skills you can gradually extend the boundaries of your skills and knowledge so that you can add to your core competence. This way, you will be able to avoid the common disability of being too wide and shallow, or even of being too deep and narrow. But width, as well as depth, are going to be important, so you need to be able to balance these optimally. What is even more important here is that you need to be able to build up a mutually beneficial mastermind alliance with those who are already specialists in your fringes. This helps you to form some new relationships and can cover you in these areas where you are falling a bit, all at the same time and in the process.

Parkinson's Law

The next thing that we need to look at is the Parkinson's Law. This one is often brought up in human resource type positions or personalities, but we are still going to take a moment to look at it here. This mental model can work well with some of the personal development that you may want to do in the process as well, so it is time to take a look at it here.

The greatest challenge that can come with personal development is how you are able to manage your time in a manner so that you can be more effective with it. This helps you get more done in a smaller amount of time while helping to boost up the amount of productivity that you are experiencing on a regular basis. You will find that there are a lot of tools out there that are going to work with this mental model. These tools sometimes work, and sometimes don't, but they are meant to help you really manage your time to get more done in the process. Often the one that you go with is going to depend on your own personal preferences and what works the best to motivate you. Some of the tools that have been devised to help you work with the Parkinson's Law mental model will include the critical path method, time Scheduler, Gantt Charts, To-Do Lists, and the Pomodoro Timer.

The Parkinson's law is not meant to be overly difficult, and you may find that it is easier to work with than you would think. Some of the steps that you can take to make sure you can properly utilize this kind of mental model for your personal development includes:

1.   Take a look at the tasks that you need to do and then break the tasks up into achievable chunks.

2.   Allocate the chunks that you made into a specific completion time.

3.   Schedule performance of each chunk using any or some of the above-mentioned tools and narrowing the time margins between each chunk so that there is some error of safety if needed. You can pick the one that you want to use in terms of methods, but make sure that at least one is in place to help you with this.

4.   Be dedicated and disciplined so that you make sure you stick with the method and the schedule that you have set up and get the work done quickly and efficiently.

Mental Models for Personal Happiness

We just looked at a few of the mental models that you are able to use to help with personal development. Now we are going to take it a bit further and look at some of the mental models that you can use to help reach your own personal happiness including tranquility, joy, peace, and satisfaction.

Happiness is a term that is sometimes hard to define, yet its feeling is such an easy one to express. Because of this, there isn't really going to be a standard that is universal when we look at happiness. Each person, culture, country and more will have their own ideas on happiness and what it entails. Even with this though, we all know what it feels like to be happy. We also have a good idea that happiness is going to be in the mind. There can be two people in similar circumstances, and one is happy and the other is not. This is why having the right mental model in place can help to condition us, and our happiness levels will go through the roof. Just by learning how to condition our minds, we will learn that happiness can be found anywhere and that we don't have to spend time searching for it any longer. There are several mental models that you are able to use that can help you to work on increasing your own personal happiness. Let's take a look at some of these mental models and how they are going to have a direct impact on your own happiness.

Entropy

Entropy is going to be a term that is borrowed from the Second Law of Thermodynamics. To keep it simple, this term is going to state that in a closed system, there is some tendency of the elements that are inside of that system to start moving towards a state of disorder. In our lives, no matter how hard we try and no matter if we give our best efforts or not, there is always going to be a few things that will go wrong. For example, no matter how healthy you try to eat, how much you try to stay active and avoid risks, you will still eventually pass on to the next world. This model is helpful because it is going to help us to understand that at some level you are going to have disorganization. This is something that is inevitable. Some things just occur randomly, that is, we can work to plan out as much as possible, but the unexpected can always sneak back in and ruin all of those best efforts. We can plan for a big party, but someone will get sick someone will be late, or something else will go wrong in the process. In some ways, we can look at the entropy model as the ideas that are found in Murphy's Law. This one talks about "anything that can go wrong, will go wrong!" This may seem a bit pessimistic, and we are not saying that you should always assume that everything is going to fail and crash around you. And you are not meant to use this to surrender yourself to fate. On the contrary, this entropy model is going to state that we need to keep on the process of ordering things, organizing ourselves, and improving ourselves each and every moment to rise above this disorder state, the state of disintegration, and the state of disorganization. For example, you should not stop eating healthy and doing physical exercise just because you are going to die anyway. You shouldn't stop taking care of yourself just because you are going to, at some point, get sick anyway.

You have to try and stay on top of the disorder and enjoy your life anyway. When you choose to do nothing, then the rate of decay and disintegration will end up catching on to you.

Instead of letting this happen, you will learn how to do something so that you are able to rise above some of the processes that are part of nature, at least do this as much as you possibly can.

The Pratfall Effect

The idea of this mental model is that your likeability is going to increase if you aren't seen as perfect all of the time. it is a common adage that perfectionists are hardly able to live a life that is happy. They are going to torment themselves for mistakes that they made. This should not be the case because we have to remember that mistakes, no matter how hard we try to avoid them are going to be a part of our human nature. People will feel bad or embarrassed when they make mistakes or do a blunder. Yet you will find that people like you better when you make these mistakes. According to psychologists, perfectionists are hardly likable at all due to their high standards causing discomfort and fear in many. This often causes them to be shunned, and that is not the right step to happiness.

When you are able to show others, and admit to others, that you are not perfect, people are going to start seeing you as more human, more normal, and more approachable rather than some perfect deity that they don't really want to be around. Thus, to help increase your happiness, you need to let go of your fear of making mistakes. Now, this doesn't mean that you can never make mistakes. In fact, this mental model is going to encourage you to make mistakes and own up to them, because this is what will make you happier. If you do make mistakes, and you will then own up to them, and accept them with grace. Don't be scared to make fun of yourself, poke at yourself, and laugh about mistakes. Overall, this is going to be the push that you need to make yourself more likable, helps you to attract more friends, and feel happier overall.

The Spotlight Effect

You look around and notice that people aren't giving you all that much attention. If this is true, isn't it also true that your mistakes are not being noticed by other people as much as you think? More often than not, we are so focused on our mistakes and some of our weaknesses, that we fail to notice some of the really neat things that we are able to do. We assume that everyone else is noticing these things too, and that makes us anxious and worried and upset overall. The truth is, most people don't even notice. They are so worried about their own mistakes and problems, they are not paying any attention to yours. More often than not, we are going to get consumed by our own weaknesses and faults that we fail to be happy at all. But deep down we have to learn that we are not unhappy because of our faults, but we are feeling unhappy because we think others are noticing our faults, and that they are judging you. The neat thing with this mental model though is that when we start to realize that a lot of people are more preoccupied with their own affairs and personal challenges and they don't have much focus left to pay attention to your own faults and defects. It is likely that they don't even notice these things. When you realize that the only person catching on to these mistakes and faults, and no one else even sees them, your life is going to become so much happier. The idea here is that we need to stop putting these imaginary spotlights into the hands of other people and then having these spotlights point back at us. It is time to just realize that we make mistakes, and it doesn't really matter if other people see them or not.

Pygmalion Effect

The idea with this mental model is that greater expectations are going to drive greater performance. Thus, to make sure that you are able to experience a greater performance like we want to see in our personal life, then we need to set expectations that are higher. Think of your expectations like the ceiling. Yes, you can't jump higher than the ceiling that you set up. But you can definitely choose the location of the ceiling.

The Pygmalion Effect is going to be the opposite of the Golem Effect. When we look at the Golem Effect, lower expectations lead to lower performance. They are similar ideas, just worked in a different manner. Psychologists assert that there is going to be a positive feedback loop between behavior and belief. If you believe you can achieve, then you will find that you can automatically gain the necessary resources and efforts towards achieving that target.

Maslow's Hierarchy of Needs

It is likely that you have heard about this particular idea, but may be curious as to how this is going to play into helping us to feel happier. Let's take a look at how this is supposed to work. Abraham Maslow is a famous psychologist who came up with what is known as Maslow's Hierarchy of Needs. When we look at this model, all of our needs are going to be grouped into three categories that are pretty broad. These include:

1. Our basic needs
2. Or psychological needs
3. Or self-fulfillment needs

Our basic needs are going to be the needs that we have in order to survive. These can be divided up into two main sub-categories to show us how they work together. The basic needs that are a part of Maslow's Hierarchy of needs will include:

1. Safety needs. These are going to be the needs necessary for one to feel secure. It could be something like protection against enemies and wild animals.

2. Physiological needs: These are going to be our needs for survival including shelter, clothing, food, water, and air.

Once we have been able to meet these needs, then it is time to move on to the psychological needs. You will not be able to meet this second group of needs unless the basic needs are met first. The two main sub-categories that help us to understand the psychological needs include:

1. Esteem needs: This is going to refer to meeting the need to feel having accomplished and achieved a great milestone in some part of our lives. It can be at work, with a goal, at school, and more.

2. Belongingness needs: These are going to include some of the social relationship needs that we have. It may include things like a need for friendship, a need for family, and more.

The self-fulfillment needs are going to be the ones that we are required to have in order to feel like we have reached our highest level of actualization. These can help us to feel happy and content with the life that we have. However, keep in mind that you are not able to reach these needs until the others have been met. This means that you can't reach the highest level of actualization if you haven't been able to meet your need for safety and for food for example, or your need to belong. While there has been some criticism that comes with the Maslow hierarchy of needs, it is a helpful tool to address our complex needs as humans. Whether you agree with it or not, it helps to break down our needs and explains why we may act in one way or another, and how each individual could be in a different section of this mental model to start with. This mental model is going to remind us to have a balanced approach to cater to the needs that we have, without accidentally (and sometimes on purpose), alienating and neglecting some. For example, while you strive to reach your basic needs, it is important to not let the other two groups of needs fall to the side and get ignored either. When of the things that makes this hierarchy so debatable with some is the way that it is going to order out the needs and pick which one is the most important. It is generally believed on this model that you have to reach your basic needs before you can start working on the psychological needs, and that you have to reach this second group of needs before you can achieve your psychological needs.

There are some who believe that this can slow us down and will prevent us from reaching our goals. Our psychological needs are no higher than our basic needs and our self-fulfillment needs are not higher than our psychological needs. These are all needs that we can pursue in any order that we want, and even at the same time. You have to decide which method of attack you would like to use to make these work. Reaching your own level of happiness and working on self-esteem and other parts of personal development can help out in so many aspects of your life. The mental models that we have discussed in this chapter are going to help you to finally take care of yourself, and reach the level of happiness and contentment that you really deserve.

Chapter 10: Case Studies of Mental Models That Actually Worked!

In this part of our guidebook, we are going to take some time to look at a few successful applications of these mental models, and some of the ways that these can be applied. We are going to take a look at some of the modern and the ancient cases of using these mental models to help leaders and more learn a new way of thinking and get themselves ahead.

The Modern Polymath

The first examples that we are going to take a look at are the modern polymath. When we look at modern conventional wisdom it is going to dictate that the specialization is the best path to take. But despite some of the negative arguments that are out there to the contrary, there are going to be those who decide that they should bear the opportunity cost of acting in an unconventional manner.

While this may not make sense to everyone, those who are considered modern polymaths are going to be a kind of jack of all trades. they want to learn as much about as many different topics as possible, learn on the go, and figure out how to get ahead in different spheres. And it has really worked out well for them. Some examples of successful individuals who are modern polymaths and jack of all trades include:

Charlie Munger

The first example that we are going to take a look at is Charlie Munger. He is known as an expert generalist. He has read widely and channeled the lessons that he learned towards his business empire, an empire that he co-founded with Warren Buffet.

Munger is the brainchild behind the latticework that comes with these mental models. Berkshire Hathaway Inc is known as an international investment company that is going to make sure that all of the investments they do on behalf of premium capitalists. Being widely learned in fields that are not necessarily going to be related back to finance and investment has been helpful because it allows Munger to navigate the company's investment decisions, no matter what environment they are in.

As an international investor, it is important to know that you can't really understand the investment climate that is going on in different jurisdictions and in different parts of the world without understanding some of the basic cultures that are found there. this means that you need to know a bit more than just their money and investments.

It is important for you to learn more about their world view, culture, and perspectives when it comes to savings and investment. And this is exactly what Charlie Munger did with his mental model of being an expert generalist.

Elon Musk

The next person that we are going to take a look at is Elon Musk. He is a well-known founder of many different enterprises that are well-known throughout the world. Some have taken off well, and others may not be as well-known, but allowed him to get things done and learn from the experience. Some of the enterprises that Elon Musk is known about includes:

1. Tesla Motors: This is a company that makes high-end tech cars, including driverless cars and electric cars.

2. SolarCity: This is a company that focuses on energy conservation.

3. SpaceX: This is a company for launching space vehicles and space travel.

4. Zip2: This is an online content management company.

5. X.com: This is going to be an online financial management company.

6. Confinity: This is a type of merger that went on with X.com and was then able to build the well-known PayPal that we know and use today.

As you can see with these different business ventures, Elon Musk has been able to voyage across a lot of diverse fields that are not really related to one another. This goes from finance to internet, from automobiles, aeronautics, and everything that is in between. He is a typical example of what is known as a modern polymath. Where would he be now if we did not try to broaden out and work with a lot of different options, and instead chose to work with just internet service technology?

Jack Ma

Jack Ma started out as an English teacher but is more known today as the founder of Alibaba. Like Larry Page, he has anchored the foundation that is his using on academics before he started to work on his own internet business. Alibaba, for those who do not know, is a big e-commerce giant that is going to be similar to Amazon in the eastern hemisphere. Some of the other enterprises that Jack Ma has been able to work on includes:

Alipay: This is a payment platform that is based on the idea of escrow.

AliExpress: This is going to be an online retail giant that allows a business to sell their products to a final consumer, no matter where they are located around the world.

Tmall: This is another example of an e-commerce enterprise, but it is going to be focused more on speakers of Chinese that are found in areas like China, Taiwan, and Hong Kong.

Think about what would have happened if Ma decided to just become a specialist and work with being an English teacher, rather than taking some of his interests to the rest of the world. We would not be able to use the multibillion-dollar enterprise known as Alibaba. And it is true that Jack Ma would not be an international personal brand either.

Jeff Bezos

The final name that we are going to take a look at here in this part of the guidebook is Jeff Bezos. He is mostly known for the venture of his known as Amazon. Although Jeff spent his time studying electronics and computer sciences, he started off working in the sector of finances. He then decided to quit his lucrative job in order to start what was originally an online bookstore, called Amazon.com.

Of course, Amazon became so much more than just an online store to buy books. Amazon has had time to diversify so much beyond books including software, gadgets, and even infrastructures. Just like what we were able to see with Larry Page and Jack Ma, but a bit different than Elon Musk, most of Bezos enterprises are going to bear the brand name of Amazon. Some of these are going to be enterprises that are big enough that they could work on their own, some are products. Some of the different enterprises and products that have become well-known within the world due to Amazon's presence includes:

1. Cloud computing
2. IoT

3. Kindle Digital Publishing: A well-known eBook publishing company
4. The platform for Amazon.com
5. The mental models that these individuals used

Now that we have had some time to look at a few well-known jack of all trades and what they have been able to do with their researching and their work, it is time to take a look at the three mental models that they used in order to get the results that they did. The three mental models that we are able to identify when we look at the names above include:

1. The 5-hour rule
2. The expert generalist
3. The T mental model

First is the T Mental model. This is given its name from the letter T. The ideas that come from this is that someone is going to acquire their knowledge in a horizontal manner, across a diverse number of fields. Then that knowledge is going to be funneled vertically down towards a given core area of specialization. This means that they are going to have one general idea that they want to be a specialist in, but then they will work on a lot of different topics and information to learn as much about that topic as possible.

Next is going to be the Expert generalist. These people are going to be the ones that know a little bit about a lot of topics, rather than a lot about a few topics. This is the natural course that shows up when the entrepreneurs from above work with the T Mental model from before.

And the third option is going to be the five-hour rule. This one is the idea that you should study for five hours a day. most of the expert generalists, as well as the polymaths, are big readers. However, they make sure that they are not reading in a narrow manner. Instead, they are going to read in a wider manner, going over a lot of different disciplines and fields. Most likely, it is this reading habit that can help them become polymaths.

Almost all of the people who fit into this kind of category are going to be ardent readers, and sometimes they would read for more than the five hours that this rule talks about. No matter the case, they not only find time to do the reading, but they are busy people. This means there may be some days when they miss out on the reading, but they still manage to average it out through the week to help them learn as much as possible.

The Big Dreams Garage

The next type of group that we are going to take a look at is the Big Dreams Garage. This one is all about startups that began in the backyard garage. This could be a real garage, a car boot, a college dorm, a sitting room couch, a bedroom, or somewhere else that is small and that you would not expect a business to start out, much less see success. It is basically going to be some kind of unconventional space for a business. Even some startups were able to establish themselves from a food café or something similar.

This is going to be a type of mental model is all about utilizing the free space that is available to start up your venture. First off, it can be cost-efficient because you do not have to worry about paying business rent to a startup. You just need to have a little space. This one is all about the sheer passion that comes from doing this whole process, rather than the sophisticated space from where you started the business. Some examples of people who fit into the Big Dreams Garage mental model will include:

Steve Jobs

At just 20 years old, Jobs was able to start up the company known as Apple with his friend Wozniak. This company was started in the basement of Job's parent's garage. To get the capital that was needed to start this venture, the $1350, Jobs sold off his Volkswagen microbus and then Wozniak sold his Hewlett-Packard calculator. During this time, Steve Jobs also dropped out of college to pursue the dream venture that was his at the time. And today, Apple is a company that is known all around the world.

Bill Gates

Staying along with the same idea with this one, we are going to move over to the start of Bill Gates and the Microsoft company. Bill Gates, with the help of his college friend Paul Allen, saw an advertisement in the magazine known as Popular Electronics. This advertising was looking for someone who could work with the Altair 8800 programming language.

Bill Gates and Paul Allen saw this as a really big opportunity for them to get ahead, and they decided to go straight for it. At this time, Gates dropped out of Harvard University to pursue his dream venture. It was a matter of the urgency of now. This shows us that if something is not that urgent, and it is not so pressing to you, then it is time to just kick it out and not pay any attention to it any longer.

Richard Branson

The next person that we are going to take a look at with this kind of mental model is going to be Richard Branson. Branson started from the streets, as a kid hawker who sold Christmas trees. Eventually, though, he rose up and established a magazine business from the Churchyard. Branson is the most famous for his enterprise brand, known as Virgin Group. Under this enterprise, there are a few different options including:

1. Virgin Atlantic: This is an airline company

2. Virgin Galactica: This is a space technology company

3. Virgin Records: This is a well-known record production company.

Just like what we saw with Elon Musk, Branson's Virgin Group was able to break out of its core and cut across a lot of diverse fields in the process. At this point, Branson owns almost 400 companies under this umbrella group, and not all of them are going to be in the same field either.

Chapter 11: A Mastermind Alliance

The next topic that we need to take a look at is going to be the mastermind alliance. This is going to be based on the master-master relationship. This is a type of alliance between independent, yet mutually interdependent persons with the aim of them all pulling together and consolidating their respective mental resources so that they are all able to meet their own goals.

The world is going to have a lot of examples out there of the master to servant relationships. This is often going to result in subjugation and domination, along with some level of exploitation of the vulnerable party in that relationship. Those who have instead chosen to go with the mastermind alliance are going to be rare and few overall. Probably, this deliberate scarcity of the mastermind alliances is out of the desire of most humans to either rule or be the one who is ruled over in the relationship.

While it is possible to have these mastermind alliances in a lot of different spheres, including in technology, science, education, religion, and politics, one of the most unique mastermind alliances that we are able to take a look at are going to show up in the sphere of entrepreneurial startups that can cut across a lot of diverse fields.

Looking a bit closer at some entrepreneurial startups, some of the ones that are the most successful in the world right now are going to be the ones driven by a unique mastermind alliance, one that is made up of passion mates. Not passion in terms of them being in a romantic relationship, but the passion in terms of pursuing a certain adventure. We are going to take a look at some of the examples out there when it comes to these mastermind alliances that are created out of the passionate entrepreneurial adventures.

The Importance of Having This Passion Mate

If you are young and you already know of a close friend of yours who would share a passion for a specific skill, know that you have not just found yourself a soul mate, but also a mind mate, a master mate, and someone who can be your passion mate. Some examples of these that we have seen throughout time include:

1. Zuckerberg and Eduardo Saverin
2. Larry Page and Sergey Bring
3. Bill Gates and Paul Allen
4. Steve Jobs and Steve Wozniak
5. Warren Buffet and Charlie Munger

Nonetheless, remember that it is never too late in the process to learn how to catch up to all of this. The earlier is the better because the biggest problem with this is that when you start a family, get married, and more, then things change, priorities shift, and it is harder to get the results that you want. Pursuing your passion can be lonely if you are trying to do it all on your own, and if you don't have someone close to you to share all of this with. Chinese proverbs often say that "if you want to walk fast, walk alone. But if you want to walk far, walk with others." A passion mate can help you to walk that far, and even further than you would imagine from before.

The Importance of Forming One of These Alliances

A mastermind alliance is not just going to be about sharing thoughts and other information for the startup. It is going to be a fusion of the minds. It is going to be a dissolution of your separate minds so it becomes one common mind. Very few startups that began with just one person running them were able to walk that far, even though they were able to start with a bit more speed than others.

Yes, there is a reason to have some of these sprints, but there is also a reason that there are marathons around. A sprinter is hardly going to fit into the marathon, and the marathoner is hardly going to be able to fit in with the sprinter because they are each created in a different manner. This means that in the beginning, you have to be able to ask yourself if you are a marathoner or a sprinter. The answer that you get to this question is going to help you know where to start.

The Mastermind Mental Model

Now that we have had some time to talk about what the mastermind alliance is all about, it is time to work with the mental model and see how this is all going to come together. Think of it this way, did it just occur to these groupings to come together and form a pair to start a business? Even friends can be mean with each other when it comes to core mind investments. While you would think that this process would make things a bit easier, there are some times when things don't go the way that we want, and in some cases, friends will keep close secrets from one another.

Even these people and group pairings that we have talked about in this guidebook didn't have just one friend to work with. They had several. So, why didn't each go alone? As we all know, and as we can see from the tone of this book, it all begins in the mind. To embrace one of these passion mates towards an endeavor that is skillful and successful is going to be a matter of having a unique mind craft. Your goal here is to seek out a passionate peer who has a similar mind. You know, whether this is consciously or not, that you are not able to capture this heavily potential moment all on your own. And any further delay means that the heavy expectancy is going to be delivered beyond you, by someone else. So, if you come to the ultimate conclusion that you are going to need someone to lend you a helping hand along the way, you have to make sure that you don't end up missing out on this opportunity or feeling overwhelmed in the process.

Chapter 12: Shifting Your Paradigm to Work with Mental Models

At this point, we have spent a good deal of time looking at these mental models and some of the great things that you are able to do with them. But it is important for you to work with these in order to improve your life and make sure that you are able to make good decisions and see some results in no time. But for some people, changing their old habits and moving over to using these mental models, and understanding how they work, can be a challenge.

In this chapter, we are going to explore the option of paradigm-shifting. This is going to be a radical and irreversible shifting to a new way of thinking and doing things. Why would we want to embrace this kind of shifting when it seems so strong and hard to do?

There are actually a few different reasons that can make it so important to embrace this kind of paradigm-shifting. One of the main reasons is that as great as any model really is, we have to remember that it is never going to be perfect. Because of this, a model is going to be just the best-fit depiction of reality. But the reality that we are in, and that we see, is never going to be perfect and it is always changing.

Reality, just like our clouds, is going to shift and change over time. Reality is in a constant state of motion, even though it is true that our focus is going to stagnate, and keep changing each and every moment. Hence, a model that was once a best-fit depiction of a specific reality will soon no longer be a best-fit when the reality ends up changing or ceases to be completely.

While a fixed mindset model is going to hold to a certain mental model as being the absolute (such as seeing it as the only good one, seeing it as the answer to everything, and turning to it in each scenario), a growth mindset is going to hold that a certain given model is going to be like a pair of oars that will enable it to navigate from one end of the shore over to the next.

With this analogy, we see that a fixed mindset is going to hold tightly onto the water as its end, and this could risk some drowning when we are swimming. But when we focus our attention on more of a growth mindset, we know that the water is a medium that can help us to travel from one end to the next.

Any time that you are working with these mental models, we have to remember that working with a fixed mindset is not always going to be a good thing. It is going to provide us with a really limited relevant range beyond which it becomes not just obsolete, but it could become a burden that is dangerous to stick with. Changing over to some growth mindsets could be the answer that you need to open up to these mental models, and actually get them to work for you.

A fixed mindset is going to limit us. It is going to see that a mental model is going to be the one and ultimate solution, or an end in itself. On the other hand, a growth mindset is going to see that these mental models are not absolute, but they can be a great tool to work on. This allows for the potential to craft up some new solutions along the way.

The fatality of having to look at these mental models just as a solution is that we end up clinging to the old tools that are no longer effective or efficient. Imagine that you stick to the tools that were used by the Homo Habilis in order to do food processing and farming. It is either that the evolution clock stops, or the species is going to become extinct, and we certainly don't want to see the latter as part of our destiny.

When we learn how to see some of these mental models as tools, we find that it is easier to understand that they are not just going to be a solution in themselves, but they become a means that we can use to reach our solution. Just as a pair of oars are not going to be our hands, and they are not our destiny, but they can be our means of reaching our destiny.

Believing is not always a bad thing. However, there are going to be certain beliefs that are more negative that end up being limiting or destructive to us. The most important thing to remember and understand here is the nature of the belief. A belief no matter if it is positive or negative is going to emanate from a lack of knowledge. It is more of a placeholder than anything else. As soon as you are able to find the right content to fill in this void, then it is unnecessary to have that placeholder any longer.

For example, at one point or another in history, some people thought that the world had to be flat. But, when the knowledge came out that the world is a sphere instead, the belief died its natural death. In the past, the idea that the earth was flat was a very simple placeholder for the lack of knowledge that people of that time had when it came to the true shape of the earth.

Thus, a belief is going to exist in the absence of knowledge. Where there is absolute knowledge, there will no longer be any beliefs in the process. A belief is just the natural mental way of the human mind to try and free up some of its energy from the anxiety that it gets from not knowing. Yet, a belief, if strongly held, is able to yield some complacency, and this is going to hinder some of the discovery and exploration that needs to happen. In this regard, you need to make sure that you don't hold yourself a slave to beliefs. You need to be able to seek to understand their true nature and free yourself from their binding attachment. I believe not because I hold the belief to be true, but because I haven't found the truth yet.

Like beliefs that are no longer relevant when you receive some new knowledge, the old mental models that no longer fit into the modern world need to be left alone to die in the old ways.

We have to learn how to think of these mental models as a kind of tool that will help us to think better, and even to make some better decisions. But we have to understand that as tools, they can be changed, and they don't have to be used forever in the same manner. When we find better tools, or newer tools that work for us, it is not necessary to hold onto the tools that no longer serve the purpose that you need.

Letting go can be really hard for a lot of people. They like the mental model that they have. They may think that this mental model is the best one for them, and they won't need to change. And letting go of it is not going to work well for them. But being more flexible in the process, and learning when to use a tool, and when it is time to let it go, is going to make sure that you get the most out of these mental models.

Conclusion

Thank for making it through to the end of *Mental Models*, let's hope it was informative and able to provide you with all of the tools you need to achieve your goals whatever they may be. The next step is to get started with using some of these mental models for our own needs. There are so many different types of mental models, and we tried to go through some of the most effective ones, the ones that will help you to make decisions, manage your time, and actually get things done. When you have the system in place that the mental model is able to provide to you, you will find that it is so much easier to get the results that you want. Your mind is now more free to think creatively, rather than focusing on things that are not all that important to you.

This guidebook took some time to look at the different mental models that are available to you. We discussed what these mental models are all about, some of the best mental models that can work for you, and the mental models and how they work with different situations in your life. This can help us to see all of the different things that come with them and will ensure that we are also using them in the right situations. When you are ready to start freeing up your mind and seeing results with using these mental models for yourself, make sure to check out this guidebook to help you get started.

STOICISM

The Manual of Ancient Stoic Philosophy as a Way of Modern Life - A Beginner's Guide to Develop Mindset Through Critical Thinking and Self-Discipline, and to Increase Your Wisdom Daily

Introduction to Stoicism

"True happiness is to enjoy the present, without anxious dependence upon the future, not to amuse ourselves with either hopes or fears but to rest satisfied with what we have, which is sufficient, for he that is so, wants nothing."

- Seneca

The following chapters will discuss the ancient philosophy of Stoicism, which is making a major comeback in the modern world. The philosophy that once guided emperors now helps CEOs, professional coaches, generals, and other leaders. The self-disciplined Stoic way of life is ideal for anyone who wants to overcome difficult or impossible situations and turn problems into advantages. Since ancient times, Stoicism has offered something unique and valuable: the secret to genuine and lasting happiness. The Stoic can meet all of life's ups and downs with untroubled serenity, secure in the knowledge of what truly matters.

This book will tell you everything you need to know about the history of Stoicism and the great Stoic thinkers Epictetus, Seneca, and Marcus Aurelius, as well as the core ideas of Stoicism, the Stoic approach to critical thinking and pragmatism, Stoic methods for building self-discipline and resilience, and methods for handling emotional turmoil with Stoic meditations. It will also tell you how history's greatest leaders and innovators have applied the wisdom of Stoicism and how modern psychology has adopted Stoic principles, with techniques and practices you can apply in your daily life. The book concludes with the advice of the Roman emperor and Stoic Marcus Aurelius on the leadership mindset.

Chapter 1: The Story of Stoicism

"Be like a rocky promontory against which the restless surf continually pounds; it stands fast while the churning sea is lulled to sleep at its feet."

– Marcus Aurelius

Stoicism is an ancient philosophy and way of life, founded by a man named Zeno of Citium about 2300 years ago. Even though Stoicism is a school of philosophy, it's very different from most of the philosophies you may be familiar with. The Stoics are not remembered for abstract debates or complex theories. Their main focus was on how to live and how to be happy.

In fact, Stoicism claims to hold the secret to happiness. The Stoic approach is counterintuitive, but many people have found it to be both compelling and effective. For thousands of years now, people have been using the insights of the great Stoic philosophers to live better lives. You can do the same by adopting the simple and practical Stoic mindset in your own life. Let's start by finding out more about the history of this remarkable philosophy, which has been guiding leaders and comforting the troubled for more than two millennia.

Socrates

The story of Stoicism begins with Socrates, the most famous and influential of all the ancient philosophers. Socrates himself didn't write any books. He was mostly remembered for having asked penetrating questions about everyday topics. Unfortunately for the philosopher, some people interpreted his persistent questioning as a deliberate attack on traditional values. Socrates was arrested and charged with corrupting the minds of his young students. Condemned to death in 399 BC, Socrates refused to flee the city and faced his execution with calm courage that amazed and impressed even his most bitter critics.

The students of Socrates took up his mantle, including the almost equally influential Plato. Most of what we know about Socrates comes from Plato's writings, including the somewhat extreme idea that virtue is the only real good there is. Socrates seems to have been deeply concerned with the question of what is good, and he often questioned his fellow Athenians about their opinions on the topic. The commonplace answers failed to satisfy him, and Socrates continued to probe the question throughout his life. Eventually, he concluded that our own ethical choices are the key to happiness.

In Plato's *Euthydemus*, Socrates teaches that nothing is truly good or bad except for human actions. The four "cardinal virtues" of wisdom, justice, temperance, and courage are genuinely good, but the random events of human life are neither good nor bad. By refusing to flee when he was condemned to death, Socrates set a powerful example of moral strength that influenced many of the philosophers who came after him.

The Cynics

Socrates's most famous student was certainly Plato, but Plato's mystical tendencies did not appeal to all his fellow disciples. Antisthenes was another student of Socrates who founded an extreme philosophy known as Cynicism, based on the idea that people should reject all social norms and live lives of absolute minimalism, focused exclusively on virtue.

Antisthenes and his followers earned the nickname of "dogs" (ancient Greek *kynikos*) because they lived outside, giving up all material possessions. The most famous Cynic philosopher—a man named Diogenes—lived in a tub in the streets of Athens. When the conqueror Alexander the Great came to visit the famous wise man, the only thing Diogenes would say to him was, "you're blocking my light!"

Cynics like Diogenes considered virtue the only good and rejected everything, from marriage to politics, as useless distractions from the ultimate goal.

Their fellow Greeks found the Cynics both fascinating and shocking at the same time, and they told many anecdotes about the outrageous behavior of Cynics like Diogenes. In one of these tales, Diogenes throws away his only possession—a simple cup—after seeing a child drink water with his bare hands.

Diogenes often acted with startling fearlessness toward the rich and powerful. (Our modern word "cynic" was inspired by his constant sarcastic comments toward the normal citizens of Athens.) Sold into slavery after being captured by pirates, Diogenes was asked what kind of work he could do. "I'm good at leading men," the philosopher replied. "That man over there looks like he needs a leader, sell me to him." With this bold reply, Diogenes secured himself a comfortable position as tutor to a rich man's children.

The Cynics were totally committed to their extreme philosophy, and the best of them did seem to be happier and freer than the average person. However, not many people would be capable of giving up everything and becoming homeless in the pursuit of happiness. Stoicism began with Zeno of Citium, a student of Cynicism who thought the original Cynic teachings went too far.

Zeno of Citium

In Zeno's opinion, the Cynics were right to say that virtue was the only real good. However, he didn't think most people would be able to live the Cynic lifestyle, and he didn't think extreme minimalism was really necessary for either virtue or happiness. By rejecting family, property, and any participation in normal society, the Cynics were treating these things as if they were bad.

The original teaching of Socrates was not that such things are bad, only that they aren't genuinely good. If something is neither good nor bad, then it must be indifferent, and that's exactly what Zeno began to teach. At a marketplace in Athens, known as the "Painted Porch" (*Stoa Poikile*), Zeno taught his students that the secret to happiness was to consider most things to be indifferent but not necessarily to give them up completely like the extremist Cynics.

For example, a follower of Zeno might happen to get married, inherit wealth, or become a political leader. Unlike a Cynic, he wouldn't be expected to reject these opportunities, but he would still be expected to remain indifferent to them, treating them as fundamentally unimportant compared to living a life of wisdom, justice, temperance, and courage.

Because Zeno and his followers met and discussed their ideas at the Painted Porch, they became known as the "Porch" school or "Stoa." Followers of the Stoa were known as Stoics.

Chryssipus

After Zeno died, the second leader of the Stoa was a man named Cleanthes. Cleanthes was succeeded in about 230 BC by the philosopher Chryssipus, who was, for many centuries, the most famous and influential of all the Stoics.

Unlike the later Stoics, such as Epictetus, Chryssipus was interested in many aspects of philosophy other than ethics. Where Epictetus and Marcus Aurelius would write mostly about how to live a good life, Chryssipus developed his own system of logic, his theories about religion and the nature of the universe, and so on.

For example, Stoic logic that was developed by Chryssipus included five types of argument:

If A, then B. A. Therefore, B.

Example: If anyone can be happy without getting married, then marriage is not needed for happiness. Some people are happy without getting married. Therefore, marriage is not needed for happiness.

If A, then B. Not B. Therefore, not A.

Example: If wealth is needed for happiness, all poor people will be unhappy. Not all poor people are unhappy. Therefore, wealth is not needed for happiness.

Not both A and B. A. Therefore, not B.

Example: It cannot be simultaneously true that unhealthy people can be happy and that health is necessary for happiness. Unhealthy people can be happy. Therefore, health is not necessary for happiness.

Either A or B. A. Therefore, not B.

Example: Either power is unnecessary for happiness, or it is necessary. Some people are happy without power. Therefore, power is not necessary for happiness.

Either A or B. Not A. Therefore, B.

Example: Either a good reputation is needed for happiness, or a good reputation is not needed for happiness. Some people are happy without a good reputation. Therefore, a good reputation is not needed for happiness.

As you can see, Stoic logic can be used to produce ethical arguments. These arguments would become the centerpiece of Stoic philosophy.

Seneca

The original Stoa was centered in Athens, but growing Roman influence over Greece eventually resulted in a Stoic diaspora. Stoic teachers left Athens and scattered all over the territories of the Roman Republic until the original Stoa in Athens faded from history.

Stoicism was a popular philosophy among the stern and self-disciplined Roman elite, especially to those like Cato the Younger, who resisted the rise of the dictator Julius Caesar. Cato committed suicide rather than accept Caesar's rule—one of several events that made Stoicism a suspect philosophy in the eyes of some Roman rulers. After all, Stoics taught that virtue was the only *real good*, and that's not a stance any Caesar follower was likely to approve.

After the Roman Republic became the Roman Empire under Caesar Augustus, Stoicism's place in Roman life was somewhat precarious. The Stoic teacher Seneca was sent into exile by the emperor Claudius in 41 AD, only to become the chief advisor to the emperor Nero in 54 AD. When the cruel and corrupt Nero suspected Seneca of joining a plot to assassinate him, he ordered the Stoic teacher to commit suicide. In keeping with Stoic principles, Seneca faced his death with self-disciplined courage.

Seneca is most remembered today for his Epistles or letters to his friend and student Lucilius. It included 124 essays on issues, such as how to face the fear of death or deal with minor daily irritations like excessive noise. He is also believed to be the first ancient writer to question the morality of the Gladiatorial games openly. Seneca is somewhat controversial for his role in Nero's government, but it is generally agreed that he did his best to provide a stabilizing influence before the tyrant turned on him.

Epictetus

Unlike the wealthy and politically connected Seneca, the great Stoic Epictetus came from the lowest levels of Roman society. Born in 55 AD, the future philosopher was a slave to Nero's secretary Epaphroditus. Even his name refers to the fact that he was a slave: Epictetus means "something acquired."

Despite his status as a slave, Epictetus was able to study under the Stoic teacher Musonius Rufus, who taught a simple and pragmatic version of Stoicism that emphasized practical questions of daily life rather than the other topics that had fascinated Chryssipus. When Epictetus began to teach, he kept the same focus on practical issues.

Freed by Epaphroditus, Epictetus was forced to go into exile when the emperor Domitian decided to persecute the Stoics. During his exile in Greece, Epictetus taught his wealthy students how to make better decisions and live better lives, often referring to them sarcastically as "slaves" because of their inability to control their own emotions.

Epictetus never wrote a book of his own, but his student Arrian took extensive notes in class and later published these as a series of books: the four-volume *Discourses* and the *Enchiridion* or "Handbook." These books proved to be hugely popular and influential, to the extent that people interested in Stoicism would study Epictetus rather than earlier Stoic works by Zeno or Chryssipus. As a result, none of the works of these early Stoics have been preserved.

It's not that Epictetus taught anything the earlier Stoics would have disagreed with, but he focused exclusively on practical advice and left the speculations to other philosophers. Most readers preferred the simple and practical life advice of Epictetus to abstract ideas about the universe, and that's what Stoicism is now remembered for. Stoic logic and Stoic physics are now known only to professors of philosophy, but the Stoic way of life has continued to guide and inspire people for thousands of years.

Stoics vs. Epicureans

The Stoics were rivals of the Epicureans, a school that believed pleasure to be the only good and pain the only evil. To the self-disciplined Stoics, this teaching must have seemed like amoral and self-serving hedonism. In reality, Epicurus taught a much more balanced way of life than his basic doctrine might suggest.

Although Epicurus believed that pleasure was the only good, he acknowledged that many pleasures lead to pain later. For example, the pleasure of eating sugary or fatty food can lead to the pain of tooth decay or other health problems. The pleasure of sex can lead to the pain of broken relationships or venereal diseases. Any pleasure to be gained from antisocial or criminal behavior would be tainted by the pain of anxiety about possible consequences.

To avoid the pain that can come from pleasure, Epicurus taught a simple and dignified lifestyle based on enjoying good food and conversation in moderation with a handful of chosen friends. Epictetus himself could hardly have objected to this sort of life, as Stoics consider friends, good food, and conversation to be pleasant things despite being "indifferent."

Despite the inoffensive nature of the Epicurean lifestyle, Epictetus often attacked the doctrine in his lectures. If pleasure is the only real good, and pain is the only real evil, then the Stoic approach to happiness has no foundation. Because he believed from his own experience as a slave that happiness has nothing to do with pleasure or pain, Epictetus did everything he could to defeat the arguments of the Epicureans. The irony of the dispute between the two schools is that they advocated similar lifestyles for completely opposite reasons.

Marcus Aurelius

Stoicism helped Epictetus endure the sufferings of a slave, but it also helped Marcus Aurelius endure the very different problems of a Roman emperor. Adopted by his uncle Antoninus Pius, Marcus became the heir to the throne when his uncle was declared emperor in 138 AD.

Although emperors, such as Vespasian and Domitian, had suppressed the philosophers, Antoninus Pius provided financial support for teachers of philosophy. His heir Marcus Aurelius was deeply affected by his study of Stoicism, and he drew comfort from the philosophy when he became emperor in 161.

During Marcus's reign, the Roman Empire faced a series of wars with Germanic tribes, such as the Marcomanni and the Quadi, as well as the Sarmatians, the Parthian Empire, and the Kingdom of Armenia. With so many enemies, the emperor was away from home on a campaign for years at a stretch, traveling with the army rather than governing from Rome.

From an army camp in the land of the Quadi, Marcus Aurelius began to keep a kind of diary, encouraging himself to face the challenges of war and leadership with a Stoic mindset. The tone of this diary is highly personal, and the emperor does not seem to have intended for other people to read it ever. Many passages are simple reminders not to get irritated with other people or not to fear death, a bad reputation, or poor health:

"What if someone despises me? Let me see to it. But I will see to it that I won't be found doing or saying anything contemptible. What if someone hates me? Let me see to that. But I will see to it that I'm kind and good-natured to all and prepared to show even the hater where they went wrong—not in a critical way or show off my patience but genuinely and usefully."

A real "philosopher king," Marcus Aurelius seems to have made every effort to govern the Roman Empire with justice and wisdom.

The diary was more of a spiritual exercise than a work of philosophy, but someone preserved it and passed it down under the name *Meditations*, and it is now at least as influential as the works of Epictetus. Despite the earlier fame of the men who founded and led the original Stoa, the much later and more personal works of the emperor and the slave now define Stoicism for most people.

Stoic Revivals

The influence of Stoicism eventually declined, but Stoic ideas were absorbed into later philosophies such as Neoplatonism. The Roman Empire turned away from pagan philosophy to embrace the new religion of Christianity, and the center of the empire switched from Rome to Byzantium. By the time the last emperor of Rome was deposed in 476 AD, Stoicism no longer existed as a distinct school of philosophy. The influence of Stoic values can be seen in the work of Boethius, a man who could be described as the last of the classical philosophers. A Roman in the service of Theodoric the Great, the King of the Ostrogoths, Boethius was arrested and condemned to death in 524 for plotting against Rome's Germanic rulers. While awaiting his execution, Boethius composed a work called *The Consolation of Philosophy*, with lines that could have been written by Epictetus or Marcus Aurelius centuries earlier:

"Nothing is miserable unless you think it so; and on the other hand, nothing brings happiness unless you are content with it."

The Consolation of Philosophy was a popular work in medieval Europe, but the Catholic Church was somewhat skeptical of what was originally a pagan way of life. However, the Stoic emphasis on virtue and self-discipline seemed perfectly acceptable to many Christians, and some monasteries even used an edited version of Epictetus's *Handbook* as a guide for monks.

The *Meditations* of Marcus Aurelius were known to a few scholars and churchmen but were not widely available until the Renaissance. Around the same time that the *Meditations* became available to the reading public, a philosopher named Justus Lipsius made a determined attempt to create a new and Christianized form of Stoicism. In his *De Constantia* of 1584, Lipsius argued that Stoic teachings could be useful for Christians facing hard times. Lipsius was criticized harshly by some religious leaders for his attempt to revive Stoicism, but philosophers like Montaigne and Spinoza adopted elements of Stoic teachings into their own systems. Immanuel Kant's theory of ethics can be traced to the influence of Epictetus.

Modern Stoicism

"No longer talk at all about the kind of man that a good man ought to be, but be such."

- Marcus Aurelius

Stoicism is now experiencing its greatest revival since ancient times, with philosophers and self-help writers like Donald Robertson, Ryan Holliday, John Sellars, Lawrence Becker, and William Irvine—all championing a modernized version of the ancient philosophy. The "Stoicism Today" blog offers daily guidance for modern Stoics, and social media sites, like Facebook, have active groups for Stoic practitioners. Mental health counselors also use Stoic ideas in a modified form in Cognitive Behavioral Therapy and other treatments. Much like Epictetus and Marcus Aurelius, today's Stoics emphasize practical questions of daily living rather than abstract ideas. Stoicism has always claimed to offer the secret to happiness, and many people are intrigued enough to want to try it for themselves.

Chapter 2: Basics of Stoicism

"Freedom is the only worthy goal in life. It is won by disregarding things that lie beyond our control."

- Epictetus

The basic principle of Stoicism is that some things are under your control, and some things are not. According to the great Stoic philosophers like Epictetus and Marcus Aurelius, the main cause of unhappiness is confusing things that are not under your control for things that are. When you seek happiness in things you can't control, you suffer from anxiety and stress. When you seek happiness only in things you really do control, you are totally free.

If this seems like a simple insight, that's because it is. You don't have to understand any abstract metaphysical ideas to get the point of Stoicism. All you have to do is accept and try to live by this one simple idea. Whatever is not under your control is not worth worrying about. Only the things that are under your control should concern you at all.

Epictetus gives four examples of things that are not under your control–your body, your property, your reputation, and the amount of authority you have over others. These are only examples, but they do cover many of the problems people run into in life.

If there's one thing most of us assume we have control over, it's our own body. Epictetus invites us to ask ourselves whether this control is real or an illusion. Can you guarantee that you'll never suffer from illness or injury? Can you keep your body from aging? Nobody can. In the most extreme circumstances, you might no longer be able to move at all. Your body is something you do not control.

The same is true of your property. "A man's home is his castle," as people say, but you can lose that home to a foreclosure or bankruptcy. Your car can be stolen. Your building can burn down. As much as you might want to, you don't control your own property.

Reputation is another example. No matter how hard you work to build up your business, anonymous social media reviews can do a lot of damage to your reputation. The same is true for your private life. You might think of yourself as a good and honest person, but you can't control what other people think of you.

Authority, or "command" as Epictetus calls it, is beyond your control as well. Your ability to command other people depends on two things–your role in whatever organization you work for and the willingness or ability of your subordinates to do whatever you ask of them. If you're not in a position of authority, you cannot command others. Even if you are, you cannot be sure they will choose to obey you. If they do obey you, you cannot be sure they will do a good job.

Think about how you would feel if you became seriously ill, if you lost your home to bankruptcy, if other people saw you as a bad person, or if you could never get other people to do what you wanted them to do. If you're like most people, you would feel unhappy if any of these things happened—yet you have no power to keep them from happening.

Epictetus tells us that we cannot be free and that we can never be truly happy, as long as our happiness depends on things we cannot control. Because we cannot control our bodies, our property, our reputations, or our ability to command others, we should think of all these things as irrelevant to our happiness.

The Power of Choice

If we have no control over our bodies, our property, our reputation, or our ability to command others, then what do we have control over? According to Epictetus:

"Things in our control are opinion, pursuit, desire, aversion, and, in a word, whatever are our own actions."

You control your opinions because you're the one who decides whether you agree with something or not. You control what you pursue in life and what you don't. For example, you can decide whether to go to college or accept a marriage proposal, among other things. You control what you avoid, for instance, by not eating certain foods when you're on a diet. Your own actions are under your control, and anything other than your own actions is not under your control. According to the Stoics, the cause of unhappiness is simple confusion. When you mistake something that isn't under your control for something that is, you chain your happiness to something that can be taken away from you at any time. The inevitable result is that you suffer whether you get what you want or not. For example, you might think you'll be happy if you find a romantic partner, but as soon as you do meet someone, you start feeling anxious about losing that person. You might think you'll be happy about getting that promotion to management, but you end up feeling stressed out because your subordinates aren't as motivated or competent as you are. The source of stress, anxiety, and other negative emotions is the desire to control things that were never yours to control in the first place. As Epictetus says:

"The things in our control are, by nature, free, unrestrained, unhindered; but those not in our control are weak, slavish, restrained, and belonging to others. Remember, then, that if you suppose that things which are slavish by nature are also free and that what belongs to others is your own, then you will be hindered. You will lament, you will be disturbed, and you will find fault both with gods and men."

So, how can you free yourself from this self-defeating tendency? In the philosophy of Stoicism, the key to genuine and lasting happiness is your own ability to recognize the difference between things you control and things you don't. If you can learn to tell the difference, you will find true freedom and true happiness.

First Impressions

There's a difference between an instinctive reaction and the type of thinking that leads to unhappiness. If you stubbed your toe, your natural reaction would be to cry out in pain. That's an instinctive response and not one that most Stoics would criticize (despite the popular use of the word "stoic" to mean a person who doesn't openly react to pain or discomfort). On the other hand, if you start telling yourself that you are having an awful day because you stubbed your toe, or if you start saying things like "why does this always happen to me," you've gone beyond the instinctive reaction and assented to the idea that stubbing your toe is "bad" and can make you unhappy.

Because you cannot do anything to guarantee that you will never stub your toe again, you've given away your control over your own happiness. The Stoics taught that we should always be careful about what we assent to, so we don't let false judgments about life ruin our happiness.

When anything happens, Epictetus says that you should avoid the impulse to classify it as good or bad immediately. Instead, you should remind yourself that your first impression may not be accurate. Whatever is causing the impression may or may not be essential to your happiness, and you don't want to make an assumption before you understand what type of thing you're dealing with. Taking a step back from your first impression, ask yourself whether this thing is under your control or not. Can it be taken away from you without your consent? If it isn't under your control, be ready to say, "this is nothing to me."

By taking this counterintuitive and radical step, you can free yourself from dependence on things that can be taken away from you, allowing you to center your happiness on things that no one can take away from you. You can apply this in situations as simple as a stubbed toe by reminding yourself that the pain is an instinctive and natural reaction but that it cannot have any effect on your happiness. You can even apply it in much more drastic situations, such as the famous example of Epictetus and his master. When Epictetus was still a slave, his cruel master deliberately broke his leg just to prove to him that he could not use Stoicism to control his emotions. By remaining calm and imperturbable, Epictetus proved that he did have that power, a demonstration that won him his freedom.

Human Nature

The Stoics considered nature to be the ultimate guide for human behavior, so why did they teach people to disregard perfectly natural emotions? To understand this particular aspect of the Stoic philosophy, we need to consider what type of nature we share with all other creatures and what type of nature is uniquely human.

Hunger is something we share with all other living beings. You could say that it's part of our shared animal nature. When a cat feels hungry, it will always eat if it has food in its bowl. A hungry wolf will always hunt, and a hungry cow will always chew grass. A hungry person will usually eat if given the opportunity, but there are situations when people choose not to eat.

For instance, a person might choose not to eat because the only available food is unhealthy or because it's against a special diet they've decided to follow. People sometimes fast for religious reasons or choose not to eat just to make a point, as in a hunger strike. While hunger is part of our shared animal nature, the ability to choose whether to eat or not is uniquely human.

This faculty of choice—what the Stoics called the "ruling faculty"—is our human nature, which we don't share with other animals. A horse that did not act like a horse would strike us as something unnatural. According to the Stoics, a human who fails to exercise the ruling faculty is equally unnatural. Because we have the natural ability to make rational choices, we cannot fulfill our nature as human beings unless we make full use of that ability. While it might be natural for a dog to gobble up all the available food even if it makes him feel sick later, it's more natural for a human to exercise restraint and avoid getting sick.

Virtue and Happiness

The ability to make rational choices is what the Stoics called "virtue," and they considered it the secret to happiness. The happiest life for a lion is to live like a lion, and the happiest life for a human being is to live like a human being. Since the one thing that sets us apart from other creatures is our ability to make rational choices, the use of that ability is the one thing we need to be truly happy. Thus, virtue and happiness are the same things to the Stoics.

There was a lot of disagreement among the ancient Greek philosophers about the nature of happiness and the best way to achieve it. Almost all the ancient Greek schools of philosophy taught that no one could be happy without living a virtuous life, but they disagreed on how central virtue was to overall happiness. For the followers of Aristotle, happiness was a combination of virtue and what we would think of as good fortune—if you were reasonably wealthy, healthy, good-looking, and virtuous, then they would say you were happy.

For the followers of Epicurus, virtue was mostly a simple matter of increasing the pleasure in your life while reducing the pain. The main reason to be virtuous, according to Epicureans, was to avoid all the stress and anxiety caused by making bad decisions.

The Stoics disagreed vehemently with both positions. If happiness depends on wealth, health, and good looks, then most people have little chance of ever being happy. The Stoics were interested in finding a way of life that could bring happiness for anyone who practiced it, regardless of life circumstances. If happiness is just a matter of experiencing as much pleasure as possible and as little pain as possible, then virtue really has little to do with it. The Stoics wanted people to be both happy and good so that happiness would be something much better than mere pleasure.

To the Stoics, the other schools of Greek philosophy sought only a partial and dependent sort of happiness, a happiness that could be lost just as easily as it was gained. They wanted more, but they also wanted it to be available to everyone. That's why the Stoics taught a different and much more unusual doctrine— true happiness and virtue are the same things, allowing a person to be perfectly happy regardless of circumstances. If you're happy, regardless of circumstances, you don't need wealth or authority or a good reputation. You don't even need health, which most people think of as a bare minimum for happiness. You have everything you need, and you can never lose it. As long as you're exercising your ruling faculty, everything else is indifferent.

Indifferent Things

Most people would describe health, wealth, a positive reputation, and authority as "good" to have, and most people would describe the opposites of all those things as "bad." According to the Stoics, none of those things are either good or bad because none of them can cause you to be happy or unhappy on their own. No one wants to be sick, but there are sick people who feel happy and healthy people who feel unhappy. No one wants to be poor, but there are poor people who feel happy and rich people who feel unhappy.

If none of these things are either good or bad, then they can only be indifferent, and that's exactly what the Stoics called them. Anything not under your own control is referred to in Stoicism as indifferent to emphasize that it isn't something essential for happiness.

It is still the case that no one would intentionally choose to be unhealthy or poor or to have a bad reputation. Even though being wealthy isn't really good, it's perfectly natural to prefer wealth to poverty. Even though being sick isn't really bad, it's also natural to try to avoid sickness.

In the Stoic philosophy, it's fine to prefer some things to others, as long as you remember that they are still "indifferent," meaning they aren't essential for your own or anyone else's happiness. Since they aren't essential, you can be happy whether you have them or not.

The one thing Stoics consider essential to happiness is the skillful and rational use of the ruling faculty or in one word, "virtue." Stoic virtue includes all the traditional virtues, such as courage, temperance, justice, and wisdom, but it defines all of them as the simple use of rational choice.

For example, if you hear a child crying for help from inside a burning building, your first impression might be that the flames are terrifying, even though you would like to save the child. A Stoic would have the same first impression but would rationally conclude that death is not actually bad and that people have a duty to help and protect each other, wherever possible. This would lead the Stoic to act with courage and save the child.

Less dramatically, a Stoic might be just as tempted as anyone else by a decadent breakfast buffet but would rationally decide to eat with temperance and preserve his health. A Stoic might be tempted to feel angry by an irritating neighbor but would act with wisdom and justice rather than giving in to the anger instinct. In every case, the Stoic uses our uniquely human power of choice (or "ruling faculty") to make rational and virtuous decisions rather than get carried away by emotional first impressions. Freed from the fear and anxiety caused by false judgments, the Stoic is happy, no matter what happens.

Pathos

If Stoics are happy by definition, why do we use the word "stoic" to describe people who don't seem to display any emotion? It's not that the Stoic is covering up all the painful emotions. That wouldn't be happy at all. Instead, the Stoic is free from certain types of emotion that cause unnecessary suffering.

In modern English, the word "pathos" refers to a feeling of sadness or pity in a movie or a book. If you find yourself feeling sorry for one of the characters, that scene has pathos in it. The word "pathos" comes from ancient Greek, and the Stoics used it to refer to the emotions that cause people to feel sorry for themselves.

For example, if your stocks suddenly increased in value, you'd probably feel delighted. If the stock market crashed, you'd probably feel depressed and upset. The value of your stocks is not under your control, so your delight in one situation is basically the cause of your distress in the other situation. To an ancient Stoic thinker named Zeno of Citium, Delight and Distress are both *pathê* or types of pathos.

If you started dating someone you found very attractive, you'd probably feel desire. If they stopped returning your calls and texts, you might feel fear. Whether someone wants to date you or not is not under your control, so your desire in one situation causes your fear in the other situation. Desire and Fear are also types of pathos.

In these pairs, a seemingly good emotion is paired with a seemingly bad emotion: Delight with Distress and Desire with Fear.

"GOOD"	"BAD"
Delight	Distress
Desire	Fear

These emotions can also be categorized by when they happen in time. Delight refers to the present and Desire to the future because Desire is the anticipation of a future Delight. Distress refers to the present and Fear to the future because Fear is the anticipation of future Distress.

PRESENT	FUTURE
Delight	Desire
Distress	Fear

These four *pathê* or "passions" are all causes of suffering.

Delight and Desire might both seem pleasant, but because they aren't under your control, they can't actually be "good." Mistaking them for genuine good only leads to suffering and anxiety. Distress and Fear both seem unpleasant, but because they aren't under your control, they can't actually be "bad." Thinking of them as genuinely bad leads to suffering and anxiety.

None of the four Passions are good or bad in and of themselves. They only become good or bad because of the false beliefs people hold about them, leading people to invest all their hopes for happiness in aspects of life they cannot control.

Good Feelings

The goal of Stoic practice is *apatheia*, which means to be "without pathos." Although this sounds like "apathy" and is the origin of the word, the original meaning of *apatheia* is to be free of painful emotions, not all emotions. Instead of pathos, the Stoic experiences "good feelings" or *eupatheiai*. A "good feeling" in the Stoic sense is one that nobody and nothing can take away from you because it is based on things that are under your control.

The Stoics acknowledged three *eupatheiai*: Joy, Caution, and Wishing. The three good feelings have something in common with the four types of pathos. However, unlike the violent passions of Delight, Desire, Distress, and Fear, the three good feelings are calm and tranquil. Joy is the calm and serene enjoyment of something you prefer, without the irrational attachment associated with pathos. Caution is the rational and dignified self-control, with which the Stoic meets danger or makes decisions about her health, without the pathos of irrational fear. Wishing is the reasonable anticipation of a future Joy, without the grasping quality of irrational Desire.

PATHOS	GOOD FEELING
Delight	Joy
Fear	Caution
Desire	Wishing

As you can see, the good feelings of a Stoic are much like those of a regular person, with one big difference. The Stoic is calmly happy under all conditions, while the regular person constantly struggles with negative feelings. By centering your happiness in your own decisions, you can experience the good feelings of Stoicism while avoiding the emotional storms of pathos.

Chapter 3: Critical Thinking

"Very little is needed to make a happy life; it

is all within yourself, in your way of thinking."

- Marcus Aurelius

Critical thinking is the core of Stoicism. Whenever anything happens, Stoicism teaches us to step back and question it. Is this situation under my control or not? If it is under my control, the only thing I need to do is make the rational choice—to act with justice and dignity. If it's not under my control, then I need to be ready to say, "this is nothing to me."

Both Epictetus and Marcus Aurelius often taught through examples, brief stories that illustrated Stoic principles. We may not live in ancient Greece or Rome, but the basics of life don't really change. As Marcus Aurelius points out, people acted more or less the same way a hundred years ago and will act more or less the same way a hundred years from now. With a little imagination, most of their examples can be applied to common daily situations in the modern world.

Everyday Problems and Stoic Solutions

Situation: Your wallet gets stolen with all your credit cards.

Solution: Think of it as a trade. You can gain something more valuable than any wallet.

Anytime something upsetting happens, it's an opportunity. From the Stoic viewpoint, an upsetting incident is a chance to practice. Ryan Holiday's Stoic self-help book *The Obstacle is the Way* is based on this simple insight. When something causes you a problem, you can turn it into a chance to become more serene and tranquil.

If you succeed, you'll get something much more valuable than whatever you lost. As Epictetus says, you should never trade something more valuable for something less valuable.

When something goes missing, especially something you use every day, the immediate temptation is to get upset. Most people would, and no one would blame you. Losing your wallet is a hassle, especially when you have to cancel all your credit cards. On the other hand, getting upset won't bring your wallet back. It won't keep you from having to cancel your cards. It won't do anything at all, except to add emotional distress to your other problems.

The prize Stoicism aims at is genuine freedom, and that's worth more than anything else. If your wallet gets stolen, you probably won't be able to help your instinctive reaction of irritation and stress. That's just an impression, but whether you assent to the impression is up to you. If you can succeed in remaining tranquil, you'll make real progress toward your own freedom.

Since freedom is worth so much more than your wallet, you can think of the theft as a successful trade. You're giving up something less valuable (the wallet) for something more valuable (your emotional freedom). It wouldn't make any sense to do the opposite, because you'd be giving up the more valuable item in exchange for the less valuable item. If you lose your wallet and get upset, you lose both the less valuable item and the more valuable item at the same time!

According to Epictetus, it's especially important to pay attention to minor irritations like these. If a ship captain lets his mind wander in a dangerous storm, the ship can go off course and hit the rocks. Daily life is like that storm, and minor irritations like losing your wallet can be enough for you to lose your way.

Situation: You can't stop thinking about getting away on vacation, perhaps to a beach house or some other relaxing place.

Solution: If it's not in your power to get away right now, seek inner peace instead. That's always available.

Marcus Aurelius, the Stoic emperor, must have occasionally wished he could get away more often. He spent much of his career along the borders of the empire, in a series of campaigns against the enemies of Rome. Despite being the emperor, he couldn't get access to new books in the remote military camps where he spent much of his time. He mentions wanting to escape his responsibilities by taking a trip to the country or perhaps to the sea or the mountains.

This sort of yearning is a pathos, specifically the pathos of Desire. Rather than "assenting" to that first impression, Marcus Aurelius reminds himself that he can get away anytime he wants. All he has to do is retreat within, to the calm tranquility of the Stoic mindset. By keeping his inner self secure from turmoil, the Stoic maintains an inner sanctuary. Unlike a vacation home or a resort hotel, this inner sanctuary cannot be taken away.

Even if you do have the opportunity to get away, the pleasant experiences you'll have on vacation are all external. It's fine to prefer them, but they can never match the deep peace that is always available to the inner self.

Situation: You're annoyed by a difference of opinion.

Solution: Remember that the person you disagree with is doing the same thing you are.

Differences in opinion cause a lot of conflicts, especially between family and friends. Perhaps someone in your life supports a candidate you don't like, goes to a church other than your own, hates your favorite band, or roots for a rival sports team. Some of these examples are fairly trivial, but that doesn't stop them from causing problems. People have fallen out for a lot less!

You may have a good and well-reasoned argument for your position, but the person you disagree with may have arguments of their own. Even if the other person's position is based on nothing at all, their opinions are not under your control. If the two of you argue with each other because of your difference of opinion, both of you are doing the same thing.

Epictetus once met a local politician who got offended when people didn't like his favorite actor. As Epictetus pointed out, their attitude wasn't really any different from his. He liked the actor, and they disliked him. Both opinions were equally partisan. He could hardly blame them for booing the actor when he ordered his slaves to cheer the same man. Differences of opinion are differences of viewpoint, and irrational attachment to one side is much the same as an irrational attachment to the other.

Situation: You're upset with the lack of ethics of a coworker.

Solution: Ask yourself whether it's possible for unethical people not to exist.

If you always work hard and do the best job you can, it can be intensely frustrating to work with someone who doesn't share your values. The coworker who doesn't show up on time or do his fair share of work, the coworker who takes credit for others' efforts, and the coworker who steals are all irritating.

As frustrating as it is to work with someone like this, unethical people are here to stay. According to Marcus Aurelius, whenever you find yourself offended at a person's shameless behavior, you should ask yourself a question. Is it possible for the shameless people in the world not to exist?

It doesn't sound very likely, does it? Shameless people have always existed, and in all likelihood, they always will. If shameless people must exist, then expecting never to meet one is expecting the impossible. Expecting the impossible would be the opposite of Stoicism since it would mean wishing for something beyond your control.

The Stoics borrowed some of their ideas from the great philosopher Socrates, who taught that evil was really a form of ignorance. People do things the wrong way because they don't know better and because they have mistaken ideas about what's really good. Expecting someone to do something they don't know would not be reasonable.

No matter what your coworker does, they can never hurt you. Their unethical actions are theirs alone and are not under your control. When a coworker is unethical, you should simply remind yourself that such people exist. Since such people exist in the world, it isn't strange that you happen to work with one.

According to Marcus Aurelius, this realization will naturally cause you to become more kind and patient toward anyone who does things wrong. You don't have to agree with what they do, and you don't have to approve. Just by thinking of them as "uninstructed," you will stop feeling stressed out and irritable. You will remain free.

Situation: Your old friends don't understand why you want to make changes in your life.

Solution: Ask yourself what's most important to you, and act accordingly.

This situation comes up often, especially for people who are trying to get over an addiction or give up a bad habit. If your friends and loved ones are not ready to change, they aren't likely to be supportive when you try to do so. They may even try to drag you down because they don't want things to change between you. Everyone who has ever tried to quit drinking or smoking has had this experience, where friends try to talk you into having "just one" and make it much harder for you to quit successfully.

That's the most obvious example, but there are others. Anytime you try to stop doing something that other people are doing, they're likely to take it as a personal criticism and would encourage you to backslide. It could even be as simple as someone urging you to "stand up for yourself" and get mad about some minor irritation because they don't understand or accept your interest in Stoicism.

As Epictetus says, you can't quit drinking and still be seen as the life of the party because those goals are incompatible. You can't be known for your crushing put-downs and cultivate Stoic tranquility at the same time because those goals are incompatible. So, which is really more important? Which one offers you more benefits? Which one can you commit?

If you really feel that the approval of your friends is the most important thing, then pursue their approval and forget about Stoicism. If you try Stoicism half-heartedly, you'll irritate your friends without gaining tranquility. If you think it's more important to be truly happy, then pursue that completely, and forget about the approval of others. Either way, ask yourself what's truly important and then live by that decision. Not everyone will understand it, but that's not a problem. Their opinions are not under your control, so they aren't essential for your happiness.

Situation: Your child is badly ill.

Solution: Focus on helping your child rather than on your fears.

Epictetus once had a conversation with an unhappy family man, who was filled with anxiety because his child was sick. We don't know exactly the sickness of the child, but in ancient times, it wasn't at all uncommon for people to die in childhood because of illnesses. Knowing this fact, we can assume that the man was deeply worried. He told Epictetus that he was miserable, and the philosopher pointed out that people don't usually marry and have children so they can be miserable.

"I can't help it," said the man. "My daughter is sick."

"If your daughter is sick, then why aren't you at home?" asked Epictetus.

"Seeing her suffer was so upsetting to me that I couldn't stay in the house anymore," the man replied. "I told my wife to send me a message when my daughter gets better."

"Do you think you handled the situation well?" asked Epictetus.

"Whether I handled it well or not, I think my reaction was understandable," said the man. "I love her too much to watch her suffer like that."

"Do you think her mother loves her any less?" asked Epictetus, pointing out the flaw in the man's thinking. If he left the house because of love, then why didn't the girl's mother leave as well? If love causes people to leave you when you need them the most, then what good is it in the first place?

It wasn't "love" that caused the man to leave his sick daughter, but the pathos of Fear. By mistaking his child's illness for something "bad," he left her to suffer alone. The girl's mother knew better and focused on helping her daughter rather than her own emotions.

This example shows the difference between two kinds of love. When love is based on intense emotions, it can easily lead you to harm the person you love. According to Epictetus, that isn't love in the first place. Stoic love is a choice and is always based on doing what's right.

Situation: You're worried about your legacy.

Solution: Remember that everything ends.

As an emperor and an author, Marcus Aurelius must have worried sometimes about how he would be remembered. Would people speak of him as wise and just or as a foolish bookworm who wasted his time on philosophy? If anyone ever read his diary, would they preserve it for future readers or throw it away as useless scrap?

As a practicing Stoic, Marcus Aurelius knew not to get too caught up in this sort of question. Even if people do remember you, those who remember you will die soon enough. If they pass down their respect for you to the next generation, those people will soon die as well. Even if you are remembered for a thousand generations, the last people who remember you will eventually die.

Of course, we now know that Marcus Aurelius is remembered as one of the greatest of the Roman emperors and that his book is considered a classic of philosophy. If he were here today, he'd be the first to remind us that these things are temporary. No matter how long it takes, the day will come when no one remembers him.

Everything ends, and that's just a fact. Whether people remember you or not is not under your control and can't possibly be bad or good. The opinions of others are not worth worrying about.

Situation: Your boss wants you to lie rather than present information that would put him in a bad light.

Solution: Ask yourself which aspect of the situation is under your control. Can your boss do anything to harm you? Would it harm you to lie?

Sometimes, we find ourselves under pressure to do something we know is wrong or beneath our dignity. Epictetus gives the example of a man named Florus, who was trying to decide whether to participate in the degrading spectacles of the tyrant emperor Nero. Agrippinus told him to go ahead, which confused Florus because he knew that Agrippinus had never attended the spectacles himself.

"Why are you saying I should go to the spectacles when you don't go to them?" asked Florus.

"Because I've never even considered going to them," was the reply.

Once you start to debate with yourself about whether or not to give in to pressure, you've already assented to the idea that something external is more important than doing what you know is right. Having made that false judgment, it will be very difficult to avoid doing wrong.

Imagine a boss who asks you to lie at an important meeting rather than present a report unfavorable to him. Your boss has the power to write a bad performance review or maybe get you fired. Does this mean your boss can harm you? No, it does not. Your boss's actions are not under your control, so they can neither harm nor help you. The only thing that could harm you would be to do something wrong.

According to Epictetus, your attitude in this situation should be like that of the Roman senator Priscus, who refused to be a yes-man at the emperor's request: "If you don't ask my opinion, I won't say anything at all. If you do ask my opinion, I have to tell the truth as I see it."

It's not that Epictetus didn't understand the pressures involved. As he says in his Discourses, pleasure is preferable to pain. Keeping your job is preferable to losing your job. Despite these obvious facts, you can never hope to be more than an ordinary person if you do something you know is wrong just to avoid an unpleasant consequence. The person who is aiming for something more will never settle for less and will never even consider trading what is truly important for what is not.

Situation: You're involved in a lawsuit.

Solution: Remember that all actions are caused by opinions.

Epictetus once spoke with a man on his way to Rome to argue a case in court. The journey was a long one, and the man risked everything from discomfort and loss of position to accidental death along the road. When Epictetus asked him why he was going, the man replied that he "had to."

"What makes you say that?" said Epictetus. "It's just an opinion, but it's enough to make you face all these dangers and inconveniences. Everything you do is because of your opinions, and that's equally true of your opponent in this case."

If you're involved in a lawsuit, it's easy to feel that your actions are fixed: the opponent does this, so you do that. The opponent makes this argument, so you make that argument. Even if you firmly believe that your arguments are correct, the opponent probably feels the same way about their own arguments. It's all opinion, just as every action is caused by opinion.

In the Stoic philosophy, the important point is not to win the lawsuit but to make sure that your own opinions are not mistaken. It would be a shame to leave your home, travel a long distance, and face all kinds of risks and inconveniences all because of false opinion.

Is there any way to avoid having false opinions? The Stoics certainly thought so. In fact, they thought it was surprisingly simple. Just don't add anything to the basic facts, and you will avoid making most kinds of false judgments.

Not Adding Anything

The Stoic approach to critical thinking is highly pragmatic. It isn't based on abstract arguments but on the basic facts of everyday life. In one passage from his Discourses, Epictetus provides a simple key for applying Stoic thinking to anything that happens: "We ought to exercise ourselves daily against appearances for these appearances also propose questions to us. What do you think of it? It is a thing beyond the power of the will; it is not evil."

Every difficulty we face is an opportunity to practice, from a minor source of stress like a traffic jam to a major life event like a divorce. Epictetus even lists extreme misfortunes like being condemned to death and denies that they can be evil because they are not within the control of the will. This example is easier to understand if you think of a soldier. Soldiers swear to serve their country, and that sometimes means that they must die in battle. If dying were evil, it would always be good for soldiers to flee. By choosing to stand and fight against overwhelming odds, the soldier prioritizes duty and treats death as unimportant.

To face death with courage and dignity is good, but to die is indifferent. By adding a judgment of "good" or "bad" to a simple fact, you tie your happiness to something you cannot control. By not adding anything to the basic facts, you can turn everything that happens in life into something good.

You didn't get the promotion. What does that mean? That you didn't get the promotion and only that. You lost thousands of dollars. What does that mean? That you lost thousands of dollars and only that. Someone cut you off in traffic or said something bad to you, tried to trick you, or even stole from you. What do any of these things mean? They're all just facts, and any judgment we make about them is added afterward. To think like a Stoic, all you have to do is to avoid adding anything else to the bare facts.

Chapter 4: Self-Discipline and Resilience

"Be tolerant of others and strict with yourself."

- Marcus Aurelius

By this point in the book, you probably think that Stoicism sounds pretty hard to apply in practice. You're not alone. The ancient Stoics recognized certain people as Sages for their ability to apply Stoicism consistently in their daily lives. Epictetus himself denied being a Sage because he could never quite get rid of anxiety about his health. His students must have been surprised by this statement because they asked him to name a real Sage. Perhaps sarcastically, he answered, "Hercules."

Any Stoic other than a Sage is called a *prokoptôn*, a "person making progress." When one of his students asked him the difference between a *prokoptôn* and a regular person, Epictetus said it was the same as the difference between drowning in 15 feet of water rather than 150 feet.

As you can see, Epictetus really didn't want his students to think of themselves as being close to Sagehood or as being wiser or more philosophical than other people. Stoicism is a process, and the most any of us can realistically hope is to make some progress toward the goal.

That doesn't mean stoicism can't help you right now—far from it. If Epictetus himself was not a sage, then you don't need to be a sage either to benefit from stoicism. The calm happiness and resilience of stoic practice is available to everyone but only through rigorous self-discipline.

As Epictetus says, you would never think of competing in the Olympic Games without the necessary training that involves a lot of toughness and self-discipline. To take up philosophy is not so different and comes with its training methods.

In the practice of stoicism, the training involves three specific disciplines.

The Three Disciplines of Stoicism

The Discipline of Desire: this means to restrict your desire to things that are under your own control. Whenever you find yourself desiring something that is not under your control—money, power, love, or admiration—transfer that feeling of desire to things that are under your own control. The desire for money can be changed into a determination to do a great job at work. The desire for power can be changed into a desire for justice, no matter who is in power. The desire for love can be changed into the desire to be a more loving person. The desire for the admiration of others can be changed into the desire to live an admirable life. In every case, you can take your yearning for something you can't control, and use it to fuel your determination to improve as a person and as a Stoic. Over time, you can teach yourself to stop desiring anything that isn't under your control.

The Discipline of Action: Stoicism distinguishes between actions that are "perfect" and actions that are merely "appropriate." Both types of action are correct, but the perfect action is done for the right reasons while the merely appropriate action is not. For example, if you don't cheat on your spouse because you don't want to get caught, your action is merely appropriate. If you don't cheat because you know it's wrong, your action is perfect. If you give money to charity so people will praise you, your action is merely appropriate. If you give money to charity for no other reason than to help other people, your action is perfect. The Sage's actions are always perfect, but the person making progress won't always be perfect. The discipline of action means to act appropriately, even when you aren't ready to take perfect actions. This is essentially a "fake it till you make it" approach. You might not be able to do the right thing with the right mentality, but you can, at least, make sure to do the right thing always. Don't think of this as hypocrisy but as practical training. Over time, the habit of doing the right thing should start to become second nature to you. More and more often, you will find yourself able to do the right thing for the right reason.

The Discipline of Assent: The discipline of assent is the Stoic practice of questioning first impressions, as in the examples given in the "Critical Thinking" chapter. By refusing to jump to conclusions about the things you experience, you can gain the distance you need to avoid being overwhelmed. Remember that Stoicism distinguishes between instinctive reactions and false judgments. There is an ancient story about a Stoic philosopher whose ship was caught in a deadly storm. When a huge wave smashed into the ship, the philosopher yelled as if he was scared. Questioned about his behavior after the incident, the Stoic said that his yell was due to an "impression" but that he had not "assented" to it. Whether he was telling the truth or not (and we'll never know!), the distinction is valid for any Stoic. You can't help having instinctive reactions, but whether you assent to them is up to you. Whenever you experience an emotional reaction, whether positive or negative, you should mentally pull back and ask yourself whether this involves something under your control or not. If it does not, be ready to say, "this is nothing to me."

The Three Disciplines can be summarized in a single sentence: restrict your desire to things you control, make sure your actions are always appropriate, and never assent too hastily to any impression.

Twelve Principles of Self-Discipline

The twelve principles discussed in this chapter are all derived from the *Enchiridion* or "Handbook" of Epictetus, one of the most accessible and useful works of ancient Stoicism. If you can remember and practice these twelve principles, you'll be well on your way to developing the self-disciplined and resilient mentality of the Stoic.

1: Control Desire

2: Keep Your Thoughts on the Ship

3: Remember That Nothing is Free

4: Let Them Laugh

5: Don't Reach for Things

6: Play Your Part

7: Avoid Envy

8: Don't Get Carried Away

9: Don't Show Off

10: Watch Yourself

11: Never Criticize Others

12: Accept Every Criticism

Control Desire

As Epictetus tells us, the feeling of desire includes the anticipation or "promise" of getting what you want. All too often, it's a false promise. If you desire something and you don't get what you desire, you'll feel disappointed. If you never want to feel disappointed, avoid desiring anything you can't be sure of getting. As Marcus Aurelius says, you can have an undefeated record in the battles of life if you never enter a battle that you aren't sure of winning. So, how can you avoid desiring things you can't be sure you'll get? The answer is through self-control and self-discipline.

Early on in your Stoic practice, Epictetus says you should "totally suppress" desire. Why does he make such an extreme statement? Desiring anything that is not under your control would only disappoint you and lead you away from Stoic practice while desiring anything under your control would be pointless until you develop more control in the first place. Desiring wisdom when you aren't capable of wisdom yet would have the same results as desiring anything else unobtainable.

Instead of desire, Epictetus says you should restrict yourself to pursuing the right things and avoiding the wrong things rationally. Even then, a beginner should pursue the right things calmly and gently, avoiding any violent emotions. Calm, unhurried patience is the basic mindset of Stoic practice.

Keep Your Thoughts on the Boat

How can you pursue anything without desiring it? Imagine you're a passenger on a ferry boat, visiting an island. When the boat docks, everyone gets off and looks around. When it's time for the last boat to leave the island and return to the mainland, a horn will sound. All the passengers know they need to listen for the horn, or they risk being left on the island until the next day.

In that situation, you might wander along the beach, looking at seashells or pretty rocks. You might climb a dune to get a look at the view. You might buy an ice cream cone or a souvenir at a little shop. The one thing you wouldn't do is ignore the horn because you wouldn't want to be stranded on the island.

As a practicing Stoic, it isn't necessary to live a life of grim privation. If anything seems fun or pleasant, you can pursue it within reason, as long as you remember what's important and avoid mistaking something trivial for something significant. Pretty seashells are nice, but they aren't important compared to listening for the horn. It's safe to look around and enjoy whatever you find, as long as you remember to keep your mind on the boat.

Remember That Nothing is Free

Nothing in life is ever free, and happiness is no exception. The price of happiness is Stoic discipline, and you pay the price whenever you react to a problem in a Stoic way. Rather than thinking about how much serenity costs, remind yourself of how valuable it truly is.

If a child knocks over an antique vase and smashes it, tell yourself, "that's the price of happiness." If an employee doesn't do something you asked them to do, tell yourself, "that's the price of serenity." If a neighbor comes over and yells at you about something trivial, tell yourself, "that's the price of tranquility."

Nothing is free, and the price of happiness is to control your reactions to the things that happen in life. Epictetus tells us to completely avoid "if-then" thoughts, such as, "if I don't get mad at my kids for breaking this vase, they won't be careful in the future," or, "if I don't come down hard on my employees, my business will fail."

Your children will learn a lot more by seeing how you handle stress than they will from any lecture you can give, but even if they don't, it's still better to have careless kids than to let it stress you out. Your employees will listen to a calm and self-controlled boss more willingly than an angry and abusive one, but even if they don't, it's better for your business to fail than for you to be unhappy.

Let Them Laugh

If you start to make progress in the Stoic way of life, other people will laugh at you. Let them laugh. Expect other people to see you as foolish or stupid. They'll say you're bad at business because you never get anxious about your business dealings. They'll say you're bad at dating because you never worry about who should call who first or how your partner might interpret something you said. They'll say you're bad at standing up for yourself because you don't get mad when people say or do insulting things.

Let them think of you as foolish because it doesn't matter. They're not going to understand your Stoic way of looking at things, and to act in a way they'd understand would mean giving up your Stoic practice.

If people aren't laughing at you for some reason, doubt yourself. Your calm and unruffled attitude could turn out to be an asset in business. Your unworried and natural demeanor might help you in dating. Your self-disciplined response to insults might earn the respect of those who previously looked down on you. These things aren't bad on their own, but they're still dangerous.

You can't pursue external things and internal things at the same time, so if you start to have a lot of success with external things, it's especially important not to attach your thoughts to them. If other people start to see you as someone important, wise, or admirable, tell yourself you are none of those things. It's safer for your Stoicism if they consider you a fool.

Don't Reach for Things

Imagine you're at a pleasant dinner party, with many fun things to eat and drink. If you see one of your favorites, would you reach across the table for it or just wait until it gets passed to you? Would you pile your plate high with everything you see or take a reasonable share so other people can enjoy it, too? If the host ran out of one of the items on the table before you got to taste it, would you complain bitterly or shrug and say, "maybe next time"? The things people pursue in life are like food and drink at a dinner party. Don't reach out for them; just wait for them patiently, and enjoy them only in moderation. If they never come to you, don't worry about it, and just enjoy one of the other items. As Epictetus says, "Do this with regard to children, to a wife, to public posts, to riches, and you will eventually be a worthy partner of the feasts of the gods."

Play Your Part

A person's life is like a play or a movie, but we don't get to write the story or pick our parts. Some movies are short, and some are longer. Some actors are admired for their beauty or talent while others have minor roles, and still, others are in the background. Some roles are tragic, some heroic, and some comedic. Whatever your part is, the most important point for an actor is to play the role naturally. Even if an actor only has a single line, he'll try to say that line as well as he can. It's not in our power to pick our parts, but it is in our power to perform them well. As Marcus Aurelius says, your only other option is to make the audience laugh at you!

Avoid Envy

When a friend or a coworker gets something you don't, avoid envy and jealousy. If what they have is good, be happy for their sake. If it isn't good, there's nothing to be jealous of in the first place.

Everything has a price, and you can't expect to get the thing without paying the price for it. Does your boss seem to like your coworker better because of her shameless flattery? The flattery was the price of the boss's favor, and your coworker paid it. Your coworker now has what she paid for, but you still have your self-respect. Is a friend more successful at dating around? The price of that kind of success is to go out and flirt, to risk rejection repeatedly, and to pursue people actively. Your friend now has what he paid for, but you still have your self-control and dignity.

The things most people consider desirable have a high price tag for a Stoic because they would force him to act or think in a non-Stoic way. If you've set your sights on real happiness, you won't be willing to waste your time and energy on lesser things. Never envy anyone who is on a different path from you. If they believe those external things are more important, let them pay the price and enjoy what they've bought.

Don't Get Carried Away

Whenever you have the opportunity to enjoy something pleasurable, take care not to get carried away by it. Pause for a moment and think before you decide to indulge, comparing the short-term pleasure with the long-term consequences.

For example, you might have a few extra dollars to buy a pint of super premium ice cream. That's a tempting option, but if you sit down and eat a whole pint of ice cream by yourself, you'll probably feel sick and regret the extra calories. After a stressful day, you might be tempted to go out to the bar and do some shots. The alcohol might make you feel better for a couple of hours, but you'll feel much worse in the morning, and you'll regret the decision. While Stoics are not forbidden from doing pleasant things, even the most innocent pleasures should be questioned in this way. It can be useful for training purposes to exercise your self-control and refuse to indulge. In this situation, Epictetus tells us to compare the immediate pleasure of indulging with the much deeper joy of gaining more self-discipline and making progress in your practice of Stoicism.

Don't Show Off

If you stop indulging in things like alcohol and gourmet ice cream as often as others, people are likely to notice. Whatever you do, don't try to show off your newfound Stoicism. Don't lecture people about philosophy or act pretentious, showing off your knowledge of obscure and complicated books. Don't try to get people to notice how Stoic you are or to think of you as unusually tough or self-disciplined or philosophical. The opinions of others are not under our control, and as such, they can neither be good nor bad. Cultivating a reputation as a Stoic would be the opposite of Stoicism, as a true Stoic wouldn't give any importance to external things like impressing other people. If you keep your Stoicism low-key, you won't set yourself to fall when you make mistakes. As a person making progress rather than a Stoic Sage, you will make mistakes and make them often. It's better for people not to know you're a Stoic than to bring Stoicism into discredit and discourage others from giving it a try. If you waste your energy on trying to impress others with your Stoicism, you'll find it especially hard to put up with their mockery when you fall short.

Watch Yourself

Epictetus says to watch yourself as if you were an enemy waiting in ambush—and most people are, in fact, their own worst enemies. Knowing your tendency to chase after external things and to give value to things that have no real value, you always have to suspect your motivations. Whenever you want to do anything, ask yourself why you want to do it. Is this a rational choice or merely a pathos?

The more progress you make in Stoicism, the more people will start to notice something different about you. They may start to see you as someone with unusual self-control and calmness. They may even describe you as wise. If you listen to any of these voices, you'll lose everything you've gained so far. You should never let anyone describe you as someone important or as someone who knows everything. If anyone praises you, you should laugh at them—but not to their face, of course.

How can you tell when you're making progress? According to the Stoics, the beginner blames others, the person making progress blames himself, but the Sage blames no one.

Never Criticize Others

One of the foundational disciplines of Stoicism is to avoid criticizing other people for anything at all. A Stoic never blames or accuses anyone of doing something the wrong way. Without knowing the principles that motivate their actions, you cannot even be sure whether they're doing wrong. Rather than saying, "he drinks too much," you should say, "he drinks." Rather than saying, "she wastes her money," you should only say, "she spends her money." Restrict your comments to the facts, without attaching any blame or judgment.

The person you blame and judge could be a Sage in disguise, acting from perfect principles for reasons you don't understand. If you avoid judging and criticizing completely, you'll never have to regret making an unfair judgment of another person's actions.

Accept Every Criticism

Although you should never blame or criticize, you should always be ready to accept criticism from others without complaint or hurt feelings. As with other opinions, the judgments of other people are beyond your control and are therefore indifferent. If someone says something bad about you, the best response is to say something like this: "he must not know much about all my faults, or he would never have mentioned such a minor one."

Immune to criticism and to praise, the Stoic is completely free from the opinions of others. No one can make Stoics feel bad about themselves, and nothing can give them a swollen ego. Their focus is inward, pursuing the only thing that really matters—inner peace.

Chapter 5: Managing the Emotions

"We suffer more often in imagination than in reality."

- Seneca

Stoic discipline is good for training, but the real test of this philosophy is how you react when things go wrong. Hardship happens to everyone, including Stoics. You will experience pain and illness. You will experience loneliness. People you love will someday die. What will you do when that happens?

The Stoics claimed that they could be happy under any circumstances. Perhaps a Sage could do that, but the philosophy should at least give you the tools to handle emotional turmoil with courage and dignity. If a negative emotion overwhelms you, remember the advice of Marcus Aurelius: you may not be able to act appropriately in every single moment, but if you do lose the way, you can always come back to it. Don't be disappointed if you slip up now and then, as long as you can see that you are steadily making progress. It's enough if most of your actions are in accord with reason. The rest will come with time.

Never be ashamed to ask for help if you need it: when a soldier stumbles on the battlefield, a nearby comrade will help him up. The only thing that matters is to keep moving forward, to keep making progress, and to keep improving.

With thoughts like these, the Stoic emperor overcame his own troubles and returned to his duties, winning one campaign after another along the Roman frontiers. Challenging emotions will come and go, but life continues. This selection of meditations from Seneca, Epictetus, and Marcus Aurelius should help you do the same.

Anxiety

The old saying "don't borrow trouble" seems like an echo of this thought from Seneca, the tutor and advisor to Emperor Nero: "He suffers more than necessary, who suffers before it is necessary."

Working for Nero would have made almost anyone anxious. The emperor was paranoid and had no real loyalty to anyone other than himself. Seneca did everything he could to reign in the emperor's worst impulses, but he did not succeed. In the end, Nero decided that Seneca had betrayed him and ordered the philosopher to commit suicide.

Seneca probably knew this was a possibility long before it happened, but his letters show no trace of anxiety. In all his *Epistles*, Seneca displays a calm and cheerful attitude. When Seneca tells us that we suffer more in imagination than in reality, he doesn't mean that our suffering is unreal somehow. He means that we add to our own suffering by anticipating it so anxiously.

Imagining all the frightening things that might happen will only add to our suffering. More often than not, the things we imagine don't end up happening anyway. Even if they do, worrying about them ahead of time won't help us deal with them. We do have the tools we need to meet them courageously, as long as we remember the lessons of Stoicism.

Accidents

Epictetus refers to the random incidents of life as "accidents" and reminds us that we always have some faculty that will allow us to meet any accident without harm to ourselves. The key to handling any accident is to apply the right tool for that particular accident.

For example, if you're married and you happen to meet an attractive person on a business trip, you can apply the faculty of self-restraint. If you have to spend time with a talkative and unpleasant person, you can apply patience. If you get hurt somehow and are in pain, you can apply fortitude.

The accidents Epictetus describes here are all fairly minor, but the same principle applies to much more challenging "accidents." Whatever happens, you can apply some tool to deal with it effectively. Through the rest of this chapter, think of every example given as a tool you can use, giving you the strength to face some hardship.

If you can do this, you should find it easier to deal with emotional turmoil when it arises. With enough practice, you can transform the accidents of life into new opportunities to make progress in Stoicism.

Welcome Trouble

In one of his letters, Seneca mentions that he is sick. Everyone in his house is sick. His income is declining, and his house is starting to get worn down. Instead of getting upset, he comments that such things are simply inevitable. Trouble happens to us all, and the longer you live, the more trouble you see. Getting sick or having a run-down house is nothing unusual for an older man, so he refuses to complain about such ordinary problems. Not only is Seneca content with all this, he actively welcomes it as an opportunity to practice his Stoicism.

If no trouble happened to us, we would never have the chance to test ourselves against adversity. We would never be sure of our inner strength, and any happiness we seemed to have would be insubstantial and unreliable. We could never be sure of what would happen if everything suddenly went badly wrong. Perhaps, we would fall apart as soon as we faced a serious test. In another letter, Seneca compares a life without trouble to a sea without wind: everything seems calm, but the boat isn't getting anywhere.

As a practicing Stoic, anything difficult that happens to you is like a chance to do battle, to prove yourself equal to the challenge. Like a sailor in a storm or a soldier on a campaign, you have the opportunity for heroism.

Check Your Principles

If death was as frightful as most people believe, why didn't it seem frightful to Socrates? With this simple question, Epictetus takes us back to the roots of Stoicism in the courageous last hours of the great philosopher.

Death seems terrible to most people because they believe it to be terrible. Death didn't seem terrible to Socrates because he didn't believe it to be terrible. His principles told him not to flee from Athens, so he faced his death with unshakeable courage.

In all of life's great troubles, it is not the actual hardship that makes us sad, scared, or angry. It's always our own beliefs about what happened, our "principles" as Epictetus calls them.

Whenever anything disturbs or grieves you, don't blame the thing itself. Blame your beliefs about the thing. Check your principles on the topic in question, and correct them if there's anything wrong with them.

Is the thing that troubles you an internal matter, something you can fix through your own will? If it is, then fix it. Is it an external matter, something not under the control of your own will? If this is the case, then disregard it.

Hindrances

Epictetus refers to troubles and hardships as "hindrances," things that stand in the way. But what do they hinder?

If you think of them as hindrances to yourself, then you will be hindered. If you think of them as hindrances to something other than yourself, you will not be hindered. Stoicism encourages you to identify yourself with the ruling faculty, the ability to make rational choices, rather than with the body. The ruling faculty is under your control, but the body is not.

Is illness a hindrance to the body, or the ruling faculty? Most illnesses do not hinder the ability to make rational choices. Whenever you're ill, tell yourself, "this illness hinders my body, but it doesn't hinder my ruling faculty." If it doesn't hinder your ruling faculty, it doesn't hinder you.

Imagine you're injured and you can no longer use your leg. Does this hinder the leg or the ruling faculty? It obviously cannot hinder your ability to choose, so it only hinders your leg and not yourself.

You can do this with any physical problem that causes you difficulty in your daily life. Yes, the hindrance may put limitations on your movements. As long as it doesn't affect your ability to choose, you can remain free of any mental turmoil.

Insult

People get so agitated by insults and disrespectful behavior that they never stop to consider whether such things can injure them in the first place. Rising to every trivial provocation, they only end up making the situation worse. Damaged relationships and unnecessary drama are the inevitable consequence, but it can sometimes be worse than that. Much of the random violence in our society is driven by one simple error in judgment: the idea that an insult or act of disrespect can harm us. If a person insults you or does something you consider disrespectful, how will you react? Will you insult them back? Will you hit them?

Doing either of these things in response to an insult can have tragic consequences. When you decide to escalate a conflict, the other person can easily do the same. Road rage incidents and random arguments get out of control, and a minor incident becomes a tragedy. People go to prison every day because of their ideas about insults. People die.

Even in much less dramatic circumstances, responding emotionally to an insult can cause bigger problems. An argument with a friend or romantic partner can get out of hand as both people say hurtful things to each other, permanently damaging the relationship.

When you feel insulted, remember that you cannot be harmed by the insult itself, but you can be harmed by your ideas about it. Whatever discomfort or emotional distress you feel, it comes from your ideas about insults. If you can change those ideas, no insult will ever touch you.

Criticism

Harsh criticism can be hard to deal with, especially when it is not intended as an insult but as an honest critique or piece of advice. Imagine you're meeting an old friend for coffee, and your friend suddenly launches into a sweeping indictment of all your recent life decisions. Most people would probably feel upset and hurt to be judged like that. Perhaps the critique is a fair one, and perhaps it isn't. Perhaps your friend doesn't understand what happened or is making some unfair assumptions about your role in the situation.

Two plus two equals four, regardless of what anybody thinks. If a person is insisting that two plus two doesn't equal four, that person is harmed by his own ignorance, but the proposition isn't hurt at all. It just goes on being true. If your friend was wrong about some choice you made, the truth cannot be changed or harmed by the misunderstanding. Whenever anyone harshly criticizes you, remind yourself that they were acting as they thought best based on their own understanding of the situation. They can't see the world through your eyes, and you can't see it through theirs.

Mistreatment

Some situations go beyond mere insult or criticism and into active mistreatment. You aren't obligated to let anyone mistreat you, and Stoicism should not be used as a reason to let yourself be abused. However, there are some situations where we may not feel it appropriate to let go of a certain relationship even though the other person is being extremely difficult to deal with. For example, if you're caring for an elderly parent who has dementia, they may say and do many hurtful things without even realizing it. A teenaged child might steal from your wallet or act out in other harmful ways. In these situations, Marcus Aurelius suggests a simple mental trick.

Imagine a heavy object with two handles—one large enough to pick it up with and one too small for that purpose. If you had to pick up that object, you wouldn't try to pick it up with the small handle, only with the large handle. The small handle is the feeling of being mistreated. The large handle is the relationship itself. You can't deal with a difficult parent by thinking about how difficult they are but by reminding yourself that this person is your mother or father. You can't deal with a problem child by thinking about what a problem they are but by reminding yourself that this person is your child. Always use the larger handle.

Misfortune

If you feel unhappy because of something that happened to you, Marcus Aurelius suggests a series of questions. Does this thing prevent you from being just? Does it prevent you from being generous? Does it prevent you from being temperate that allows you to respond to your problem in a calm and self-controlled way? Does it prevent you from being prudent? Does it force you to accept any false opinions or make any poor judgments? Does it take away your mental freedom?

If you can answer "no" to all these questions, then whatever happened has not truly harmed you. Someone else might have broken under the same pressure you just faced, but you didn't break. You're still here. Even if you didn't succeed in being completely Stoic, you haven't been thrown too far off course. Instead of being unhappy at your apparent misfortune, remind yourself to be happy that you have borne it well.

Contagious Emotions

Emotions can be contagious, especially negative emotions. You can become anxious by spending time with an anxious person or sad by spending time with a sad person—but only if you adopt their view of the matter.

To guard against this, Epictetus warns us not to get caught up in the intense emotions the people around us may be experiencing. If you see someone crying, by all means, try to help them somehow, but don't start crying along with them.

Instead, remind yourself that this person is crying because of the beliefs they hold and not because of whatever happened.

Ambition

If you're an ambitious person with big dreams and goals, it can be hard to watch other people earn the honors, promotions, or awards you've always dreamed of having. It's easy to start feeling envious or wonder why you haven't received the same kind of recognition. You may even start to feel depressed and self-critical, seeing yourself as a failure compared to others.

Ambition is a potent force, and there's nothing wrong with dreaming big. A Stoic practicing to become a Sage is an ambitious person, but she focuses her ambition on her actions and her own will. Rather than asking you not to dream big, Stoicism asks you dream even bigger. Don't set your sights on anything as limited and temporary as the recognition of others. Set your sights on becoming free, and don't be satisfied with anything less. As Epictetus reminds us, there is only one battle where your success is under your control: the battle of the will. If you focus all your ambition on that battle, you can be sure of winning.

Difficult People

When you have to deal with an unreasonable person, Marcus Aurelius says that you should think of them as a training partner at a wrestling or boxing gym. Some training partners are unusually rough, and you might get extra bruises when you train with them. It's nothing personal. If anything, the need to protect yourself will keep you on your toes, and the training will be more valuable than usual.

If you think of a difficult coworker or family member as an especially rough training partner, you should find it easier not to lose your patience with them. You may even be grateful for the valuable training.

Illness

In one of his letters to Seneca, Lucilius challenges the Stoic teachings on illness and other hardships. According to the Stoics, a person can be happy under any circumstances—even when suffering the pain and discomfort of a serious illness. No one ever prays for illness or suffering. Doesn't that prove that such things are actually bad and not merely "indifferent"?

Seneca disagrees, pointing out that the happiness of the Stoic does not come from hardship but from the courage with which he is able to meet it:

"Nor am I so mad as to crave illness; but if I must suffer an illness, I shall desire that I may do nothing which shows lack of restraint... The conclusion is, not that hardships are desirable, but that virtue is desirable, which enables us patiently to endure hardships."

- Seneca

Severe illness can cause intense suffering, and no one would ever want to go through that experience. Even so, a Stoic can meet the challenge of illness with courage and fortitude, and that's where his happiness comes from.

Loss

The things we have in life are basically borrowed, and we never know when we'll have to give them back. That's true of everything from a childhood toy to the people you love the most. Sooner or later, you'll have to return all these things. Rather than thinking of a loss as something precious that has been taken away from you, think of it as a thing you borrowed and are now giving back. When you suffer some loss, whether large or small, you can apply this meditation to help you deal with it.

Instead of thinking, "I've lost my favorite book," tell yourself, "I've given it back."

Instead of thinking, "I've lost my job," tell yourself, "I've given it back."

Instead of thinking, "my pet has died," tell yourself, "I've given her back."

Epictetus suggests using this technique even with the most challenging of life's events such as divorce or a death in the family. As hard as it might be to apply this idea in such difficult circumstances, it's always healthy to remember that we don't own other people. We might feel like we've "lost" them, but the truth is we own only ourselves and our ability to make choices.

Grief

Seneca also addresses grief, perhaps with a little more empathy than the stern Epictetus. In one of his letters to Lucilius, Seneca seeks to comfort his student on the death of a close friend. Rather than asking him not to grieve at all, he asks him only to keep his grief within the limits of reason.

"Let not the eyes be dry when we have lost a friend, nor let them overflow. We may weep, but we must not wail."

- Seneca

Seneca does acknowledge the Stoic doctrine that the Sage could meet even the death of a close friend with total equanimity, but he is not so harsh as to insist that Lucilius live up to that demanding standard. He only tells him not to grieve too long or with any kind of melodramatic display.

Death comes to everyone, and almost all of us will lose friends and other loved ones at some point. To make sure we aren't surprised by grief, Seneca encourages Lucilius to keep the mortality of all his friends in the back of his mind. That way, when someone dies, we won't be so shocked that we lose our sense of balance.

Depression

"Sometimes, even to live is an act of courage."

- Seneca

While Stoicism can help with many of the problems that make people unhappy, clinical depression is not just a matter of feeling unhappy. If you suffer from depression, you may not have it in your power to reverse those feelings just by applying Stoicism.

On the other hand, you do have it in your power to handle depression the way a Stoic would. If you can't help being depressed, then it isn't under your control. What's under your control is how you respond to it. As with any other illness, it is possible to face your depression with Stoic courage.

Death

Most of us suffer from the fear of death to a greater or lesser degree. Marcus Aurelius was no exception. On campaign far away from home, he must have known that he could die in battle or from a disease, especially the disastrous Antonine Plague that killed five million Romans during his reign.

Many of the passages in the *Meditations* address the fear of death, implying that this was something the emperor struggled with frequently. In one passage, he reminds himself that the past and future are both illusions of the mind. The only thing that ever really exists is the present moment, and the only thing any of us can ever lose in death is the single moment in which we die.

The emperor's insight may or may not be helpful for you, but to a Stoic, the fear of death is like any other fear. You can't control the fact that you'll die someday, so death cannot be good or bad. Adopting this viewpoint can remove much of the fear.

Chapter 6: Great Stoics and Admirers of Stoicism

"Bitter are the roots of study, but how sweet their fruit."

- Cato

The Stoic way of life has inspired many people over the past 2300 years, including some of the most influential leaders in politics, sports, business, and the arts. Some of them practiced Stoicism as their daily philosophy, while others drew comfort and inspiration from the Stoic classics. From the committed Stoics to the merely curious, here are some of the greatest leaders and innovators who have applied the wisdom of Stoicism in their lives and careers.

Political Leaders

Considering that Stoicism is such a practical philosophy, it's not surprising that some of the greatest Stoics were political and military leaders rather than professional philosophers. In ancient times, the most influential and revered of these "practical Stoics" was probably Cato the Younger, a Roman statesman who fought to preserve the Republic and prevent the rise of Julius Caesar.

Cato was famous for his Stoic lifestyle, his uncompromising moral standards, and his physical courage. He dressed as a poor man, shoeless, and bareheaded in every weather. As a general of the Roman legions, he lived and worked as a common soldier. As a Senator, he refused bribes and scorned any attempt to influence his vote. When attacked by assassins during a Roman election, Cato refused to flee and made his way to the polls, still bleeding from his wounds.

Though some people mocked him at first for his inflexible rigidity, the consistency of Cato's character was deeply impressive. Over time, he gained so much moral authority that his fellow citizens saw him as the quintessential Roman and paid close attention to his opinion on any important issue. Unfortunately for Cato, he was unable to prevent the ambitious general and politician Julius Caesar from building popular support and assuming power.

When it became clear that Caesar would become the dictator of Rome—the development that eventually led to the end of the Republic and the birth of the Empire—Cato literally fell on his own sword in protest. Refusing all offers of help, he died as bravely as he had lived.

Cato was friends with another statesman named Cicero. Unlike Cato, Cicero was far from being a dogmatic Stoic. Despite being unwilling to commit completely to Stoicism, Cicero tried to live by Stoic principles in his career as a Roman politician. He was personally responsible for putting down a coup attempt through his decisive action in executing the leading conspirators. Just like Cato, Cicero was a defender of the Republic and an opponent of Caesar. Unlike Cato, Cicero outlived Caesar and went on to oppose his successor Mark Anthony.

Of course, the most famous Stoic political leader is probably Marcus Aurelius, who is remembered as the wisest and best of all the Roman emperors, as well as an important Stoic philosopher in his own right. To get some sense of what his life might have been like, watch the first scene of the movie *Gladiator*—the wise old emperor at the beginning of the movie is supposed to be him.

When Stoicism faded out of public awareness as the Roman Empire became Christian, leaders turned to other sources of inspiration for a time. The Renaissance brought Stoicism back into the public eye, and eventually, the Stoic classics became a standard part of the educational curriculum and influenced generations of leaders.

American president Theodore Roosevelt, in his long and grueling mission to explore the River of Doubt in the Amazon rain forest, brought only eight books in his luggage. One of those books was by Epictetus and another by Marcus Aurelius.

Chinese prime minister Wen Jiabao, in an interview with *Newsweek*, revealed that he had read the *Meditations* of Marcus Aurelius over a hundred times. Other leaders who have claimed to be inspired by the Stoics—whether or not they actually lived according to Stoic principles—include Thomas Jefferson, Bill Clinton, and Cory Booker.

Military Leaders

The Prussian ruler and military leader Frederick the Great took up the practice of Stoicism in a moment of despair after his armies were nearly wiped out in the Seven Years War of 1756-1763. Going on to eventual triumph and great renown as a general, Frederick was so grateful to Marcus Aurelius for his inspiration that he filled his summer home with statues of the philosopher-emperor and referred to Marcus Aurelius as his personal hero. Frederick the Great wasn't exactly a Stoic—his ambition for glory wasn't Stoic at all—but he was able to use Stoic principles to overcome disaster and go on to victory.

During the American Revolution, George Washington used his admiration for Cato the Younger to rally his dispirited troops at Valley Forge. Cato the Younger was a hugely popular figure among the American leaders, who saw him as a symbol of both the Stoic virtues and resistance to tyranny. Washington arranged for a play about Cato's life to be performed for the troops, inspiring them to endure the winter at Valley Forge with the same Stoic resolve Cato the Younger would have shown.

Washington wasn't the only leader of that period to be inspired by the Stoics. Toussaint Louverture, one of the leading figures in the Haitian War of Independence against Napoleon's France, was said to have been guided by his study of Epictetus. Incidentally, the Haitian Revolution is still the only successful slave rebellion in human history, so the writings of the slave Epictetus influenced the liberation of the Haitian slaves many centuries after the philosopher's death.

More recently, Vice Admiral James Stockdale used the teachings of Epictetus to help him endure his seven years of captivity at the "Hanoi Hilton" POW prison in North Vietnam. Stockdale's fortitude and courage in this situation are legendary. He not only held up under torture repeatedly but succeeded in inspiring his fellow prisoners to commit to unyielding resistance against their captors. Later in life, Stockdale could still recite any passage of Epictetus's "Handbook" from memory.

The writings of the Stoics remain popular with soldiers. According to Nancy Sherman, a Professor of Philosophy who wrote a book called *Stoic Warriors: The Ancient Philosophy Behind the Military Mind*, the works of Epictetus are especially popular with soldiers because of his straightforward and unpretentious style. Former Defense Secretary James Mattis carried a copy of the *Meditations* of Marcus Aurelius in his rucksack as a young soldier and credited it with helping him endure the hardships of combat. While serving as Defense Secretary, he described it as the one book every American should make a point of reading.

Entertainers

Although Stoicism offers the most to those who practice it wholeheartedly, the Stoic classics can provide support and emotional resilience to anyone who reads them. Several popular entertainers have expressed an interest in Stoicism or one of the Stoic thinkers. For example, Anna Kendrick—singer, actor, and author of *Scrappy Little Nobody*—turns to Marcus Aurelius for emotional comfort even though she doesn't consider herself a practicing Stoic. In a *New York Times* interview, Kendrick described the *Meditations* as a "soothing" book, even though she doesn't agree with everything Marcus Aurelius has to say. You can get a lot of great advice for daily life just by keeping a copy of one of the Stoic classics by your bed and reading a short passage every night before you go to sleep. That's probably why Thomas Jefferson had one of Seneca's books on his nightstand when he died, but he's not the only one to keep the Stoics close at hand. Brie Larson of *Community* and *21 Jump Street* tweeted a screenshot of one of her favorite passages from Marcus Aurelius in 2017. The passage she chose was about philosophy as a guide for daily life, encouraging her fans and Twitter followers to find out more about the Stoics.

Similarly, English actor Tom Hiddleston tweeted a screenshot from Seneca's "On the Shortness of Life" in 2011, adding that the Stoic philosopher "knew a thing or two." In this passage, Seneca talks about how different people are driven by different things—greed, ambition, or simple restlessness—but few are capable of simply slowing down and enjoying their lives. According to Seneca, life only seems so short to us because we spend most of it distracted. Hiddleston has appeared in Marvel superhero movies such as *Thor* and *The Avengers* and was the star of the BBC miniseries *The Night Manager*.

Stoicism seems to be especially popular among hip hop performers. Lupe Fiasco mentioned Marcus Aurelius in the track "Lightwork," and encouraged fans to read *Meditations* first if they wanted to talk to him. Twista claimed to be "as sick as" Marcus Aurelius in his track "Get Me," and rap superstar LL Cool J is a fan of Neo-Stoic self-help guru Ryan Holiday. Stoicism is also in vogue with at least a few major R&B performers, including Grammy-winning T-Pain, creator of the album *Stoicville: The Phoenix* and the mixtape *Stoic*. T-Pain has stated that he identifies with the Stoic's ability to endure pain without complaint. Dutch musician and artist Nick van Hofwegen, also known as Young & Sick, helped the Daily Stoic blog design a poster based on a quote from Marcus Aurelius. These entertainers might not be deeply involved in the Stoic practice, but they have all drawn on Stoic ideas to one degree or another in dealing with the ups and downs of life in the public eye. By using their fame to promote the works of Seneca or Marcus Aurelius, they may influence at least some of their fans to give Stoicism a try.

Athletes

Stoicism has been surprisingly influential in the world of professional sports, largely due to a chance gift NFL executive Michael Lombardi received from his wife. When she gave him a copy of the *Meditations* of Marcus Aurelius for Christmas one year, the two-time Superbowl winner became so intrigued that he took a challenge to try to live like a Stoic for 30 days. Lombardi went on to take a course in Stoicism from writer and teacher Donald Robertson, author of *How to Think Like a Roman Emperor*.

Lombardi began to encourage other people in professional football to study the Stoics, especially the members of the New England Patriots. Rather than asking the players to read the original Stoic classics, Lombardi encouraged them to read *The Obstacle is the Way* by Ryan Holiday, which updates and popularizes Stoicism as a "life-hack" or technique for modern people to improve their lives.

The book proved to be highly popular with Tom Brady and the other players, who used it to overcome the widespread public criticism of the team over the Deflategate controversy. When the Patriots beat the Seattle Seahawks to win the Superbowl, they were kind enough to recommend the book to their defeated rivals. Seattle Seahawks head coach Pete Carroll has since become known for his interest in Stoicism, as has Seahawks General Manager Schneider. Holiday's work is now popular throughout the NFL.

Interest in Stoicism is spreading to college football as well. University of Alabama coach Nick Saban relies on the advice of Marcus Aurelius, as well as on Ryan Holiday's modern interpretation.

In an interview with *Sports Illustrated* about his interest in Stoicism, Lombardi points out that great leaders in all areas of life are always looking for new ways to improve their leadership qualities. Studying the great leaders of the past is an obvious choice—the ideas that helped Marcus Aurelius in his wars with the enemies of Rome can certainly help the New England Patriots in their struggles with other teams. Lombardi didn't stop with Marcus Aurelius; in the same interview, he also mentions reading and enjoying Seneca.

Interest in Stoicism among professional athletes and coaches is not confined to football. Chicago Cubs manager Joe Maddon is a fan of Holiday's version of Stoicism, as is University of

Texas basketball coach Shaka Smart. Chandra Crawford, a cross-country skier and Olympic gold medalist, is also known as a practicing Stoic.

Stoicism's appeal to athletes isn't hard to understand. Athletes have to engage in harsh training to achieve their goals, and all athletes experience both defeats and victories. A philosophy like Stoicism is ideally suited to the athlete's lifestyle, giving them the mental fortitude to handle both the rigors of training and the uncertainties of competition. Marcus Aurelius and Epictetus both use athletic metaphors in their works on Stoicism. Epictetus compares training in Stoic philosophy to training for the Olympics, and Marcus Aurelius suggests treating difficult people as unusually rough training partners. The connection between athletics and Stoicism may have been just as clear in ancient times as it is today.

Authors

Most writers are also voracious readers, and some of the most influential writers of all time have counted the works of the Stoics among their favorite books.

Ambrose Bierce, the author of the satirical classic *The Devil's Dictionary*, was fond of the *Enchiridion* of Epictetus. In a letter to a friend, he echoed a passage from that work by saying that the study of Stoicism would make him worthy of being a dinner guest of the gods themselves. Bierce is mostly remembered today for his witty and cynical definitions of common words, but he was also a journalist, poet, and author of powerful short stories about the Civil War.

John Steinbeck, the author of some of the greatest American novels ever written, has one of his characters read a passage from Marcus Aurelius in his 1952 novel *East of Eden*. Steinbeck described the *Meditations* as one of his two favorite books.

JK Rowling—perhaps the most famous writer of modern times for her Harry Potter series—has also described herself as a fan of Marcus Aurelius.

Of course, being a fan of a book is one thing, and incorporating its ideas into your own life is another. Author and philosopher Ralph Waldo Emerson was a fan of the Stoics, but he also incorporated some of their ideas when developing his own philosophy of Transcendentalism.

More recently, philosopher Nassim Nicholas Taleb has mentioned his love of Seneca in two of his works—*The Black Swan* (which deals with the often world-changing consequences of highly improbable events) and *Antifragile* (which explores societies and systems resilient enough to avoid sudden collapse).

Robert Greene (author of *The 48 Laws of Power*) and Neil Strauss (author of *The Game: Penetrating the Secret Society of Pickup Artists*) have also expressed enthusiasm for Stoicism, though it should be noted that neither pickup artists nor power-seekers can be described as Stoics.

Business Leaders

Stoicism began when Zeno of Citium took up philosophy to console himself after losing his fortune in a disastrous shipwreck. He later described this shipwreck as the most profitable voyage he had ever undertaken. Stoicism can help entrepreneurs and business leaders overcome adversity and achieve the heights of professional success. Paradoxically, it does so by teaching them to stop getting emotionally invested in concepts like defeat and victory and profit and loss.

In the words of Musonius Rufus, the Stoic teacher of Epictetus, "the person in training must seek to rise above, so as to stop seeking out pleasure and steering away from pain; to stop clinging to living and abhorring death; and in the case of property and money, to stop valuing receiving over giving." By detaching from the endless pursuit of profit and competition with other companies, the Stoic business leader can see things as they truly are and act appropriately. Stoicism does not teach us to ignore our roles in society just because they are "indifferent" to genuine happiness.

A Stoic emperor cannot neglect his duties but must seek to govern wisely and well—as Marcus Aurelius did. A Stoic businessperson, without allowing himself to think of profit as good and loss as bad, must still conduct the affairs of his company with all the skill and strategic intelligence he can manage. As Epictetus says, we don't get to pick our roles in the play of life, but we still need to perform them with all our skill. Several prominent business leaders have been inspired by Stoicism. Jack Dorsey, a co-founder of Twitter, is one of several well-known tech leaders who are admirers of Stoicism. Others include Foundry Group investor Brad Feld and GoDaddy CEO Blake Irving, as well as many lesser-known designers and engineers in Silicon Valley. In fact, Stoicism has become so popular among Silicon Valley tech workers that it inspired an article on the topic by *Quartz's* Olivia Goldhill.

Kevin Rose, a highly successful investor and entrepreneur, is a fan of the book *The Ego is the Enemy* by modern Stoic Ryan Holiday. Angel investor Tim Ferriss is so enthusiastic about Stoicism that he republished Seneca's *Epistles* under the title *The Tao of Seneca*, and recorded excerpts from Seneca's letters on his own podcast.

Condé Nast CEO Jonathan Newhouse won't travel without copies of the Stoic classics on hand. David Heinemeier Hansson, the founder of project management company Basecamp, mentioned his admiration for the Stoics in an interview with Tim Ferriss.

Stoicism: Life-Hack or Way of Life?

As you can see, Stoicism has appealed to many people, including some who have had a tremendous influence. If George Washington had never been inspired by the example of Cato the Younger, who knows if the United States would even exist? If Frederick the Great had not turned to Stoicism after his early defeats, would he have ever gone on to win his greatest victories?

Although Stoicism has given courage and fortitude to some of the greatest leaders, writers, and even entertainers, there's a difference between using Stoicism as a "life hack" to make you more effective and practicing Stoicism as a way of life. Kai Whiting and Leonidas Konstantakos, writing for the "Partially Examined Life" blog, encourage readers interested in Stoicism to take their interest deeper. You can turn to Stoicism for comfort and inspiration when things don't go well, and you can use it to give you the fortitude to overcome a challenge and go on to victory. But, neither of these things can produce genuine and lasting happiness.

Epictetus once described students with "a little philosophy" as the most challenging of all, since they were harder to help than students with no experience. He also described the condition of a "person making progress" as being similar to drowning in shallow water—you're closer to safety, but you're not there yet.

If you don't completely agree with Stoicism, you can still apply the parts of it you do agree with to help you live a better and more fulfilling life. That's what Cicero did, despite going on record as a critic of some Stoic ideas. If Stoicism does strike you as a valid philosophy, you'll probably get a lot more out of it by practicing it seriously than by using it as a mere technique for getting ahead in life. As Whiting and Konstantakos point out in their article, the pursuit of success for its own sake binds you to something not under your control. According to Stoicism, this makes it impossible for you to be free or happy. If you pursue Stoicism with a full commitment, you may also end up being a success in business or whatever field you decide to pursue. The clear-headed mentality of Stoicism can be a tremendous asset. If you pursue Stoicism half-heartedly, you may find yourself unsuccessful at both career and philosophy. As Epictetus says, it's not possible to put equal effort and intensity into two separate goals.

This is not to imply that you cannot have a career while pursuing Stoicism. The Stoics believed it was possible to practice philosophy within the everyday world of career and family, or they would never have split away from the Cynics over that issue. However, your best chance of achieving both happiness and success is to focus on happiness, letting success happen along the way. The Stoic approach to life and work is one of the most enduring guides to making that happen.

Chapter 7: Stoicism and Psychology

"The philosophical origins of cognitive therapy can be traced back to the Stoic philosophers."

- Aaron T. Beck

Everyone has not welcomed the renewed popularity of Stoicism. Stoicism is sometimes criticized as an outdated philosophy, a relic of ancient thinking with no place in the modern world. Some people say it's unrealistic, that we can't really control our emotions just by changing our belief system. Other people say we shouldn't even try and that Stoicism would keep us from ever experiencing love or joy. Does Stoicism increase good feelings as its practitioners claim, or does the rejection of the passions lead to a gray life with no emotional depth?

The great Stoics, like Epictetus, taught that our thoughts are the main source of our happiness and unhappiness in life. So, how well does Stoicism match up with what we know about the brain? If Stoic ideas have any validity, they should be confirmed by modern psychology and cognitive science.

There are many different therapies in the practice of psychology, including everything from traditional Freudian psychotherapy to acceptance and commitment therapy. One of the most effective and widely used treatments is known as Cognitive Behavioral Therapy or CBT.

CBT is used in the treatment of anxiety, mood disorders, eating disorders, depression, gambling addiction, substance abuse, and many other common problems. Studies have shown it to be one of the most effective and practical types of therapy, and it is considered the preferred treatment for a wide range of cognitive and behavioral issues. Studies have shown it to be just as effective as medication in some cases, making it the ideal option for people who want to address their problems without medication if possible.

Although CBT is a treatment method rather than a philosophy, the core ideas of this therapy are based on ancient Stoicism. Practicing Stoicism is not the same thing as receiving treatment in Cognitive Behavioral Therapy from a qualified professional, and receiving CBT treatment won't make you a philosopher. The two are distinct. Nevertheless, the tools CBT therapists use are based on the insights of Epictetus, Seneca, and Marcus Aurelius—a powerful argument for the validity of the Stoic worldview.

Cognitive Behavioral Therapy is a broad term, encompassing several different methods. Cognitive Emotional Behavioral Therapy, Structured Cognitive Behavioral Training, Moral Reconation Therapy, Stress Inoculation Training, Unified Protocol, Mindfulness-based Cognitive Behavioral Hypnotherapy, and Brief Cognitive Behavioral Therapy are all types of CBT.

All these therapies have slightly different theories and techniques, and some incorporate other influences along with Stoicism. For instance, Mindfulness-based Cognitive Behavioral Hypnotherapy incorporates some ideas from Buddhism. However, the basic insights and assumptions of CBT are shared by all the variations, and all of them share the same roots in ancient Stoicism.

Development of CBT

CBT can be traced back to an earlier method called Cognitive Therapy, which is now considered one of the subtypes of CBT. Cognitive Therapy was developed in the 1960s by a psychoanalyst named Aaron Beck, who felt that traditional psychotherapy was too focused on the unconscious to be practical for most patients.

Beck's reading of the Stoics had convinced him that psychological problems are often influenced by how people think and what they believe about the world. This matches several passages in the *Meditations* of Marcus Aurelius, where the emperor reminds himself that our beliefs and opinions are the prime cause of all our actions.

According to Beck, negative feelings and behaviors are often the direct consequence of negative beliefs and thoughts. He wanted to help patients recognize distorted thought patterns so that they could transform them over time into more positive and functional thought patterns. Beck believed that this would naturally lead to a decrease in dysfunctional behaviors, making Cognitive Therapy an effective treatment for substance abuse and other behavioral problems.

Cognitive Therapy is based on Beck's Cognitive Model, which divides human thought into three categories: automatic thoughts, intermediate beliefs, and core beliefs. Automatic thoughts are involuntary negative reactions based on the patient's underlying beliefs about the self, other people, or the future.

For example, a person suffering from an eating disorder might have a feeling of revulsion and self-hatred when looking in a mirror, imagining herself to be much heavier than she really is. Automatic thoughts derive from intermediate beliefs in an "if-then" pattern, for example, "if I lose enough weight, I'll finally be popular." Intermediate beliefs derive from core beliefs such as, "nobody likes me." By tracing the automatic thought all the way back to the core belief that ultimately inspired it, it becomes clear that this patient's eating disorder is based in a deep belief that she is unlikeable and that treating this belief is key to treating the behavior.

In Cognitive Therapy, the therapist helps the patient learn to recognize automatic thoughts, then identifies the intermediate and core beliefs driving automatic thoughts. By asking a series of questions (a method borrowed from Socrates), the therapist demonstrates the irrational nature of these beliefs. Finally, the therapist helps the patient understand that these beliefs and automatic thoughts are distorted and inaccurate.

This process mirrors the Stoic approach to cognition, in which automatic reactions or "impressions" are subjected to questioning and only "assented to" if they seem rational by Stoic standards. Essentially, the Cognitive Therapist teaches the patient to question his impressions and assent only to those who turn out to be rational after close examination. Epictetus would certainly approve.

Cognitive Behavioral Therapy takes the basic idea of Cognitive Therapy and adds additional techniques from Behaviorism, especially the use of desensitization and conditioning techniques to help patients overcome neuroses such as phobias. The Cognitive aspect of CBT is the aspect most heavily influenced by Stoic philosophy, but the Behaviorist aspect has proven to be very helpful for patients suffering from deep underlying fears and compulsions.

Thoughts, Emotions, and Actions

In the CBT model of how the mind works, thoughts influence emotions, and emotions influence actions or behaviors. Our actions confirm our thoughts about the world, and the cycle then repeats itself.

For example, you might think that you can't relax and destress without some wine. This thought leads you to feel stressed out and tense until you do drink some wine, at which point, you feel a little bit more relaxed. The next time you have the same thought, you're more likely to act on it because your experience of drinking the wine confirmed the validity of the thought. Of course, drinking too much wine causes other problems over time, but it's hard to break out of the loop because the connection between thought, feeling, and action seems so convincing. Even if you suspect that drinking too much is ultimately causing you much more stress, it's hard for you to accept that it won't help you right now.

At a deeper level, CBT holds that our core beliefs drive our thoughts. As in Cognitive Therapy, core beliefs are divided into three categories: beliefs about the self, beliefs about other people, and beliefs about the world. For example, the thought that it is not possible to relax without wine might be driven by core beliefs that the world is a threatening and stressful place, that other people cannot or will not offer emotional support, and that you can't rely on anyone except yourself when you feel overwhelmed. Not knowing any other ways to relax effectively, you then convince yourself that drinking wine is the only realistic option.

This is only a simplified version of how CBT works, but the connection to Stoicism is easy to see. Epictetus would certainly agree that our core beliefs about the world inform our opinions about specific situations, generating negative emotions or *pathé*, such as fear, and finally leading us to make unhealthy decisions. Stoicism and Cognitive Behavioral Therapy share the same basic and practical assumption that our actions are driven mostly by what we believe about the world, and the most effective way to make positive changes in our life is to change what we believe. However, CBT does not focus on the central doctrine of Stoicism that all cognitive distortions ultimately come from the same source.

Cognitive Distortions

The main difference between the Stoic approach and the CBT approach is in the definition of what makes a thought "distorted" or unhelpful. In classical Stoicism, defining anything outside your own control as "good" or "bad" is a cognitive distortion. This is the basic error the Stoic wants to avoid. In CBT, there are four types of cognitive distortion: catastrophizing, overgeneralizing, minimizing positives, and maximizing negatives.

Catastrophizing is a type of if-then thinking in which the worst-case scenario is assumed to be true without any evidence. For example, "if I don't keep my house spotlessly clean, I'll catch a disease and die," or "if I don't get this report perfect, I'll be fired, and my career will be ruined."

Overgeneralizing is drawing a sweeping conclusion without enough evidence to support the conclusion. For example, if you go to a party, and no one talks to you, it would be an overgeneralization to assume that no one ever likes you or wants to talk to you. Your experience at a single party just isn't enough evidence for the generalization.

Minimizing positives is the habit of disregarding any evidence that things are going well for you. For instance, you might tell yourself that your new promotion doesn't matter because you'll just be overwhelmed with stress and mess things up.

Maximizing negatives is the habit of focusing too much on whatever is difficult or challenging in your life. For example, you might tell yourself you're all alone because you don't have a girlfriend, ignoring the fact that you have several close friends.

The four cognitive distortions of CBT do show some influence from Stoicism. Marcus Aurelius and Epictetus both warn us not to indulge in any "what if" thinking but to stick to the basic facts about the situation. It's not harmful to say, "my mother is sick," but it is harmful to say, "my mother is sick; what if she dies?" Avoiding "what if" thinking prevents catastrophizing.

Sticking to the facts is also a good defense against overgeneralizing. "I went to the party, and no one talked to me" is just a fact, with no value judgment attached to it. "I went to the party, and no one talked to me because no one ever wants to talk to me" is an overgeneralization. By just not adding anything to factual account, you can avoid this type of cognitive distortion.

The other two types of cognitive distortion are a bit more distant from Stoic thought because a Stoic would never admit that any external event could be positive or negative in the first place. Minimizing positives would just be "minimizing preferred *indifferents*," and maximizing negatives would just be "maximizing dispreferred *indifferents*." The Stoic way of thinking about life doesn't grant any true importance to either one.

That's the difference between Stoicism as a philosophy and CBT as a therapy. To practice Stoicism, you have to accept Stoic teachings about what really matters and what does not. Without accepting that virtue is the only good, it would be hard to practice Stoicism. To benefit from CBT, you don't have to accept any particular belief. You just have to be willing to question your existing beliefs with the therapist's help and guidance.

Cognitive Behavioral Therapy is a practical application of Stoic insights for people who don't necessarily know anything about Stoicism.

Stages of Cognitive Behavioural Therapy

Cognitive Behavioral Therapy begins with an assessment, in which the therapist attempts to determine which critical behaviors are having an effect on the client's life. Next, the therapist decides whether these behaviors are excessive or deficient—too much or too little for the real situation. The therapist finds out how often the behavior is happening, how long it usually lasts, and how intense it is. This becomes the baseline, and the goal of the therapy is then to increase or reduce the frequency of the behavior based on the circumstances.

For example, the behavior might be excessive handwashing, a typical compulsive symptom. The therapist would find out how often the client washes his hands and how much time he spends doing so. The goal of therapy would be to reduce the frequency and duration of the behavior, so it stops causing problems in the client's life.

The next phase in CBT is reconceptualization, where the client is encouraged to think about his problem differently. This phase is similar to the Stoic approach because it's based on changing the client's beliefs about the world.

This phase is followed by skill acquisition, where the patient practices specific exercises to help him modify the behavior. Once these skills are consolidated, the therapist helps the patient generalize what he has learned in therapy. By learning how to spot the four basic cognitive distortions, the patient is given the tools to become his own therapist in the future.

That doesn't mean it's all smooth sailing from this point forward. Patients typically need some follow-up sessions to make sure they haven't slipped back into old ways of thinking.

Stoicism in Positive Psychology

Of course, Cognitive Behavioral Therapy only supports Stoicism to a limited extent because the creators of CBT didn't incorporate every aspect of Stoicism into the practical therapies they were designing. The success of CBT suggests that Stoicism is right about a few key points, especially that our happiness or unhappiness is largely determined by our beliefs.

However, CBT's effectiveness cannot be interpreted as evidence for Stoicism's most important assertions. For that, psychologists would need to test Stoicism itself, not a therapy derived from Stoicism. The purpose of therapy is to correct a disorder, but the goal of philosophy like Stoicism is to achieve well-being and happiness. This is the domain of positive psychology, a movement to redirect psychology away from the exclusive study of psychological disorders and toward the study of human well-being. Some researchers in this field have decided to test whether Stoicism can live up to its claims and improve people's lives.

In 2013, Professor Christopher Gill of the University of Exeter conducted a research study on the benefits of Stoicism with Tim LeBon of the Modern Stoicism website. The goal of the study was to determine whether Stoic training would help participants experience more life satisfaction and more positive emotions.

Participants in the study were taught the basics of Stoic practice and assigned a set of daily exercises. Exercises included a morning meditation on Stoic principles, daily study of Stoic principles and techniques, a Stoic worksheet, and evening meditation on things done well and poorly during the day. All these exercises were based on specific passages in the Stoic classics.

Some of the participants were recruited from existing Stoic discussion groups, and others were recruited from the public at large. The study lasted for a single week, after which participants were asked a series of questions to determine what effect a one-week training course in Stoicism had on their daily lives.

At the end of the week, the amount of life satisfaction reported by participants had increased by 14%. The frequency/intensity of negative emotion was down by 11%, and the frequency/intensity of positive emotion was up by 9%. Feelings of optimism were up by 18%, and 56% of participants described themselves as having behaved more ethically than usual. These are significant improvements for a study that lasted for just a single week, providing strong scientific support for Stoicism as a path toward increased well-being, happiness, and virtue.

The Stoic Attitudes and Behaviours Self-Rating Scale

In an attempt to further study the relationship between Stoicism and well-being, modern Stoic Donald Robertson has developed the Stoic Attitudes and Behaviors Self-Rating Scale or SABSS. This scale is a test anyone can take at home to determine how closely their own beliefs match Stoic attitudes.

The SABSS test consists of 20 statements about Stoic beliefs and attitudes, followed by 10 statements about Stoic behaviors and life strategies. There is also one question to determine whether participants consider themselves to be practicing Stoics. Depending on the individual, identifying as a Stoic may or may not go along with holding Stoic principles or using Stoic strategies.

Participants are asked to rate every statement on a scale of one to five, with five meaning "strongly agree" and one meaning "strongly disagree." This allows shades of agreement and disagreement with Stoic principles. For instance, you might give a five rating to the statement that the goal of life is happiness but a three to the statement that virtue is the only thing needed for happiness.

Study of the SABSS questionnaire has produced some interesting results. As Stoicism predicts, prioritizing pleasure over virtue seems to be correlated with low levels of happiness and well-being. Stoic beliefs and attitudes were correlated with higher levels of happiness. However, Stoic life strategies and behaviors turned out to be more important for well-being than Stoic beliefs.

The study is not yet enough to establish causality, but it seems to imply that living like a Stoic will do more for your overall well-being than simply thinking like a Stoic. Given a choice between Stoic habits and Stoic beliefs, you should focus on building good habits and let the beliefs take care of themselves. Cognitive Behavioral Therapy teaches us that thoughts, emotions, and actions are all part of a feedback loop. By taking Stoic types of action, you can change your thoughts, which will result in changing your feelings as well.

Stoic Habits

The SABSS study identified four specific Stoic habits as most important in promoting happiness and overall well-being. The first was "mindfulness," defined as paying close attention to your actions and to the judgments you make in daily life. Rather than acting without thinking or making judgments without consideration, you should carefully weigh both your thoughts and acts.

The second was questioning your mental impressions before assenting to them. The ancient Stoics compared this practice to a sentry questioning anyone who approaches the guard-post. Don't let just any thought come in through the gate—be suspicious of your impressions.

The third was thinking of yourself as part of the social whole rather than an isolated individual. Marcus Aurelius talks about this constantly in his *Meditations*, reminding himself that "whatever does not harm the hive does not harm the bee."

The fourth was negative visualization, desensitizing yourself to potentially upsetting experiences by imagining them ahead of time. This practice could be the original inspiration behind the desensitization practices in Cognitive Behavioral Therapy. Of course, it's important not only to visualize whatever scares you but also to visualize yourself handling it in a Stoic way. It wouldn't do you any good to visualize breaking down or going into a tailspin of negative emotions!

These four practices on their own are an excellent introduction to the Stoic practice. Be mindful of your actions and judgments, be suspicious of your impressions, think of yourself as part of a social whole, and imagine the worst before it happens. With such a simple set of daily goals, anyone can get started practicing Stoicism right away.

In Stoic practice, right actions done for the wrong reason are merely appropriate, while right actions done for the right reason are referred to as "perfect." Appropriate behavior is the first step toward happiness, and perfect behavior is the culmination. The SABSS study suggests that appropriate behavior is enough to bring significant improvements in your life even if you aren't yet capable of perfect behavior.

In practical terms, this means that a "person making progress" can become significantly happier by practicing Stoicism and that greater well-being and freedom are not restricted to the Sage. While many more studies will have to be done before we can say anything definitive about the effects of Stoic practice, there is certainly enough evidence to be optimistic. Rather than being an outdated and irrelevant philosophy from the distant past, Stoicism is beginning to receive support from the most up-to-date research in positive psychology.

Chapter 8: Everyday Stoicism

"Let sleep not come upon thy languid eyes

Before each daily action thou hast scann'd;

What's done amiss, what done, what left

undone; From first to last examine all, and then

Blame what is wrong in what is right rejoice."

- Epictetus

Now that you understand the basics of Stoicism and how Stoics go about dealing with daily problems and emotional turmoil, you might be wondering how to get started. The Stoic idea is surprisingly simple, but making progress as a Stoic is not so simple. As with any skill, Stoic thinking takes a lot of practice. These simple exercises are not absolutely required in the practice of Stoicism but are likely to be helpful in the early stages. Some of them might seem a little harsh and puritanical the first time you read them, but they are based on the practical everyday psychology of the Stoic school. By being strict on yourself in the early stages, you'll find it a lot easier to build Stoic resilience and self-discipline into your daily life.

Broaden Your Affection: Let's say you have a favorite coffee mug or an old and well-loved fishing pole or any other object you're especially fond of. People often get emotionally attached to favorite objects like this. As a beginner at Stoicism, you would probably be upset if you dropped your favorite mug and shattered it or if your beloved old fishing pole fell off the back of the boat and disappeared into the lake. Every time you pick up this well-loved object of yours, ask yourself what it is and answer honestly. It's only a coffee mug, and there are many other good coffee mugs out there. It's only a fishing pole, and there are plenty of good fishing poles. Instead of focusing on the specific object, try to broaden your feeling of affection to include the broader category the object belongs to. Epictetus suggests doing this even when you kiss your child goodnight or put your arms around your spouse, telling yourself that you are simply kissing or hugging a human being. As with anything else in Stoicism, it's probably wiser to start small rather than trying to take this advice to such an extreme setting right away.

These Things Happen: Sometimes, we understand things better from a little distance. We usually don't overreact to a situation unless it affects us personally because we find it easier to see the situation for what it really is. For example, if you were over at a friend's house and your friend's child spilled a glass of milk, you certainly wouldn't get irritated over such a minor incident. What would you say? Probably, "these things happen" or something of the sort because it is true that these things will happen. What happens when your child spills a glass of milk? If you're like a lot of other parents, you'd probably get irritated at your child's carelessness and say something like, "I've asked you a thousand times to be more careful." Is there any real difference between the two situations? There is—only the amount of distance between you and the source of stress. Practice telling yourself, "these things happen," even in situations where you're directly involved. If you can make this a habit, you'll start to find it easier to look at your own life the way you would look at someone's else's life, with just enough distance to remember that "these things happen."

Don't Chatter: The phrase "strong but silent" is a cliché and might remind you of a John Wayne type of character: stoic on the outside, whatever emotional turmoil might lie beneath. In the practice of Stoicism, "appropriate" actions are considered good training for "perfect" actions, so being stoic on the outside can help you become Stoic on the inside over time. Epictetus advises his students not to talk too much, saying only a few words and only when necessary. He doesn't go as far as to forbid conversation, but he does tell his students to avoid any of the "common topics" that tend to get people worked up emotionally. Most importantly, Epictetus says to avoid talking about other people and their actions. Don't praise them, don't blame them, and don't compare them to each other. Why? Some actions are praiseworthy, and some are not. Some actions deserve blame or embarrassment. People can easily be compared to each other in various ways—this one is smarter, that one stronger. It doesn't matter. Blaming, praising, and comparing all have the same problem. They divert your mind from its proper focus, which is always your own actions and never anything external. According to Epictetus, your silence during an inappropriate conversation may even bring it to a halt, stopping people from repeating harmful gossip and innuendo.

Control Your Laughter: Epictetus says not to laugh too often and not to laugh too long or too loudly. This might seem a little harsh, and Epictetus is probably the harshest of all the Stoics. It's not that there's anything wrong with laughter, though. After all, joy is one of the "good feelings" even a Sage can safely indulge. The reminder to control your laughter is a training exercise to keep your mind as focused and self-disciplined as a Stoic's should be. In addition, laughter is frequently cruel in some way. Imagine a coworker telling a funny story, the theme of which is the stupidity and incompetence of one of your other coworkers. Is that a story you can laugh at safely or a situation where you should remain silent? If you can control your laughter in that situation, you will also avoid the mistake of criticizing others. Like the speech of a Stoic, the laughter of a Stoic should be relatively infrequent.

Avoid Vulgar Language: It would probably take a Sage not to swear in some circumstances, such as hitting your thumb with a hammer. Epictetus knows this, but he still asks his students not to swear, if possible, and to keep it to a bare minimum, if swearing simply cannot be avoided. Yelling out something colorful when you hit your thumb with a hammer is more like an "impression," an involuntary reaction rather than a choice. Swearing casually or excessively is more like "assent," the acceptance of false judgment. Like all the other exercises in this chapter, you should think of this more as a training exercise than an absolute rule. Having said that, it's hard to imagine a Stoic swearing often or loudly.

Avoid Vulgar Entertainment: Again, it's not that any particular type of entertainment is good or bad. In the Stoic view, good and bad are never found in external things but only in your reaction to them. From rock shows to professional wrestling to a horror movie, the things people do to pass the time are all indifferent. However, popular forms of entertainment usually try to provoke intense emotions. The better the entertainment is, the more emotion it provokes. For training purposes, it's usually better for a Stoic to avoid popular (and especially vulgar) entertainment. If you happen to find yourself at such an event, you can still use it as an opportunity for Stoic practice. First, try not to get caught up in the emotions around you. If everyone else is shouting and stamping their feet, avoid doing the same. Second, avoid any display of superiority or condescension. Try to stay calm and unaffected, without seeming to disapprove of everyone else. If you can avoid being swept away on the tide of emotion, you'll find it easier to do so in your daily life as well. It should be noted that Stoic philosopher Seneca wrote plays, including at least eight tragedies. A Stoic should avoid any entertainment based on the crude manipulation of extreme emotion, but that doesn't mean you can't enjoy a good movie or a good book.

Avoid Luxury: To teach yourself how to do without, Epictetus advises living a life of intentional minimalism. Don't buy the fanciest cut of steak or that bottle of expensive single malt Scotch. Don't wear designer clothes. Don't buy or build the most luxurious house. Epictetus actually says to confine yourself to what is merely useful, never going beyond bare necessity. The much wealthier Seneca wasn't anywhere near as harsh. He only advocated living such a minimalist lifestyle a few days out of every month. Both approaches are training methods rather than absolute rules. Minimalism, like luxury and refinement, is an external thing. However, having the bare necessities won't cause you to become addicted to luxury, but living a luxurious lifestyle will probably make it much harder for you to deal with hardship if it ever becomes necessary. To achieve Stoic independence from external things, it can be helpful to reduce your need for such things before you have to.

Be Careful About Sex: Sexuality is such a powerful biological instinct that most people would find it difficult to abstain from sex completely. If you aren't in a committed long-term relationship, Epictetus says it's better to abstain if possible, but he acknowledges that it won't be possible for everyone. If you don't think you can abstain, it's best to be careful. Don't overindulge, and don't participate in anything harmful or exploitative. While holding yourself to the highest standard that you can manage, avoid giving the impression that you look down on people who do things differently than you. In general, Stoicism teaches us to be stern with ourselves but easy on others. Making a point of your high standard of behavior is just as contrary to Stoicism as having no standard of behavior. This is a difficult line to walk since people who notice that you do things differently will often assume that you're looking down on them even if you haven't given them any reason to think so. While holding your actions to a high standard, try to project an easygoing and nonjudgmental attitude about the actions of others. That way, you can avoid both extremes.

"May the Best Man Win": This saying exemplifies the Stoic attitude to athletic competition. The way Epictetus phrases it is slightly different. He says that you should wish the winner to be whoever ends up winning. Strictly speaking, the better man could lose due to a fluke, and a Stoic still wouldn't get upset about that because it would still be something beyond the control of the will. Still, "may the best man win" is close enough for our purposes and will keep you from getting too worked up about the outcome of any particular game. A lot of people get wildly emotional about their favorite team—elated when their team wins, despondent when it loses. Your team's win-loss record is not under your control, so like any other external thing, it is indifferent to a Stoic. That doesn't mean you can't have a "preferred team" as a practicing Stoic. Remember, indifferent things can still be preferred or not preferred. Even if you do have a preferred team, your underlying attitude should still be "let the best man win." If you watch the game with that mentality, you won't be disappointed by the results, no matter what they are.

What Would Epictetus Do?: Epictetus himself doesn't say "what would Epictetus do." He tells us to imagine what Socrates or Zeno would do, especially when meeting an important person. It's hard to imagine the fearless Socrates or the noble-minded Zeno behaving without dignity and self-respect in front of anyone alive—not even a powerful and dangerous ruler. For the modern Stoic, asking, "what would Epictetus do?" is an equivalent exercise. If you have to meet the CEO of the company or perhaps a politician, don't say or do anything you couldn't imagine Epictetus doing in the same situation. This exercise can help you avoid doing or saying anything you might regret later on, no matter how nervous you feel about meeting the big man in person. This exercise can also be helpful if you happen to meet a celebrity for some reason.

Don't Tell Too Many War Stories: Even if you've lived a life filled with action and excitement, other people may not want to hear about it as often as you think. The ups and downs of life can be entertaining, and often, the worst experiences make the wildest anecdotes. At social events, such as parties, people often tell stories about their adventures. For a Stoic in training, the risk is that you will become too focused on the opinions and reactions of your audience. Do you want them to laugh and think you're funny, to be amazed at your courage, or to envy your exciting experiences? In all those situations, your mental focus is on something outside your control. Some of the most entertaining anecdotes involve bad decisions and their consequences. Are people laughing with you, or are they laughing at you? As with swearing and sex, Epictetus doesn't ban anecdotes completely, but he does say not to tell stories about your adventures very frequently. In addition, if someone else is telling an anecdote about something reprehensible, you should make it clear, through your response, that you don't want to hear that kind of story.

Be a Fatalist: The ancient Stoics were fatalists, believing much of life to be predestined by the gods. To Marcus Aurelius or Seneca, complaining too loudly about your life is like telling the gods they made a mistake. It won't fix whatever problems you have, but it will tend to alienate you from the gods. Of course, you don't have to believe everything is predestined or worry about angering God to practice Stoicism. Even if events are not predestined, you can still accept whatever is beyond your control. Still, thinking of events as decrees of Fate can be a useful exercise because it reduces the tendency to wish things were different when you can't do anything about it. Epictetus suggests using a line by the Greek playwright Euripides as a maxim:

"I follow cheerfully; and, did I not,

Wicked and wretched, I must follow still."

When something can't be changed, you just have to live with it. If you accept it cheerfully, you won't feel bad about it. If you don't accept it, you'll have to go through it anyway, but you'll be wretched. As Euripides says, accepting fate without complaint is a sign of genuine wisdom.

Memento Mori: The Latin phrase *memento mori* means "remember death." It's not meant to be grim, but a simple reminder that our time is limited. We all have to die, and none of us knows when our time will end. In one of his letters, Seneca talks about checking the time. Some people always want to know the time of day, but never give any more thought to how much time they have left to live. If you knew that you had exactly ten more years, how would you spend your remaining time? What if it was only ten more months or ten more hours or ten more minutes? If you weren't sure how much more money you had left in your checking account, you'd be wary of spending a single dollar for fear of an overdraft. According to

Seneca, we'd all be much more conscious of how we spent our time if we understood the fact that life could end at any moment. By reminding yourself constantly of the reality of death, you can focus your mind on what is truly essential and make every minute count.

Negative Visualization: The phrase "negative visualization" probably sounds like the exact opposite of all the feel-good, positive-thinking advice you've ever heard. As counterintuitive as it might be, negative visualization is a foundational technique of Stoic daily practice. It's not intended to make you sad or anxious but to inoculate you against sadness and anxiety—like a mental vaccine. The basic idea behind negative visualization is a simple one. Instead of telling yourself that bad things won't happen, you tell yourself that they *will* happen but that you can handle it.

It's a good idea to start small, rather than trying to tackle the big anxieties of life right away. Before you do anything, you should visualize the irritating things that usually happen. For example, if you're going to the movies, you should imagine people talking or a tall man sitting in front of you without taking off his hat. Remind yourself that you aren't just planning to go to the movies; you are going to the movies while keeping your mind calm and settled. If people do end up talking during the movie or blocking your view, you should find it easier not to get irritated because you prepared yourself ahead of time.

Once you have some experience at negative visualization, start applying it to things that are more serious than trivial irritations. For example, if you want to ask your boss to approve a major project, tell yourself that she won't agree to meet you. If she does agree to meet you, she'll cancel or reschedule the meeting. If the meeting happens, she'll ignore or disagree with everything you say. If she approves the project, she'll insist on changing your plans and micromanaging the process. By picturing all the things that would usually stress you out in that kind of situation, you can avoid getting stressed out when and if they actually happen. Paradoxically, this can even reduce the odds that any of these things will end up happening. Your boss is much more likely to trust your judgment if you come across as calm and self-controlled than if you seem anxious and needy.

As an experienced practitioner of negative visualization, you should deliberately visualize the worst things that can possibly happen. Illness, homelessness, injury, death—anything that scares you should be the subject of a negative visualization exercise. By imagining frightening things in the safety of your mind, you can reduce your fear reaction until it disappears, leaving you free from that particular anxiety.

Review Your Actions: Just before you go to sleep, think back over everything you said and did. Which actions were appropriate and which actions were inappropriate? Do you have anything to be proud of, any moment in which you lived as a

247

Stoic? For example, did you succeed in remaining calm and dignified in a stressful situation or self-disciplined in the face of temptation? Allow yourself to feel proud and happy because you're making progress toward genuine freedom. Is there any moment you regret, any action unworthy of a Stoic? For instance, did you lose your temper or indulge in something that wasn't good for you? Admit your fault, and fill yourself with a firm determination to do better tomorrow. Some Stoics find journaling to be the most effective way to do this exercise because you can go back and review your journal later to track your progress. The *Meditations* of Marcus Aurelius began as a diary, showing that this exercise was known to the ancient Stoics. Your diary probably won't have readers a thousand years from now, but it can still help you practice Stoicism daily. As you gain experience, you should find your ability to live philosophically improve over time. When you look back at earlier entries and see how far you've come, you'll gain confidence and a sense of quiet happiness at how much Stoicism has already done for you.

Chapter 9: The Stoic Leader

"Where a man can live, there he can also live well. But he must live in a palace; well then, he can also live well in a palace."

- Marcus Aurelius

Stoicism has long been considered the ideal philosophy for leaders, perhaps because of its association with powerful rulers like Marcus Aurelius, Frederick the Great, and George Washington. Modern political leaders like Wen Jiabao, business leaders like Jack Dorsey, and even athletic leaders like Michael Lombardi still base their leadership styles on Stoic principles.

There's a bit of a paradox here because "command" is one of the things we have no control over. Rank and authority are external things, and all external things are indifferent to a Stoic. A practicing Stoic may even find a leadership position to be a little bit awkward because it makes the practice of Stoicism much harder. For example, Marcus Aurelius didn't seem to have been particularly interested in the position of emperor and was tempted to resent all the demands it placed on him. He didn't use this as an excuse to neglect his responsibilities. Instead, he used his responsibilities as an opportunity to practice Stoicism.

In his *Meditations*, the emperor compared the imperial court to a stepmother and philosophy to a mother. A good man would never neglect his stepmother and would always treat her with respect, but his warmth and affection for his birth mother would always be stronger. The Stoic leader governs well but never loves power for its own sake.

The Nine Rules of Stoic Leadership

In his *Meditations*, Marcus Aurelius wrote a list of nine rules for the Stoic leader. These rules emphasize the importance of not losing your temper with the mistakes of your subordinates, an important consideration for an emperor with the power of life and death. Even though few modern leaders have so much power, the same principles still apply. Before making a decision that can affect someone else's life, consider these nine points.

> 1. Think of yourself as a bull leading a herd of cows or a ram leading a flock of sheep. The role of the bull or the ram is to protect and guide, knowing that all the members of the group exist to help each other and that none could thrive without the others.

2. Ask yourself what kind of people your subordinates are. What are they like at work? What are they like at home? What are they like among their friends? What opinions do they hold, and what do they seem to take pride in?

3. Whenever a subordinate does well, be pleased with them. Whenever they do poorly, remember that they don't do so intentionally but because of their own ignorance of the best way to act.

4. Always remember your faults and bad habits before judging others. Even if you do have better habits, remember the poor motives that often underlie them. For instance, if you work longer hours because you want other people to see you as hard-working, then your actions are still only appropriate rather than perfect.

5. Consider the circumstances before making a decision, and remember that you may not have complete information. Sometimes, it seems like a mistake has been made only because the full context is not yet known.

6. If you're so angry that you just can't let it go, remind yourself that nothing lasts forever and that all this will seem trivial and not worth worrying about once enough times has passed.

7. Remind yourself that the actions of another can never hurt you. The only thing that can ever hurt you is your own opinion.

8.   Remind yourself that far more trouble is caused by anger than by the things that usually make people angry.

9.   Correct the errors of your subordinates gently and with patience, with the goal of teaching rather than punishing.

The Advice of the Emperor

The nine rules are intended to protect you from the consequences of a hasty judgment based on a momentary flash of anger, but there's a lot more to leadership than just being patient with the people who work for you. Gems of useful leadership advice are scattered throughout the *Meditations*, which is not surprising because Marcus Aurelius was responsible for leading an entire empire. Here are some of the Stoic emperor's tips for leaders.

Lead by Mentoring: The entire first book of the *Meditations* is a list of the people the emperor learned from and what they taught him. He thanks his grandfather for teaching him to control his temper, his father for teaching him modesty, his mother for teaching him to live simply, and a series of tutors for teaching him the principles of the Stoic life. Marcus Aurelius often reminds himself to think of leadership as a teaching opportunity, guiding others on the right path in life through a combination of patient instruction and his own example. Your goal as a leader should be to mentor all those who work under your authority.

Consider the Whole: Always remember the whole and your part in it. That means considering the whole organization, your role within the organization, and what responsibilities flow from that role. The responsibilities of the role may sometimes go against your inclinations, but as the leader, you still need to fulfill your role. Never think of yourself as merely an individual but always as an individual embedded in a network of relationships. No matter what might be going on, no one can prevent you from fulfilling the responsibilities associated with your role to the best of your ability.

Appreciate Imperfection: Marcus Aurelius uses the example of a loaf of bread that has split in baking. This is something bakers usually try to avoid, but to a customer buying a loaf of bread, there is still something appetizing about the sight of a split loaf. Imperfections can be appealing, especially if you know how to put them to good use. A timid person can be useful in a position requiring meticulous attention to detail. A reckless person might spot opportunities other people would miss. Leading people effectively is often a matter of making good use of their imperfections.

Embrace Change: Change is inevitable, yet people fear and resist it all too often. Marcus Aurelius compares the flow of events in human life to the flow of water. On one level, nothing changes, but on another level, change is all there is. That's because there is nothing about change that prevents an underlying continuity. There is nothing harmful about change, though our fear of change often causes us harm. If you encounter any resistance to a planned change, remind the people who work for you that nothing happens without change. You can't take a shower without changing the water from one form to another, and you can't eat dinner without changing the food. If you find yourself resisting change, remind yourself that change is the one precondition for every single thing that happens. Pushing back against change is like pushing back against life.

Don't Be Too Suspicious: In one passage of his *Meditations*, the emperor cautions himself against being too suspicious. Rather than worrying about what other people are doing or what their real motives might be, he reminds himself to concentrate on his actions and motivations. The alternative is paranoia, an easy and very dangerous temptation for any leader. The emperor's goal was to be able to answer the question "what are you thinking?" immediately and directly, without needing to leave any of his thoughts unsaid. This is only possible if you guard your thoughts just as carefully as you guard your actions.

Be Willing to Change Your Opinions: In a position of leadership, it's easy to interpret any disagreement as a direct challenge to your authority. Even if you don't take disagreement personally, it can still be hard to let go of your own opinions.

Marcus Aurelius reminds us that it is not a sign of weakness or lack of authority to change your opinions when presented with a convincing argument. A leader who can never change his mind seems brittle and fragile. Only yes-men and sycophants will voluntarily follow a leader like that. If you show yourself willing to be convinced, your subordinates won't be afraid to present you with new ideas or point out possible issues before they develop into serious problems.

Keep a Sense of Proportion: Don't give anything more attention than it really deserves, especially the petty dramas of office politics. It can help to imagine a scene from the past, such as your own organization before you joined it or some other organization a hundred years ago. People were flirting, flattering, plotting against each other, stealing from the company, having birthday parties, getting promoted, taking vacations, and so on. Technology changes, but people don't. Don't give too much attention to things that will never change.

Get Up and Get at It: The sound of the alarm clock is often unwelcome, but most people have little choice except to drag themselves out of bed and get to work. For a Roman emperor like Marcus Aurelius, the temptation to remain in bed must have been a strong one. After all, who's going to tell Caesar to stop lying around and get to work? To motivate himself on mornings like these, the emperor had several mental tricks. One was to remind himself that he was a member of society and that it was time to get up and contribute to society. Another trick was to think about the ants and the birds that get up and do their work without needing anyone to nag at them. He also reminded himself of artists and people obsessed with a personal project and who will often go without sufficient sleep just to get a chance to work. Whatever it takes to get you moving, don't let the relative privilege of your position make you lazy and unfocused. Get up and get started, thinking of your work as an opportunity to practice your philosophy.

Don't Keep Track of Favors: Some people will never do a good deed for anyone without considering it a debt. Treating every human relationship as a *quid pro quo* is a losing strategy because not everyone will pay you back as you think you deserve, and you will be repeatedly disappointed. Marcus Aurelius compares a good leader to a grapevine, which naturally produces new grapes every season without ever expecting a reward for it. Help your subordinates at every opportunity without calling attention to yourself or expecting anything in return for your benevolence. Those who understand and appreciate what you've done for them will be loyal in return, while those who do not would have been ungrateful anyway. You'll get all the benefits of the *quid pro quo* approach without any of the drawbacks.

Look in the Mirror: Constantly ask yourself what kind of personality or character you currently have—what kind of "soul," as Marcus Aurelius says. Looking in the mirror may not be easy, but you can't hope to improve unless you're brutally honest in your self-assessment. Do you have the character of an inspiring leader, or would some other word describe you more accurately? The emperor mentions several possibilities—a child, a wild beast, a tyrant, and a weakling. If you can't describe yourself as a strong leader with a straight face, that's a sign that you need to change something.

Live Well Wherever You Are: Unlike the followers of Aristotle, the Stoics never considered wealth or power a prerequisite for living well. As Marcus Aurelius says, a good person can live well anywhere. If this is the case, then it follows that a good person can live well "in a palace." The possession of wealth and power is not a prerequisite for wisdom or happiness, but neither is it an impediment to them. In a position of authority, it's important to remind yourself that you are deeply responsible for the well-being of everyone who works for you. Since you happen to be in the palace, you must do your best to govern well.

Don't Take Things Personally: All your subordinates will make mistakes, but a few will do something that goes far beyond a mere mistake. Actions such as embezzlement or sexual misconduct reveal deep flaws in a person's character and also expose the company to legal risk. When you discover misconduct, take firm action, but don't take it personally. It's irrational to expect a person of poor character not to do bad things, so misconduct is simply evidence that the person responsible has that type of character. You can take whatever action is needed without letting it shake you, knowing that they simply did what a person of that type will always do.

Obstacles are Indifferent: Rivals and competitors will always exist, and sometimes, they will prevent you from achieving your goals. For example, a rival on the board of directors might sabotage your project, or a competing company may land the contract you were going for.

The Stoic should always think of other people as fellow members of the human community to be helped wherever possible, except when they interfere with your goals and become obstacles. In this case, Marcus Aurelius says you should think of them the same way you would think of the weather or a dangerous animal. You might not be able to go outside in the pouring rain, but you'd think of the rain as a mere obstacle, not an enemy. You might not walk down a street with a fierce dog on it, but you wouldn't see the dog as a personal foe. To a Stoic, all obstacles are equally indifferent, including people who stand in the way.

No Harm to the Hive: When you're part of a group or a community with a common goal and purpose, you identify yourself with that goal and stop thinking in a self-centered way.

As Marcus Aurelius says, nothing is harmful to the bee unless it harms the hive. Whenever you're frustrated in your role as a leader, ask yourself whether the situation that's frustrating you harms the whole organization or is just a hassle. Unless it prevents the organization from achieving its goals, it's probably not worth so much stress in the first place.

If It Needs to be Done, Do it Right: Anything that ever needs to be done can be done well or poorly, including the things that are most laborious, unpleasant, or uncomfortable. Whatever you have to do to fulfill your responsibilities as a leader, ask yourself what the best way to do that thing is, and make sure to do it that way. For example, many companies have fallen victim to attacks by hackers because they failed to download and install critical updates soon enough. Patching software is a thankless task and frequently slows down the whole company until the task is done.

Some business leaders prefer to put off such a bothersome task, patching infrequently or inconsistently. Their desire to keep the company running smoothly is understandable. That doesn't change the fact that patching is necessary and procrastinating is dangerous. Getting taken over by hackers typically costs far, more than updating software regularly. If it has to be done, there's no advantage in waiting just because it's a hassle. By doing things the right way no matter how inconvenient, you can save yourself a lot more trouble down the road.

The Stain of Power: Marcus Aurelius compares habits of the mind to a bright dye, easy to be stained by and hard to wash out. In ancient Rome, purple was a color reserved for emperors. Although he was the emperor himself, Marcus Aurelius expressed concern in his diary about being "stained" by the dye of Caesar. A leadership position is a grave responsibility, and the power that comes with the position can easily change how you think if you don't watch out for it.

Once you start to think of yourself as the person who *should* be in charge rather than the person who *happens* to be in charge, it will be hard to keep your equilibrium. Stoic leadership is servant leadership. The goal is the general welfare, not your personal power. According to Marcus Aurelius, a Stoic leader should be, "simple, good, pure, serious, free from affectation, a friend of justice, kind, affectionate, and strenuous in all proper acts." From the moment you assume a leadership role, you should be on guard not to let any of the "imperial purple" spill on you and stain your thoughts. The craving for power is an especially hard dye to wash out.

Stand in a High Place: This technique is often called "The View From Above," and comes from Plato originally. To get a big-picture view, imagine yourself standing in a high place, such as a mountaintop or a balcony on a very tall building. Look down from above and see everything all at once in your mind's eye. Watch the factories where your products are made, the container ships carrying your company's products across the ocean, or the accountant driving home to the suburbs when the day is done. Try to imagine how everything is interconnected and how all the different parts affect each other on a daily basis. The more often you do this exercise, the better you will understand how your organization works, and what it needs from you as a leader.

Understand the Past to Understand the Future: Look back on the history of your organization and of similar organizations before your own. If you're a coach, study the history of the great teams. What made them so successful, and what led them to stop winning championships, eventually? If you lead a company, research the history of your industry. What companies used to dominate and no longer do? What changes happened and why? Whatever happened before will happen again, always in new forms but always the same. The purpose of studying history is to recognize patterns so that you can use those patterns appropriately and strategically in your role as a leader.

Actions Show Principles: When you're considering someone for a position of responsibility, the most important point is to know what principles they live by. You can't always find this out by asking questions because most people will tell you what they think you want to hear. The best way to find out their real opinions is to observe their actions because they'll give away what they believe. Do they do things the right way when they think you're watching but slack off when they think you aren't paying attention? Do they try to sacrifice others for their advantage or claim credit for work that is not their own? The things people do in life show what they think, no matter what principles they claim to hold. To discover their real principles, observe their actions. The secrets of human character are in what we do, not what we say.

Let All Your Actions Be Social: As a leader of others, your role in society is for the good of the whole. According to Marcus Aurelius, all your actions should serve a social purpose, and you should think of any purely personal action as something that tears your life into two pieces. Rather than compartmentalizing our lives into the personal and the public as so many people do, the emperor advises us to keep an undivided focus on general welfare. Of course, this doesn't mean to neglect your family and friendships to focus solely on work. Our actions toward friends and family members are also social and part of the leader's social responsibility.

To sum up the Stoic approach to leadership, the Stoic leader is a mentor and public servant who always puts the well-being of the whole above any narrow concerns. The Stoic leader is patient and forgiving and looks for ways to use imperfections as advantages wherever possible but hires and promotes based on character. The Stoic leader seeks the View From Above, always looking for the big picture. The Stoic leader is always willing to change when appropriate and never loves power for its own sake.

Conclusion

In this book, you've learned about the history of Stoicism and the great Stoic thinkers whose ideas have survived to the present day. You've learned the basics of the Stoic practice, including the four passions to avoid and the three good feelings to cultivate. You've learned how to respond to first impressions with Stoic pragmatism and critical thinking, how to cultivate more resilience and self-discipline, and how to manage emotional turmoil with the Stoic mindset. You've learned how Stoicism has inspired some of history's greatest leaders, how it has influenced modern psychology, and how you can apply it in your daily life. The next step is to get started with the four most important and helpful Stoic habits:

- Practice being mindful of your actions and judgments.
- Question your first impressions.
- Remember that you are part of a whole.
- Imagine what can go wrong and see yourself overcoming it.

With these four habits as a starting point, you can go on to cultivate the serenity and untroubled happiness of the Stoic way of life. The most important to remember is a simple one: focus on what is under your control and disregard everything that isn't.

MASTER YOUR EMOTIONS

A Practical Guide to Overcome Negativity through Emotional Intelligence, Manage Your Feelings with Anger Management Techniques and Declutter Your Deceptive Tricky Mind

Introduction to Master Your Emotions

This book is a step-by-step guide for a more fulfilling life which demonstrates clearly how to identify and redirect harmful thoughts.

It teaches specific tactics to use when emotions get out of control trough a lot of examples to illustrate how the techniques described work.

Among others, this book contains the following topics:

- What emotions are and how they work
- How to control and change emotions through emotional intelligence concepts
- Strategies to eliminate negative thoughts, stress and fears
- Strategies of anger management to reach calmness and build up self-control
- How to use your emotions for personal growth and to improve relationships

Chapter 1: What Emotions Are and How They Work

Emotions are the mental state in line with feelings that change how a person behaves and their judgments towards different people, situations or events. Emotions alter the normal feelings of a person depending on their current mental state. These emotions include hate, anger, love, depression, loneliness, excitement, embarrassment, pride and shame.

Scientifically, emotions are connected to the nerves that determine how we feel and think about people, situations and events. They dictate our movements, actions and every single idea that we make. Our relationship with other people is determined by the state of our emotions. Sometimes communication becomes difficult when we are not in the right state of emotions and when everything is well, communication becomes better.

Emotions influence a person's personality and have a great impact on how they relate with others. It determines their interpretation of events and actions. People respond differently to every action and how their responses are normally contributed to by their current state of emotions. How a person feels towards a particular event or another person can never be the same way we all think about them. Our different feelings and opinions are always as a result of the different emotions.

Overexcitement can make someone overreact, overpromise or do something in excess that will spoil the fun of it. Sometimes it makes a person and forgets something important that will cost them in the future. This usually happens as a result of being too much obsessed about an event or situation that takes away your mind and focus it all towards a single event. You are subjected to doing things beyond normal when you get too much excited about something.

A person can also underestimate or overestimate something depending on their level of excitement. Excitement is the key determinant of our judgment and reaction towards everything. It makes us to either judge so low or too high based on how it makes us feel about the situation or person. It can make us have an excess urge of doing something or lose interest in it completely.

Depression, as well as a state of emotions, determines how we feel, how we act and our response to different reactions and also how we perceive things. Someone who is depressed is subjected to always seeing the negative out of everything. They in most circumstances attend to compare everything that happens to then to what they had experienced in the past that led to that state of mind. It makes them think that nothing is worth being happy for. They are made to believe that only made things are meant for them and that nothing good can happen to their life that will ever make them feel like other people.

Post-Traumatic stress also makes a person to fear facing life as it is. They are scared of trying something new for the fear of landing in the same state that they were in before. Maybe this person was involved in an accident that killed all other passengers leaving him or her as the only survivor of the scenario. The scene that they witnessed will ever be fresh in their mind that any time they want to travel, they will always have the fear of getting involved in a fatal accident. Some victims end up refusing to ever travel and this is all because of fear and trauma that never ends.

Some people after surviving an accident that killed many people are always left feeling guilty of themselves. They normally think that it was their fault that many died but they survived. They carry in their heart a burden that they should not carry because they don't deserve it. Guilt affects the mental state of any normal person making them think too much about a situation that it even becomes harmful to their health. These kind of people are always fragile to any kind of attack and generally, appear weak all the time.

Someone can also be traumatized after losing something that meant a lot to them. A person can lose a lot of money through theft or a failed business. This will leave these victims subjected to too much stress that they never planned for. They will be thinking of how to recover their lost money but will be afraid to invest again for the fear of losing for yet another time. This kind of emotional stress affects many people that even lead to them not focusing on their goals and are taken many steps behind.

Curiosity also makes a person think constantly of a particular thing that they are always in a hurry to know more about it. They can go to an extreme extent without thinking of the danger involved. Their minds are taken away out of this state of emotions and the only thing they think about is knowing more about a particular event, where it took place and when and even how it happened. If they don't get someone to give them full information of whatever it is that they are anxious about, they feel so incomplete and the constant struggle to gather the full information about it can even lead them to some kind of trouble that they never expected and that could have been avoided if only they let go of that particular event.

A person can usually feel so lonely that they attempt to think that no one in the society wants to be around them and that they don't deserve to be treated in a better way. This emotional state makes many people start distancing themselves from other people and prefer to spend time away from other people and also keep their thoughts and ideas to themselves. Such people are never ready to share how they feel even if they need help.

They will always choose to keep everything to themselves and this is because they normally fear no one will be ready to listen to them or give solutions to their worries.

Being so lonely can make a person start thinking of odd things that are sometimes dangerous to them or other people. Some people will think of taking away their lives because they will think that they are leaving a useless life and that they have no reason to stay alive. This sometimes occurs as a result of pressure from work, school or from within the family. These people will feel so isolated and unfit in society that is full of different kind of people from different backgrounds.

Having low self-esteem makes a person feel so rejected and very weird of themselves. Their failure to see their worth and think that other people are more important than them and that their living standards are so low as compared to how other people live their lives. They start comparing themselves with others and feel bad every time they fail to achieve what others have achieved. What they normally forget and that is very important is that their destination is far much different from the destinations of other people and that there are always different routes that lead to the same destination. They don't realize that they don't have to do exactly what others do to lead a better life as them and that everything takes time. They can never start and finish at the same time.

Some emotions lead a person to hate other people and events to an extent that there can never stand the thought of them. They are dragged by their emotions to think that these people or events are a disgrace to them and a threat to their happiness. They can never bear the feeling of being around these people and whenever they come around them, they are made to either walk away or treat them with silence and wrath. They are so much annoyed by the fact that they have to be around such people. Any single mistake that these people make appear to them as the worst mistake ever and that does not deserve to be forgiven. They will keep talking about it over and over again to express how bad they feel towards the people that are involved. Hatred can make a person overreact towards anything that is done by the person they don't like. They become too cross with these people's opinions that they never calm down to give them a listening ear. Everything done or said by these people disgust them too much and none of their ideas is never right according to them. They think of the other person as the worst enemy all the time and they never think of making up for things to work well between them.

Anger is also influenced by emotions. It makes a person feel so bitter towards something that offends them. It normally leads to fights that become difficult to control and reconcile. If anger is not well handled, it can lead to a person saying hurting words that can never be retracted or doing things that can never be undone but leaves a scar that is never-ending on someone's heart. Some people murder because of anger and some kill themselves. However, emotionally intelligent people will always find it easy to control their emotions to manage their anger and avoid things that cost them a lifetime to forget.

Anger can destroy the relationship between friends, family, and colleagues when someone overreacts to a given event. Not everyone will be in a position to control their emotions and change how they feel about something that has already happened. It takes a lot of maturity and courage to handle things calmly without hurting other people's feelings or making them feel unwanted.

Emotions driven by anxiety makes a person be too much alert and expects anything to happen anytime. They bring curiosity and fear in a person that they can never relax and feel normal all the time. They always believe that something must happen whether good or bad. The mentally that something must happen is what makes some people go insane. This is because they tend to have the fear of experiencing a bad situation that may affect their mental status and distract their brains.

Emotions are connected to the nerves that direct our feelings. The nerves signal the brain about an event that is just about to take place or that is already taking place. How the brain responds to the alarm of the nerves with determining how we will react to that event. It allows us to either react positively or negatively depending on the signal that the brain receives. A feeling that supply bitter signals to the brain resulting in negative reactions and thoughts.

Someone can feel embarrassed by something which will make them afraid and uncomfortable around other people. They won't be able to interact freely as they used to before and facing situations becomes difficult to them. They are controlled by the result of what they did that did not turn out as they expected or as was expected by the people who interact with them. Taking about that thing in their presence makes them feel so bad and unfit.

Embarrassment also lowers a person's confidence in what they are doing. They think that everything they do will turn out imperfect making other people to underrate their ability. It makes them do everything unwillingly or filled with doughnuts about their ability and the far they can go if they focus much on their duties and responsibilities without recalling something that had happened and cannot be retrieved.

To understand how emotions work, you first need to understand the possible causes of emotions. Emotions are normally a result of our own thoughts. They occur from the experiences that we get involved in our day to day life activities. It is true that we do encounter different experiences from different situations that may have involved several people. According to scientists, many people may be involved in a similar event but this will impact different emotions in them usually because of the different thoughts that are involved in each of them.

These can be noticed anywhere maybe in school, in church, at work or at home. It may involve your coworkers, family or friends. For an instant, imagine a situation where two or three people have a walk together then you happen to come across a dog. One person can feel scared at the thought that this dog can be harmful and maybe scream or run away from it. This is a feeling that is usually experienced by someone who had never had a pet dog earlier. On the other hand, the other person will get attracted to the dog and admire its appearance. This person may comment "oh, this dog is so cute." This is common with people who grew up with the mentality of pet dogs in their lives. This brings out a picture of different people with different experiences having different thoughts and ideas of the same event.

People attempt to think differently about different events and other people. These different thoughts can result in different feelings and changes in what the body does, what you think about or get interested in, what action you want to take and how you respond to different reactions. These different changes are what we use to figure out our feelings and emotions.

Scientists say that different state of thoughts will definitely lead to a different state of emotions. For example, when someone thinks "I have failed exams" that person will normally panic and feel some sense of fear within them. Someone who thinks "I have made it" will probably feel so happy and excited while a person who thinks they have been wronged or badly threatened by other people will automatically feel angry and anxious.

Thoughts that are leading to different emotions always have different questions involved like;

- Did it happen as per the expectations
- Is it worth celebrating
- What is its impact on what I wanted to achieve
- Will it lead me to what I wanted or take me a step backward
- What will happen next
- Am I in a position to control what will follow
- Do I have the ability to endure what has already taken place
- Who's the fault is it that this particular situation was encountered

Anything that happens will call for different feelings and emotions depending on your mind and thoughts and how you will interpret and respond to these questions. For example, if you business fails or gets robbed, you will definitely feel sad if you are not sure you can have a solution to it or invest in a different way to recover what you have lost. You will feel so depressed and think that this is the end of everything for you. However, someone else may quickly think of a possible solution, maybe an insurance cover that they had taken before and feel relieved because this kind of event will not have severe impact on their business, or, they will strike out a plan for a different and alternative way of investing the little cash they are left with that will be more profitable to cover up for the loss they had experienced.

You can also feel sad when you lose someone you were so attached to and have never imagined being away from them. Maybe you broke up with your partner after being in a relationship for so many years. You may feel so worried about this particular situation and find it unbearable and hard for you to let go. You will get stack at the thought of having lost the best person in your life and moving on will be such a hard task for you. This situation can impact different feelings in your heart. You may be filled with so much hatred that you do not feel like falling in love anymore. You may find yourself having a totally negative attitude towards the opposite sex right from the experience that you got involved in.

In some situations, you can encounter some emotions but you don't have even a single idea as to why you feel so. Sometimes you will feel some emotions but you will not be in a position to notice any thoughts that can result in such kind of emotions. Understanding this situation can sometimes be hard. However, it is said that sometimes your brain can signal an emotion out of unconsciousness. This implies that our brains might trigger an emotional reaction to something they have noticed about our situations but we might totally have no idea about this and we can never notice it. The scientist has found out that our brains get involved in so many activities that we never notice.

When emotions are triggered, the brain changes the body us doing too much the emotions. For example, when you are overexcited about something, the speed of your heartbeat will increase and you will feel so nervous. The same apple when you feel so scared and afraid. You become so uncomfortable and feel uneasy all the time.

People can also think differently at the same time. For example, someone can be happy but find themselves around another person who is so sad. The sad person will normally think about the sad situations in the past that match their current feelings and think that nothing good will ever happen to make them happy while in the other hand, the person who is happy will only think of what they can do to enjoy themselves or some past situations that ever made them feel so happy and they would like to bring it back to their lives one more time so that they get to feel the same for another time.

The different thoughts and feelings are signaled by our brains that make the muscles to react differently making us to either smile, shed tears or have a frowned faces. When we learn to balance our thoughts, balancing our emotions becomes easy as well. Emotions and thoughts go hand in hand with each other. When we have negative thoughts, we will only have negative emotions and positive thoughts result in positive emotions.

Emotions push us to do weird things and act differently from how we normally act. For example, emotions can make you want to destroy something completely or hit someone so hard when you are angry. You can also fee as you should really run away whenever you feel scared or distance yourself from other people when you are sad. You will only want to be left alone to think about yourself and everything that is happening to you. Everyone will seem like a bother to you whenever they try to be close to you or talk to you. When a person is happy, they will always have an excess urge of jumping here and there or talking to anyone that they come across. Emotions make them to badly want to do something that is not normal or that to engage in activities that they do not usually engage in. Their feelings are ever beyond the normal feelings of a normal person.

It is normal for a person to be unsure of what they are feeling. This is because at times our emotions and feelings tend to be so confusing and need too much time and effort to understand. The same kind of emotions can subject different feelings in different events, while different types of emotions can subject to similar feelings towards a given situation. This leaves everyone wondering what has come over them and how they can control it. However, controlling this mental state is never easy since at times you don't even realize when your brain triggers some types of feelings and emotions.

When you come to realize you are experiencing and emotional reaction, you still have an added task of figuring out what it is that you are feeling and why. For example when you go to a neighbor who has a pet, when the pet dog looks at you your heart might start racing and you will think that the emotions you ate feeling is fear. You will easily think that you are undergoing fear because you are afraid this dog can hurt you. However, is such situations, some people will act strong and courageous that they don't feel the fear of being hurt by the pet dog. Their emotions will react differently from those of a person that has never been used to being around pet dogs.

I have come across a number of people who get their relatives and friends admitted to a hospital. Most f these people are always filled with the fear of losing their relatives and friends to the hands of death. They are taken away with panic and anxiety that they even start thinking of how life will be without these people. They allow their minds to imagine that these people are gone already and start fantasizing the kind of life they will live without the people they were used to and that they cherished too much.

On the other hand, others are always hopeful that their loved ones will recover and be with them again. They think positively about the situation and keep praying to God that these people get well soon and join them in living a normal life that is free from sickness and pain. When these people do not recover, their friends and families are left traumatized and filled with regret. Some people will think that it is their fault that this situation came along and Starr blaming themselves for not being in a position to stop everything from happening the way it happened. This traumatizes the people involved in leaving their minds occupied by too much stress about the situation.

Not everyone is in a position to figure out what they feel towards something and this has been proven by scientists. They again extend it and say that a person who does not find it easy to figure out how they feel and understand their emotions does not have to struggle to make themselves feel comfortable. It is ever easy for them to feel better at any time. Unlike the others who can easily tell what they are feeling. It makes it difficult for them to come out of the situation and feel better.

Paying close attention to your emotions is very important. It helps you to start practicing how to figure out what you are feeling and how you can come out of it with much ease. When you train yourself this way, it will be easy for you to overcome a difficult situation and feel better whenever you are down. It makes healing easier and faster and also helps you to understand what you have learned from different situations when you felt angry, sad or anxious. Handling similar situations in the future becomes easier when you get to deal with them from the start.

Understanding your emotions comes with a lot of advantages. It helps you figure out how you can overcome different situations without feeling so awkward and weak. It also helps you figure out how you can respond to your emotions in different situations by helping you to tell whether your current emotions much the current situation and if not, what can you do about it to balance it with the situation.

Emotional reactions sometimes become helpful in some events. For example, when a child sees fire and gets scared of getting close to it. The fear of not going around a fireplace will help to prevent the child from getting burnt. Also in a situation where someone goes out with their friends and see other people swim in the ocean but they are scared of getting into the water to swim with them. That fear helps to protect them from being drowned or getting attacked by ocean animals. Lastly, someone who fears to invest in forex trade for the first time will protect themselves from the risk of losing their capital.

However, when these emotions happen in the wrong situation, they become unhelpful. For example when you get mad at your boss because they corrected you over something that you did not do according to their expectations. This can make you quit your job or get fired when you react rudely to them. This only leads to a loss instead of again. Or when you are scared of asking a question in class to get more clarification about a point that is mentioned by your lecturer. This will hinder you from getting the information you need and you might end up failing a test just because you were afraid of asking a question in class.

It is good to listen to what your emotions are telling you if it so helpful but you can also dodge your emotions and reorganize your thoughts when they are unhelpful and likely to cause trouble. For example, when you feel affected by what your boss or colleague said, you can rethink about your job and assume them to protect your job or think of an alternative way of earning then quit that particular job. Also when you are afraid of asking a question in class during an ongoing lecture, you can opt for consulting a different lecturer who is familiar with that field or your fellow student who understood better what was taught.

Some emotions can be controlled by exercise or activities. For example, when you are angry, you can engage yourself in activities like swimming, jogging or take a walk. These activities will help you feel relaxed and let go of the anger that was previously burning within you. You will feel relieved and let go of the past situation that made you feel so angry. Sadness can also be controlled easily by engaging in some activities. When you sit home alone and think of past sad experience all the time, you will never get over it. You will always feel so low and depressed but when you get out and get yourself involved in different activities, you will be able to come back to your normal state of mind and let go of what happened that made you sad.

Going out to spend time with friends is also another way of healing from negative emotions. It helps you forget the sad event by distracting your mind through the conversations that you hold with friends. For an instant, when you get invited to a party, you make up your mind to go out and join your friends to party with them. You would have freed yourself from the circle of thinking about the past situation and getting hurt more by more. You will feel some sort of joy and positive feelings within you. Emotions can control a person's decisions when we allow them to overpower us. We can become prisoners of our own emotions when we let emotions control what we do all the time. Look at a situation where you feel angry at your sibling. You can be highly tempered and fight them back. What if this fight leads to one person getting injured, or you hit a sensitive place and kill your brother. You will have involved yourself in another difficult situation that you did not plan for and that you would have avoided if you did not allow yourself to be controlled by harsh emotions.

Emotions are triggered by the brain but should be managed by us immediately we realize that we are in a state of emotions that is dangerous to us and to those around us. It can be difficult to deal with the emotions if you don't understand them and cannot figure out how it is and how to come over it. You will be left stranded between decisions and if you don't make the right choice then you are doomed.

Emotions are manipulative. If they take over us, they attempt to dictate our actions and responses towards different reactions. Emotions can make you do something that you would not have done if you were in the right state of mind. It can influence you to hate someone for no good reason and only see the worst in them despite their struggles to make things straight. Negative emotions will only make you think of doing something negative without thinking of the possible results. Emotions can lead to revenge a bad action with the same treatment. This will gain you nothing but only lead you to problems and make things worse for you. Coming out of a bad experience that was influenced by your own emotions is not an easy task. You will have struggle and fight your thoughts to feel normal and if you can't come out of it, your emotions will still suggest negative solutions to you. Things like running away from home or committing suicide or even killing someone who makes you feel bad.

Emotions disturb our minds and increase our passion for something that we have in mind. They can impose conflict in our mind trying to overcome a bad feeling or trying to avoid a particular event to prevent something from happening. People who are led by their emotions are always in trouble trying to go against their own feelings to save the situation. Having to do everything as dictated by your emotions only makes you a slave of your own thoughts. It becomes more burden to us than anything else. Emotions can make someone too possessed with another person or event. This normally occurs in the event of relationships. You can be too much into someone that you don't see their faults at all. Anything they do will sound right according to you and no one can ever convince you that some wrong is happening to your relationship because you chose to trust your emotions too much to an extent of giving up your happiness for the sake of your partner.

Remember your partner have emotions too and when they realize that you are too much into them that you can't avoid them at any cost, their emotions will lead them to take advantage of your feelings for them and use you to achieve what they have been longing for over a very long time. You will have no choice but to serve their interests because you have allowed yourself to fall in the trap of your own emotions and the manipulative emotions of your partner.

Scientists have discovered that emotions take over someone if they are not strong enough to stand against them. They control every single decision that these people make leading them to a destination that they never prepared for. This can make a person do several things unknowingly and only realize it when they are already in trouble with other things. It disorients their minds leading to failure of plans that would have been productive and profitable. Emotions are the worst rulers of a person's mind. Psychologists have said that most mentally unstable people are always victims of their own emotions. They are controlled by their negative emotions to destroy things and put the blame on someone else. Or, they are forced to get too much affected by the absence of something in their life that they can never have peace without that thing or person but again when they get what they want, they attempt to misuse them under the influence of these negative emotions that can never be controlled by them.

Such people in most cases end up losing more than they gain. It is because their emotions make them want to start away from other people and because of their bad attitude towards other people, most people also attempt to avoid interacting with them to stay away from troubles that are always caused by these people. Their emotions take full control of them and people are made to believe that they are insane even if they are not.

Children are easily affected by their emotions and those of the people around them. If their emotions make them believe that a particular thing can hurt them, they will be convinced that it is dangerous for them to be found around such things and the fear of getting hurt will always keep them away. It will be difficult to make them believe that they can be around these things without getting hurt. What their own emotions tell them can never be taken away by anyone.

Children too when they observe a negative attitude towards them in someone much older than them, they will be scared of interacting with this person. They fear of being treated harshly will make them avoid this person by all the possible means. No one can ever come between them and their thoughts to convince them that this person cannot hurt them. They are highly affected by the thought of being involved with the person that they are scared of. Emotions control even the toughest people. For example, when it is announced that terrorists are attacking people in a given region within your country, and you happen to be in the region or someone who is very close to you is within that region. You will be filled with the fear of you getting attacked or your friends or family members. This fear will eat over your mind making you become restless all the time.

Someone who is not in that region will also be scared of going to that region for the fear of getting involved in the terror attack. They are driven by the emotions of fear to believe that if they get to that region they will never be spared of the attack. They fear losing their lives can even lead to some people being helplessly depressed.

People who happen to witness a terror attack or human slaughter, or just get to watch the clips of such events are exposed to the trauma of what the saw. They develop fear within them that gets them scared all the time. Such people are exposed to weak and fragile personalities that they can't even stand simple jokes that are relating to such events. These people are driven by their emotions to get scared of anything. They can panic at the sight of any even that raises attention.

According to scientific studies and proves, emotions do not choose anyone's personality. Everyone has a nervous system that is connected to the brain. Once the responsible nerves signal the brain of a particular situation, the brain will trigger the related emotions before you realize it. The impact of this emotion in someone's reactions will depend on their psychology and emotional experience. Someone who is emotionally week will automatically follow the commands of their emotions and end up doing something that was not their intention.

On the other end, a person who studied and understand the psychology of emotions will find it easy to change their thoughts and go for an alternative way of overcoming the situation without causing any trouble. They can never react according to their emotions when they understand that the resulting situation may affect them negatively or inconvenience other people. They will divert their attention to a possible and positive solution even if it means they have to go against their own emotions.

People who are psychologically stable have active mind control techniques to control their mind and those of other people. These people can easily detect manipulative emotions within them or in the people that they interact with. This will direct them on how to apply the mind control techniques to prevent these emotions from negatively ruling the situation. They can then come up with a positive solution that makes everyone fill good about the situation. Emotions are two-phased and can either result in something positive or the opposite of what was expected. They can help us come out of the trap when we use them carefully but again when they come the opposite way, they can land us into trouble and even spoil our relationship with others.

Chapter 2: How to Control and Change Emotions through Emotional Intelligence Concepts

A Comprehensive Definition of Emotional Intelligence

Emotional intelligence is also referred to as emotional quotient (EQ). This is the ability of understanding, using and managing your emotions in a positive way.

This is meant to relieve oneself from stress, be able to effectively communicate, to overcome challenges, show empathy to others and defusing conflicts. Emotional intelligence can be of great need in building stronger relationships, achievement of personal goals and in career, and also succeeding at work and at school. Apart from that, it can also assist you in connecting with feelings, turning intentions into actions and even making informed decisions.

Attributes that defines Emotional Intelligence

The following are some attributes that are commonly used to define emotional intelligence:

Self-awareness

This entails you identifying your own emotions and the effects that they have on your behavior and thoughts. This will, therefore, help you to realize where your weaknesses and strengths lie thus gain self-confidence.

Relationship management

This entails you know the way you can develop and also maintain a perfect relationship, inspire, communicate clearly, influence others, manage conflict and also be able to work well with a team.

Social awareness

This basically refers to you having empathy towards others. You can, therefore, be able to understand other people's needs, concerns, and even emotions. You will also be able to understand the various emotional cues and pick up on them, have a comfortable social status and also recognizing the power of change in an organization or a group.

Self-management

This refers to your own ability to manage impulsive behaviors and feelings. It also entails managing your own emotions in good approaches, adapting to the changing circumstances and following up commitments.

Benefits of Teaching Emotional Intelligence in Schools

As children and teens develop and grow, emotional intelligence is very vital. Much evidence has been put up to demonstrate how it positively helps students to handle stressful conditions, be comfortable during transitions they face and even develop relationships with other students. Knowledge of emotional intelligence is very important to students especially those who are still in their teenage. It helps students to effectively employ emotions to be productive in their studies and adapt to the school system without going through many challenges. The following are a few benefits that students will gain by having this knowledge at hand:

- Students will improve and achieve more in their academics.
- Students will learn and gain active listening skills.
- Students will be self-aware thus know their capabilities.

In the recent past, emotional intelligence studies have been so popular among teens and generally students. One of the critical ideas is that emotional intelligence should be incorporated into the school curriculum and not isolated. This, therefore, means that there has been more focus on the way in which we can put more focus on social and emotional learning.

This program will help schools to have the emotional intelligence principles in their curriculum. Through the coaching of students, teacher training and other resources such as evidence-based, emotional intelligence will be taught at all levels of studies. This will be of great help to students as they will be able to know the skills and approaches needed to manage and change their emotions. As a result of this, the job market in the near future will be flooded with the brilliant mind of people who are capable of dealing with stressful conditions in the workplace. These are people who will also have a good relationship and achieve many successes in their lives both professionally or even personally.

Importance of Emotional Intelligence

Emotional Intelligence is linked to various aspects in one's life if not all. It can, therefore, be said that it can be linked to our careers, job performance, and even our success. The following are, therefore, the various ways which have depicted the importance of emotional intelligence:

Emotional Intelligence and Job Performance

In the recent past, there has been a rise in emotional intelligence awareness in management-focused literature together with leadership training summits. This gives us an indication that there exists a very strong relationship between job performance and emotional intelligence. It not only proves to exist but also has depicted an array of value in different areas. One's workplace is a representation of a social community that is very separate from their personal lives. This is also a place where increased appreciation of emotional intelligence has been on the rise allowing people to have an understanding of themselves and even others, be conversant with hard situations and communicating in a more effective manner. This, therefore, means that employing emotional intelligence at your workplace might greatly improve your personal and even other individuals' social capabilities.

Emotional Intelligence entails management of emotions which improves job performance, which in turn helps people to stay calm and think logically thus establishing good working relationships and achievement of goals. Apart from that, there is an evident relationship between emotional intelligence and how senior employees manage their juniors. A manager who has got a high emotional intelligence is well conversant with the stress management skills and also how recognize and manage the stress in other people. Therefore, if we put emotional intelligence in the stress management perspective, then the relationship between job performance and emotional intelligence is crystal clear. This is because one's commitment to their job is highly and positively impacted by stress management.

In many instances, emotional intelligence usually applies to all kinds of employees and not only those at the management level. The employees that are at the lower rank in the hierarchy of an organization and have a high emotional intelligence usually have got desires and abilities to establish and maintain good relationships at the workplace. Apart from that, these individuals are good in management and resolution of conflicts. This, therefore, means that they have the capability of sustaining relationships that exists in the workplace as compared to those with either low or moderate emotional intelligence. In the current job market, many organizations are undergoing revolution and changes in different sectors. This has made organizations to have the need of employees who can easily cope up with these changes and respond to them easily. This indicates that emotional intelligence is an important factor in job performance in both group and individual levels. This thus clearly describes the way in which emotional intelligence is of value.

Emotional Intelligence and Resilience

Emotional intelligence has proved to be a valuable tool in adversity as it has the potential of enhancing not only teamwork effectiveness and leadership abilities but it is also an important tool in enhancing personal resilience. The impact of emotional intelligence on the resilience of a person is the ability of that person to cope up with situations that are stressful. It has been clearly demonstrated by research that a person who has got high emotional intelligence usually easily overcome stressors and their negative impacts.

Focusing on leadership, a leader is usually expected to have increased responsibilities which usually are accompanied by potential stressors. In such a case, it is important for the person to have strong emotional intelligence in order to be resilient and battle with these stressful conditions. From research where investigations were done into the link existing between emotional intelligence and stress, it was found out that people who showed high emotional intelligence levels were not negatively affected by stressors. These participants did an emotional intelligence ability-based test before the threat level that was posed by the two stressors was rated. After that, they reported their emotional reactions the stressors before being subjected to physiological stress to also assess their responses. The findings of this research showed that emotional intelligence has a relationship with lower threats. This study, therefore, provides us with a valid prediction that stress resilience is facilitated by emotional intelligence.

From further research done, the relationship between high levels of emotional intelligence, the tendency to depressive behaviors and resilience was drawn. It was found out that there was a positive correlation that exists between mindfulness, self-compassion, and resilience with the rate of burnout. In conclusion, individuals who have got high emotional intelligence levels were more resilient and could not easily fall into depression or burnout. Emotional intelligence has a strong link to the individual's advancement and also their performance. Evidence also suggests that there is a significant link between their resilience and their motivation to achieve. Apart from that, it also made a suggestion that resilience acts as a mediator between self-motivated achievement and resilience. Resilience, in this case, has got a perseverance component that acts as a motivation to motivation when facing obstacles. From the various research findings and theories, we have seen a strong relationship between emotional intelligence and resilience. We have clearly seen how one's emotional intelligence levels affect their resilience. This, therefore, has proved emotional intelligence to be very important.

Emotional Intelligence and Motivation

Emotional intelligence is one of the key ingredients for motivation which in turn is very vital in the achievement of success. An emotionally intelligent person will always have an understanding of what they aspire and the necessary motivation skills that they would need to achieve these aspirations. There are four elements that are said to make up motivation; how we commit ourselves to the goals we set, how ready we are to utilize opportunities, self-drive to improve and how resilient we are. Motivation is said to be a psychological process that which we use to psyche ourselves into action in order to realize a desirable outcome. It doesn't matter the action we are doing, whether dedication of much time to work on a project or just changing the TV channel using a remote, without being motivated we cannot act.

This is because motivation energizes, arouses, sustains and directs performance and behavior. The motivation that usually comes from within, also known as intrinsic motivation usually drives us to the achievement of our full capability. A person who is emotionally intelligent has got both skills required to motivate themselves and those needed to motivate other people too. This is a very useful skill to possess especially if you are in a management position in your job. Self-motivation is the key to the achievement of one's goals. With self-motivation, emotionally intelligent people will always be capable of impacting the motivation of employees. The ability to determine the emotions and needs or concerns of others is a great skill to possess in relation to the determination of perfect methods of motivating individuals and teams.

From a study and research did, it was found out that the emotional intelligence of a first-year graduate was positively linked to their self-motivation to studying the respective course and choosing that course. Another study of senior employees with very high emotional intelligence found out that they are good in arguments, have good behavior and great work outcomes. It, therefore, means that a happy employee is a motivated employee. The capability to be conversant with anxiety and stress is a very useful emotional intelligence tool when it comes to motivation. From the above studies and research findings, it is clear that emotional intelligence plays a major role in one's motivation. Since motivation is a very vital tool in our actions, then emotional intelligence is also very important.

Emotional Intelligence and Decision-Making

Emotional intelligence plays a key role in both professional and personal development. It not only has an impact on the way in which we handle our behaviors and control our social complexities but also the approaches we take in decision-making. Having an in-depth understanding of the emotions you feel and the reason as to why you are feeling them can heavily impact your decision-making capabilities. This, therefore, means that if we carefully look into our emotions, then we can avoid making misleading and misguided decisions. Emotional intelligence is a very vital tool required in the prevention of making poor decisions based on our emotions whereby lower emotional intelligence can make you anxious and result in you making a poor misguided decision. This does not mean that we should keep emotions aside when making decisions but discovering these emotions which might not have any relationship with the problem and ensuring that they do not influence the decision that you are going to make. Negative emotions can be a stumbling block to decision making and problem-solving in either your workplace or even personal circumstances. Being able to recognize emotions that are becoming a stumbling block to making rational decisions and being able to effectively ignore the emotions will prevent their negative influence on your decision. This, therefore, means that decision making at this stage will be much favored as it will not be negatively influenced in any way.

From research done through observations and administering a series of questions, it was discovered that people and organizations reaped big benefits from a practical application of emotional intelligence in making decisions. This study had the aim of improving emotional intelligence awareness and how emotional intelligence skills can be employed in decision making. From the observations, it was discovered that having training sessions on emotional intelligence is one of the most effective ways to incorporate decision-making skills and also helps you to understand the possible consequences of poor decision-making.

Having an understanding of the causes and possible consequences of emotions gives you the freedom to manage and make a decision about the feeling. For instance, if you have an argument with your spouse the go to work without resolving it you will probably stay angry the whole day. Being angry at work, your colleague might make an offer to you but you dismiss it without even paying attention to it. This is a kind of emotional interference that can be very dangerous to your decision-making. If you have high emotional intelligence, then you can be able to identify this form of emotional interference and manage it thus avoiding making decisions that are emotionally driven. This, therefore, means that emotional intelligence is vital when making decisions.

Emotional Intelligence and Success

There are things which mean different to different people. As happiness is so is a success which everyone has a different version of defining it. But no matter no success is defined, it is clear that emotional intelligence plays an important part in its achievement. From history, most intelligent individuals are usually not attributed to greatest successes. This is because IQ is not sufficient on its own to enable one to succeed in life. In regards to this, you can be the most intelligent person but if you lack emotional quotient, you may fail to turn down people with negative thoughts about you and even manage stress. This shows that emotional intelligence is sometimes even more powerful as compared to IQ in life success. Your emotional intelligence is the actual thing that helps you to achieve your life objectives and realize great successes. Therefore, developing emotional intelligence would influence your achievements through contribution to your morale, cooperation and most importantly motivation by a great margin. In a workplace, the managers and employees who perform well as compared to others usually employ strategies that are associated with emotional intelligence in the management of conflicts, reduction of stress and thus achieving their goals. In the recent past, there has been blooming evidence of a range of activities said to constitute emotional intelligence are now vital in determining success.

This refers to success both in the workplace and also one's personal life. It incorporates applications that we associate with in our daily lives in relationships, businesses, and even parenting. Emotional intelligence guides one to easily manage their emotions in situations that are likely to provoke anxiety. These situations include when taking examinations at the university. It is also positively associated with success in social functioning and personal relationships.

In social relationships, success achievable with the employment of emotional intelligence skills to determine other people's emotions, then adopt their emotional states and thus regulate the way they behave. This briefly shows how important emotional intelligence is in achieving success in the different spheres of life.

Emotional Intelligence and Communication

One's ability to have the knowledge and understanding of their emotions might aid them to be aware and understand the feelings that other people are experiencing. This has got an impact on the way in which we communicate in our daily lives.

Considering communication in conflict resolution in the workplace, people with great emotional intelligence levels would most probably approach the conflict in the most reasonable way possible and negotiate together with others to finally come up with a reasonable outcome. On the contrary, a person with lower levels of emotional intelligence will not be able to solve the conflict in a reasonable calm manner thus might even end up without a solution at the end.

In the workplace, relationships are usually affected by the manner in which we can manage our emotions and also understanding the emotions of those around us. The capability to do this helps us in communicating without necessarily resorting to confrontation. If you have high emotional intelligence, then it is beyond doubt that you are equipped with conflict management skills and thus you will be able to put up a meaningful relationship guaranteed capacity to understand and address needs of those they engage with.

In recent years, emotional intelligence has been able to receive much attention that drives effective communication within individuals and even teams. On close examination of emotional intelligence as a reason for team success, you will find that it does not only do it drives the viability of a team but also affects communication quality in a positive way.

Achievement of successful communication in relation to successful negotiation and conflict has a very close relationship with high emotional intelligence levels. In this case, individuals with lower emotional intelligence would be so defensive in such stressful situations. This will instead escalate the conflict instead of managing it. If you have high emotional intelligence, then this means that you have got the necessary skills to ensure effective communication without resulting in a confrontation. From this, we can easily derive the importance and great contribution that high levels of emotional intelligence add to the achievement of effective communication.

Emotional Intelligence and Happiness

Just like any other word or felling, happiness seems something easy but actually getting to understand it is when you will realize that it is a hard nut to crack. This is because different people have got different instances and experiences that they describe them to mean happiness to them. Truly, happiness means different to different people but undoubtedly, emotional intelligence is a great requirement to have despite the kind of interpretation you prefer. Happiness is an emotional intelligence facilitator that contributes to each and everyone's self-actualization which positively impacts our happiness.

From a study where the relationship between different interpersonal relations and emotional intelligence was examined, it was discovered that individuals with high emotional intelligence scored highly in self-monitoring, social skills and taking empathic perspective. Apart from that, they also scored highly in affectionate relationships, satisfaction in relationships, and cooperation with their partners.

Emotional intelligence skills are very important when it comes to reducing stress, thus, in turn, will positively impact on one's happiness and wellbeing in general. Apart from the motivational value that it possesses, happiness acts as a monitor to the wellbeing of an individual. It is also a source of a positive mood to the manner in which the person copes up and meets daily needs, pressures and challenges.

Positivity is what actually encourages the emotional energy required in the increment of an individual's motivational levels which is responsible for getting things done. It actually helps one to be successful in what they are doing and even gets to the extent of telling them the extent of success they are actually achieving. From a study done by Furnham, it was realized that a large section of variance that is evident in the wellbeing and happiness of a person is determined by their emotional intelligence levels. This refers to their ability to stabilize their emotions, social competence, and even relationship skills. Although these emotional intelligence skills are not the only source of one's happiness, it is very vital to realize that they contribute and impacts our happiness up to 50%. This, therefore, prove it to be a very vital thing which should always be put into consideration.

Happiness has, therefore, proven to be closely linked to emotional intelligence if the research and studies detailed above are to go by. A person with high emotional intelligence will have the necessary skills to dodge any obstructions that might act as a hindrance to happiness. On the other hand, a person who has low levels of emotional intelligence will not be able to cope up with these obstructions and end up always sad and stressed up. This thus proves emotional intelligence to be vital.

Emotional Intelligence and Goals

In life, each and every person has got goals and achievements that they hope to achieve someday in life. In order to achieve these goals, there are various conditions that usually impact it either positively or negatively. In this case, emotional intelligence also plays a key role in the achievement of these goals. Emotional intelligence will drive you to realize self-actualization which requires you to first get motivated. In order to have the motivation, you will need to be happy with whatever you do. This is because lack of happiness will challenge you in pursuit of the motivational levels that are required to achieve your goals.

In order to realize success and eventually achieve your dreams and goals, there is a need to employ emotional intelligence skills. If you have high emotional intelligence levels, you will definitely perform excellently in what you are doing in all aspects. The effectiveness of a person or a team in a certain process directly reflects their emotional intelligence skill level. Those with high emotional intelligence levels will perform well while those with lower intelligence levels would perform dismally and might never achieve their goals.

If we want to produce best results in what we do and achieve the goals we might have set, then all we need is a positive self-regard, effective skills to solve problems, skills to make informed decisions and informed self-awareness. All these are directly attributed to one's emotional intelligence. This, therefore, means that our levels of emotional intelligence dictate if we will achieve our goals or not. Low emotional intelligence will see you fail and never achieve the set goals. On the other hand, high emotional intelligence levels with required emotional skills are very important and they will positively contribute to the achievement of your goals in life.

How to Control and Change Emotions through Emotional Intelligence Concepts

In life generally, we go through diverse situations that might sometimes arouse emotions within us. Being emotional is also not a good thing as such but if we can be able to change and control our emotions in these situations, then we are better off. There are various approaches that can be employed to effectively manage the emotions that we experience. Among these approaches is the emotional intelligence concepts which are very ideal and one of the best.

The following are ways in which one can use to control and change emotions using these concepts:

Self-management

Engaging your emotional intelligence requires you to employ your emotions in making sane decisions regarding your behavior. Sometimes you may go through hard and stressful conditions such that they overpower you. At this time, you might find yourself emotionally weak thus lacking the power of managing and controlling your emotions. This may end up making you bitter and even more stressful thus might end up causing more serious problems like mental illnesses such as depression and the likes. This means that you may not be able to think or even act in a thoughtful and appropriate manner. When overwhelmed with stress, it is true that making sane and rational decisions might not be a walk in the park. At this stage, you will tend to compromise the ability to clearly organize your thoughts and even to manage your emotions, both your own and those of others in this case.

Emotions make up the most important source of information that gives you the ability to understand yourself and even tell about others around you. Apparently, in stressful situations, we get overwhelmed and might end up losing control over ourselves. With the ability to manage stress and other similar situations, we will get to stay emotionally upright and strong. This will, therefore, mean that you may receive information that tends to upset you but being emotionally strong you will not allow it to take over your emotions and thoughts. At this point, you will be able to decide and sanely make reasonable choices which will control and manage any form of impulsive behaviors or feelings. Apart from that, it is a healthy way in which you can be able to manage your emotions.

Self-management is a way in which you are able to understand your inner self thus getting to know whatever triggers your emotions, both positive and negative. By first having a full understanding of yourself, is now when you can easily relate to other people and their emotions too. At this point, it is beyond doubt that you shall be able to manage and control your emotions and even those of others at stressful circumstances that tend to provoke your emotions.

Social awareness

Social awareness entails having empathy towards others in pursuit of gaining some understanding of their emotions. This enables you to easily identify and possibly interpret the cues, mainly non-verbal cues that others use when you are communicating. From these cues, you may get to understand the other person's feelings and emotional state. You can also get to understand the manner in which their emotional state changes from one moment to the other and more so whatever they term to be important. If the same non-verbal cues are used by a group of people, then that is a clear indication that these people are experiencing the same emotional crisis. Social awareness is a concept of emotional intelligence that employs mindfulness a great deal. To be able to have strong social awareness, you might need to dig into understanding the vital importance of being mindful when socializing. This is a concept that requires you to always be present at every moment of that time as you cannot be able to identify recognize and note non-verbal cues when thinking of something else. Therefore, you should be ready to sacrifice and set aside some thoughts that might hinder your social goals. Instead, you should solemnly focus on the interaction. You should also keep track of the other person's emotions and their flow. This will ensure that you pay full attention to the manner in which your own emotions are also changing with time.

When you take time to focus on someone else's emotions, does not necessarily mean that you will be diminishing own self-awareness. In contrary to this, focusing on other people's emotions will actually aid the development of your own emotional experience and even your beliefs and values too. Therefore, through social awareness, it is very evident that you will be able to understand yourself too in the process. It is also a very good opportunity where you might get a chance of managing and possibly changing their emotions without negatively impacting them in any way. Apart from that, if you feel that something someone is talking about does not please you, then you will be learning something. From such situations is where you can be able to understand your emotions from a social perspective and thus be able to manage and possibly change them accordingly.

Relationship management

Being able to identify and understand the experiences that other people go through together with emotional awareness is the basis of working with other people. With emotional awareness in place, then it means that you can perfectly now develop emotional skills which will be important to your relationship by making it more fulfilling, fruitful and effective.

Relationship management enables you to be aware of the effectiveness of how you use non-verbal cues. When communicating with others on matters linked to your feelings, it is very hard to avoid using non-verbal cues. These non-verbal cues act as stressors which loudly convey your emotions and can also aid you in reading the emotional intent of other people. Therefore, if you can recognize and understand the non-verbal cues then it means that you get the message behind it. From this, you will be able to understand one's emotions and even those of your own thus strengthening your relationship a great deal.

Relationship management also incorporates using humor as a way of relieving stress or any stressful conditions. For long humor has been regarded as the best approach to overcoming stress. This is because humor frees you from stressful thoughts that might be a burden to you and helps you to keep focus and in the right perspective. As a result of laughter, your nervous system comes into balance. You also get to be calm and stress-free thus making you be more of empathic. In the process of being calm, you get to understand the emotions of others and most importantly your own. This will be a strong basis for managing and possibly changing emotions.

Through relationship management, you will also get to learn seeing conflicts as a great chance of growing closer to those around you. Disagreements and conflicts are very common and inevitable in human relationships.

This is because two people cannot ever have the same and exact opinions, expectations or needs at all instances. This, therefore, means that conflicts and disagreeing with others are not a very bad thing but somehow normal. Being able to resolve the conflicts in a healthy and organized manner is the best approach to strengthening bonds between each one of you. This is when you can now have a chance of understanding their emotions and how they change over time. This will make it easy for you to control and change emotions easily.

Self-awareness

In order to achieve fully built emotional intelligence and be able to have control and change your emotions, self-awareness is the most basic step of it all. Science of attachment usually tries to describe that a person's current emotional state is usually the result of what they have gone through earlier in life. The way in which you are capable of managing your feelings such as sadness, joy, fear, and even anger usually depends on the consistency and nature of your emotional experience earlier in life. If you were brought up by someone who cared and valued your emotions, then you would obviously grow up with your emotions being a great value to you. On the other hand, if as a young child you had confusing and painful emotions, it is much likely that you will grow up wanting to distance yourself from such emotions. Having the ability to connect and understand your emotions and how they change from time to time is the best way to understand your emotions and how they impact your actions and thoughts.

In order to build and strengthen your emotional intelligence, you need to be emotionally healthy and have the capability of reconnecting with your inner emotions and being comfortable experiencing them. This can be easily achieved by practicing mindfulness and keeping focus. Mindfulness is the act of focusing on what is going on at the present purposefully without judging.

Mindfulness helps you to avoid bad scenarios of the past that make you emotional and focus on the present while appreciating it. It, therefore, keeps you calm and makes you become focused. In this process of being calm and focused, you will be able to be more aware of yourself and more specifically your emotions. Being self-aware and practicing mindfulness is one of the best approaches to controlling and changing your emotions. This is because you will get to understand the inner you and the circumstances which make you emotional. The act of mindfulness will allow you to forget the past that evokes emotions that might be haunting you.

This will thus mean that you shall have the leeway of understanding your emotions and the way in which they keep changing from time to time. Having achieved all these, then it means that you will have control over your emotions and thus can easily change them.

Advantages of Managing Emotions Using Emotional Intelligence Concepts

Being able to control and change emotions at different circumstance accrues with various advantages in different life aspects. These advantages incorporate the end product which might be success or goal achievement. The following are some of the advantages that management and change of emotions has:

Achievement of set goals

Having the ability to control and change emotions enables you to achieve the life goals that you might have set. Being able to change and control emotions enables you to focus on and embrace the present. This, therefore, means that you will forget the sad experiences of the past that may make you lose focus and in turn focus on your goals instead. This will, in turn, enable you to achieve the goals and life objectives that you might have set.

Keep effective communication

If you are able to control and change your emotions, then this means that you can also understand the emotions and feelings that other people have.

When communicating you will be very careful not to say what may revoke bitterness and make the other person so emotional. You will, therefore, be able to communicate with people effectively and not going to the extent of hurting their emotions and feelings.

Making informed decisions

A person who is capable of controlling and changing their emotions are always focused and calm. They usually have nothing destructing them from their focus as there is no emotional interference affecting them. In this state, it means that they can calmly think about certain issues which they need to make decisions and come up with great reasonable and informed decisions.

Be successful

Having the ability to control and change emotions is a calming and satisfying feeling ever. This will enable you to focus on what you are doing and avoid any distractions that might be experienced. If you are still learning, then this means that you will focus and put all your hard work into the studies. In the long run, you will notice that this will start bearing fruits and success will be on your way.

Embrace resilience

Emotional management by being able to control and change emotions always makes one be hard and does not easily 'burnout'. This is because you will have the motivation to do what you like doing and not easily swayed by emotions or feelings. With time you will get focused and resilient. This means that you will be able to cope with hard situations that are very stressful at some point in life. This, therefore, proves this ability to be very vital and useful in facing the daily life activities that are usually filled with hard and challenging situations.

Always be happy

People who are emotionally intelligent and can change and control their emotions usually are free from any form of stress.

This is because, at situations where they feel uncomfortable with a certain emotional condition, they can easily articulate and change their emotions to favor them. In this way, they will be able to dodge all stressful situations. This will allow them to focus on situations that they feel they can handle and remain happy. If not possible to control, they can change their emotions to suit the situation and thus overcome the challenge. In this way, they will ensure that they are always happy.

Chapter 3: Strategies to Eliminate Negative Thoughts, Stress, and Fears

In this chapter, we are going to look at how to get rid of negative thoughts, stress, and fears. As we know stress, negative thoughts, and our fears can drive us into paths we never expected to end up to. We should, therefore, try as much as we can to eliminate these barriers to progress. One cannot move forward if they have negative thoughts, stress or has fears about something or someone.

Some of us are fearing things and people and we come to realize that fears are dangerous when we become old. It is, therefore, necessary to try as much as we can to get rid of our fears so that we can become of importance to ourselves and to the society at large.

Negative thoughts make us perceive almost everything negatively. Negativity can cause so much harm to a person. Someone might have planned about something and all was going on well until the person started being negative. The negative thoughts make someone live a 'don't care life'. They prevent someone from accomplishing their goals in life. Stress can make someone depressed or even get sick. We should eliminate stress, negative thoughts, and fears.

Strategies to Overcome Negative Thoughts

Always strive to find the positive side of the situation

To get rid of negative thoughts, one should always be positive despite the situation you are in. A student may be preparing for assessment tests but remembers how terribly he/she had failed in the previous tests. The student might be tempted to start having negative thoughts and says that exams do not define who we are or that maybe he/she is not gifted in academics. One should not let this happen. The student should view that as a motivation to work hard. The student should tell himself/herself that if they work hard they will be praised and admired by the teachers and staff. One should continuously work hard without giving room to negativity. Being positive about a situation helps us to overcome negative thoughts.

Do not listen to people's opinions

To overcome negative thoughts, one should not dwell much on people's thoughts and opinions. People will always have different opinions from yours and if you listen to them you will be negative about a situation. A person might say that they do not like a particular person or thing because of a particular reason and you listen to them.

Chances are you will be convinced to think as they do and this might make you be negative about something. One might want to start a car industry but then someone comes and tells you that the industry has so much difficulty, that the taxes paid are so high or that it is not a profitable business. After hearing all this, one might start thinking negatively about the car industry and even stops all plans they had in place of starting the business. One should only listen to scientifically proven facts but not mere opinions. Opinions should not be listened to if one wants to overcome negative thoughts.

Stop thinking about the thought

One should end a negative thought as soon as they realize they are being negative. One should not try to break the thought down. One should find a whole different thought about something that is not related and start thinking about it. One should not wait after hours, days or weeks so as to get rid of the thought. It should be stopped as soon as you realize it is a negative thought. If you want to stop being addicted to a drug but some time later you tell yourselves how good drugs are, that they relieve stress and they help one to relax their minds, you should stop those thoughts immediately. One may start thinking about something different like how their kids are performing at school and by that, you will have tried to eliminate negative thoughts. To eliminate negative thoughts, one should try to stop the thought and think about something else.

Talk to someone

To get rid of negative thoughts, one should find someone to talk to. There is that one person or a number of people that we always find ourselves talking to whenever we have an issue. One who has negative thoughts should reach out to that person and talk to him/her. A problem shared is a problem half solved. When we talk to someone we feel like the burden is less. By talking to someone, we feel that there is someone who cares about us and there is someone who is always there for us. When we talk to a person about what we think, the person can help us get another dimension of thinking about the thing. Our thoughts are also made to be. One should try as much as they can not to put some thoughts into themselves. Talking to a person you trust is a great way of eliminating negative thoughts.

List down the negative thoughts

Writing down the thoughts can eliminate the thoughts. If one is thinking negatively about something, you should write it down. By writing it down, one feels like they are talking to someone. You can even picture your feelings and draw a map or a chart about something. One can even use crayons to draw what they think they are feeling. Writing helps one channel all their anger and thoughts on paper. One feels relieve d. It is similar to talking to someone but in writing, no one is listening to you. You are all by yourself and you are channeling your thoughts to the paper. Writing helps one overcome negative thoughts.

Avoid using negative terms

Negative terms should be avoided so as to eliminate negative thoughts. Negative thoughts are mostly accompanied by negative terms and negative words. Words like I am unable, I will not, It is hard, she/he also did not make it too, let it be, I am always a failure and it has never been easy among others are all terms that one should avoid. One may be used to such terms and it may seem normal saying them to oneself but one should avoid such terms. They make one not to go the extra mile. One may be saying the terms to oneself or to others. What you feed your mind is what it eats. If you tell your mind that whatever you want to do is hard, your mind will not struggle to do it since it knows it is already hard. One should get rid of words that are just negative in nature. Words like disastrous and failure should be avoided if one wants to eliminate negative thoughts. One who wants to eliminate negative thoughts should avoid the use of negative terms and words.

Talk to yourself about the thought

If you want to overcome negative thoughts, you should talk to yourself about the thought. One should hold a small meeting with oneself and try to find the cause of the thought and what he/she can do to stop thinking about it. When you get some time to yourself, you might even realize that you are just overthinking over nothing or because of a small issue that is not worth it.

One can even have a special statement or word that reminds you not to be negative. One may have a statement like, 'I am a conqueror'. Whenever you are in a situation that your thoughts tell you is difficult and you say that to yourself, you always change the way you think and become positive. One can also decide to always say 'Relax you will make it' or 'Relax it is not hard'. One can decide to always include the word relax in what they say and that will always remind them to be positive when faced with a difficult situation. Use of encouraging statements can help to get rid of negative thoughts.

Understand and accept that you are thinking negatively

One who wants to get over negative thoughts should accept their thoughts. The first step is accepting who we are and what we do. Once we do that, it becomes easy for everything else. The first thing is to accept that you are thinking negatively. After accepting, you start understanding why you are thinking that way. One should try to find the reason why you have such thoughts. One may be having negative thoughts because someone said something about the issue or because they just do not feel like it. Once you understand why you are thinking like that, you try to find a solution to your problem. If you have negative thoughts about a situation like hitting the gym because you think you might not even lose weight, ask yourself why you are thinking that way. There are people who have tremendously loosed weight due to hitting the gym and you can be among them. To eliminate negative thoughts, one should understand and accept their negative thoughts.

One can stop negative thoughts in many different ways. One can always be positive about a situation and try to find the good out of everything. One can get one of his/her confidants and tell what they are thinking and the person will help or advise accordingly. One can list his/her thoughts and get creative with what he/she is thinking. One who wants to get rid of negative thoughts should stop listening to other people's opinions and only listen to empirical-based statements and facts. One should try and talk to oneself about the thought and find out why he/she has such thoughts. One should stop the thoughts as soon as they realize they have such thoughts. One should avoid using negative statements and words when talking to oneself and when talking to others. One should understand and accept his/her thoughts so as to stop negative thinking. There are many ways to avoid negative thoughts. These are just a few which negative thinkers should try to implement.

Strategies to Eliminate Stress

Identify the root of the stress

Finding the cause of why you are stressed is an important step that can help to eliminate stress. There are times when one feels stresses or one feels uncomfortable and thinks a lot about something yet the person is not sure what the issue is. To get rid of stress, one should find what is causing you to be stressed up. One should commit some 'lone time' and talk to oneself and find out why they are stressed out. To find what makes you stressed, you should ask yourself questions like; who is concerned in this? Why did I do yesterday? Who was I with when this happened? Such questions help one identify the cause of the stress easily. Identifying what causes stress is the first step to eliminating stress.

Get rid of commitments that are not necessary

One should avoid getting committed to things that are not necessary. Depending on who you are and what you do, we all have different commitments. One may be committed to their children, their marriage partner, their work, their education, their spiritual knowledge and much more. It is for a person to know what commitments are necessary and which are not.

One should only concentrate on things that are important to them. You might find a person putting so much effort into something that should be done by another person. You should let everyone play their role. It is through having all those commitments that are not necessary for your thoughts, that you find yourself stressed. The moment one gets rid of unnecessary commitments, one becomes focused and does not get stressed up. One should only be committed to necessary things only.

Avoid postponing

Postponing should be avoided if one wants to get rid of stress. At times we say we will do things at a later time or at a later date mostly because we are lazy or because we have something else we are doing at the moment. Procrastination is the thief of time. One should do tasks and things immediately as they emerge to avoid having so many things to do at a particular time. When one postpones, you come to realize later that you have no time left and you have loads of work to do. This makes one stressed out thinking of how they will manage to be done perfectly and on time. A simpler solution to all this is to do things the scheduled time. By this, you will always meet the timeline and will not be stressed out. One who wants to get rid of stress should do things the scheduled time and avoid postponing.

Be organized

One should do things in an organized manner and in a neat way to avoid stress. At times we might plan things and everything falls into place but there is that one time that we slide and try to squeeze in something. This squeezing in may make us stressed up as there is no place for what we have squeezed in. Disorganization may also stress out someone when you urgently need something but you cannot find it because you are not sure where it is. One might be looking for a certain certificate that is needed for a job interview and it is urgent but you do not find it because you are disorganized. This will make you lose the chance to get the job and in turn, you become stressed. If the person was organized they would have known the certificate is in a certain drawer or bag and they get it out and they get a chance to get the job. One who wants to avoid stress should not be disorganized but should plan everything in an organized manner.

Do not be late

One who wants to be stress-free should always do things on time. When one is behind his/her schedule, one tends to be stressed up. We should try as much as we can to be punctual enough so as to start things on time and finish on time. When one is late when doing something, you always feel stressed up. When you have an exam at 8 and you are not in the exam room by 8 you get stressed. One thinks of the many possibilities that could happen if one missed the chance. If you are late you will have to redo the exam. This will make you stressed and you will start blaming yourself for not being punctual enough. If you are late to go to the bus station and the bus leaves before you are there you will have to get other means of traveling, this makes you stressed up while searching for another means of transport. One should try as much as possible to always be punctual and do things at the right time.

Do not control others or things

If you do not want to get stressed out, do not control things or other people. We do not have the power to do that and whenever we force ourselves to do that, we get stressed because things might not really turn out as we expect. One might think that if you control a person and tell them to do a certain job for you will make it easier for you. The person may or may not do the job, whatever they do is under their control not under your control. If they decide not to do what you had told them, you will have to do the job. Doing the job means you will have to fix that at a particular time which means you will have to do it in a hurry. You can only give directions and controls to yourself. A person of sound mind will do what they want regardless of whether it is right or wrong. You should just let things flow as planned but not as you wish. You should respect other people's decisions and the way they control their things. One who wants to avoid stress does not control other people but only controls himself/herself.

Avoid people who stress you out

To avoid stress, one should avoid people who stress him/her. There are people who when we meet we just feel stressed out. They can be our employers, teachers, parents, colleagues, relatives or even friends. One should avoid being in the presence of such people because they will always stress you out. If your employer stresses you out, try to avoid him/her. It can be that whenever your employer sees you in the wrong they remind you of a past event that stresses you out. An employer might see you trying to fix live wires and they start mocking you saying how the last time you tried doing that the firm lost a lot of property in a fire. Maybe whenever you remember that incident you get stressed out. One should avoid such people as they will only do you more harm than good. One who wants to avoid stress should avoid people that cause them to be stressed.

Appreciate everything and everyone in life

If you want to avoid stress, always appreciate everyone and everything life gives you. One should learn to show gratitude. Sometimes we stress up because things did not end up as we expected. Maybe you were doing an exam and you get a grade B while you were expecting to get an A. You should appreciate whatever life offers you. When life gives you lemons, make a cocktail out of it. Do not ask for more. That is what you got and that is what is yours. You will not get another so you should just accept and strive to do better the next time. If you want to be associated with a particular group of people because you think they are cool but you end up being in another group of people, appreciate them. You can still be happy with them if not happier. When we learn to appreciate what we have, we will not get stressed up.

Exercise and eat foods that are healthy

If you want to reduce stress, eat healthy foods and do a lot of exercises. Exercise rejuvenates our body and makes us stronger. When you exercise your mood changes and you become happy. Exercise and eating healthy go hand in hand. There are foods that make one moody and there are foods that do not have mood effects on a person. A healthy person is less prone to stress. Exercise does not leave room for stress in a person's body. Exercise also gives one some time for himself/herself. As you exercise, you think more about yourself and the situations you are in. This prevents one from getting stressed as they have a plan of their lives. Eating healthily and doing exercise regularly can help reduce stress.

Plan to do important things only

If you want to avoid stress, have a to-do-list of important things only. One should not put loads of works on their list. There are things that even if you do they will not impact on you. One should get rid of such activities. Concentrate on things and activities that are important and necessary. If you think something does not help you in any way get rid of it. One who keeps a long to-do-list without caring whether it is helpful or not is prone to be stressed. This is because the person has each 0f their minute planned on and whenever they try to fix some time for themselves in between they will mess things up. One should only strive to do things that are important to you and leave out other things. To avoid stress, one should create a to-do-list of important activities only.

Do what you like most

One who wants to reduce stress levels or get rid of it completely should practice doing what they like doing most. We are all different and we have different preferences. Our talents, hobbies, and abilities are different. Different people may like doing different things like listening to music, taking a walk, going to the movies, skating, playing tennis, helping others, playing soccer, reading novels and books or even writing blogs. One should put so much attention to what they like. The body wants what it wants. If you give the body what it wants, you will not become stressed up easily. People find their happiness from small things. I personally listen to music find myself in a fantasy world. When you do what you like doing, you will spend most of your time being happy. One who wants to get rid of stress should spend their free time doing activities that they find fun doing.

Talk to someone

One who is stressed should find someone to talk to. The person can be a friend. A relative or anyone you trust. When you talk to someone you feel better. It is through talking to someone that you get to exchange thoughts. When you talk to someone the person gives his/her ideas and thoughts on a particular issue. The thoughts of the person can help you get a new perspective to a new thing. When you talk to someone you feel you have gotten something off your chest. It is important to talk to someone when stressed out. Talking to another person when stressed prevents depression. To avoid stress one should reach out and talk to someone about the issue at hand.

Be assertive

One who wants to eliminate stress should always mean what they say. When one says yes, they should mean their yes and when they say no they should mean their no. One should not be influenced by others to do things or not to do things. You might do things because you were influenced by someone then when the consequences come to be you regret alone and be stressed out. Everything has its own consequences. One should, therefore, make assertive decisions after critical thinking. One should not do something because his/her friends have done it but should do what is right. The right thing is usually hard to do but we should strive to do it. The simpler thing is mostly the wrong thing. Wrong things have negative consequences which will get you stressed. To avoid stress, one should mean and do what they say.

Take caffeine in regular amounts

Caffeine should be taken in the correct amounts by someone who wants to get rid of stress. Caffeine is a stimulant. It is found in a drink like tea and coffee. One should take such drinks in regular amounts as they contain caffeine which increases anxiety levels. People are different and each person has a maximum caffeine intake. One should try not to exceed it as it will increase anxiety and stress levels. Stress should be avoided and in case one gets to be stressed they should try to eliminate it. There are many ways in which one can avoid stress. One should avoid situations and people that make him/her stressed. One should avoid commitments that are not necessary. One should not postpone things and do things at the scheduled time. One should always be organized and never be late to do anything. One should not give himself/herself the mandate to control another person or thing. One should have a simple to-do-list that is made up of important things only. One who wants to get rid of stress should exercise and eat healthy foods. One should use their free time to do what they like doing most. One should have a regular caffeine intake depending on their threshold. One should practice gratitude and appreciate others and whatever they get to have in life. One should always be assertive and strive to do the right thing always. One should talk to someone if they feel stressed out. There are many ways of eliminating stress. Above are just a few.

Strategies to Eliminate Our Fears

Know what your fears are

One who wants to eliminate their fears should start knowing what his/her fears are. We all have different fears. Each person has his/her own fear. One can fear height, water, darkness, spiders, being alone or flying just to name a few. When one realizes that they fear a particular thing or person, they should accept that they fear those things. After one has accepted, they should not try to hide from them. If you fear something, you should realize that it will never end. If you fear darkness, there is no time that will come for darkness to cease to exist. Knowledge is power. When you have the knowledge of your fears, you will not find yourself in hard situations when faced with your fears. Knowing your fears should be the first step taken by one who wants to get rid of their fears.

Learn to appreciate

One who wants to overcome fear should learn how to show gratitude. When you learn to be appreciative of things you have and situations you are in, you will get rid of fear. If you fear flying on a plane, be appreciative that you got the chance to fly in a plane. If you fear to lose a job, appreciate that you currently are doing the job and you have not lost the job. When you learn to show gratitude when faced with your fears, you will view the positive side of you will have fewer emotions connected to the fear. When you show gratitude to someone or something, one feels good. It is good to appreciate something if it is nice. One who wants to eliminate stress should practice the act of gratitude.

Discover what emotions are associated with fear

One who wants to eliminate fear should identify the feeling or emotion connected to the fear they have. One might have different feelings or thoughts for different fears. You might feel shocked when you see a spider, you might feel anxious when flying on a plane and you do not know when you will get down, you might feel sad when you think of losing your job and when you think of everything that will happen when you lose the job.

Mostly when someone thinks of their fear they start to overthink and they get different emotions while thinking. You might be having the fear of failing an exam and when you think about it you feel pitiful for yourself, then you remember how much your parents have struggled to see you in school you start hating yourself and much more feelings. These are the reasons why one should identify the emotions and feelings they get when they face their fears.

List them down

One who wants to get over their fears will list them down. Most times thinking about our fears only gets us stressed. At times it makes us even more stressed than we were before. It is therefore wise for someone to list their fears down if they want to get rid of them. When you list them down, you feel better and you feel relieved just a little bit. Writing helps us to express what is in our thoughts and what we feel. When writing, one should not be restricted to a particular concern but should list all that is in their mind. One can even go further and start drawing what they think they feel or have in their chest when they are associated with that fear. One who wants to get rid of their fears should write them down.

Talk to someone

Talking to someone about your fears will help you eliminate your fears. One might have had a fear of flying and they decide to talk to someone. When talking to the person about your fear, they tell you that they have flown several times and it is fun and maybe you should try it out with them. This might help you get a better image of flying. When you talk to a person about your fears and what you feel about your fears, the person tries as much as they can to change the situation. One might not necessarily change your perception towards your fear but they might help you know how to face it. They might give you stories or testimonies of people who have made it through and you encourage yourself and hope all will be well. One should make sure that after talking to a person they should not leave the person the way they came in terms of facing and handling the fear. Talking to someone can be a great way of eliminating our fears.

Learn not to control things

To eliminate fear, one should not control situations or things. A person might think that because they are good at something they can never fail or make a slight mistake at it. We are humans and we can never be perfect. You might be a punctual employee always on doing your tasks and obedient but one day you might delay a bit and you will get your fear from that. You will not know how to face your employer because you have always told yourself you are the best and no one can beat you at being punctual. You start fearing that the employer might fire you or you start fearing that the employer might but you down there in the hierarchy. We should not control things or people if we want to get rid of our fears.

Learn from others

One who wants to get rid of their fear should learn from others. There are many people who share a common fear. Some have managed to get through it while some are struggling to get over it. One who wants to eliminate their fears should reach out to such people. If someone already made it overcome the fear, find out what they did to overcome the fear. If you find people who are still struggling to get over it, learn what they are doing. Every day should be a learning day to someone who wants to get rid of their fears. You should even try to associate yourselves with people who have the same fear as you have and are trying to overcome it. One may fear to break up with a spouse and when you go to your friends who have the same issue, they tell you what they do to always see they are together. To eliminate your fears, you should learn from other people who have or who had the same fear as you.

Pray or meditate

One who wants to get rid of their fears should pray and ask for help. Christians are taught that God listens and answers our prayers. There are times you struggle with something so much that you do not know what to do next. One who has reached this stage should try and seek help from a religious perspective. Christians should ask God for help and Muslims should ask Allah to answer their prayers. This depends on the religious background of a person. I am a Christian and I personally believe that whatever you ask shall be given unto you. If one is not religious or finds it hard to pray, one can meditate. Meditation is as good as praying and helps one to overcome their fears too. One should choose whatever they think will be effective for them. A person who wants to get rid of his/her fears should pray or meditate.

Accept that everyone makes mistakes

One who wants to get rid of his/her fears should understand that no one is perfect and we all make mistakes. Some of our fears are caused by failing. One might have the fear of failing a test, of not doing well at the place of work, of not emerging the best in a fashion show or of not meeting the sales of a particular item. We should, however, understand that we have all experienced points in our lives when we failed at a particular thing. One cannot always be successful at everything you do and if that happens you are not doing something right. One should, therefore, understand that failure opens a road for success. When you fail chances are people will mock or laugh at you while others will hold your hand and show you the way. It is therefore up to us to decide what we emerge out as after failure. We should not be defined by failure. One who wants to get rid of fear should not let failure put them down.

Let life be

One who wants to get rid 0f his/her fears should flow with the events of life. If you want to live life peacefully, just flow with the

339

way things are. At times we create fears because of people's opinions about us and how they judge us. One fears to talk in front of a large crowd because you are afraid of the impression you have on people or because you are afraid that people will talk about you. One should not let their fears be based on such small issues. People will always speak their views and thoughts about something or someone and because we all have different preferences we should not let that bother us. Maybe when you do something great some people will not notice because they are not destined for greatness. After all, people have talked about you severally and life went on after that. Even with our fears, we should just flow with life in case we face them. One might be at 45 years and have a fear of losing his/her job and they eventually lose it. Being 45 years that might not be the first job you have lost. After losing the first job life continued as usual. We do not know what life holds for each one of us. One who wants to get rid of his/her fear should just let life be and flow with everything as it happens.

There are many strategies one can use to eliminate his/her fears. One should start with identifying his/her fear and dig to know what emotions and feelings are associated with fear. Once one has known what emotions are connected with the fear, they should find a way to control the emotion or feeling. One should talk to someone about their fears or talk to trained personnel and if they find that hard they can write their thoughts about the fear down. One should seek religious help by praying and if they find that hard they can meditate. One should understand that failure is not permanent and everyone at some point has failed in a particular thing. One should not create fears because they are afraid of peoples' opinions and thoughts. One should flow with life because even after everything happens life will go on. One should learn to appreciate the opportunities they have and not view them as fears.

Negative thoughts, stress, and fears are all things that can cause us to be mentally ill and depressed. They are concerned with our cognitive behavior and one should try to eliminate them as soon as they realize they have developed them. They can be hard to avoid and eliminate but one should try as much as they can to get rid of them. There are strategies that apply to all three issues. Strategies, like talking to someone, writing them down, exercising and eating healthy and praying or meditating, can all help eliminate the issues. One who wants to eliminate negative thinking, stress or his/her fears should struggle as much as they can since it is not easy. There are times when one gets halfway there and loses hope because they cannot see the fruits their efforts but that should not be a reason for them to stop. One who has made a personal decision to eliminate all these do not turn back.

Chapter 4: Strategies of Anger Management to Reach Calmness and Build-Up Self Control

It is normal to have anger issues. It is an emotion that is normal and it is not bad or good. When we get angry, we are communicating that we are not happy about the things people have told us. It is just a way of telling people around us that we were not happy about their actions. Anger can also be said to be a way that one uses to communicate their frustrations or even issues that may be threatening their peace.

There are those times when one finds themselves just angry for no reason.

When it becomes extreme, it can cost people relationships and also make them psychologically disturbed which may make them lose focus and also deprive them of a good quality of life. There are people who do not show anger and so they will pile it up. Piling up anger may have very negative effects on one's well-being. They may have long term negative impact which becomes difficult when not controlled.

Anger is something that can be managed with proper control. It is important for people to understand that anger is not bad when it is under control. It becomes bad when it makes people behave in a way that can make the people around them uncomfortable. It also becomes an issue when people harm themselves as a result of anger.

People will get angry when they see someone abusing children when they are mental or emotionally abused and also when they find themselves in traumatic situations. They may also become angry when they lack sleep when they have low self-esteem and also when they are stressed and anxious. It is important to ensure that you look for help early enough in order to avoid anger at all costs.

One is required to ensure that they find a solution to this problem early enough in order for them to ensure that they remain calm and for them to avoid anger. When one wants to manage anger, they do not need to hold it inside them. They should talk about it and take measures to ensure that they are free from it. For one to be able to manage their anger, they should be able to accept that they actually have anger issues. When one finds out that their anger issues are making them lose control, they would need to look for help.

There are those signs that will stand out when one has anger issues. However, there are those extreme cases which will tell you that you need help from a professional. I have listed some of the signs that one will experience and make a decision to look for professional help.

1. When they find themselves on the wrong side of the law

2. When they find themselves suppressing their anger all the time

3. Having fights with people around them and also their family from time to time

4. When they find themselves confronting people around them because of petty issues

5. Becoming violent towards people an even threatening them

6. When they find themselves breaking things in the house when they get angry

7. When they lose their temper over small issues

When you find yourself in any of the above cases, then you need help. It is at this point that one might need help with managing their anger since it will be evident that the anger is having some negative influence on them. It will also be having some negative impact on the people around which may make them judge you wrongly. It is also said that anger can have some effects on one's health as well as causing them to have an issue with people around them.

When one has anger issues, they may get heart diseases and insomnia as well as finding themselves with high blood pressure. It may also hinder your concentration which may make you feel frustrated since you may not be able to handle all the things around you with ease. This will also make it hard for you to enjoy life since you will not have an easy time interacting with people.

Whenever people find themselves struggling with anger, they should look for help from counselors. This will enable them to live a life that is free from stress. You will also be able to relate well with your friends, colleagues, and employers without experiencing any challenges. For one to be able to control their anger, they should follow the following steps:

- Being able to recognize signs of anger early enough
- Giving yourself time to think about it and identify the triggers
- Using strategies that will be of help in control of anger

There are many things that one can apply in life in order for them to be able to manage their anger. I have discussed some of them below.

Find Out Reasons for your Anger

Am sure most of you have gotten into a fight because of some things that would be considered petty. After thinking through the things that made you fight, you may have discovered that it was something that you could actually have solved without an issue. For someone to make sure that they are in control of their anger, they have to ensure that they find its real cause.

When you know the cause of your anger, you will be able to use the means possible to eliminate it. You will also be able to look for strategies which would help you to be able to overcome your frustrations which will help you to deal with the anger issues as they arise. Frustrations will mostly come as a result of not being understood or when one is not understanding the people around them. it would be important to identify the things that make you angry and ensure that you get away from them. This will help a lot in avoiding anger.

When you find out the reasons for your anger, you will also be able to keep away from the things that make you angry. There are people who may have anger issues as a result of growing up a place that they were not given a chance to express how they feel. This means that they could stomach all kinds of mistreatments without saying a word. As a result of their frustrations, they become so sensitive to the things said to them. A very minor thing can accelerate their anger to a level that all the people around them cannot even understand.

When you have grown up in an area that does not allow you to express your feelings, you will always find yourself using anger to solve issues. This is because you were only trained to bottle up feelings. It would be advisable to seek counseling in order for you to learn some strategies that you can apply when something angers you. Counselors are skilled and knowledgeable about the things that may be of help to you when it comes to handling anger issues.

It is very easy to manage anger when you know its cause. You can even learn how to control it by yourself. This is because there is a lot of information about it on the internet which I will be helpful to you. This means that a person who has accepted that they have anger issues can look for information that can help them overcome it from anywhere.

Acting on Anger Signs Early Enough

You may find yourself just exploding as a result of anger without any warning. Even before you get angry, you feel it in yourself some emotions which could be making you feel uncomfortable about various situations. Those are the signs that you need to be aware of since they are the ones that make you feel angry. Being aware of such emotions is very important since one will be able to get away from the people who may be making them angry. They are also able to control their anger when faced with situations that require them to control themselves.

By doing this, one will be able to control their anger before it comes out since the anger may affect people around them. One is required to listen to their body and when they are angry and convince their mind that it isn't right to get angry over issues. They can choose to walk away which will be of help to them since they will be able to avoid getting angry.

When people with anger issues feel the signs of anger, they should be able to choose not to get angry. They can even choose to see the good sign of the situation that is making them angry. By doing this they will be able to live a positive life that is free from anger. They will also be able to have good relationships with people around them which will make them relate well with them without any conflicts.

Identifying your Triggers

It is important for one to identify the things that make them angry. They may be getting easily irritable because of stressful situations. The stressful situations do not mean that one must get angry, they should be able to take control of their anger even when they are under pressure. One can check on their day to day activities and identify those activities that trigger anger in them. By doing this, they can choose to change the routine and come up with one that is not too stressful for them. They can also choose to avoid those activities and replace them with a positive thing or something that they love doing.

One may be going out with a group of people and the end results become fights and abuses which make them angry.

They can avoid going out with such people as it will help them to be able to avoid getting angry. It is important for one to ensure that they get rid of the bad company since they will make sure that their anger levels are controlled and they may also avoid getting triggered into getting angry.

People may think that their anger comes from internal sources but the truth is that they may come from your interpretation of the issues you may be facing. Someone may be giving out ideas that may change a situation but someone with anger issues will interpret them depending on their mood about it. They may be triggering their anger through overgeneralizing issues and also through jumping into conclusions about them.

Triggers may also come from blaming people for your misfortunes and also your failures. It is therefore important for people to be able to discover the things that trigger anger in them in order for them to be able to avoid getting angry. By doing so, they will be able to have a good relationship with the people around them.

Identify Ways of Cooling Down Quickly

When one is trying to manage their anger, they should be able to look for ways to ensure that they cool down when anger issues arise. They should be able to tell that they are about to get angry through the triggers. By identifying that, they will be able to avoid things that make them angry in order for them to feel better about themselves. There are many strategies that one can apply in order for them to be able to cool down easily after an argument. I have listed them below.

Taking Some Deep Breath: When one gets some anger triggers, they should be able to calm down, take a deep breath in order for them to release any tension within them. The deep breath will help them to relax and feel better about the situation that they may be going through. They will also be able to avoid feeling angry which will be of great help to them.

Focusing on Other Things: When one feels angry, they can try to focus on other things that are not related to the situation that they may be facing. Focusing on those things will make them forget the issues that are making them angry. They may also find other positive things that may make them keep going. They may also get some distractions which will make them cool down and even forget about the issues that may be making them angry.

Taking a Walk: When one feels angry, taking a walk will be of great help in lowering their anger levels. As they walk, they will get some distractions along the way which will make them forget that there were things that were making them angry. They may meet friends along the way and may end up catching up on various things. This helps a lot in lowering their levels of anger. Walking helpful in so many ways. It helps people to be able to freshen up and release all the tension within them. They are also able to look at nature and appreciate it. They will feel peaceful since by the time they get back they will have cooled down.

Engaging in Physical Activities: There are people who join the gym or do some physical activities at home. The activities are very important in helping one to cool down when they are angry. This is because one releases a lot of tension when doing them. People who may have gone there when angry will leave the place having cooled down as a result of the activities they will have carried out in the gym.

As they carry out different activities, they get distracted from the challenges that they may be experiencing which make them forget that they were angry. It is therefore important for one to take part in physical activities in order for them to be able to cool down when they suspect that they are going to get angry.

Whenever one is feeling angry they need to ask themselves some questions like whether it is really worth it to get angry about a given issue. They should also ask themselves if the issue making them angry is really worth ruining their day. They can also ask themselves if there is something they can do about the issue that may be making them angry and also whether taking any action will be worth their time.

By asking yourself those questions, one will be able to decide whether to get angry about the situation or not. In case any of the issues making them angry needs them to act on them, one will be able to act on them without regretting the consequences of the outcome. People around you will also understand you when you get angry because the issue that may have made you angry will be genuine unlike when you get angry because of small issues.

Find Healthy Ways of Expressing Anger

When one gets angry for a situation that is worth getting angry about, they should ensure that they look for mature solutions to the problems they may be facing. They need to ensure that however severe the situation is, they come up with ways of solving the issues without complicating the issue more. They should come up with ways of ensuring that they deal with the issues in a healthy manner which ensures that nobody comes out of it hurt. When one comes up with better ways of solving issues, they maintain good relationships with the people around them. They are able to interact with people around them easily without conflicting or experiencing any challenges.

People who were one quick to anger are able to build healthy relationships with people when they learn ways of dealing with their anger. People will start relating well with them because they will see that they are changed and that they are able to control their anger. It is therefore important to ensure that one finds of dealing with their anger issues in order for them to build healthier relationships with people. People who are determined to make their relationship work should ensure that they work on making the relationships stronger rather than being the winner in the relationship. This will help them to gain trust with the people around them and also respect is automatically cultivated amongst themselves.

When people are arguing, it is important to ensure that they do not focus on the disagreements they had in the past. They should focus on just the current issues in order for them to avoid complicated issues. When you focus on the issues that may be making you angry now, you will be able to ensure that you solve the issue without experiencing any challenges.

One needs to also ensure that they have the willingness to forgive those who make them angry. They should learn that forgiveness is the only thing that can lessen the burden in their heart. It is easier to deal with issues when you do not have a grudge with anyone. When you have a burden in your heart, you make easily irritable. This is because you still have some underlying issues. It is important to ensure that you handle all the issues as they come in order for you to avoid pilling up issues with people in your heart.

It is also important to ensure that you know the right time to let go. Whenever you find yourself in a disagreement, you should be able to tell when it is the right time to stop it. Whenever you find out that you cannot disagree on anything, you would need to end the argument by taking the burden. In this case, no one will win or lose the argument. This will make things neutral and will leave everybody in peace.

Staying Calm by Taking Care of Yourself

When one decides to take care of themselves, they are likely to achieve overall mental, physical and emotional health. They will remain peaceful since they know and understand the things that make them angry and those that don't. They are able to manage their stress well which enables them to be in control of the issues that stress them and avoid them completely.

When one is calm, they are able to think through all the issues before acting on them. If they figure out that reacting to some issues will not benefit them in any way, they should avoid getting angry because of them. This will help a lot in ensuring that you stay calm and avoid trouble. There are those people who will only be able to stay calm by they talk to a trusted friend. They have to open up to someone in order for them to remain calm. If you are that type of person, ensure that you open up to someone that you can trust.

There are people who will spread the things you share with them with other people. This will only complicate things more. The trust you had for them will break as a result of that. Lastly, ensure that you get enough sleep. When you have enough sleep, you will be able to eliminate any negative thoughts that you may be having. You will also have enough rest which will help in improving your focus on other things so you won't have time to get involved in issues that will make you angry.

Using Humor to Relieve Tension

When things get tough, it is important to apply humor in order to lighten people's mood. Humor makes people forget the challenges they are facing for a moment. One can also use humor when they want to pass sensitive information. Humor will help a lot in ensuring that people who are likely to get mad at you do not get mad. This enables you to be able to communicate your point without making people angry.

It is important to note that you are supposed to laugh with them and not laugh at them. By doing this, you will be able to ensure that they are all comfortable with the joke. Humor is, therefore, able to reduce stress, lower tension levels and also lower one's anger. This helps a great deal in ensuring that you avoid conflicts with people around you. This gives people a good environment to work and relax.

Know When You Need Professional Help

You may be able to put all the measures to ensure that you manage your anger but you may still need professional help. You should be in a position to tell that you have done your best but you still need professional help. There are people who try their best to ensure that they control their anger but they hit their dead-end on this. It is at this time that they will need to look for a professional counselor who will help them to be able to manage their anger.

When you decide to look for professional help, it will help you a great deal. This is because you will be able to meet other people battling anger which will give you the motivation to know that you are not battling anger issues alone. It will motivate you to work on your anger in order for you to be able to achieve better results. When there, you will be able to get therapies and counseling which will help you to be able to achieve your goal. Seeing a professional is therefore very important in ensuring that you finally manage to handle your anger issues.

Make sure that you Think Before you speak

Many are times when you find yourself overreacting to issues because of not thinking them through before you speak. You will find yourself regretting because of speaking about the issue when you are still angry. It is important to ensure that when you feel angry, you take your time to collect your thoughts before you speak. By doing this, you will be able to only speak about the things that make sense. You will also be able to control your anger which will help in making sure that you are reasonable enough.

There are those times when you will find yourself arguing with someone who is not reasonable. This will make you angrier. The best thing to do is to give the person time to calm down. Once they calm down, you will be able to discuss the issue with them which will help in ensuring that you achieve the best results.

Therapy

Therapy is one of the things that have been used by people in order for them to be able to control their anger. They may attend the therapy sessions as individuals or as groups. Through the sessions, they are able to get help in the identification of triggers that may be making them angry. They also get to learn the ways of handling the triggers and making sure that they do not cause anger in you. Therapists also teach people techniques to apply in order for them to overcome anger. They ensure that they see things positively which enables them to solve problems without experiencing any challenges.

Keeping an Anger Diary

An anger diary is a record that people keep for them to be able to follow up on their anger patterns. They can list all the things that made them angry that day and the reasons why they got angry. This helps them a lot in ensuring that they are able to anticipate when triggers are likely to happen. Once they predict them, they will be able to cope with them effectively which helps them to cope with anger.

When writing down the information, they can also note down the strategies that worked and those that did not work. This will help them to be able to apply those that they are sure they will work and get rid of those did not work. By doing all this, they will be able to control their anger which will help them to lead a better healthier life.

Through the diary, one can also write down the positive things that happened to them during the day. This will be of great help in ensuring that one sees that apart from the negative things, there were also positive things that happened to them. This will act as a motivation to achieve more positive things each day than the negative ones. It is very important for people to have self-control if at all they want to be able to manage their anger. One will have to ensure that they are consistent with what they choose to have some self-control in order for them to eliminate anger in their lives. They may be required to practice some of the things that I have listed below in order for them to be able to control their anger.

• Having a Positive Attitude

When one has a positive attitude, it becomes very easy for them to handle issues. This is because they believe that they can do it and they put all the necessary measures to ensure that they achieve all the set goals. It also feels great when one is in control of their situations. It motivates them to do even better since they are determined to conquer everything. With a positive attitude, it is likely that you will not feel angry about the issues that are meant to annoy you. This is because you will look at the bright side of it and be able to face it and solve it successfully.

• Setting Goals

It is important for people to set goals if they want to be in control of the issues facing them. They need to come up with rules to follow when people or situations make them angry. They are then expected to follow those rules to the latter. They have to ensure that they are disciplined enough to deal with the issues without breaking the rules. This will help them to be able to control their anger since they have no room for making mistakes.

By achieving those goals, they will have made a step ahead which will ensure that they are self-controlled. Achieving the goals makes them motivated since. They will even go an extra mile in order to ensure that they achieve the goals. They should also ensure that they set achievable goals. They can even start with short term goals before they set long term goals. Once the short term ones, they will be able to slowly add the goals in order for them to be able to be consistent which in return will enable them to achieve the goals.

• Self-Monitoring

One will be able to tell whether they are achieving the set goals through monitoring the progress they are making in all the areas. Self-monitoring gives them feedback on their progress. When you monitor yourself, you will ensure that you are following all the rules that you are required to follow. You will make sure that all the goals are achieved within the given timelines. By doing this, you will be able to control your anger issues and with time, you will be free from anger.

Self-monitoring is also said to help one to avoid losing track of the goals they have set. They will make sure that they are following all the rules in order to ensure that they lower their anger issues. Once they succeed in this, they will note that their anger levels will have gone lower by great levels.

- **Through motivation**

Motivation works so well, especially with children. They can be given presents for not getting angry for a given period of time. They get motivated to achieve the goal within the set period. Motivation also works for adults. The may get rewarded for controlling their anger. The rewards make them strive to be able to achieve their goals which enables them to also feel better about themselves.

People will mostly stick to something as a result of the value they get from it. No one will stick to something that is not benefiting them in any way. One gets motivated through their achievements so little or no achievements makes them less motivated. People need to, therefore, ensure that they set goals that they can achieve in order for them to get the motivation to control their anger and to also work on the things that may be making them angry.

• Confidence

Confidence is so important in so many areas of our lives. When one has confidence that they will achieve a certain goal, they will definitely achieve the goals. When they decide that they will work on their anger issues, they will achieve that since they have the confidence required to achieve it. They will, therefore, take up the issue and work on it and believe that they will lower their anger issues. It is therefore important to ensure that one gathers confidence to say no to anger and by doing so, they will be able to get rid of the burden of anger.

• Have the Willpower

Willpower is referred to as having the strength and also psychological energy which one needs in order for them to be able to set goals and achieve them. It's also having the strength to overcome any kinds of temptations which will enable them to be able to achieve all the goals that they have set. Having willpower is very important as it helps one to keep moving even after the going gets tough. They do not give up since they are only focussed on the goal.

Through willpower, they are also able to have some self-control which helps them to control their anger even when they are tempted to feel angry. When one is able to control themselves, they get rid of anger little by little. This means that they are able to achieve their goal with the set time.

• Monitor their pattern of behavior

It is important for people with anger issues to ensure that they monitor their pattern of behavior. This will help them to tell the things that make them angry and those that do not. They should be able to get rid of the behaviors that make them angry even as they try to work on their anger. Monitoring your pattern is crucial since it enables you to ensure that you maintain discipline which will in return help you to get rid of anger issues.

Monitoring your pattern of behavior will also ensure that you do not repeat the mistakes that you did in the past. This is because you will be able to apply self-control whenever the issues arise which will help you avoid getting angry. It is also through monitoring your behavior patterns that you will be able to avoid situations that make you angry and also be able to remain calm even when you are provoked by the people around you.

There are very many reasons why people chose to control their anger. One of the reasons being the benefits that come with it. Below are some of the benefits that one gets from being able to control their anger.

Being Able to Deal with Issues Soberly

When one overcomes their anger, they are able to deal with the issues that arise in a sober manner. This means that they do not have conflicts with the people around them since you will be in control of your emotions and also feelings. One is also able to have meaningful relationships since there will be no fights between them. Whenever any of them is angry, they will be able to talk about it and solve the issues without getting angry. They will be able to agree that there is a problem and deal with it without experiencing any kind of conflict.

One Becomes more Empathetic

When one is in control of their anger, they are able to have empathy for others. This is because they are more understanding and reasonable. Whenever they get angry, they are able to get away from it without experiencing any challenges.

It is very important for people to ensure that they deal with their anger issues. This will enable them to be able to look at issues in a positive manner. By doing this, they will be able to see issues in other peoples perspective which will help them to understand them. Doing this will help people to understand each other and build better relationships amongst themselves.

One Gains New Insights

When one decides to deal with their anger issues, they get to learn from their mistakes. As they go through the healing process, they are able to see where they went wrong which helps them to work on the issue. They are also able to be in control of all the issues they are going through since they are now fully aware of the issues. They are able to treat people better, cooperate with them which in the ends enables them to build healthy connections with people.

They are Less Stressed

When people are angry, they are likely to be stressed throughout that period. This is because they do not have peace within themselves so they will tend to quarrel, everyone, they interact with. Many are times which they will be involved in confrontations as a result of piled up issues. Once they deal with the anger issues, they are able to calm down, make peace with other people and also relate well with them. By doing this, they are able to make better friends and maintain them since they are in control of their feelings. This makes them have some peace of mind which helps them to live well with the people around them.

One Becomes Less Aggressive and More Assertive

When one is angry, they become unreasonable. This is because they are selfish and think that they are the only ones being made angry. What they don't know is that the situations making them angry can be avoided. They can communicate well which would help them in understanding each other better. They need to be assertive when it comes to communication in order for them to be able to have a clear channel of communication which they can use. Through it, they will be able to become less aggressive and more aggressive.

One Becomes Responsible for their Actions

It is important for one to know that they are the only ones who are responsible for their actions when angry. Everything they do should be thought through in order to ensure that you do not regret your actions later. This means that when one manages their anger, they are able to identify issues that may annoy them and be able to avoid them. It also means that they have learned to keep all annoying situations in control which makes them calm down when they are angry. Being responsible for your actions is therefore very important as it helps one to be cautious when dealing with issues.

One Gets to Build Better Relationships

When one has anger issues, they tend to push the people they love away. They may avoid holding conversations with them since they feel angry at everybody around them. Most of them will do this when they realize that they are hurting them. There are others who will keep away from their loved ones when they make them angry. One, therefore, makes good relationships with them as a result of controlling their anger. They will bring them closer and ensure that they do not hurt them again.

It is therefore important for people to ensure that they work on their anger issues early enough in order to ensure that they do not spread the anger to the people around them. By doing this, they will not only have helped themselves but also the people they engage in their day to day lives. Whenever they are not able to handle the anger themselves, they should look for help from professionals who are experienced in this area. At the end of it all, they will be able to live a happy life which is free from anger.

Chapter 5: How to Use Your Emotions for Personal Growth and to Improve Relationships

To manage our anger, as we have seen in chapter four, is vital towards improving our general emotions. Passion has led to the destruction of a lot of relationships and the chequered history of humanity.

Many philosophers, among them, Seneca and Marcus Aurelius talked about the negative impact of anger and taught us how we could go through life without giving in to anger.

As we saw in chapter one, emotions are complex, and when in their full swing, they can be overwhelming. Consider the situation where you became so overwhelmed by anger that you did something that you regretted. Or feeling so fearful that you ended up in an embarrassing situation, or almost lost your life to the object of your fear. Emotions can and often are overpowering. As we saw in the beginning, we can control them, and we should be able to easily influence how we react when we feel overwhelmed by fear or shame or guilt or anger. Emotions are stimuli that nature intended to be what drives us to action. We act to rid ourselves of the excitement, rather than let the emotion act on our behalf.

After looking through ways in which you can subdue how you react to your emotions from chapter two through to four, in this chapter, we tie it all together. How do you use what you have learned to become a better person and build better relationships? How do you become a more emotionally adjusted person who has regard for others?

Become Aware of Yourself

Do you ever take the time to consider how you come across to others? Do you ever make the connection between how people act around you and how you act around them?

When you eventually learn how to control your emotions, to progress from here, you will then need to know how your emotional reaction to things and issues affect how others look at you. You will then achieve this by taking the time to sit with yourself and learn about how you put yourself forth to the environment around you. Stoicism gives us three virtues in for life - wisdom, morality, courage, and moderation. The stoic philosophy is one of the best philosophies that you can use to build better self-awareness.

It is through observing our thoughts that we become able to make the connection between them and how we act and react to the outside world and how it then acts and reacts towards us. Our bodies release chemicals with each thought, and it is these chemicals that then determine how we respond. When we are scared, our body produces adrenaline and osteocalcin that then lets us flee or fight off the threat. When stressed, the body produces cortisol, which sends signals in us that we are stressed and should act appropriately. When we are angry, our brain produces neurotransmitters called catecholamines, which then is what lead to how we bust out in anger. All this often happens before the part of the brain responsible for judgment, the cortex, kicks into action. In succession, the body then produces adrenaline and noradrenaline, which then puts you in a state of arousal, making you now ready to come to blows.

The thing about anger is that it tends to last long, even after the object of our hatred has gone. This situation then means that you will then express this anger in minor irritations. You will direct the anger to people that are not responsible for making you angry, thus costing you relationships. No wonder the Stoics call on us to altogether avoid getting angry. It harms you a lot more and stops you from processing things a bit more clearly.

It is through self-awareness that you will be able to judge better how you come across to others. Do you believe in the virtues that you claim? If you do not find what you claim, then chances are, people will read this, and they will then avoid you. This cognitive dissonance can be damaging to your relationships. You say that you care about others but then despise it when someone in the street asks you for money. You claim to be moral but then have no sense of it when someone you are close to is on the wrong. When you reflect within yourself, you will be able to know where your strengths lie, what your weaknesses are, what you do not embody and espouse. You will understand what triggers emotional reactions in you and how you will then work towards having to reduce the influence they have on you. Self-reflection is one of the key ways to build emotional intelligence as what we put out into the world is a reflection of how we are within. With a more accurate perception of who you are, you will begin to know where you need to improve to become better, where you are doing well and building on it and what you do not tolerate and won't work with when you come across someone.

This self-perception and acknowledgment of who you are, allows you to connect between your actions to how other people relate to you, something that many people, unfortunately, seem to lack. Have you ever come across someone so insufferable, yet lacking self-awareness such that you wonder just how they manage to get along in this world? Instead, pointing outwards for every error and mistake. Such is the effect of a lack of self-awareness. You will only see how the world reacts to you and remain blind to how you act out to the world. You will be unable to identify areas that you need to improve, which means that you will not build on yourself. Of course, when you are always blaming the other person, the relationship will not last.

Self-reflection improves how you present yourself to other people, and they will then respond positively, leading to better relationships. So, take time, each day to look at yourself.

Practice Self-Management

After self-awareness, comes self-management.

Self-management is the ability to direct yourself in a specific direction while being mindful and aware of your actions.

Let's try to think back at the time when you made a rational, favorable decision when you were under the temporary madness that emotions put us. Can you honestly remember? How many times did you then do this once you become aware of it? As we have seen above, the chemical reaction in the brain when we become emotionally charged usually happens so fast before the part of our brain responsible for judgment kicks in. This reason is why you will come across instances of people making irrational, and sometimes stupid mistakes when they are highly emotively charged. It is for this reason that young couples in the throes of passion elope, or marry in haste. It is for our inability to be rational that we have fought wars that we could have avoided if we had taken just a little more time to think through before acting. It is possibly this reason that has led to people losing their jobs and broken relationships. But, once you begin to practice self-awareness, this second part becomes rather easy to follow through. If anything, it is directly tied to self-awareness. Once you become aware of what triggers you, you will then become better at assessing situations and make preemptive measures on how you will act when the other person or the event push you to the edge. When you choose to be emotionally present, you will then become able to take in devastating news or be in a stressful situation without it having to compromise your rational. So, if you are someone who struggled with anger, this would mean that by becoming self-aware, you will then identify what triggers rage in you. Then, self-management follows through. Since you will be aware of what makes you angry, you will begin to make decisions that will help you fight the anger before it has taken complete control of you.

If you are extremely fearful, you will learn why you are nervous and then, make more deliberate actions towards overcoming that fear. But to push through with this stage, you will need commitment and to put a lot of deliberate thought into it. Because we tend to want to stay the same, our brains will often talk us out of a movement for change. Yes, your mind is stopping you from pursuing your path to greater things. Change is scary. For this reason, you will find that you will want to stay in familiar territory. Becoming deliberate in how you move and navigate around the world can be overwhelming. It will mean that you then get uncomfortable with the things you once enjoyed. It means coming to terms with your failings, becoming aware of how your actions, which you may have been doing without thought, affect your relationships and your overall mental health. So, it will not be easy to make the step towards managing how you react to your emotions. Plus, there is always that feeling of great satisfaction that comes with acting out your feelings. You feel you are justified in your actions. The adrenaline at that moment makes it seem like what you are doing is heroic. You are bold and courageous and not just emotional and irrational. So, it can then become addictive to want to keep yourself in this cycle of emotional turmoil. But while it may be for a moment, in the long-term, the effects of an emotional reaction to any situation is lasting. When you become in touch with your emotions, you will then be able also to be more forgiving to other people that are struggling with their issues and will want to help them. As you become more forgiving of yourself, so do you become of others? When you are not in tune with your emotions, you will reflect that state other people. You become angry at another person with a short temper because you are also short-tempered. You mock another fearful person because you struggle with dread. All these issues work to make you unsociable. When you manage your emotions better, it improves how you relate to people. Rather than reduce them to their emotional state of being, you see their struggle, because it is something that you have also struggled with/are struggling with and thus, can relate. You then exude charisma because you understand how the other person feels and help them begin the first steps towards managing their emotions better.

Improve Your Conflict Resolution Skills

We all want to be able to manage a situation without any adverse outcome, or at least, with minimal negative consequences. But how many of us really can do that? How many times have you intervened at a situation and arrived at an amicable conclusion? Conflicts trigger strong emotions in us, which, when we do not resolve correctly, results in hurt and disappointment, and this could lead to breaking relationships. Conflicts are often a sign of healthy relationships. When you can share your view with another person even when they do not agree with you, it shows that the relationship is open and the parties are open with each other. However, it is during conflicts that a lot of negative emotions arise. In battle, you become stressed, angry, fearful. Because of the high-voltage emotions, the chances of acting irrationally and in a way that damages the relationship are high. How, then, do you manage this delicate situation? How do you and the other party/parties get through this situation by maintaining the core of the relationship yet without being dishonest with each other just for civility? So, how do you improve your conflict resolution skills?

Understand the conflict

During the conflict, it goes beyond just a disagreement. A battle stresses the body to see to it that there is a threat, even when there is none. So, to understand the conflict, be able to realize that the other person, just like you, is fearful and therefore, know that they do not have an issue with you. So, take the time to know what caused the conflict? Were you on the wrong? If so, make a sincere apology? If your partner was on the wrong, you could bring them round in a respectful, non-condescending manner to their fault.

Throughout this process, it is essential to keep in mind that your problem is not with the other person, but rather, with an issue. So, avoid making remarks about the other person and instead, always ensure that you are speaking on the subject. So, rather than say "you are always hurting me', say instead "whatever you say always hurts me.' the second part brings attention to the person's utterances, rather than accuse them as a whole as is the first statement.

Understand the Needs of The Other Person

A second part of resolving a conflict is always to keep the other person in mind. With each back and forth, try to see their point of view. We all deserve to be respected and have our opinions considered.

Therefore, to manage conflict better, always keep in mind the humanity of the other person. The understanding of other people is our role to humankind - to acknowledge the other person and their feelings, their needs, and their views. To see where they are coming from and why they see the world as they do, even when we do not agree with it.

Be Willing to Compromise

We all get the feeling of wanting to be right in a conflict. Thus, when the other person says something, you counter them with your hot-take, the result then being that throughout the battle, none of you listens to the other. This emotive back and forth will most often result in resentment and will lead to further breakdown in communication.

To manage conflict better, is necessary that you listen to the other person, and they then listen to you, and the two of you come to a compromise that will take into account the views of the other person.

Compromising doesn't mean that you waver on your principles. Instead, it shows that you value the relationship and the needs of the other person.

However, also note when you become the only one compromising, or the one making the most significant compromises after a conflict. This one-sided compromise is a symptom of a toxic relationship. While it is challenging to split settlement down the middle in a way that satisfies both parties, you can make it better by making sure that none of you holds the heavy side of things during every conflict. When you make winning an argument or being right a priority, you will then not be willing to listen to the other person, and this will break down the communication further.

Focus on the Conflict In Front of You

It is often tempting to throw in previous encounters into a new conflict. You and the other person are arguing about whether or not to buy a new item, and then suddenly, you get a boost. "Remember that time you didn't (insert unrelated issue here)' you say. Suddenly, it devolves into the two of you just going on and on about an issue that wasn't part of the day's argument.

When we hold on to what was past, we become less able to make rational decisions. Rather than look to resolve the present conflict, we begin to dig deep into the past, trying to dig up something that will help you to win the argument or shut the other person up.

Be Willing to Let Go

Letting go can be a very delicate thing to do since you will often be conflicted as to whether you are making go or if you are sweeping the issue under the carpet. But it is important to note that you should make a point of resolving the issue before you consider letting it go. You need to get to a situation where you can confidently answer "no' if you ask yourself if the problem still bothers you. When you sweep things under the carpet, you will often still be bothered by them and would just be postponing them. So, to decide to let go, do so at a time when you are less angry or stressed and volatile. That will allow you to weigh the outcome of your decision rationally. If you still find yourself unable to let go, then you may not have resolved the issue.

Pick Your Battles

Not every potential conflict will need your input. When you become more in touch with your emotions, you will be able to know what is worth your effort and what is not. Conflicts are high-stress situations and will drain you of your strength. So it is key to then, engage in only those conflicts that will result in an improvement of your perspective, well-being, and better understanding.

A lot of the time, most of the conflict we may find ourselves getting into will not be worth it. In economics, there is a principle called the Pareto Principle. We took this principle from Italian economist Vilfredo Pareto and it stated how he found that most of the land in Italy was under the control of a small percentage of the population (80% of land to 20% of the population). From this, came the belief that 20% of our actions shape 80% of the consequences. Using this rule, you will then realize that you should focus your efforts on conflicts and relationships that give you the best state of mind, the best instances for growth. This rule will give you a peaceful state of mind as it will force you to sit down and try to identify what gives you great satisfaction as such, what requires your attention.

Relationship/Social Awareness How do you tell if someone is saying what they mean when they aren't straightforward? How do you pry someone open when they aren't willing to be opened up?

In order to become emotionally intelligent and grow from the situations that you have faced, it is essential that you then channel your understanding of your emotional state also to understand the emotional being of the other person. Social awareness is what allows us to develop relationships and maintain them. When you make it a priority to understand the other person beyond the words that they speak, you will be able to gain a better understanding of them. So, how then, do you build social awareness?

Listen Keenly

Listening is one of those skills that, while important, is one that has hardly mastered. It is tough to listen, especially when you also have issues of your own going on. To relate well, or better with others, you must listen. Listening allows you to hear, and the process then understands where the other person is coming from, how they see the world. Actively listening, which means repeating to the person what they say after they have said it, allows you to build a connection with the other person. When you listen, you can put yourself in the other person's shoes, thus, understanding them better.

Be Aware of Non-verbal Cues

Psychologists say that we say a lot without speaking than we do speaking. But let us not dwell too much on whether this is true or not and instead, put ourselves in the situation where we do not feel comfortable expressing ourselves verbally. What do you often do?

If you are waiting for someone at a place where there are many other people, you may find yourself tapping impatiently at something, perhaps a table or the armrest of your chair. Or you may begin fiddling with something in your hands when you become anxious and restless. We often send out these signals without our knowledge sometimes. Therefore, even when we say something that is in dissonance with our emotional state, our body language may betray us. Thus, to build on your social awareness, be keen on what people are not saying. Look at how they carry themselves when they aren't speaking. Look at how they act when they cannot talk. Learning how to read these signals will help you become better at tailoring your message to match their state of being at the moment. So, you will try to make the anxious person relax by, say, cracking a joke before you proceed with your point.

When you show high awareness of people's actions during interactions, you will come across as someone who value them and what they say. This awareness will help you build a rapport faster with them. However, it is essential to note that you should do this expertly as you will come off as creepy if you are not careful. The key is to notice their non-verbal cues and interact with them in ways that make them feel the opposite of their reaction, all without making them feel watched.

Be Empathetic

To have empathy is the most significant way to build rapport. As we have seen earlier in chapter five, to develop your compassion, you need to be aware of who you are first. But, empathy is a problematic state of being to master. Because of our belief in the superiority of our being and ideas, to be empathetic will mean that you look at other people with an acknowledgment of their humanity. Empathy means that you will try to put yourself in their shoes and interact with them from their perspective. It is easier said than done, though.

How many instances have you found yourself unable to understand why a person will believe the things that they do? How many times have you made final judgments about someone without giving yourself a chance to glimpse from where they are coming?

We often make this oversight a lot of the times, which then shows that empathy is something that we should practice. To be empathetic is to acknowledge the humanity of the other person, even when we do not agree with them. It means that you know that the person that was rude to you may have been under their stresses. It means that you understand why someone else made a drastic decision that seemed illogical and stupid. Allowing others the room to be human and to err is a significant strand of emotional growth and intelligence. It means then that in your interactions with people, you will listen to them more, you will agree with them more and contradict them without belittling them. To be empathetic will make you cherish your friendships and play your part because you understand our human need of wanting love and recognition, called the law of esteem. So, practice empathy when you interact with others. To begin this, whenever you are talking to someone, and they say something that you do not agree with, rather than interrupt them with your beliefs, as them why they view the world as they do. Once you learn about them, you can then use persuasion to try and give them a different perspective.

This practice, of course, will be hard in situations where the issue of contention is highly emotive and divisive. And it becomes even harder to empathize with the other person when they appear hell-bent on remaining to their ways. Well, it is here that you apply the earlier lesson in conflict management - know when to walk away/cut your losses. You cannot empathize someone out of their ignorance that they want to maintain. If they are willing to have a sobering discussion about it, then beautiful. However, if they seem to not listen to you as much as you listen to them, walk away, because emotional intelligence is also about knowing when to walk away.

Channel Emotions Productively

To bring your emotions under control is not to mean that you cannot feel these emotions. It is also not that you cannot find ways to express them. Mark Manson, of the *Subtle Art of Not Giving a Fuck* fame, stated that you could not control yourself from feeling, but how you react to how you think is what is essential. Intense emotions have a way of rewiring our brains. They are disruptive and cause us disequilibrium. Since we are learning how to become more emotionally intelligent, I will not mention destructive, but we have seen how they can be catastrophic, even more, positive feelings like joy or happiness. When emotions within us begin to run, significant, the chemical reactions in the body lead to various changes in us, which then means that we become more focused, the focal point of our attention being the person or event that is causing us the joy or happiness or distress and anger. And to be emotional is then to be ripe for various surges of human feats. When we look at the annals of our history, we often get to see how people turned their emotions into art or literature or social movement. Think of how people who suffered great grief and a sense of loss used to make social movements. We can look at how mothers who suffered significant injury make movements that address the issue that led to their loss, e.g., Mothers Against Drunken Driving.

When we look at anger, we see it as a negative emotion. And it is true. Anger is a passion which we can live better with when we have it under our control. We can also see how we can use passion to do good. Human rights movements and many movements for social change often have people who are fed up with the situation as they are and so, use the frustration to make their voices heard. When you begin to make yourself more self-aware, you will realize that through every emotional upheaval that you experience, there are ways in which you can channel it positively. Your grief could make you more willing to address the situation that led to your loss. Your joy could make you want to discuss what made you miserable so that you do not experience it again. Anger can drive you to become more focused and drive social change. All these help you become a more valuable member of society, even when you do not get recognition or applause for it. You do it to improve your surroundings. This act of channeling our emotions to constructive activity is known as positive psychology, which calls us to not only embrace our positive emotions but also come to terms with our negative ones and embrace them too. They exist for a reason, the reason being that, more than positive emotions, negative emotions are great catalysts for change. So, how do you begin to channel the emotions more constructively?

Think if It's Worth Exploring

When we say that you can use your emotions to drive change and make a positive impact, be in the know that it may not always be the case and that sometimes, your desire to channel your emotions could not be compelling because whatever makes you angry could be something beyond your control. So, in this case, take a moment to think of expressing the emotions is necessary. At times, you are better off taking time out to let the emotions cool down as you avoid high-octane situations that could trigger you.

Monitor and Correct

To be able to channel your emotions positively means to be in constant touch with what triggers you, how you react to it, and how it affects your moods and actions. Then, map out the adverse reactions you take when in your emotional trance. Then, create ways to make it work for you, and as well as for others. When angry, for example, you can use the razor-sharp focus of the rage to work on your projects or to begin your workout routine. When in grief, you can use the muse that that clouds us during pain to create art or literature to express it. Always make a point of monitoring your reactions. Every. Time. This monitoring is hard, as it will need you to be always alert, but if you want to become a better person, a more social person, you will need to be aware of your emotional reactions.

Know Your Limits

Embracing your emotions should also come with the knowledge that you have your limits. Become aware of whether you are becoming addicted to getting a high out of your feelings. Remember, the key is not to make the emotions your muse for expression but rather, using your inspiration to channel your creativity when you are emotional.

This call then means that you should be aware of how you act when you have calmed down. Create a situation where you give yourself a short time within which you hold onto emotion and channel it. After which, be willing to let go. Scientists have noted that anger especially, tends to remain active in the body for hours or even days after the initial trigger of your anger has passed. This revelation then means that you become susceptible to triggering at the slightest inconveniences. The reaction can then destroy relationships and make you unwilling to compromise with others. So, become aware of your limits and know when just to let go. This awareness will improve your well-being generally, as well as make you better in your relationship with others.

Boost Your Performance

We all experience self-doubt in different scenarios. Even when we are confident in our skills, there will still be situations where you find yourself lacking confidence in your abilities. Self-doubt can be crippling. But just like any other emotion, you can use it to make yourself become a higher performer. So, when you experience self-doubt, make a point of seeking out someone more experienced in your field and learn from them. Alternatively, since self-doubt makes you doubt your abilities or skills, you can leverage it as a motivation to keep doing it in a bid to improve yourself. When you do it, you become better at what you. In time, you find that you are in a level of mastery of your skills or abilities. You can do this with regret too. If you made a wrong choice, you could use the guilt that comes with it to push yourself forward. You create a situation in your head where you do not want to go back to feeling regret, so you use it to propel yourself forward. Who will stop you?

When you learn to channel emotions more positively, you will quickly realize that you will not need to have an external motivator to propel yourself. The surges of emotions will be enough to give you the propulsion you need.

Share Your Knowledge

When we get into relationships, whether friendships or romances, we always want to feel part of the other person. Through an exchange of ideas and experiences, we make each other comfortable and vulnerable, creating a bond that we trust will be productive to us in the end. When you have gone through all the steps to become a better person, it is vital that you then make a point of making those around you become aware of their failings and learn from you. Sharing is one of the profound ways in which we show that we are vulnerable with each other. It is the result of you being able to relate to the other person. For many reasons, and to many of us, sharing is often something that we either are unwilling to do or uncomfortable doing.

This reaction is often born from our insecurity, one of the biggest causes of failure in relationships. Because of the fear of being upstaged, people will avoid sharing knowledge, skills with others. This situation, of course, causes friction and will result in a breakdown of communication in the relationship and eventually a break-up. When you become a more emotionally intelligent person, you become comfortable in the knowledge that you are not perfect, and that's okay. You know that the other person is better than you in some instances and areas and that is okay. What you are focused on is self-improvement, and your understanding of our emotional needs means that you will be willing to share your improvement tips with the others, as you know that, even at their best, your friends or partner(s) remain human as so, still have a crippling doubt of themselves. When you share, you communicate that you care. Our relationships flourish when we show the other people that love us that we are on the lookout for them. In turn, they also develop the same towards us.

However, this may not be the case sometimes. There are many cases where one party was more generous and giving, and the other party just took it all for granted. Still giving is often a sign of the other person being a narcissist or at the very least, a self-absorbed asshole. They consider the fact that someone committed to them is a sign of their charm and superiority. To them, the other person and their needs are worthless. What is important is what they want. This selfishness, of course, creates a delicate balance. But, as someone who is developing your emotional intelligence, you will be able to pick this out before you establish a secure connection with the person.

Keep Secrets

One of how we build connections, according to psychologists, is often through gossip. Many researchers have concluded that we usually bond better when we find common ground about another person which allows us to then create a rapport with the other person as it gives us something mutual that we often need when we want to create a connection.

However, this revelation has meant that many people, especially those that lack emotional intelligence, become more willing to share their secrets and those of their loved ones with any charming stranger.

One of the ways that we can build and maintain relationships is through respect of the other person's confidentiality. This result is because when you respect the other person and are emotionally astute, you will want to maintain their trust. It is trust that develops from all the others. When you are empathetic, you become more understanding of the other person, and thus, gain their confidence. When you are honest, you communicate that you are trustworthy. When you make a point of helping others become better people, you tell them that they can put their belief in you. It all builds up to trust as you can see. It is trust when the other person becomes vulnerable to you and shares their deepest secrets.

So, as you get more in touch with your emotions and who you are, then you will be in a position to want to maintain the relationships, you value the bond and thus, will do the right things to sustain them, which includes confidentiality.

When you find yourself eager to share your friends' secrets just because the person you have met sounds and looks decent, you may not be emotionally mature. Take a moment and pause. Why do you want to share your friends' secrets with this stranger? Do you value them if you do?

Gaining trust and maintaining it is hard. To do that requires that you are a person who has a high EQ (emotional quotient). You understand that the other person is sharing with you, not because they are stupid, but because they feel like they have an ear in you. Don't break it. Always make a point of maintaining and keeping your end of the agreement. But, what if the other person is the one that breaks my trust? You ask.

It is true that not every person that we meet will turn out to be a great friend. Because of our bias on first impressions, many people with sinister intentions will often be charming and accommodating at first. The charm is so that they can gain our trust. If you find yourself having to deal with the other person breaking your confidence, the best thing to do is to acknowledge what you are going through. You will be angry and confused and at a loss. Acknowledge these feelings, then practice what you have learned to help you cope.

Conclusion

Emotions are necessary, and they are with us in everything that we do. In every decision that we make, there is an emotion connected to it. Thus, mastering it is the key. In this book, we have learned:

- What emotions are and how they work. This understanding has allowed us to delve deeper into the essence of emotions into our being.

- We have looked at how emotions, when they become active, can be destructive and thus, looked at how emotional intelligence can help us cope.

- We have also looked into how we can manage stress, fears, and crippling negative thoughts. Emotions have a way of shaping how we view the world; thus, keeping track to them to keep them in check is vital.

- You have also learned how to manage our anger and how to make the best of our emotions to build our relationships. After all, emotions help us build relationships and are also critical in how we destroy them. Thus, looking at how we can develop better relationships around our emotions is worth learning.

OVERESTHINKING

The Fast Cure for Women and Men Who Think Too Much and Want to Stop Procrastinating - Proven Tips to Turn Off Relentless Negative Thoughts in Place of Optimism and Strong Focus

Introduction to Overthinking

This helpful guide was designed to be not only informative and educational but also fun to read and encouraging to everyone who is ready to learn the best ways to start making positive changes in every part of their life from personal connections to professional reputation.

In the following chapters, the guide will discuss   and provide helpful details on subjects including and connected to habitual overthinking and how to overcome it, such as:

- Common negative side effects and health conditions that have been tied to psychological habits like procrastination and overthinking
- The connection between procrastination and overthinking
- Benefits and other positive effects people have experienced after overcoming their habitual psychological compulsions
- Detailed explanations of what habitual overthinking is and what it is not so that readers can better understand where these types of psychological habits come from
- What causes overthinking and procrastination habits to develop and how to identify their origins to better design an action plan for conquering them

Throughout the course of the guide, readers will also learn about factors and variables involved with the development of overthinking and procrastination habits like:

- What kinds of people and personality types are more likely to develop overthinking and procrastination habits
- How to create personal mantras or start meditating in order to gain better control over one's emotions and stay motivated during times of doubt or lack of energy
- How to improve communication and become more emotionally open with the people they trust to create an encouraging and supportive network
- Helpful activities, tips and tricks for increasing their own self-esteem and becoming more confident in anything they do
- How to stay focused and determined on the path toward their goals, regardless of their current emotional state or unexpected complications and challenges that may arise throughout the course of this personal adventure toward an improved life!

By the end of this educational and informative guide, our hope is that readers are more confident in themselves, have more faith in their own abilities and feel ready to not only conquer their negative psychological habits, but any challenges or mountain that has stood in their way but seemed impossible to master before. Within this guide are the skills, basic facts and most cutting-edge methods and techniques that every person can use to reach their personal improvement goals, regardless of their individual factors and variables.

We know that there are no shortage of self-help guides and other books of this nature on this subject on the market and every effort was made to ensure it is full of as much useful information as possible.

Chapter 1: An Introduction to Overthinking & The Ways It Can Affect People

We are lucky to live in a time where it is not just scientists and medical professionals that are able to earnestly understand and learn to adjust how the human mind works. Since the acceptance of psychology as a valuable and respectable form of health science, massive amounts of information have been collected and studied by experts all over the world in order to better understand human thoughts, behaviors and actions and how they are shaped by the psychological variables that each individual faces throughout their personal life paths. There are a seemingly endless number of psychological concerns people can face, but one of the most commonly experienced and reported across the globe is overthinking. While many people find ways to cope with their personal overthinking struggles so that it does not take too much control over their lives, there are also many out there who end up seeking help after missing out on opportunities, distancing themselves from personal relationships and other negative impacts that can come from the inability to take action because of habitual overthinking.

What Is Overthinking?

The definition of overthinking is typically listed in the simplest terms as "thinking about something for too long". While the definition makes it seem like something that is easy to understand and obvious to recognize, the habit itself is much more complex and damaging, particularly when experienced over long periods of time without understanding or relief. Specifically, habitual overthinking is different for each person and can come with a variety of variables and negative effects that will also be different for each person. The key to discovering the causes and origins for each person's individual overthinking habit comes with a focus on self-awareness which includes the individual being more aware of not only their current emotional state during times of overthinking, but also:

- Their emotions regarding the events, subjects or responsibilities they are overthinking about
- Any common factors between different overthinking sessions
  - For example, some people may notice that they only have difficulty overcoming their overthinking habit when they are stressed or under unusual pressure at work. Others may notice that their overthinking sessions are focused around someone in particular and the individual's previous or upcoming interactions with them.
- Their thoughts and actions in similar situations in the past (if there have been any similar situations) and what they learned from that experience

- Any other particular variables like the number of people they are working with on a specific issue, recommendations they have received from others trying to help ease their current situation or emotional state and all tasks, resolutions or responsibilities that are included in their current concerns

In psychological terms, overthinking is not just thinking about something for longer than is required, recommended or accepted as normal. The main reason for this is because everyone has their own ways of thinking about things and every subject, option, opportunity or question comes with a variety of variables that can determine how long something needs to be contemplated or what needs to be considered before taking action, such as:

- How many choices the individual has to make to come to a solution
- The urgency or importance of the subject
- How many other people may be affected by their potential decisions or actions
- Pros and cons or risks and benefits related to the subject

Just thinking about overthinking can be enough to inspire anxious responses and impulses in people, especially those who struggle with overthinking as a psychological habit. These people are set apart from those who fall into the leadership category with their organization, strategy and readiness because their overthinking does not lead to efficiency or productivity. Their thinking never stops- with options, risks, rewards, involvement and any other number of variables spinning around in their thoughts without ever leading to helpful or successful action. For those who have never experienced it, overthinking and its various negative effects can be difficult to explain or understand. In fact, in many cases, describing what overthinking *isn't* is more effective than trying to describe what it is.

What overthinking is *not*:

- A conscious decision that can just be stopped on command
    - Overthinking is a psychological impulse, often a response to anxiety, that becomes habitual over time
- An unbreakable habit or impossible to overcome
    - There are lots of steps and actions people can take in order to change the way they think about and approach different situations
- Something to be taken lightly as it can be damaging emotionally and psychologically over time

- People who suffer from habitual overthinking often have other psychological issues that affect their ability make a solid decision and move forward with it without regret or increased levels of stress
- A disorder on its own
    - Overthinking can be controlling and dominant for those who struggle with it, but in the end, it is caused by a larger psychological concern and not a disease or disorder by itself

What overthinking *is*:

- A symptom of a larger psychological concern that leads to an inability to take action when faced with decisions or responsibilities of varying urgency or importance

The Most Common Causes for Overthinking in Men & Women

It's connection to previous experiences, environmental influences and situational variables can make it difficult to pinpoint specific causes of overthinking in individuals. However, recent studies have shown that there are several common causes and factors reported in men and women around the world.

One of the most common causes that has given scientists and doctors insight into overthinking is a as an indicator or sign of psychological disorders such as Post-Traumatic Stress Disorder (PTSD), various anxiety disorders and various phobias. Anxiety disorders are the most prevalent in today's society, many believe that it is due to the overstimulation from technology (televisions, advertisements, radios, and all of the handheld devices that media can be carried around and played on). For those with anxiety disorders, the overthinking comes with a more intense version of anxiety known as meta-anxiety, which is a stage of anxious behavior in which an individual is getting anxious about their own anxiety and the potential for panic attacks or similar episodes in the near future.

In some cases, and often those not related to psychological issues, the cause for this type of overthinking is related to a lack of self-confidence, self-esteem or questioning one's own abilities with regards to the subject or problem at hand. Some of the most reported overthinking experiences described by study subjects in this category include:

- Fixating on things that should or should not have been said after the event, situation or issue has been resolved
- Comparing themselves to others at work, school or whatever specific environment in which

they will have their performance observed or appraised

- Assuming the worst before, during and after a situation that leads to anxious behaviors, a feeling of uncertainty and a vulnerability that causes overthinking

Overthinking is often an emotional response in some people whenever they are faced with an important task or decision they need to make. It begins with a knock to their self-esteem as they worry about their ability to accomplish what has been asked of them. This doubt in themselves leads them to feel poorly about the task or subject from the very start and only increases the impulse to overthink in most people. Since the individual in this example is already doubting themselves and their abilities, they are now faced with the fear that others will see it in their results or solution and from here their mind can take a few different actionable paths including overthinking or procrastinating. Overthinking happens more often when someone feels the need to prove themselves through their task while many turn to procrastination in an effort to distract themselves from their concerns regarding their responsibilities.

The Difference Between Overthinking & Being Prepared

Most people know at least one person who is always prepared for anything that comes up or at least has the appearance of control and organization. In some cases, this may be the individual themselves. The ability to maintain control (or the illusion of control) in any given situation, particularly when others involved are giving in to the stress, is a valuable talent and a developed skill that is commonly sought after in leadership and management roles. It is not only those with psychological conditions that are prone to overthinking. It is one of the most common complaints for adults living in the 21st century who find themselves hesitating or needing a break from their current environment in order to clear their minds enough to make a solid plan or decision. At some point in their life (often many times throughout), every individual finds themselves overthinking or ruminating about something that they should be able to let go of or move on from. This is a natural response as humans related to our survival instincts and need to have control over situations. Since people cannot see the future, it is natural desire for everyone to be as prepared as possible for any situation that arises. One of the most common excuses for people trying to avoid facing their issues with overthinking in their daily lives is to claim that they are not overthinking but being cautious, thorough or paying attention to detail in order to set themselves up for success. This could be for minor inconveniences or encounters throughout their daily routines or for larger, more stressful or emotional issues that do require consideration and caution before coming to a conclusion. If there are times, situations or concerns that require more thinking than others, how is it possible to tell when someone is taking their time to make sure they are coming to the best decision and when someone is just habitually overthinking? Unlike much of what is known about overthinking, this answer is simple:

- People who are taking their time to make solid decisions they are confident in and won't come to regret will take action or announce their decision when they have considered all of their options and concerns.
- People who are overthinking will run through all of their options and concerns only continue run through their thoughts until it evolves from being thorough to becoming obsessive. These people will never take action or announce a decision, preferring the repetition and safety of their own thoughts until someone else eventually takes control, withdraws their offer or makes a decision on their behalf.

The Most Common Signs That Your Overthinking Is Controlling Your Behavior

Before steps can be taken to ease and even eliminate habitual overthinking, it is important to know whether or not you (or someone you are concerned for) is overthinking as a matter of psychological impulse related to anxiety or fears, or if overthinking is a sign of a larger issue that needs to be explored and addressed. Here are some of the most common warning signs and indicative behaviors that those who are prone to damaging overthinking habits exhibit, especially when put under pressured or faced with a new task.

Pessimism: One sign that many overthinkers tend to overlook (or fail to accept) is their tendency to assume the worst in any given situation. Claiming to be a realist and not a pessimist is a common assertion with overthinkers in denial about their issue, but the truth is that overthinking and the negative psychological and emotional symptoms connected to it grow to pollute the way individuals see the world around them. Hope and excitement for life are replaced with anxiety and fear of change leading to a completely negative view of the world around them that can be difficult to see beyond.

Repetition: One of the main descriptions used by those trying to explain what overthinking feels like is circling or whirling thoughts in their mind. No matter where a thought starts, what logical path it follows or what other thoughts it ends up inspiring, those who are overthinking and unable to take action find their thought process right back at the beginning where their initial concerns and thoughts evolved from. Once overthinkers have reached the point where actions or decisions should be initiated, followed all of their related thoughts through their logical paths and have nothing else to obsess over, instead of making their move, they will just go back to the beginning and start the overthinking process all over.

Inability to Move Forward: People who overthink about things (from encounters with other people to opportunities they have taken or passed up) have very little confidence in their own ability to make the right decision, regardless of the situation. It can be something major like deciding to take one job over another or something small like whether they said or did not say something they should have when they spoke to someone new at the coffee shop. For various amounts of time (sometimes years) after a particular event or meeting, habitual overthinkers will replay everything that was done or said, questioning every point of concern and their vocal or actionable responses to them. Even if nothing came from the subject in question or there is nothing that can be done to change any related events that followed or continue around them, people who overthink will continue to relive the scenario until something else becomes more stressful or urgent for them to worry about.

Too Inwardly Focused: One of the causes for overthinking in people is the fear that comes with social interactions or maintaining relationships, both personal and professional. This fear causes people, particularly those who are also prone to expecting the worst, to worry over every word they exchange or even how their facial expressions are interpreted by those they encounter on a daily basis. These people can often have issues with empathizing or focusing their thoughts on others, making come across as anti-social or even unpleasant. This is not always the case though. There are many overthinkers that maintain healthy social interactions without regret or concern dominating their thoughts after each night out or lunch with friends. It is all a matter of how self-aware an individual is, how developed their emotional intelligence is and how in control they are over their habitual overthinking or procrastinating impulses.

The Negative Effects of Overthinking

For those who are concerned for themselves or for others they know are struggling with getting control of their overthinking habit, knowing the negative ways overthinking can affect both the mind and body is a good way of waking up even the most stubborn of friends and family. While not everyone who deals with overthinking will experience all of the connected effects discussed in this chapter, here is a closer look at some of the most prevalent and widely experienced negative effects caused or aggravated by habitual overthinking.

Absence of Inner Peace: Since overthinking is often connected to anxiety and stress-related impulses, one common negative effect is a persistent and inescapable feeling of negativity that can manifest as a number of traits such as:

- Depression
- Pessimism
- Reclusiveness
- Disinterest in being social (even with close relations like family or romantic connections)

For people who overthink, this habit does not just affect their decision-making abilities. It can spread to affect all aspects of their life, leaving a negative impact wherever it touches. Since they are always worried about what is happening around them, it is often impossible for overthinkers to find their emotional center or any kind of psychological stability that brings peace and relaxation throughout their mind and body.

Physically & Mentally Exhausting: One negative effect overthinking has on people is that it consumes and burns away energy from the mind and body that could be used more effectively. People who struggle with habitual overthinking typically also suffer from mental and emotional burn out, constant or regular fatigue and tend to get sick more often than those around them (whether it is at work, home or both).

Respond Emotionally to Situations That Do Not Call For It: Another negative effect overthinkers face is that over time, they lose their ability to respond rationally or logically to statements others make to them or situations that are purely professional. Whether it is getting excessively or unreasonably defensive about comments, observations or criticisms made to them or having emotional breakdowns in situations that do not require it. Habitual overthinkers spend so much time and energy focusing on the hypothetical or repetitive thoughts whirring around their minds that when they are faced with minor inconveniences or unexpected interruptions (especially if they require immediately responses or actions).

Warped View of the World Around Them: Arguably, the most damaging effect of overthinking is that throughout the years and as individuals struggle through their personal challenges, overthinkers start to believe the things they tell themselves during their episodes of overthinking. This would not be as concerning if people focused on positive and encouraging thoughts when they were overthinking, but the harm in overthinking comes from centering one's thoughts on negative subjects or events and replaying them in their mind until nothing else is able to break through their thoughts. This can warp people's view of the world in a number of ways like making them assume that everyone they encounter is thinking negatively about them or that everything they say is being criticized or obsessed over the same way they obsess about them when overthinking. The more someone focuses on thoughts like these, the more they become the automatic response to new encounters or unfamiliar surroundings. When these thoughts become normal for someone, they become difficult to break free from and start to affect all aspects of their lives so that soon, even events or situations that should be enjoyable take on a negative tone as the individual overthinks about how each person around them is thinking about them and whatever they are (or are not) doing.

Less Social & More Inclined to Separation: People who spend massive amounts of their free time (or times they are supposed to be focused on other, more productive habits or tasks) have very little time to spend with their friends and family. The main reason for this is that they are too consumed by their cyclical and repetitive thoughts about regular social situations and experiences like what other people think about them, analyzing each and every word they say or wish they had said, and coming up with hypothetical encounters to prepare themselves for imaginary conversations that may never take place. In many cases, the stress of all these thoughts and pressures becomes overwhelming and the individual decides it is best to just stay home and get lost in their favorite television shows or whatever activity they take part in within the safety and protection of their own home and private space.

411

In addition to all of these concerns, overthinking is also the most commonly recognized negative effect connected to procrastination in men and women of all ages. While a dangerous psychological habit on its own, overthinking becomes even more restrictive and harmful when paired with habits like procrastination.

Chapter 2: What Is Procrastination & Why Is It Such A Difficult Habit to Break?

The definition of procrastination is widely accepted as the act of delaying or avoidance of an action or decision. While this definition is accurate, as with the definition of overthinking, it is also overly simplistic when trying to understand procrastination as a psychological concern. It is a major factor and common practice for those who also struggle with controlling their tendency to overthink.

What Is Procrastination & Where Does It Come From?

More than just a popular word in the English vocabulary, procrastination is a negative habit that has existed and been recorded since the early days of humanity. Most prevalently connected with a Greek poet named Hesiod, one famous view of the human impulse to procrastinate was published "work prospers with care; he who postpones wrestles with ruin". In fact, the word "procrastinate" originally comes from the Latin term *procrastinare* which translates into "put off until tomorrow". The psychological theory connected to the word "procrastination" comes more from the early Greek phrase *akrasia*, a word which means to do something against one's better instinct or judgment.

This is a repetitive theme amongst procrastinators regardless of location, situation, age or experience: even while they put off their responsibilities, they know that there will be consequences to face if they are not able to get it done in time or by when it is expected to be resolved. However, this knowledge is not enough to inspire action or decision, instead only serving to fuel the procrastination habit by putting the individual in a deeper and more tumultuous emotional state that only continues to strengthen the urge to hide from their current situation. As their deadline or time limit grows ever closer, they begin to remember their real-life responsibilities and consequences and panic sets in. Now they fully realize the amount of work or the weight they needed to get done or the weight of the decision they needed to make begins to weigh heavy on their shoulders. They rush to get everything completed and come to a solution for the situation they've been procrastinating with. In many cases, they are unable to complete it and have to face the real consequences such as having to work off the clock or having to request an extension, their dedication to their position called into question by their superiors. In some cases however, procrastinators are able to get everything completed and instead of having to regret their decision to procrastinate, they convince themselves that they do their best work under such pressures and the habit is born.

Other famous sayings related to procrastination (and the importance of handling it efficiently) include:

- Don't put off until tomorrow what you can do today- Benjamin Franklin
- While we waste our time hesitating & postponing, life is slipping away- Roman Philosopher, Seneca

The first quote is intended to help individuals reach their full potential by inspiring them to take more control over their actions and get themselves moving today. This may work for some as a personal mantra or a reminding poster on their office wall, but for those who struggle with procrastination as a compulsion and as a habit, quotes like Mr. Franklin's have very little effect. Seneca's quote on the other hand (and the poem that it comes from) serves to remind individuals that procrastinating does nothing but waste time and energy that could be spent on other activities like trips they could be taking with the extra time or promotions they could be working towards with the extra energy once their avoided tasks are finished.

One of the most common misconceptions connected with procrastination is that it is a matter of laziness or lack of discipline on the part of the individual, but the truth is that procrastination has nothing to do with how much self-control a person has. In this chapter, we will cover the finer details of procrastination and reveal some surprising facts about the condition and how it affects men and women of all ages.

Pro Tip: Art is a great way analyze and process difficult emotions of thoughts about anything! It exercises the creative part of the brain which helps with emotional control and strengthening over time. Using art as a means of emotion and thought processing in place of obsessive or compulsive overthinking gives individuals a unique, productive and effective way of expressing their personal thoughts, desires, goals, fears and any other factors or variables they are looking for help with understanding and controlling.

Why Is Procrastination Such A Hot Issue When It Comes to Understanding & Conquering Overthinking?

Procrastination is something that all adults wrestle with throughout their lives. However, just because it is a widespread habit, that does not mean that it is natural or healthy for those who find themselves procrastinating regularly or compulsively. The negative side effects (which we will be discussing later in this chapter) can take a severe toll on a person's mental and emotional health. One of the main reasons for this is because the majority of people looking for answers on how to beat their procrastination have enough psychological self-awareness to know how unproductive and hindering the habit can be. They can see how behaviors like procrastination and overthinking are holding them back from reaching their full potential and even with this knowledge, they are unable make themselves take any action or make any solid decisions. This knowledge throughout each of their procrastination processes eats away at their self-esteem, causing them to feel even worse and more stressed out as their deadline approaches or the pressure they are under continues to increase. It isn't just the mind that feels the effects of procrastination over time. In fact, the long-term negative effects of this habit can be damaging not only psychologically and emotionally, but it can also affect people physically as stress levels (and the physical body processes connected to stress like blood pressure levels and breathing speed) fluctuate into unsafe regions. This fluctuation and inconsistency can lead to muscle weakness (especially in the heart) and even blood clots in more extreme cases.

Many psychological professionals are taking an interest in procrastination and overthinking as serious health concerns with some even going as far as to categorize them as self-harm behaviors. These types of behaviors and related habits are getting more and more attention as depression, anxiety and suicidal numbers increase across the globe. The more information that is gathered and studies that are performed on habits like overthinking and procrastination, the more society as a whole will be able to understand the difficulties related to these types of conditions and the more solutions can be found for those who have had trouble finding the answers they need for their specific concerns.

The Difference Between Habitual Procrastination & Poor Time Management Skills

One criticism that procrastinators often hear is that they would not be as stressed or pressured in life if they knew how to use their time better. While this seems like a logical solution to a problem that is notorious for burning energy and letting time pass inefficiently, but when it comes down to it, poor time management and procrastination are not the same issue.

Those with poor time management skills have a much easier path ahead of them when it comes to stopping the delay or avoidance of their responsibilities and replacing it with better and more productive habits. This is because in many cases, their poor time management impulses come from a lack of knowledge about how best to prioritize or organize their time to reach their most efficient and productive level. Once these individuals learn the necessary skills they require in order to take control of their time management behaviors, they may find themselves procrastinating from time to time, but now it is not related to their inability to see the problem as a whole or come up with a plan to accomplish their goals in an effective and reasonable time frame.

Procrastination is different in that many people who are aware that they struggle with procrastinating in various aspects of their life are also aware that they possess the time management skills that should be helping them through every episode of procrastination.

Pro Tip: Take the time to analyze your own behaviors or the behaviors of someone you are concerned is struggling with procrastination. If there are tasks they come across that they can get planned out or put together with little to no additional stress, then this is a good sign that this person already has effective time management skills. However, if they then avoid taking actions or making any kind of starting motion on their plan, then this person is most likely having difficulty overcoming their habitual procrastination.

- If the person being analyzed is you, then you have already made a major accomplishment in conquering your procrastination habit: accepting the issue as reality and recognizing the damaging behaviors that make it such a concerning habit.

- If you are concerned about someone else's habitual procrastination or lack of time management skills then the best course of action once you have identified their particular behaviors and habits is to speak openly with the person about your concerns. This conversation may help them see the problem in a new light, knowing that others have been able to see it as well, which may also help them to understand and accept the challenge they are facing. Like with any trial or challenge, there is no way to help someone change their ways (even if it would be the best course of action for them) until they are willing to admit, accept and begin to learn about their condition and where it comes from.

Those who are unwilling to accept their habitual procrastination often do so because they are not currently under stress, are feeling fine or are in a positive frame of mind. In this type of mental state, procrastinators are able to justify their actions or push them to the back of their mind until their mood starts to slip to the more negative end of the spectrum and the overthinking spiral starts.

The Health Dangers & Other Negative Effects of Procrastination

There are as many different types of effects and dangers associated with procrastination as there are different types of personalities. While some may be common or at least reported in various different situations and studies, each person has their own struggle and individual variables that cause and fuel their procrastination so not every person will experience each of the different negative effects in a way that makes a lasting impact (or at all).

Loss of Time: One of the most obvious negative effects of procrastination is the amount of time that is allowed to just pass or be burned on unproductive tasks. Some people say this is not directly connected with procrastination but with a person's time management skills (a disconnect that many psychologists are supporting as studies show that procrastination and poor time management skills are not necessarily the same issue or even connected in some cases). There are those procrastinators that are lucky enough to have enough trivial tasks or things that they've been meaning to do to occupy their procrastination time but those who do not spend this time searching for something to do to appear productive so that they can justify their procrastination to their logical selves in some way.

Loss of Energy: Many may see procrastination as a form of laziness, but the truth is the amount of energy it takes to procrastinate is often more exhausting on the mind and body of the individual than just doing their task or making their decision would have been. Instead of just getting done what they need to finish, procrastinators spend massive amounts of energy on anxious behaviors such as pacing or waste energy up at night overthinking about their responsibilities and how they need to get them done, keeping the person from getting any sleep to restore the energy that they're wasting on the stress and panic that comes with procrastination.

Track Record of Bad Decisions: Procrastinators often struggle with regret and obsess over past decisions during their episodes of overthinking that only make them feel worse about themselves and their abilities over time. When people doubt themselves, they become less concerned with thinking about their options or trying to plan things out because they lose hope and begin to believe that anything they chose to do will end poorly so why bother putting time and energy into weighing options. When decisions are made in this mind set, people are not concerned with potential consequences, figuring any path is full of them so just pick one and roll with the punches. Their low self-esteem leads to lack of hope, motivation and passion over the years. This behavior can also become habitual over time and people who are not concerned with the benefits or consequences of their actions have very little chance of building a successful future for themselves.

Damage to Reputation: This could be professionally or personally as one behavior often associated with procrastination is making promises or plans only to break or cancel them at the last minute. Professionally, this could ruin someone's career if allowed to get out of hand. Personally, many people who wrestle with procrastination impulses have ended up alienating themselves from friends and loved ones by avoiding or skipping social situations.

Long-Term Negative Health Risks: The stress and sleeping issues that affect procrastinators are just some of the ways procrastination damages people's health. Individuals that struggle with procrastination in their personal and professional lives are more inclined to letting the habit seep into other aspects of their life such as exercising and going to the doctor. The exercising skipping as a habit starts innocently enough, typically with the individual missing a regular session or a planned lesson for a reasonable circumstance. Sometimes this circumstance or change may be out of the person's control. The issue is not that they have missed the one workout, the issue is that everything was okay while they missed that one exercise window, in fact, they may have felt better that day than they normally do after exercising because they are not all sore and sweaty.

This positive feeling they remember the next time they don't feel like exercising at their regular time or skipping their lesson and the procrastination habit takes control. Adults should attend regular annual check-ups to ensure their health and always check in with their doctors when health concerns are starting to worry them. Procrastinators often avoid going to the doctor under nearly any circumstance and others may make appointments with the best intentions only to skip them when the time comes. One of the most repeated excuses for procrastinators with this habit is that they feel fine in the moment and that the appointment is just time that could be used on the task or responsibility they have been procrastinating on. Using their favored reasoning or justification, they talk themselves out of getting their check-up or going to see their doctor, cancelling their appointment often never to reschedule it until there is an emergency or their loved ones hold an intervention.

Other negative health effects that have been linked to habitual procrastination include:

- Heart damage, particularly for individuals already at risk of heart disease for lifestyle or genetic reasons
- Inconsistent sleep patterns that lead to mental and emotional stress and burnout throughout the day
- Damage to emotional health and wellbeing with continuous trials and suffering of the emotions and psychological processes on an individual as they try to beat or justify their procrastination tendencies

Once procrastinators see the health risks and potential dangers associated with habitual procrastination, many are more likely to be willing to start taking steps toward taking control of the impulses and psychological compulsions that are commonly practiced with their condition. Now that we've covered the health risks, keep reading for a closer look at some of the most common warnings signs and indicative behaviors seen in procrastinators of all ages.

What Are Actions, Signs & Indicators of Procrastination in Men & Women?

While procrastination is widespread phenomenon amongst adults of all ages, races and locations, it is not a healthy habit (as we discussed above) and one that is difficult to break once it has reached a point that the individual is experiencing more negative effects than benefits to their procrastination practice. The good news for procrastinators everywhere is that with some patience and practice, anyone can stop procrastinating and start living up to their full potential! One way to accomplish this is first by checking for warnings signs or indicators in oneself or others to determine whether they are a habitual procrastinator or just someone who struggles with time management.

They Are Often Distracted: Those who fall into the category of habitual procrastinators often struggle in social situations as they tend to be distracted, looking for topics, conversations or activities they can take part in to avoid whatever task or responsibility they are procrastinating with. One of the most prevalent indicators of a procrastinator is the habit of searching for distractions. These are the more active procrastinators that are unable to talk themselves into getting a specific task done but is also have trouble with letting time pass without productivity. These types of procrastinators will often make lists of other tasks they have been meaning to get done or less important tasks that they can convince themselves they will be able to knock out quickly so they can focus all of their attention on the one main issue or subject. Their past experiences with procrastination and the negative side effects they've had to deal with will tell these types or procrastinators that they are setting themselves up for unnecessary stress or even failure, but the compulsion to avoid tasks or make decisions is more powerful than their logical thoughts.

They Are Often Overwhelmed By A New Task or Assignment: Procrastination is a habit directly tied to emotional and psychological impulses, factors and desires, depending on the individual. This is why many habitual procrastinators can overreact or give into rising feelings of panic or frustration whenever they are presented with a new responsibility, tasks or opportunity. Even if it is something that will affect them in a positive way, either through the process of completing in or once the activity or solution in question is reached, many procrastinators only see the negative side of it: more work, something else to do, another decision *they* are going to have to make or another plan *they* have to come up with. Whatever an individual's specific reasons or excuses, their first reaction to new situations is often an emotional one triggered by stress and fear that affect their thoughts and behaviors in ways that make them difficult to work with or even be around, depending on the situation.

They Have Difficulty Dealing with Unexpected Changes or Disruptions: One thing procrastinators are often good at is making plans for what they need to get done within their specific time frame. In most cases, it is the only way for them to be able to justify their procrastination because they know they have a solid plan of action laid out and prepared for when they are ready to get started. This plan of action is often their only comfort and fallback when the panic from time constraint or pressure starts to take its toll and they begin to regret their procrastinating.

This is why when unexpected difficulties, tasks or decisions arise, procrastinators often have difficulty emotionally or logically handling the change because they most likely did not plan any spare or free space in their time frame for anything to go sideways or come up. Planning additional time is not something that procrastinators think about, although it is a time management skill that many adults already possess. It is an invaluable part of organization and preparation for any task that many people make sure to leave room for as fear of the future and the uncertainty that something could disrupt even the best laid plans are natural human reactions.

They Have a Bad Habit of Showing Up Late: Whether it is to work, class or social events, habitual procrastinators are often known in their professional or social groups as the person who is most likely to show up not only late, but most likely unprepared for whatever it is they are facing that day. This bad habit leads to a reputation of unreliability that can damage someone's professional and personal relationships or connections.

This known habit of being late regardless of consequence or importance gives procrastinators a disadvantage when it comes to building their futures as it gives them a reputation for being unreliable that can penetrate all aspects of their life from their professional responsibilities to their social, familial or romantic relationships. Since they are always late, or at least late often enough that others have begun to notice or remark on it as a regular behavior, they are not as trusted as their peers or other members of their group and can often alienate themselves over time or start to get left out of events and gathers since the people they would be going to see may have started to just assume the individual would be bailing anyway. It is not just personal relationships that can be affected. Their superiors may observe this habit of being late and see it as a weakness in their employee, that person then finds themselves missing opportunities or getting passed up for projects or assignments that could further their standing or career.

They Focus on Trivial or Non-Essential Activities Before Getting Their Necessary Tasks Completed: Another one of the most common traits displayed by habitual procrastinators is a strong reliance (even a dependence) on lists and organization, regardless if it is at home or work. The lists themselves can range in length or priority but are typically filled with smaller tasks or lighter decisions that the individual may have been thinking about for some time, but that he or she is using as a means of distraction from the more pressing tasks they are procrastinating with.

The only thing about these lists is that while they may be informative and impressive when looked at on first glance, but if someone were to investigate how many of those tasks have actually been marked off or even started, they would be highly disappointed. Despite their lists, their preparation and their organization, most procrastinators never end up checking off their entire lists, or even the majority of them. Of course, this varies from person to person and how out of control their procrastination impulses are, but it is one of the few behaviors that most habitual procrastinators share as it gives them viewable proof to use against or wave at people who question their productivity.

Procrastination Habits Identified: Now What Can Be Done to Help Fix Them & Solve or Come to Terms with the Issue as A Whole?

The first step in finding a solution to any problem is to understand how it starts, where it comes from and how it connects to overthinking. While many people may find the cause of their procrastination is similar to others working to conquer with the same matter, every individual will have their own variables and specific situations that may set them on a different path to understanding and overcoming their personal struggle. Keep reading, as these are topics we will cover thoroughly in the next chapter!

Chapter 3: The Causes & Stress Triggers That Lead People to Procrastinate

Coming to terms with procrastination and overthinking starts with finding out where they come from. As with any psychological issue or concern, the answers regarding origins and what lifestyle points might affect them will be different for each individual. Fortunately, modern psychologists and health professionals have spent plenty of time studying these behavioral phenomena and the amount of knowledge related to overcoming them has grown exponentially in the last few decades.

Through various studies and surveys, professionals across the globe are discovering and sharing their findings with regards to who is most at risk for developing psychological habits, how to identify them and how they can be treated. As with any medical or health-related topics, not all symptoms and traits are going to be true for every person who struggles overthinking or procrastination habits. The point of gaining this knowledge is to determine which factors or variables each individual is facing so that a plan can be formed for how best to tackle their personal situation.

Now that we've provided a better understanding of what overthinking and procrastination are, let's take a closer look at where they come from and what types of personalities are more likely to cave to their emotionally driven psychological compulsions.

What Causes Procrastination?

If procrastination is something that everyone has to deal with at multiple points throughout their life, can it really be all that bad? Despite the many health and well-being risks associated with habitual procrastinating and overthinking, there are still those who refuse to believe that their personal habits and compulsions are under control and far from being dangerous to their mind or body.

Pro Tip: This denial is one of the challenges all people wanting to take control of their habits and behaviors must overcome before any forward progress can be made. If someone is unwilling to acknowledge their issue and make a conscious decision to change, then they are not going to be able to improve their behaviors or psychological habits.

However, there is plenty of hope and proven techniques out there that have made all the difference for those wanting to give up procrastinating and overthinking. The most recent studies have shown that the development of habitual procrastination can be traced back to four main psychological causes:

• **Unable to Focus or Gain Control of Thoughts:** Sometimes people who have difficulty with controlling their thoughts or getting themselves to focus have their behaviors being controlled by their emotions rather than their logical thoughts. Emotions are truthful and powerful, but they are also unpredictable and capable of changing without warning, especially for those with existing psychological conditions.

• **Fear of Failure & Fear of the Unknown:** These are perfectly natural phobias that every person faces at some point in their life. While for many the fear disappears once a plan has been made or more information has been gathered, but for others these types of fears (which can be encountered in nearly any given situation) can lead to full-blown panic attacks and other emotional reactions can affect their behavior and inspire psychological habits like procrastination and overthinking to take control of all thought and action.

- **Lack of Motivation & Low Levels of Energy:** These two traits are often connected as many who find themselves trying to cope with procrastination also have experience with larger psychological concerns like depressive states, suicidal behaviors in extreme cases, and the development of anti-social behaviors related to lack of confidence or faith in their own talents, abilities or future potential. This negative thinking constantly circling through their mind can leave damage on an individual's self-esteem, a negative emotion that comes with physical side effects such as fatigue, low immune system efficiency and muscle soreness throughout the body with little to no physical strain to cause it.

- **Need to Reach Perfection:** This is a common trait that comes with the fear of failure and is one of the main causes of procrastination. Through their previous experiences with procrastination and their tendency to overthink, they begin to believe that the only way they will be able to complete something or come to a proper resolution is if their application is totally flawless. Of course, perfection is an often impossible bar for people to reach, particularly when distractions, interruptions and unwelcome challenges can arise at any time and throw off even the most well-planned solutions.

There are still those out there that argue habits like procrastination and overthink cannot be nearly as harmful as people claim they are since everyone deals with them at some point but not everyone falls prey to their control of behaviors and reactions to situations throughout life. Recent studies have looked into this fact as well as determined that the reason not everyone develops dangerous psychological habits because there are those in the population that are more susceptible to the negative and long-term effects than others.

While the image itself may have a comical tone, it is an accurate and widely relatable visual of the types of thoughts that dominate someone's mind when procrastination habits have control over a person's mind, emotions and behaviors.

What Kinds of People Are Most Likely to Become Procrastinators?

Like with all psychological habits and behaviors there are some with different personalities and lifestyle variables that can be more or less likely to develop procrastination or overthinking habits. Some of these common variables and personality types include:

Perfectionists: People who struggle with being a perfectionist often also have difficulties controlling their impulse to procrastinate. One of the main reasons for this is because people who take pride in perfection and faultless execution in everything they do are less concerned with not getting a task done than they are finishing something that is flawed in any form. However, for many procrastinating perfectionists, the closer their deadline comes or the higher the pressure gets for them to take action, the more panic sets in an they find themselves in a panicked frenzy to complete their task.

Students: Students, regardless of age or education level, are some of the most common victims of procrastination and overthinking. One of the reasons for this is often connected to a lack of confidence in their own talents and abilities that causes them to obsess about each and every detail of their assignments until they are trapped in a whirlwind of thoughts that keeps them from completing their task. Another one of the main reasons for student procrastination is the self-deception that comes with the belief that they perform better under the pressure of a nearly impossible deadline. Despite being told over and over by their friends and family that they will not only feel better, but that the quality of their work will improve if they didn't procrastinate, the impulse is too strong in many cases and the need to put off their responsibilities takes over.

Pro Tip: Those who use this excuse are able to convince themselves that they will be able to complete their task to their best ability even in the shortened amount of time typically because they have done it before. It only takes one successful event for the habit to start and take control. The first time someone procrastinates and is still able to complete their task or find their solution in time for someone to start procrastinating as a matter of habit and compulsion.

People Pleasers: Those who find themselves constantly surrounded or often outnumbered by people who are difficult to please often become procrastinators. These types of people are eager for those around them (both peers and superiors) to see them in a certain light. It could be that they lied or fictionalized something about themselves in order to paint this picture for their friends or co-workers, or it could be that there is no reason for the person to feel inferior to those around them because they are just as experienced or talented, but do not see it because their self-esteem has been so wrecked by their procrastinating and overthinking habits.

Those Who Have Learned Through Experience: Those who procrastinated until they were under the gun and managed to come out on top without consequence once or twice by accident are more likely to develop a problem with habitual procrastination because their experience has taught them that they are still able to put out quality work or make solid decisions without having to spend the effort and energy on the time management skills and patience it would take to achieve their goal in a timely and comparatively stress-free manner. While they may consider themselves lucky at first, the longer this habit is allowed to develop and is practiced by the individual, the further the quality of their work and performance (often in various aspects of their life) will slip until those they work or interact with take notice and action.

The Connection Between Procrastination & Overthinking

While the two are often symptoms of a larger psychological concern that should be acknowledged and explored, habitual procrastinating and overthinking have also been linking as being the cause for one another.

Overthinkers who consider themselves driven and motivated in everything they do find that over time, their psychological habit of obsessing over small interactions or replaying regrets through their mind can develop into habitual procrastination over time as these individuals try to find ways to distract themselves from their dominating thoughts and emotions, often pushing aside responsibilities or pressing tasks to avoid having to think about them.

Alternately, those who start as procrastinators may find over time that they are overthinking more and more about the things happening around them, personally and professionally. One of the main reasons for this is that those who are self-aware enough to recognize their impulse to procrastinate in matters from choosing where they want to eat dinner to delivering a major presentation to their employers are also emotionally intelligent enough to realize that the anxiety and panicked emotions that come with that habit are only increasing their stress and decreasing their chances of success.

Unfortunately, although they are aware of their habitual procrastinating and overthinking, the compulsive behaviors associated with those habits are more powerful than rational thinking and are often determined by how the individual is feeling at any given moment. This only makes the habitual overthinking worse as it brings up questions like why the person can't just make themselves take an action or make a decision and why they start procrastinating every time they face something, knowing how much stress, regret and guilt comes with the process.

Another connection that is common between the development of procrastination and overthinking habits is a third psychological stage that is fueled by emotions like the fear of failing and the awareness of passing time and burning energy that could be used more productively. This stage is an overwhelming guilt that also comes with negative health and wellness effects like fluctuating stress levels and uncertainty of one's ability to accomplish anything.

Use This Newly Gained Knowledge & Get the Answers You Have Been Searching For!

After the last few chapters, we hope you're feeling better informed and more confident in your knowledge of overthinking, procrastinating and where they come from. Now that the knowledge has been collected, it is time to put it to use and start preparing for those first steps forward with taking control of your mind, behaviors and emotions in order to conquer your habitual overthinking and/or procrastination.

As with any plan, the first step is to take a step back and analyze the situation as a whole. Answer these questions about yourself or the person you are concerned for to get a better read on the big picture and the individual factors that may affect treatment:

- What behaviors have you noticed that could be connected to habitual procrastination or overthinking?
- What is the individual's personality type? Do they fall into the category of higher risk personalities?

- What specific factors could be causing the habitual procrastination or overthinking?

- Are there certain situations where their behaviors, thoughts and actions (or lack thereof) can be identified as compulsive or driven by emotion rather than rational decisions?

- Have you (or the individual in question) acknowledged and accepted that there is a problem with these habitual compulsions that is hindering their ability to function at their full potential?

The Origins Have Been Explored. Traits Have Been Analyzed. What's Next for Breaking These Habits?

Now that the foundation has been laid for better understanding of psychological concerns like procrastination and overthinking habits and information has been shared about who is statistically most likely to develop these habits over others, it is time to start making an actionable plan for how to change the way the mind thinks and views the world so that impulses like procrastination and overthinking lose their power over your behaviors.

Answer the following questions to determine whether or not you are prepared to begin taking control of your mental and psychological health in order to improve the health of your whole being:

- Have you fully acknowledged your individual negative psychological habit or multiple habits?
- Are you prepared to make conscious decisions and alterations to your behaviors and reactions?
- Can you stick to these changes, overcoming your emotional impulses that may arise and challenge your determination?
- Are you ready for a better life packed with as much fulfillment, success and discovery as you can fit into each day?

If the answers to these questions are all *yes*, then it is time to get started and time to take control of any and all psychological behaviors to make the most of life and everything it has to offer! Congratulations on gaining the knowledge and preparing yourself for the first steps to overcoming overthinking for a less stressful and more efficient life at home, work, school and/or any other situations where you find emotional responses and irrational behaviors setting the pace for you. In the chapters to come, we will be discussing tips, tricks and the most cutting-edge techniques in use around the world today from some of the most trusted and respected professionals and experts in the field!

Chapter 4: Taking Your First Steps (From Harmful Procrastination to Incredible Productivity)

There is not one easy solution when it comes to finding the best way to conquer one's habitual procrastination. The main reason behind this is that procrastination comes in varying urgency levels. For some people, they are only experiencing the compulsion to skip, shrug or put off their responsibilities in this moment but may have had no trouble getting things done on any other day. This type of procrastination is often connected to the person's current emotional state. Perhaps they have had a bad day or are fatigued from a lack of sleep the night before, and often times giving in to the procrastination habit is not as dangerous and may even be the best option for their mental and emotional health. This type of procrastination is not habitual but rather inspired by unusual circumstance. For others, their procrastination is something they have to battle with every time they have set a goal for themselves, have a deadline to meet or an obligation to fulfill. This type of procrastination is more damaging as it becomes habit easily, a habit that is widely accepted as one of the most difficult to break. The good news for people with this type of procrastination struggle is that there have been people around the world searching for and perfecting different methods and techniques, tips and tricks for how to overcome procrastination for those with the motivation and determination to get started! As you have read, there are so many different origins and variables that can give a procrastination habit its power within a person's mind. Since there are so many different variations, it only makes sense that there are just as many different courses of action that can be taken in the quest to overcome procrastination. In this chapter, we will be covering (in detail and with as much information as possible) the most proven, practiced and professionally recommended methods for beating habitual procrastination available today!

The Baby Steps Method: All It Takes Is Two Minutes!

One popular method making its mark on the psychological and business communities is the *Baby Step* or *Two Minute Method*. With this method, people are able to lay the foundations and start taking action toward breaking their procrastination habit and building positive habits in its place.

This method confronts and tackles procrastination habits head-on with actionable plans that begin with taking a step back from the individual's problem or task, analyzing it and listing the steps to completion from the simplest to the most difficult or time-consuming, depending on the person's priorities. Once the situation has been analyzed and broken down into its simplest and most basic steps, the person needs to make a plan of action for their task and list each step they need to take from the beginning to the resolution. The trick to mastering this method is that each step should take no more than two minutes to complete.

If the different stages of the task become too complicated to complete in two minutes and the person is not in a situation where they are not procrastinating, then the next step of this method is to break each of the remaining, more complicated steps down into two minute tasks and continue to do so until the entire task is completed their satisfaction. It may sound more complicated in explanation than it is in practice, so here is an example to provide a clearer picture of the Baby Steps Method in action:

- Someone has been trying to finish a manual for a new work program that are going to have to start using regularly next week. Their procrastination has told them that they have plenty of time (seven whole days) before they have o have the manual completed so they don't need to worry about it now.
  - Potential Situation A: The person listens to their procrastination thoughts and doesn't touch the manual until five days have passed. Now the panic begins to set in as they realize they now have 48 hours before they're supposed to have the manual completed. From here, there are two main courses of action:

- The person can grab the manual and skip everything they had planned for the next two days in order to dedicate the entire amount of time to making their way through the manual before work starts again in 48 hours.

- The person can become overwhelmed by the pressure and end up just skimming or flipping through the manual to try and collect as much information as possible in order to improvise or "wing it" when they get to work and have to start the new program.

- In either of these situations, the individual is putting themselves at a disadvantage, either because they have had to cancel plans with friends and family, put off errands or chores they needed to get done, or just gone in blindly to a situation that can have a serious impact on their productivity, success and quality of work.

o The Baby Steps Method: Instead of putting off reading the manual until later in the week, the individual looks at how many pages there are or how many chapters or sections there are and splits them up evenly over the seven days they have to complete the manual before work starts again. This way, they have just set their first goal for the task: reading a little bit each day to help with content absorption and stress control.

▪ Now that the goal has been set, they have a rational plan that they understand carries the most benefits for them. The challenge now is to not let their procrastination habit start to whisper in their ear when the time comes to start their reading each day that it is not that much if they wanted to skip their reading goal one night. The rationalizing behind this is that they still have tomorrow and that the additional section is not that much to make up.

▪ When thoughts like this start to take over, the next step is look back at the basics of the task, in this case, getting the section of the manual read for the day.

• What is the first thing a person needs to do if they want to get something read? Pull out and open the manual. Once this task is completed, it will be easier and feel more natural to start reading.

• Once the manual is open, the next step is to get the reading started. The next step is to then get one complete page read.

- At this point, the person is more likely to keep reading until they reach their daily goal because they have already done the hardest part: pulled out the book and started reading.

- Even if the person decides to stop reading and play catch-up with their reading tomorrow, they can still take pride in having made a forward and positive step toward conquering their habitual procrastination.

Why This Method Works: The reason the Baby Steps Method has proven so effective for men and women around the world is that it is based on the positive reinforcement of actionable behaviors, instead of focusing solely on the negativity of the procrastination habit. The purpose of the Baby Steps Method has little to do with the procrastination behavior itself and instead gives the individual the skills they need to master the practice of showing up. What this means is that even though there are times where the habitual procrastination will come out on top in the struggles, but as long as the person has taken the first of their two minute steps and completed it (and hopefully more of their two minute steps in the process), then they have already made progress on overpowering the habit by simply showing up and beginning the goal they set for themselves as opposed to completely avoiding any positive action.

There are a number of reasons why people who are using the Baby Steps Method should still feel good about their progress, even in the situations where they complete each of their two minutes steps and the procrastination still takes control:

- Habits are not built or broken in one try! It takes practice and dedication to stop procrastination and replace it with efficient and productive habits.

- Procrastinators often have reputations for breaking promises, cancelling plans and showing up late to important events or responsibilities (if they show up at all). By learning to just take some kind of action toward their smaller goals, they are learning how to show up and the more they are able to practice that skill, the more it will start to positively affect their behavior in other aspects of their life where procrastination has kept them from showing where and when they are supposed to.

Who This Method Works Best For: This method works for anyone who is looking to start a new habit or build a positive behavior in place of one they are trying to break free from. Those who have habitual procrastination habits will benefit from this practice in any aspect of their lives and will see the most progress over time.

The Teamwork Method: Have Someone Hold You Responsible & Accept Their Help!

From the dawn of time, humans have always proven stronger when working together than trying to survive on their own. The Teamwork Method uses this base instinct between humans to band together in a way that helps with breaking their bad habit in a way that they are also receiving the support and encouragement of the people around them. At its basic level, the Teamwork Method involves:

- Analyzing the task, responsibility or action that needs to be completed and design a plan of action from start to finish.
    - If there is a deadline or date when everything needs to get done, then do not forget to include it in the plan during this step.
- Once the plan has been made, the person then shares it with one to five people who they trust to keep them on task when they get distracted or to offer positive support when they start to shirk their responsibilities.
    - This could be friends or family who already know about their issues with procrastination and want to help. These people could also be others who are involved in the task or subject the person is working on.

Why This Method Works: People are more likely to meet their responsibilities and reach their goals when they know that others are counting on them or cheering them on. When a person shares their goals with people they trust and people they respect the opinion of, they build a network of positive energy that they can call upon whenever they are feeling low or unproductive. That positive reinforcement helps to boost them up and keep them motivated throughout their trials and challenges.

Pro Tip: The most important part of mastering this method is free and open communication between friends, family or co-workers and anyone else included in the person's support team. Those who struggle with asking for help or have difficulty sharing how they are feeling or what they are thinking even with those they are closest to will not find this method effective for improving their lifestyle and breaking their bad habits.

Who This Method Works Best For: Those this method will work best for those who have already been open with the people they trust about their struggles and are ready to not only ask for help, but to accept it when it is offered. Even if someone has difficultly with open communication, if that is something they are working on along with overcoming procrastination or any other positive changes they are trying to make, then they will be able to work on that with this method as well as those who have already mastered or are already pleased with their communication skills.

When in Doubt, Get the App & Leave All of The Hard Work to Technology!

For those who are not great communicators or do not have the support network that others may have, there are still options for getting control of those psychological compulsions! One of the most popular options in today's technology driven society is to download an app and get started with virtual scheduling programs and personal assistants. Depending on the individual's specific needs and challenges, there are a variety of apps available for androids and iPhones that can help! Here is a more detailed look at some of the most popular apps available now:

- **1-3-5 List:** This app was designed to target those who find that their habitual procrastination is most closely linked to their difficulty with prioritizing their tasks. With this app, users choose a number of tasks they are hoping to complete each day: one large, three medium and five smaller tasks that need to be completed, actions that need to be taken or decisions that need to be made. Once these various goals and responsibilities have been entered into the program, the app helps the user prioritize and plan the order in which to complete the tasks so that they make the most out of their time and energy each and every day!

- **Simple Habit:** This app was designed for those who have heard about the ease and health benefits connected with meditation and have wanted to try it for themselves but have not yet started. This could be because of simply not knowing where or how to start, or because it is one of the big concerns they have been procrastinating with. This app is perfect for those who find their procrastination is connected closely with the pressure stress or performance anxiety that comes with having to complete a task, make a decision or attend an event and function in a social situation. With easy and pressure free meditation sessions available in a variety of time intervals, anyone can find a meditation track that targets their specific needs. In addition to offering a variety of programs, this app also personalizes meditation recommendations based on the user's individual preferences so that it is most productive and effective over time.

- **Mindly:** This app works best for those whose procrastination habits are tied to their difficulty with getting focused and organized. Many apps rely on to-do lists and other organization methods that work best for linear minds. Instead, this app connects related thoughts, events, responsibilities, tasks and goals in interconnected circles that allows the user to move around and organize anything on their mind from things they have to do and when they are do to things they want to accomplish and how long they are hoping that will take. This is app has proven invaluable for those who are better able to stay organized or focus their mental tracks in a way that creates a picture or that allows them to visualize to suit their best preferences.

Why These Apps Work: These apps work by keeping track of an individual's responsibilities, events or deadlines and sending them regular reminders (that can often be controlled and timed to fit the person's preferences) in order to keep their task or project in the front of their mind. By keeping their goals in the front of their thoughts, more people see success in getting started and staying focused or motivated in situations similar to those they have had difficulty managing before. These apps work best by not just focusing on breaking the procrastination habits, but also helping to increase the user's overall productivity, whether it is in personal or professional settings. One of the other reasons these apps are so productive for some people is that they are for those who like to take action and just need help focusing their energy or their thoughts on tasks at hand. Another benefit of working with these apps is that different apps are designed to target different variables that can contribute to a person's individual procrastination habits. Some apps can target multiple variables such as scheduling, notification reminders and communication options. Others focus on just one for those who have targeted their main issue and are looking for a tool to help them gain control over it.

Pro Tip: Not all of these apps are free. Some of them have a use fee or a monthly subscription. If they offer a free trial then that is the best way to start, but for those who are serious about breaking their procrastination habit and find during the trial that the app if helping with their struggle, then the price might be worth the reward. However, if you do try an app (free trial, with a temporary subscription or just by diving in with both feet to give it a shot), and find that you are not using it as much as you thought you were or that it is not helping as much as you had hoped, do not continue to pay for it! There are so many different methods and options available for conquering procrastination that

Who These Apps Work Best For: These apps are designed for people who do not have issues with procrastination due to lack of motivation or need for perfection. Instead, they are designed to help with organization, scheduling, communication reminders and keeping lists. They are designed for people who procrastinate because of the sheer number of things they have to do, those who find themselves overwhelmed by everything being asked of them. Whether this overwhelming pressure is coming from one current situation or is a consistent and regular matter of a busy lifestyle, these apps can help by working as a virtual personal assistant.

Pro Tip: One of the downsides to these apps is that most of them only work if the individual enters the deadline, information and other details they need to have in order to achieve their goal into the app's scheduling or assistant program. If a person downloads that app but is unable to stay on top of entering their tasks and action plans, then the apps will not help with their personal psychological habits and just take up space on their phone.

Take A Breather: Find a Fresh Perspective & Change the Way Things Look

One simple step for those who get anxious when trying to make changes or overcome their more dominant impulses is to get out of their current surroundings. Whether it is getting up to stretch and take a short walk around the room or in more extreme cases, taking a weekend trip to visit a friend or family member, finding somewhere else to think about and plan out your responsibilities or tasks can make all the difference in coming up with a logical resolution instead of giving in to procrastination habits or other negative psychological impulses. Not taking an annual vacation or even taking some time off to support one's personal physical, emotional and mental health is one of the most common issues facing adults in the 21st century. This is another major cause of anxiety and high levels of stress in men and women of working age across the globe. In some cases, a person's psychological habits such as procrastination are a direct result of not having any personal time to relax or ruminate on their own health. Adults become so focused on building their careers and getting those promotions that they become fatigued and even exhausted, physically and mentally. Over time, this lack of support for personal health takes its toll on a variety of factors such as motivation and quality of work.

Why This Method Works: There are experts in just about any field (medical, private or professional) across the globe that will testify to the benefits of taking a step out of one's current surroundings in order to gain a fresh perspective. There are an endless umber of health and wellness benefits like overall emotional status improvement for those who find that the stress of their jobs or their home situation is the cause of their procrastination habits and overthinking. Planning for vacations (or even for just taking a mental health day off from work and other pressures) gives people something to look forward to. That alone is often enough to help individuals feel more positively about the tasks the need to complete, plans they need to design, solutions they need to come up with and decisions that need to be made in the days or weeks between their current emotional state and the time their break starts. Positive people have better control over their emotions and a more confident understanding of their thoughts and feelings regarding stresses and pressures that their procrastination habit is trying to encourage them to avoid.

Who This Method Works Best For: This method is beneficial for everybody, regardless of the intensity or dominance level of their habitual psychological compulsions. During surveys and interviews, experts interested in the development of anxiety, negative psychological habits and related subjects found that the majority of people could not remember their last vacation, the last time they took some time off for their personal physical or mental health, or even regularly take breaks that are required by law or recommended by their employer.

Pro Tip: If there is not one single method, tip, trick or technique that makes a difference for your specific concerns or getting control of your psychological habits, design your own plan that focuses on your specific hopes and goals! Combine effective methods and abandon those that you have tried without any noticeable success. Never be afraid to ask more questions, seek out more information and pull together from multiple sources to form the most effective, inspiring and successful plan you can! The trick to mastering this technique is to stay organized and not be afraid to share with others what you are doing and how you are feeling in order to keep focused and motivated throughout your personal experience. Regardless of where someone's personal struggle lies or where it comes from, there is some kind of action or path that they can start with in order to overcome their habitual procrastination. It just comes

down to finding the right information and getting together the
drive and motivation to take the first steps!

Chapter 5: To Overcome Overthinking, You Simply Have to Get Moving

Similar to procrastination, overthinking is a psychological habit that does people more harm than good over time. As a compulsion and emotional response to stress, overthinking is not something that people can just stop doing by simply wishing it into being. It takes work, effort, dedication and above all, planning! Before the anxiety or stress starts to kick in, there is a wide range of action plans and proven steps that people can take to put an end to their overthinking. This mean that no matter what factors cause or enflame the overthinking habits, individuals can find a solution that works for their situation and helps them to take control of their mind and thinking process in a way that is effective, productive and successful! In this chapter, we will we going into detail for some of the most tried, tested and recommended options for those ready to take control of their thoughts and stop falling prey to the dangers of overthinking.

Pro Tip: Before choosing or designing a specific plan of action, the first step overthinkers need to take is to increase their self-awareness, psychologically, emotionally and mentally. The more self-aware someone can be in the moment, the more control they will be able to maintain over their thoughts, actions and behaviors in situations that put pressure on them. People who are more self-aware are also better able to live in the moment which means that they have less regrets about the things they say and do (or do not say and do, depending on which variables are causing them the most stress and increasing their impulse to overthink).

Benefits of Breaking the Habit of Overthinking for Men & Women

Overthinking has a lot of potential negative side effects that can damage the mental, physical, emotional and psychological health of any individual. For those who are tired of having to deal with these negative effects and make positive changes in order to break their overthinking habit, there are a number of benefits to get excited about! Some of the most widely reported and talked about for men and women of all ages include:

- One of the most encouraging benefits of not overthinking regularly includes a more improved ability to live in the moment. Instead of thinking about past regrets or worrying about things that may never come to pass, people who do not spend their time and energy on overthinking are more involved in what is happening around them and better able to form strong and lasting connections with the people they interact with regularly or may not see all the time but care about and want to be better about communicating with.

- People who do not overthink tend to be better leaders and supervisors because they are able to make decisions based on thought and logical instead of emotionally or in a panic as many who suffer from habitual overthinking have to deal with. Even if management is not their goal, their self-motivation that comes with the confidence and pride in their own abilities means that people who are able to beat their overthinking habit into submission are better able to reach their goals, no matter what they are because they are not distracted by constantly circling negative thoughts and the damaging effects that come with those thoughts.

- For most, their anxiety is the cause of their overthinking, but there are also those who find that they do not have issues with anxiety until their overthinking habit kicks in. Those who have discovered a connection between their anxiety and their habitual overthinking (regardless of which causes the other) see positive changes and unexpected benefits when they make the conscious decision to get control over their overthinking. By developing the skills needed to change their thoughts, emotions and the way they think about things, people who find effective ways to conquer or cope with their overthinking habits become better able to control their anxiety in other aspects of their life.

These are just some of the benefits that come with finding a way to beat habitual overthinking! Each person has their own reasons for wanting to stop and their own benefits they are hoping to experience when they do achieve this goal. Keep reading to learn more about those methods, tips and techniques that can help people with both their overthinking habits and personal anxiety concerns.

The Most Important Step: Accept That No One Can Predict the Future or Change the Past

One of the main causes of overthinking in men and women all over the world is the fear of what is unknown and the fear of what cannot be predicted. Another is the loss of control that comes with obsessing over past events or encounters that in hindsight could have been handled been or more to a person's personal satisfaction.

The first step to stopping overthinking and all of the negative effects that come with it is to understand that there are things that no one can see coming and that there will always be things we think could have been handled better or that we wish we could change, and then accept these thoughts as fact. Once these facts have been accepting, the sense of freedom that most people feel is enough to get them through their difficult times and move forward from getting their thoughts stuck in a repetitive cycle that becomes habitual overthinking. That freedom and the positive emotions that come with it help with motivation and staying on track when people hang on to those good feelings and call on them when situations start to become difficult or overwhelming. Until these facts are understood and embraced, no one will be able to successfully get control of their habitual overthinking. Like with those who are concerned for others but have not been able to help because the person in question is unwilling to acknowledge that they have an issue. Without the self-awareness and acceptance of the unknown, overthinkers will continue to get lost in negative thought cycles and the become victim to their dangerous and negative side effects.

Walk on Sunshine: Embrace the Encouraging Influence of Positive Thoughts

One trait that many overthinkers share is that they focus on the negative aspects of their tasks or situations and what can go wrong over what can go right or how the person can benefit. They get some overwhelmed by issues that can arise, negative effects their actions or words may have, and any other bad factors and variables that could mess up their plans or decision process. What many overthinkers do not realize is that these negative thoughts are the most powerful fuel behind their habitual overthinking and until they find a way to see the world around them or process what happens around them in a more positive light, they will not be able to get the best of their habitual overthinking.

Many will dismiss this behavior as being prepared for anything or as their being a realist instead of being naïve. However, there is a big difference between positivity and naivety. Those with a positive demeanor or view of the world are better able to control their emotions in stressful situations because they are more practiced at finding rational and thoughtful solutions to their problems or challenges instead of caving to emotional responses fueled by negative thoughts and feelings about their current situation. Those who are naïve are often described as being positive to the point of delusion. They hold on to their positive thoughts and feelings regardless of whether or not their individual situation needed a stricter or more confident course of action. They deny negative emotions and push them aside instead of finding a way to deal with them. This action is only further damaging their mental and emotional health while strengthening their compulsion to give in to their habitual overthinking instead of facing negative situations.

People who focus on positive thoughts are able to acknowledge and react reasonably to negative emotions that arise in their different interactions and responsibilities. These types of people are more energized, better at socializing and typically more driven in their tasks because their mind is not burdened with stressful or painful thoughts that they are unable to break free from the repetition of.

Get Up, Get Moving & Be More Active

One of the best techniques in practice for those looking to stop their habitual overthinking is to get the blood pumping and find a way to get moving! Overthinking tends to happen most frequently when people have nothing else to occupy their thoughts productively. It is during those down times, or in those times when the person is looking for a distraction (like those who also struggle with procrastination as a habit), that people start to ruminate about past actions or possible issues they expect in the future. That is why most people report that the majority of their overthinking begins in places like the shower or while they are waiting for their ride and becomes the most dominant in their thoughts around bedtime as they try to fall asleep (or when have difficulty falling asleep).

One change people make when trying this method for overcoming their habitual overthinking is picking up a new habit! Preferably this habit is one that gets either the mind or the body active and distracted from repetitive, stressful thoughts that kick off the overthinking sessions. Increased blood flow, air flow and muscle stretching are all physical benefits involved with most extracurricular activities and they also have psychological benefits like improving focus and boosting positive energies. For some, they may have better luck with an artistic or creative habit like taking a painting class or going out and getting involved with their community theater. For others, this habit could be more focused on physical fitness and activities. Some people may take this opportunity to start a regular exercise routine like going to the gym for a set amount of time two to three times a week (maybe even with extra sessions when their overthinking gets really out of control). For others, this could be an opportunity to try an activity they have always wanted to learn but never quite had the motivation to stat like taking a dancing class, going rock climbing or joining a free running group.

The point of this method is to get individuals out of the house and put them in unfamiliar situations that often require socializing (sometimes with strangers in the beginning, but with the potential to become new friends). By giving people something else to focus on and also a solid means of using up manic energy, picking up a new habit or starting a new routine is one of the most trusted and proven methods of beating overthinking habits and replacing them with something that carries its own benefits for any person's physical, emotional and mental health.

Invest in A Timer & Start Settings Limits for Yourself

One step overthinkers can take in an effort to overcome the negative effects connected to the habit is to go to the store and pick up a timer or download a timer app on your phone (if it does not have one already). This method has proven the most effective for those who have struggled with conquering their habitual overthinking with more direct efforts in the past without any success or noticeable progress.

Many psychological habits have some of the same effects as addiction. Overthinking is one of those habits. Symptoms similar to those associated with withdrawal in addicts are something that overthinkers have had to experience when they try to stop their overthinking cold turkey through distractions or denial. These individuals focus all of their mental and emotional energy on denying their thoughts or distracting themselves when negative overthinking takes over their mind.

There is no positive effect associated with this type of denial and that it only serves to make the overthinking worse by making the habit and not caving to it all that they can think about. Obsessing about overthinking is just as damaging and dangerous to a person's mental, emotional and physical health as habitual overthinking itself. Instead of trying to stop overthinking, this method allows individuals to let their overthinking run throughout their mind, but on their terms and within their chosen time frame. The first step in this practice is to find a timer. Once that has been done, the person needs to decide how long they want to devote to their overthinking habit.

- This can be based on a certain amount of time per day or it can be determined by the urgency or severity of the specific task, action or event that they have been overthinking about.

  o For example, if someone struggles with habitual overthinking every time they lay down or have a moment of quiet time then they will most likely want to schedule their overthinking sessions for a set amount of time each day before bed or earlier in the day so that they are less likely to think about it before bed. If someone is just overthinking about a certain event or action that has happened recently or is in the process of happening, they may want to pick a larger window of free time in which they can schedule an overthinking session.

- More than anything, the benefit of this method is that it helps the individual putting it into practice weaken their overthinking habit by breaking it out of its regular time frame (before bed or during shower time, whenever the person faces it the most frequently) and giving the person the power to choose when they will let their overthinking run free so they can better focus on what they should be doing and thinking about outside of that time frame.

- If you find yourself needing to dedicate time to thinking about something you are worried will turn into an overthinking session, then it is fine to schedule one that you were not expecting. In these types of situations, the most important part is to make sure you stick to your set time limit whether it is five minutes or an hour. Once you schedule an unexpected overthinking session and then do not stick to the time limit, the habit has control over your thoughts, actions and behaviors again and the individual has taken a step backwards in their progress.

One of the main reasons this method has proven to be so effective for a variety of men and women is that is easy to adapt to nearly any schedule and can be altered and arranged when unexpected life events pop up and interfere with previously laid plans or pop up and upset the emotional state of the person and those around them.

Change the Way You Think: Gratitude Vs Regret

One issue that the majority of overthinkers struggle with is thinking about the past (recent events or situations that happened years ago) and replaying their words and actions or inability to react through their mind. These overthinking sessions fill the person's mind with thoughts of what they should have said or done or that they should have walked away from something negative instead of getting involved and making the situation worse for themselves. There will always be things in the past that people want to forget about or wish they could have done better, but as we discussed earlier, there is no way to predict the future or change the past. This is where overthinkers need to abandon their regrets, releasing them from their thoughts and trying to move forward in a more positive lifestyle path. Once they are willing to let go of these negative thoughts and emotions, they can be replaced with a more positive way of thinking that will help people not only break their overthinking habit but also improve the way they see the world around them.

Gratitude is the opposite of regret. Knowing this, people who use this technique in order to overcome their habitual overthinking start by making a list of everything in their life that they are grateful for. It could be the basics like their family, friends and other loved ones or be related to the situation currently inspiring their overthinking habit like being grateful for their being employed when difficulties at work are causing stress and panic within their personal emotions, thoughts and behaviors. Once a person is able to see in writing or digitally on a phone or computer screen in front of them all the good and positive influences in their life that they are grateful for, it is easier to push away those negative repetitive thoughts that are most powerful during times of overthinking.

People who know why they should be grateful and what they have that they are grateful for, it is easier to take a more positive view of the world around them be it at work or in their personal life. Some people recommend carrying their list in a jacket pocket, purse or wallet. If the list was done virtually then keeping a screenshot or copy of it saved on their phone or tablet, anywhere that it is easily accessible, no matter where they are, has proven to be the most helpful and most recommended technique for achieving success with this method.

HOW TO STOP OVERTHINKING:
1) WRITE IT DOWN
2) PLAN A TIME TO THINK ABOUT IT
3) ALLOW YOURSELF 15 MINUTES TO THINK ABOUT IT

Think & Act with Confidence: Stop Asking "What If"?

Obsessing over what could have been or what could be is counterproductive for everyone who is trying to live more in the moment or find practical means of reaching their goals. While hypothetical situations can be beneficial in certain situations, when they start to become all that a person can think about whenever faced with a task or challenge then it has reached a point of being out of control that is damaging to their personal health.

The best way to stop focusing on the potential options and start taking control of your present situation is to practice being more self-aware of your thoughts and impulses when you realize you are starting to get lost in a whirlwind of hypotheticals. When individuals notice that they are stuck in a cycle of "what ifs", the best course of action is to change their thinking from the emotional, fearful and panic-driven to the rational. Most people who practice this method take a step back to analyze their current thoughts or whatever concern is causing them to overthink in terms of the Big Picture.

Once this is done and they have taken a moment to calm their dominant emotions, the next step is to take their improved understanding of the situation and make a list of pros and cons or risks and benefits, the specifics of the list or chart will depend on what works best for the situation. The purpose of this is not just to make a list and get their thoughts organized, but to give the person a collection of practical reasons why or why not they should be doing something. Those practical reasons help them to make a logical and reasonable decision based on productive thinking instead of an impulsive course of action inspired by fear or other strong emotion.

Ask for Help: Reach Out to the People Who Love You & Build A Network of Support Around You

No one is strongest when they are on their own, despite what the anti-social and aggressive personality types may try to argue about it. Like with any psychological habit or negative behavior, people have a better chance of conquering it if they let others know what they are doing and recruit people to join their fight and help hold them responsible. By building a support network of people who love them and want to see them succeed, people are better able to stick to the goals they create for themselves and also have a security net to help keep the focused, motivated and on track on days when the person feels low or is less interested in what their mind is doing than just using their overthinking habit as a way to escape their current problems and concerns.

This can be difficult for those who have difficulty communicating with others about their feelings, thoughts or concerns. However, studies have shown that those who have people holding them accountable and those who swallow their pride and ask for help have higher success rates in all aspects of their life than those who bottle their emotions and separate themselves from people who could boost their spirits and encourage them when they are feeling down.

The Music Method: Take Control of Thoughts by Turning to Your Favorite Tunes

The part of the brain that fuels habitual overthinking and the part that is most active when a person is enjoying music are separate areas that do not actively function at the same time. What this means for people who are trying to defeat their impulses to overthink about things is that with this method, they stand their best chances of taking control of their thoughts and emotions by plugging in their headphones and getting lost in their favorite songs, channels or stations.

Music has a strong connection to a person's emotional state and can affect the way a person feels in the moment or even boost the brain's overall performance! There have been countless studies done on the effects of classical music on the brain with most of them showing an improvement in total understanding, thought processing, creativity and the absorption and processing of newly learned information. If someone is trying to stop their overthinking using the Music Method, then the first step is to become aware of their current emotional status and their emotions connected to the concern or issue that is causing their overthinking. Once that emotion (or collection of emotions) has been identified, the next step is to choose songs, styles or artists that inspire the opposite emotions in you when you let go of stress and allow yourself to get lost in the sounds.

For example:

- If someone is feeling depressed and saddened by past events that are continuously playing through their thoughts, then they should choose music that makes them smile or relaxes them. Maybe the songs they choose are once that affect them not only emotionally but physically, making them want to dance or sway, maybe run or go for a walk around the neighborhood Anything to just get their blood pumping in some way or another.

- If someone is overwhelmed by the number of disconnected or distracted thoughts running around their mind during their current overthinking session, then they should put on some music that relaxes their mind and body. The beat should be slower or more gentle and should help steady the person's heart so that they feel more calm and in control while they listen to it.

Whatever the reason they are panicked and trapped in a negative cycle of habitual overthinking, as long as they choose music that inspires an equally strong but opposite reaction in their mind or body, they will be able to break their repetitive and damaging thoughts in place of a more favorable emotional state in which rational thoughts can make themselves known.

Meditation & Mantras: There's No Limit to Their Usefulness!

These techniques have a habit of showing up on just about any self-help call to action or to-do list. As over-published and talked about as some people claim they are, there is a reason for their popularity and widespread appeal: they work for just about anything they are put to use for. Meditation is a mental and spiritual exercise that helps individuals become more aware of their physical, mental and emotional state in order to better understand themselves as a whole. The ultimate impact of a meditation session is different from person to person depending on their specific concerns and the task or goal they are trying to reach. There are hundreds of free meditation tracks available on sites like YouTube for no cost at all and a wide range of meditation apps and channels available for free or subscription throughout the internet and in the app stores. For those who are not interested or have not had any noticeable progress with practices like meditation or for those who want to personalize their meditation experience, creating a personal mantra is a great first step!

Many overthinkers trying to regain control over their mind and emotions have seen amazing success with mantras. Mantras are a short statement, phrase or question that a person repeats (mentally or out loud) repetitively in order to inspire a change of emotion or a break in a certain cycle of thinking. The repetition of this personal statement is intended to reinforce something that the person is hoping to achieve or something they need to remind themselves in an attempt to stay motivated or improve a stressed or depressed mood that is negatively affecting their thoughts or behaviors. The best mantras are those that address or are connected to the struggle an individual is trying to get a handle on. Examples of simple but powerful mantras that also have a wide range of uses include:

- I believe, I can.
- Breathe in. Exhale.
- Get up. Just move.
- Let it go. Release.

These are just simple ones that address some of the most common causes and triggers behind overthinking in men and women of all ages. If none of these work for you or address your problem, then choose a phrase that does! The main reason that mantras have proven to be such a powerful tool for overthinkers looking to break their habit is that every overthinker's brain is already acting in a cyclical and repetitive manner. If a person's brain is already repeating thoughts and ideas, then why not put that behavior to good use and start to make it a productive and positive habit by repeating a phrase that strengthens them instead of damages their self-esteem or confidence in themselves?

Get Out of the House & Volunteer: Turn Your Thoughts to the Needs of Others

One of the most commonly shared traits of overthinkers is that they tend to be focused on their own thoughts, concerns and responsibilities (sometimes real but often imagined through hypothetical situations and anxious thought circling). This centralized thinking can often come across as narcissism or even pride, even though in many cases the person in question also struggles with low self-esteem or a lack of confidence.

Pro Tip: One of the key tricks anyone needs in order to master the art of building a new habit or before changing their behaviors is to become aware of their self-esteem and confidence levels. These traits create the foundation for each and every habit or personality shaping behavior that someone is hoping to start or strengthen. (This is something we will cover in further depth and detail in the next chapter).

One of the actions someone can when they are trying to overcome their damaging and habitual overthinking is to take themselves out of their familiar surroundings and change their perspective in order to get a more open and wider view of the world around them. Often times, people who try this method for conquering their overthinking find that they do not even have to travel very far, but that there are people within their own community that can benefit from volunteering efforts like feeding underprivileged families or collecting donations for the homeless community in their area. These are just some of the most popular and widely available activities that can be found in nearly any community or nearby city for those who live in smaller or more secluded areas.

The Conversational Exercise: Stretch Out All of Those Social Muscles & Skills

For those who do not have the time to get involved with a volunteer program and are searching for a smaller exercise that they can take part in whenever or wherever they may find themselves throughout the day, another popular exercise for those looking to focus on the needs of others is as follows:

1. Pick three people you have been wanting to contact or catch up with

2. Once the three people have been chosen, send each of them a message or an email letting them know that you have been thinking about them and asking about how they are. For those who are trying to be more direct with their connections and interactions, a phone call (even if it leads to a leaving a voicemail) is always a great course of action as well!

3.   Give them a few days to respond before following up if you would like to, but in terms of the exercise, whether or not they respond is not important. The reason for this is because the purpose of this exercise is to turn your thoughts to someone else when you notice yourself starting to overthink. As long as you chose three friends or family members and sent them some form of message to see how they are, you have achieved your goal and taken the first step into building a positive habit of changing the way your mind works when you start to habitually and compulsively overthink.

Alternately, you can choose three strangers, co-workers or others you may encounter throughout the day and start a conversation with them, making sure to ask about their current life status, events you know have recently happened or that they are preparing for, or just if there is anything they need to talk about.

If you are uncomfortable bringing up sensitive or emotional subjects with people you have just met or do not know very well, then go ahead and start a conversation with lighter topics such as weekend plans or movies they are interested in seeing, following after whatever comes up or whatever course the conversation naturally takes. The key to making the exercise work in situations like this is to just make sure the conversation stays focused on the person you are speaking with and their concerns.

Why This Exercise Works: This method and exercise are effective because they encourage the individual putting them to use to become more active in their community and more social with the people they encounter daily. In some cases, people have even been able to reconnect with friends or family members that they had strained relationships with or lost contact with years before.

Even if the message ends up going nowhere, the person has made steps toward building a positive social habit to replace their habitual overthinking. This exercise teaches people through stress-free experience that it is okay to make the first move when it comes to speaking to other people and helps with building confidence over time, helping people to become more bold with their actions or voicing their opinions in personal and professional situations.

Who This Exercise Works Best For: This method and exercise are most effective for anyone who is wanting to expand their social skills or just their social circle, anyone who is trying to overcome their habitual overthinking, anyone who is trying to build their confidence levels and anyone who is trying to gain new skills and train their brain to be more positive when it comes to interacting with other people.

Regardless of where a person's anxieties and habitual overthinking come from, there is always a way to expand their emotional intelligence, understand their personal factors and variables and make a plan of action that will help them see the most progress with practice and better control over time!

Chapter 6: Confidence is Key When It Comes to Building Positive Habits

There is a strong connection between confidence, emotional control and the conquering of psychological habits. Over the years, through all of the surveys, interviews and studies conducted, this is the most common and repeated truth from those participating in them and those performing them: no matter what a person is trying to attempt, confidence is key! There are lots of different life factors that can affect a person's self-esteem and confidence with adolescence taking the largest toll on a person's view of themselves. During adolescence, humans It is in these years that men and women receive the majority of their emotional education as it has the highest inclusion of factors like the following for most people:

- First romantic relationships (often tumultuous with lots of highs and lows)
- First deep friendships that are tested by adjusting hormones, changing personalities and other life factors that may arise without warning
- First major successes and accomplishments like national awards and recognition, college scholarships and summer internships
- Learning to drive and understanding the responsibility that comes with getting behind the wheel of a car

- Developing decision-making skills that are shaped by how adolescents handle things like peer pressure, balancing their school, work and social lives, and making their first life-affecting decisions like if they want to further their education after their required schooling is completed

With all of these exciting changes taking place, how could someone's self-esteem and confidence levels be hindered or even damaged? Unfortunately, for all of the positive events men and women experience during their teenage years, there are also a lot of negative events and factors they face (in their highest quantity and intensity than most people see throughout the rest of their lives) such as:

- Learning to differentiate affectionate teasing from friends and loved ones with harmful teasing and bullying that comes from those with the intention to cause harm
- Physical changes to their skin, muscles and other parts of the body that may require attention from over-the-counter medical products or even prescriptions from medical professionals
- Emotional changes that are often unexpected and out of control as skills are developed through experience and education
- Lots of fear and uncertainty as everything seems to be changing around them without a sense of direction or stopping point in sight

Not everyone has come out of adolescence with more negative memories than positive ones, but for those that did and find those negative experiences or memories affecting their adult lives, never fear! There is always action that can be taken to improve your self-esteem and confidence levels in order to improve your overall life satisfaction and path to reaching your goals!

Self-Esteem & Confidence Levels: How Are They Connected & How Are They Different?

Many times, when people talk about self-esteem and confidence, they speak about them as if they are one and the same. However, in truth, self-esteem and confidence are two separate personality traits that are often interconnected but can be damaged or weakened on their own and need individualized attention in order to help rebuild and strengthen them.

Pro Tip: Self-awareness is one of the skills people should try to master or at least become more familiar and practiced at before turning their energies to self-esteem and confidence. Without knowing where you stand psychologically, mentally and emotionally, it is difficult to determine where your focus should be aimed and what kinds of goals you should set to reach your ultimate hopes and aspirations.

A Self-Awareness Exercise: Listen to Your Self Talk & Learn from What You Say

One of the best ways for someone to understand their emotional status and why they are feeling a certain way about something is to listen to how they are speaking to themselves, either vocally or in their mind. Everyone has a little voice in their thoughts that voices their opinions about what they are thinking or what they are doing in a way that is honest, even if sometimes it can be discouraging or even cruel. The reason this voice can be trusted as a person's most honest thoughts is because these are the thoughts, ideas and opinions that only circle through someone's mind when they are alone (especially if they are voiced audibly) or whenever they have the opportunity (for those who play the voice in their minds where only they ever hear them).

Those with lower self-esteem and confidence levels often find that their private voice is a negative one, repeating Self Talk that further damages their view of themselves or opinion of their abilities. For this exercise, the goal is to teach individuals how to be more aware of this Self Talk and its tone so that they know how to change their current thought process or emotional status any time their Self Talk takes a negative turn.

- When you feel yourself inner voice becoming negative, whether this is because you are unsatisfied with something about your physical appearance or because of a broken sentence in an earlier social interaction, it will start to make critical comments or try to target other fragile or underdeveloped aspects of your personality in order to bring your mood further down.

    o   Self-depreciation and attacks on one's own status or abilities are some of the most damaging behaviors someone can take part in and in many cases, this voice develops subconsciously, only voicing fears and concerns when the brain knows the person is emotionally vulnerable.

• When this behavior starts to take over your thoughts, take a step back and calm your mind. Listen to those thoughts and how your inner voice sounds (or your vocal tone) when the Self Talk starts.

    o   What kind of tone does your voice or inner voice take?

        ▪   Is it angry, sad or hurtful?

        ▪   Does it express any kind of emotion or does it come across as a more neutral side to your character?

    o   What kind of words is that voice using?

        ▪   Are they offensive?

        ▪   Are they words you do not normally use when talking to other people?

    o   When is this voice most active?

- Does the Self Talk get most negative or most targeted during times of stress? Or any time you are not thinking about something else?
- Do your own thoughts, actions and behaviors determine how active the voice is? Or is it more active after encounters with others?

Why This Exercise Works: This exercise works because it is based around a natural human behavior that all men and women have in common, an inner voice that takes charge of conveying our deepest and most private thoughts about the things we do and say each day. When regularly practiced, it has proven to be one of the most effective exercises in helping people expand their emotional intelligence and their understanding of themselves and how they view their private thoughts.

Who This Exercise Works Best For: This exercise has proven the most effective for those who are dedicated and motivated to take control of their emotional and psychological health. Anyone who is ready to better understand who they are and what makes them tick in order to improve their interactions with others or saying yes to more opportunities will also see noticeable progress when this exercise becomes habit and makes its way into their daily routine.

Once a person becomes comfortable with self-awareness habits and has a better understanding of where their emotional health is, they are better able to make an actionable plan for how to first improve their self-esteem and confidence levels before moving on to more stubborn and difficult to break psychological habits like compulsive overthinking and procrastination. But what is self-esteem and why is it such an important element to master when it comes to expanding emotional knowledge and health?

What Is Self-Esteem?

Self-esteem is most commonly defined as how a person feels about themselves as a whole. There is often an emotional connection to a person's self-esteem that is not shared with someone's confidence levels.

This trait is one that covers how an individual may feel about:

- Their current life status
- Their current job status
- Their relationship status
- Their main hopes and how they are working toward them
- The people around them like friends and family

- Their physical strengths and where they want to work more

These are just some of the individual factors and variables that can go into shaping a person's view of themselves and their self-esteem. If everyone in the world made a list of the points and traits they think about when they think about their view of themselves, you would most likely see a lot of repeated important factors. However, another certainty that many experts and professionals who study the effects of self-esteem on people is that there will also be as many differences as there are similarities. The reason for this is that everyone has different values or expectations for themselves based on an additional variety of factors such as:

- The environment they were raised in
- The family values instilled in them throughout childhood
- Their personal beliefs and values that have developed throughout their individual life experiences
- The expectations they set and the standards they hold themselves and those around them

These are just some of those additional factors that can help to shape an individual. The more in-depth someone looks into their own thoughts, feelings, ideas, hopes and dreams, the more they will know about themselves and the higher their self-esteem will grow to be.

Where It Comes From: A person's self-esteem is most commonly shaped by their emotional experiences and encounters. The mistakes, triumphs, accidents and successes that come throughout life all carry their own emotional and psychological influences with them. It's these influences that are most powerful when it comes to shaping how a person views themselves and their current lifestyle or life situation. The more positive influences and experiences a person is able to collect, the better their self-esteem will be and the more emotionally in control they will find themselves when stressful situations arise.

What Is Confidence (or Self-Confidence)?

Confidence (particularly when described as self-confidence) refers to faith a person has in their own knowledge, experience, skills and abilities. Depending on how much belief someone has in the things they know, the things they say, and the things they do during their personal or professional interactions, the higher a person's confidence levels will be.

Where It Comes From: A person's confidence comes from their opinion of and trust in their own strengths and abilities. This trust and faith most often are the result of positive experiences such as promotions at work or awards at school.

The more experience they have and proof they have been able to collect that they know what they are doing or what they are talking about, then the higher their self-confidence will be and the more that will start to positively affect other areas of their life.

There are lots of people who have a high level of self-esteem but find that they lack confidence, especially in certain situations like when they are asked to do something without time to prepare or when they want to ask a question, but are concerned with how others will react to it so they decide to just keep their hand down. Alternately, people may have high levels of self-confidence and belief in their personal abilities, but also have poor levels of self-esteem from having their heart broken in a failed relationship or from trust issues that developed after being double-crossed by a friend or a co-worker.

Why Are These Traits So Important for Men & Women to Embrace, Develop & Strengthen?

As different as they can be, there are also plenty of situations and experiences that can be caused by interconnected levels of self-esteem and confidence. The more understanding, experienced and control a person has over their personal self-esteem and confidence levels, the better off they will be in all opportunities they attempt or goals they strive for throughout their life.

Strengthening these traits not only helps with improving a person's overall mental, psychological and emotional health, but it also comes with a variety of other benefits that can help improve someone's personal health and wellness in a wide range of styles.

The Many Benefits of Building Self-Esteem & Confidence

Even for those who are happy with their control over their habitual overthinking and procrastination, there are an endless number of reasons to keep focused on and motivated to work on for anyone and everyone building self-esteem and confidence levels. Here is a look at some of the most popular and widely reported benefits people have experienced in their quests for higher self-esteem and confidence!

- Those with higher self-esteem and personal confidence are less likely to be people pleasers or develop people pleasing habits than those with lower opinions of themselves or their abilities
- They also tend to have better performance ratings and higher success rates in leadership roles
  - Not only are they more personable with customers or other audiences, but they are also

more empathetic with employers or co-workers and better able to boost morale during times of high demand or increased stress levels

- They are also more likely to have higher success rates with setting and reaching personal and professional goals because they are more self-aware of their mental, psychological an emotional changes and how it affects their daily performance

- Those with higher self-esteem and confidence levels report more personal and professional satisfaction throughout the course of their lives

  o They are more likely to take up opportunities when offered

  o They also tend to be bolder and more dominant in their professional teams and social circles as they are more likely to openly share their opinions and start conversations with even those they do not know with more confidence than those who question themselves and hesitate around others

These are just a handful of the benefits that study and research subjects of all ages and lifestyles have reported when tracked over time and throughout the course of their personal improvement journey! Each person will find a whole new array of benefits and progress markers that are specialized and more tailored to their individual needs based on the techniques they choose to put into practice, how dedicated they are able to remain to their self-improvement plan and of course, what specific issues and concerns that are working to improve or eliminate.

How to Get Started with Building Self-Esteem & Confidence Levels

Like with developing any new positive habits to replace the damaging negative ones, the first step to getting started revolves around a person's self-awareness of their thoughts and emotions. The first thing anyone should do when trying to build their self-confidence and self-esteem is to take a look at their points of strength and points of concern. The following is an example of a self-awareness exercise that many people have reported progress with during their own quests for higher self-esteem.

A Self-Awareness Exercise: Get to Know Yourself & Your Restrictions

This self-awareness exercise is one f the most basic, one of the most widely used and one of the most effective, proven techniques for anyone trying to get a better idea of their personal highs and points where they may want to work on improving in order to make the most of their personal potential.

- Set aside a time where you can clear your mind and focus on the concerns at hand
    - Make sure to deal with any potential distractions such as silencing your cell phone and turning off your television, perhaps even closing the door to the room you are going to be contemplating in so that you are not interrupted by anyone else in the building
- Lay out a clean piece of paper and get the kind of pens that you when working on organizational thinking
    - For some, they may just use a basic blue or black pen for anything they need to write, but when it comes to organization, some people prefer multiple colors or types of tips to choose from in order to separate different thoughts, ideas or options into color-coded or differently shaped areas
- Make a list of your strengths
    - This can be emotional strengths like being able to remain calm in high stress situations or always responding to friends and family the same day they message you
    - This can be professional strengths like mastering a certain skill or getting recognition for something you accomplished in your department

o   This can be personal strengths like organization and discipline, anything that you take pride in and use on a regular basis

- Now flip the paper over or draw a line to separate your lists and make a list of your weaker points or skills that you want to develop and master

o   Again, these points can be emotional like a tendency to breakdown when challenges arise in your personal or professional life

o   They can be professional points of concern like wanting to be better at communicating with customers or being bolder when it comes to discussing a promotion with your employer

o   They can also be personal, like a bad habit snapping at people who speak to you early in the morning or late in the day

- You do not have to make lists!

o   Some people find that this exercise works better when they form connecting circles of related thoughts or pie charts of strengths, weaknesses and action plans

o   The point is not to force your mind to start thinking in lists, but rather to find a way to organize your thoughts related to personal strengths, weaknesses and goals for self-improvement

Why This Exercise Works: This exercise has proven so effective for a variety of different personality types and characters because it can be tailored to work for any individual's particular way of thinking. Unlike most of the exercises and methods for overcoming negative psychological habits, this exercise does not require the person involved to change their mind or their thought processes, but rather can be altered and specialized in order to work best for their particular way of organizing their thoughts.

Who This Exercise Works Best For: Thanks to its ability to be altered and shaped to be an effective tool for nearly anybody, this exercise and those who strongly support its benefits can easily claim to work best for anyone who is willing to give it a try. Those who have been searching for a way to better understand themselves and learn about where their personal restrictions come from will also find this exercise to be a powerful tool. Mainly, anyone who is hoping to expand their self-awareness and be honest with themselves about points of weakness they fear or try to ignore will find this exercise to be not only helpful and informational, but illuminating and even may serve as a source of inspiration for those who have been trying to get motivated into self-improvement for some time without success.

Confidence Building Tip: Fake It Until You Make It

Often associated with Hollywood movie stars, this quote, *fake it until you make it*, is another popular saying that is being shared around social media support groups and self-improvement classes around the world. The basic meaning of this phrase is that if someone wants to build their confidence, all they need to do is project an air of confidence in everything they do, or pretend to be more confident than they feel when confronted and in time, this will become habit. Once someone is in the habit of pretending to be confident, this practice becomes their instinct and begins to feel natural in situations where the individual has been practicing their self-confidence building skills through faking it until they make it.

There are some people who do not like talking about building their confidence or projecting an air of confidence whenever they tackle a challenge! It makes them feel selfish and desperate for attention due to negative experiences with being open about their lack of confidence with others (most likely toxic people) in the past. For other individuals, they avoid the subject because they have learned to connect self-confidence with arrogance or other negative emotions that people feel around those people that make confidence seem like a negative quality.

Habitual overconfidence is one of the biggest causes of these negative attachments. Overconfidence is an unhealthy emotion based in delusion where someone is bold, arrogant and sometimes even aggressive in voicing their opinions despite not having any knowledge or experience with a topic. Self-confidence is not the same thing for those who struggle with this concern. Self-confidence is based on a person's view of their own abilities and how much trust they have in them. It has nothing to do with negativity or delusional behaviors and actions that affect other people and their opinion of a person.

Check Who Is Around You: Surround Yourself with Positive People

"Toxic person" is a popular phrase in virtual circles with people who are taking a step back to take a wider and more detailed view of their life and the people they come in contact with each day. Someone who is described as *toxic* is typically someone who, through their behaviors, opinions or actions, is having a negative effect on the people around them.

- They could be someone who pretends to be the individual's friend only to take advantage of them without gratitude or to the point of harming them
- They could be someone who smiles in front of people only to speak negatively about them or making up falsehoods about them when their back is turned

- They could be someone who criticizes their friends whenever they are having a bad day so that the people around them are always feeling as badly as they are

How to Identify A Toxic Connection or Relationship

The first step to breaking out of any toxic relationship is to identify the signs around you, acknowledge and then accept them as a truth that is negative to your health and needs to be amended. Everyone's relationships are different, but here is a closer look at some of the most common signs connection to toxic relationships:

- Emotional manipulation is one sign that is prominent in any kind of toxic relationship or connection
  - The definition of this symptom varies because it can include a wide range of actions and behaviors that vary from case to case
  - At its core though, emotional manipulation refers to the intentional alteration of behaviors or way of speaking in order to avoid or manage the emotions of someone else
    - In the case of the toxic person, this can refer to an intentional intensification of tense emotions and responses when their friend or partner is talking in order to get

them to leave the room or feel powerless in their current situation

- In the case of the victim, they know that when their friend or partner is in this mood that their tense emotions will only intensify if they try to talk to them so instead they intentionally find something to do in a different room to avoid talking to their friend or partner until they are in a better headspace

- Isolating oneself from other close connections with family or friends to spend more time with their toxic friend or partner

  o In many cases, this isolation is directly linked to and even the result of their friends and family seeing the way their loved one has changed in this relationship or connection and confronted them about it

  o This confrontation is seen as an act of aggression by the individual and they get defensive, siding with their toxic friend or partner and hindering their relationship with their supportive loved one

- Being dismissed as overly emotional or overreacting to things whenever you voice your feelings or opinions (particularly if they are counter to the toxic friend or partner)

- In some cases, the individual is not dismissed but rather teased and ridiculed making them feel even worse about speaking their mind
- They can be accused of imaging problems that do not exist if there is an issue the toxic friend or partner does not want to deal with
- Some toxic partners might try to make the individual feel selfish or guilty if their thoughts, opinions or desires are centered around anything they need or want

- A variety of controlling behaviors have been associated with toxic relationships and connections
  - Calling a person names and speaking with a sarcastic tone in situations where it is inappropriate or hurtful
  - Endless and harmful criticism that is meant to damage their self-esteem and confidence so that they are easier to control and manipulate
  - Using intimidation and fear tactics when the person becomes too bold or exploratory for their liking
  - Blaming the person from things they had no control over or were not even connected to and throwing out unnecessary accusations in an attempt to make their partner feel guilty about something that may not even have happened

Whatever the specifics are with toxic people, they are unhealthy influences on men and women of any age or profession. The more toxic people that are around and the longer or more connected their relationship with the individual becomes, the more power and negative influence they will have on the person. These types of relationships are often neglectful and even dangerous, and they can be some of the most difficult to break free from.

Tips & Techniques for Shaking Toxic Relationships from Your Life

It is not something that everyone gets experience with or training for early in life, but most people find themselves with at least one toxic connection throughout their adult life. This may be with a friend or co-worker, with a family member or with a romantic partner, but regardless of the specifics and the intensity, every person needs to remember that they deserve better and that as hard as at may be to cut ties, the rewards will be well-worth the effort. One thing that people who are free of toxic connections have in common is higher levels of confidence and self-esteem than those who do not have the self-awareness, knowledge, support or motivation to end toxic relationships before they take their negative tolls.

Here is a closer look at some tips, tricks and techniques from those who have successfully ended toxic connections and wanted to share their experience in order to help others do the same:

- Focus on how you need to do in order to not be as dependent on the toxic friend or partner
  - Do you need to build your self-esteem and confidence before confronting the person?
  - Should you confront the toxic friend or partner, or would it be better to just leave?
- What do you need in order to successfully end this relationship or connection without guilt or excessive stress?
  - Do you need to save up some money in order to move your things or find a place of your own?
  - Do you need to have someone come stay with you to help with emotional support and strength?
- Do not get distracted by each and every step you need to take
  - While it is important to know what you need to do in order to make an effective plan of action, getting hooked on every little detail can serve to only increase a person's stress levels and hold them back from reaching their freedom

- Instead, people trying to rid themselves of toxic relationships and connections should focus on their solution and their goals in order to keep themselves motivated and looking toward the future when things start to get tough

For those who have been able to break free from their toxic friendships and other connections, the next step is to fill that void left in your social life with positive influences, new friends and relationships that will help to strengthen your emotional control, self-awareness and self-esteem over time. We have already spoken about the importance of building a supportive network of people who you trust and respect the opinion of who are willing to help you on your quest for self-improvement. This advice, above all other recommendations and tips, is repeated and shared the most by those who with experience in identifying toxic people and clearing them from their lives.

Improve Your Own Self-Esteem by Helping Others Build Their Own

One positive habit people trying to improve their self-esteem and overall confidence levels like to talk about is the practice of improving their own mood, attitude and emotional status by helping others feel better about themselves. The reason for this is simple: Spread positivity and it spreads like fire! Positivity, positive comments and vibrant emotions are all just as contagious as negativity can be, it is just a matter of people being able to embrace it, even on difficult or painful days, and share with the people you come in contact with. There are any number of ways to accomplish this as well, so that anyone can find a way that works for them and their personality type!

- Set a goal to hand out three to five compliments to other people every day
    - Not only does this make the people you come into contact with smile and feel better about themselves, but it also helps improve the individual's confidence by encouraging conversations throughout the day that they may not have attempted if they did not have a goal they were trying to meet
    - With practice and over time, this technique becomes habit and individuals find that they are viewing the whole world around them in a more positive light and feeling better about themselves and others in general

- Set a goal to hand out three to five compliments to yourself every day
    - As important as it is to help others feel better (both for their personal self-esteem growth

and your own) it is also important to start looking at yourself in a positive light

    o   By picking out three to five things each day that you are proud of yourself for or that you are pleased with about your appearance, behaviors or interactions, you are directly boosting your own self-esteem and confidence

    o   Being more positive to yourself also makes it easier to feel more confident in social situations where an individual may have previously had difficulty becoming active or connecting with others

- Do you love cooking or baking? Surprise your friends, family or co-workers with a new recipe you have been meaning to try but may not have had the opportunity!

    o   Not only is this a chance to make others smile, but it also provides a fun opportunity to reach a goal you have perhaps been procrastinating in a way that boosts both your confidence and the positive mood of the people around you

    o   This also provides an opportunity to open lines of conversation with people that you may have been wanting to speak with but have not been sure how to approach

- Acknowledge other people's accomplishments
  - o Not everyone likes attention when they reach a goal or are successful in some excursion, but most people feel better about themselves and their efforts if they know others have recognized and appreciated their efforts

- Plan a fun activity with friends, family or co-workers and help everyone let loose!
  - o Maybe it is a day of mini golf with your siblings or a movie day with the people from work, as long as it is something that gets people out of their familiar surroundings for a period of time and gets them doing something out of their ordinary routine
  - o It does not have to be expensive or even cost anything
    - ▪ A picnic day at the local park or group walk at a local trail are also good ideas for those who want to plan something but are not sure about the budgets of their friends, family or co-workers

- Volunteer to be a mentor, a counselor or a teacher to kids, men and women who need them in your community o   If you have a special skill or are even just a good listener, there are plenty of community programs that provide volunteers the opportunity to connect with underprivileged individuals in their community

o   Sometimes there are coaching opportunities or community centers that need art teachers for local classes

o   It all comes down to reaching out and finding your niche!

Invest in A Journal & Create A Record of All of Your Forward Progress

Many adults who did not keep journals in their youth picture journals as something that high schoolers empty all of their emotional poems, secret crush information and angry doodles in. Those who did actually get into the habit of keeping a journal in their adolescence or even starting at a younger age may already still keep one as an adult, but if not, they are already aware of the benefits they carry on dealing with intense emotions, developing fears and painful doubts.

They do not only keep a record of negative thoughts, feelings and emotions but also the moments of pride, happy events that became positive memories, new achievements and detailed hopes or dreams for the future. The best part about looking back on all of the entries and the comments they contain is that the individual can trust that these are their truest and most honest comments. They can be certain of this because they know that they are writing each time they open their journal in thoughts and emotions that they will never have to worry about explaining to anyone else.

Here is a closer look at some of the most influential benefits men and women of all ages can take advantage of by building the habit of entering their thoughts, feelings, concerns and goals into a journal at regular intervals such as every night before bed or each morning while they are drinking their coffee, or even every other day if this is an easier schedule for them to keep and habit for them to develop.

Pro Tip: Journals are also a great place to practice the three to five compliments to yourself each day! That way you not only have a record of negative and positive fluctuations each day, but you can also look back at your previous entries or look forward to each regular entry because you know each one has at least three positive statements to help boost your self-esteem a little more every time you open the journal.

The Benefits of Keeping A Journal in Adulthood

- Keeping a journal helps adults (particularly those with difficulty expressing with or processing emotions) expand their emotional intelligence
  - One way this happens is by creating a consistent record of how their emotions have changed in the time they have been keeping the journal that the individual can look back on and learn from
  - Journals create a record of events, notable emotions or interactions, accomplishments and major regrets (all kinds of major factors that can affect how a person is feeling and controlling their thoughts, emotions and behaviors)
- Men and women who grow accustomed to honestly sharing their thoughts in written form are more confident in opening up about their thoughts and feelings in daily conversation
- Journaling has proven an effective method for people looking for ways to organize their thoughts when they fall victim to their habitual overthinking or getting themselves motivated when procrastination habits take over
  - The main reason behind this is that writing out their thoughts or concerns helps individuals to

calm themselves down to a point where their rational thoughts are able to take over for in controlling their behaviors, decisions and actions than their emotional impulses or psychological habits

- People who journal about their fears and weaknesses, strengths and hopes, and actions or reactions in their present situations are better at seeing the Big Picture in any situation they need to
  - This is a valuable character skill that is common in those who hold leadership roles
  - These people also work better in group situations and have more open minds than the people around them who are less empathetic or willing to accept the flaws and shortcomings of themselves, their friends, family or co-workers
- Those who journal become more confident in how they speak and how they express themselves to others
  - This is why keeping a journal is one of the most recommended and respected practices in use for those who are hoping to improve their communication skills
- Journaling can help to strengthen and even speed up the emotional healing process
  - Many people have difficulty expressing their deepest thoughts and feelings with others even when it would b the best thing for them

o   After traumas like surviving a car crash or being in some other kind of serious accident

o   Losing someone you love or being betrayed by someone you trusted

o   Nearly any kind of event that leaves a psychological, emotional or even physical mark or scar can increase their chances of healing in a timely manner and without permanent damage when the individual does not bottle up their emotions

o   If someone does not want to share their emotions openly with people around them, then keeping a journal can help with the processing of painful or harmful emotions and help with seeing progress made over time for those situations, accidents or traumatic events that may take more than a few months to a year to overcome

Be creative, always ask questions and never stop exploring! Even if these techniques are not suited for you, there is always a way to boost your self-esteem and confidence levels so that you reach your full potential and achieve inner peace throughout the course of your life. Reach out to others either by sharing your feelings throughout your process and quest or by sharing your successes and struggles after you have seen a noticeable change. Everyone has their private concerns and worries, and you never know who you may inspire to start bettering themselves and their lives after hearing how you have been working so hard to improve yours!

Chapter 7: Moving Forward & Staying Strong in the Face of Every Challenge

You have now read through and collected some of the most productive, effective and widely respect information available on overthinking, procrastination and everything that can cause or enflame them in men and women of all ages! Armed with all this knowledge, you hopefully now have everything you need in order to conquer your negative psychological habits, build new positive ones and start moving toward a successful life path that is full of satisfaction and self-respect.

In this final chapter, we will cover some proven and well-practiced next steps that readers can take if they find themselves getting stuck, needing motivation, still seeking answers to some specifics they have experienced that may not have been covered in our thorough and informative guide, or run into any other kind of trouble! Never forget that whenever you are in doubt or having a difficult time:

- This situation, your feelings towards it and how it is affecting you is temporary
  - Take a step back, take a deep breath and use your self-awareness skills to get a better picture of the specifics and requirements connected to the situation

- Get out and get some fresh air

  o Get your blood moving and soon your mood and emotional state will improve right behind it!

  o Remember that changing your current surroundings provides fresh perspective and can help with clearing your thoughts

- Call up your friends and make some plans!

  o Many times, overthinkers and procrastinators have lost their social connections and personal relationships to their psychological compulsions

  o Sometimes one of the best ways to encourage yourself to keep moving forward or to get back in the right mindset to keep progressing is to just swallow your fears and anxieties and reach out to the people you love

  o Those who reach back are often the best people for your network of support as they already have some kind of affection or even just conversational connection with you and are happy to reconnect

  o Do not let yourself get concerned about those who do not reach back after you make the first move! Just sending the first message or asking others to get involved with some social plans is a huge step to overcoming habitual overthinking and procrastination

Looking for more options or actions? Keep reading for more exercises and recommendations on how to gain control of your negative habits and become happier and more confident in yourself and your mind!

Don't Let Others Determine How You View Yourself

This issue is often directly connected to a person's level of self-esteem. How high someone's self-esteem levels may or may not be is directly connected to how positively a person sees themselves and their emotions toward their behaviors, thoughts and actions. One of the most popular quotes currently circling self-improvement groups on virtually every social media site is:

- What anyone else thinks about you is none of your business
  - o The purpose of this quote is not to make anyone feel worse about themselves or about how they perceive how others see them
  - o Rather, its purpose and full intent is to provide people with a way to remind themselves when they start to worry about what people around them are thinking that they are better off letting it

go and turning their attention to more positive and productive thoughts

    o   This is where those skills, methods and techniques that the person is putting into practice become their most powerful tools for building self-esteem and confidence levels

Those who seek the approval and affection of everyone they meet will never find their true happiness or be able to gain any control over their psychological habits. The main reason for this is that people who are constantly letting the opinion of others affect how they speak or behave never find their true selves as they constantly change to please the people around them.

Find ways to change the way your mind is thinking and practice those skills and techniques that focus on seeing things more positively and optimistically. Focus on activities that clear your mind, balance your emotions and make you more aware of who you are and what you want for yourself. This is the only way to enjoy some inner peace and live more in the moment, instead of in memory and regret or hypothetical scenarios.

Never Accept Failure & Always Plan for Success

Make changing the way your mind works to see the challenges you face and the people you encounter, even your own mind and actions, in a more positive light. That positivity, no matter where in your life it needs to be strengthened, exercised and practiced, comes with so many encouraging and inspiring benefits (mentally, emotionally, psychologically and physically as we've discussed in previous chapters) and those benefits all serve to help people reach their goals and achieve success!

Even in those situations when you are struggling to come up with a plan of action or get motivated to get moving toward a resolution, if you start your thought process under the assumption that you are going to succeed then your chances of success are already higher than they would have been if negative psychological habits like overthinking and procrastination were allowed to take over and become dominant in the brain.

This goes back to the technique of faking it until you make it, or basically if you believe that you can do it you will be able to as long as you take action. The more you practice this technique, the more habitual it will become until it replaces overthinking and procrastination habits as your compulsion in times of stress or overwhelming responsibility.

There will be times that you stumble and times that you fall. There will be tasks where you are forced to ask for help or may cave to procrastination habits due to a lack of knowledge and help or a desire to avoid a stressful situation. The trick to mastering discipline and reaching your ultimate success goals is not to keep yourself from ever falling, but rather to never accept that failing as the peak of your abilities or potential. Instead, achieving success is about giving up the quest for perfection by understanding that everyone (including you) makes mistakes throughout the course of their life and always picking yourself back up when you are down, falling or hitting the ground.

If You Cannot Make A Solid Decision, Don't Be Afraid to Play Devil's Advocate with Yourself

Devil's Advocate is a hypothetical exercise that has a long history of use and success, particularly in political, judgment matters and throughout the business world. Often sold as a strategic thinking exercise, the purpose of Devil's Advocate is to teach the user how to see opposing viewpoints to their main point or opinion.

Before Devil's Advocate can be an effective tool for forming and developing strategic thinking skills and strengthening one's own arguments or theories, the person must first be strong in their understanding and development of their own thoughts and opinions on the topic. Without that certainty and confidence, there is no way someone will be able to defend their opinion or idea against someone who is questioning them (even is that someone is themselves).

How to play Devil's Advocate:

1. Know your thought, opinion or argument with total confidence

    - Use whatever organization techniques that work for you until you are certain that your piece can stan up to criticism

2. Lay out your information as if you were your target audience

    - This can be done literally by laying out note cards or showing posters or graphs that have been created for the presentation or argument
    - This can also be done by simply performing your sales pitch or argument in a mirror so that you can gain experience in delivering it to an audience while also presenting it as if a member of that audience

3. Once that is done, take a step back and clear your mind

    - Try to look at your notes or graphics objectively

- If you find yourself unable to look objectively at one aspect, look at your notes or presentation again and start asking "why?" every time you go back over a point

4. Question everything, even if you already know the answer (especially if you know the answer)

- The purpose of this exercise is to search for weaknesses or flaws in an argument or presentation in order to fix them before the event itself, thereby strengthening your stance and your delivery before anyone else ever even sees it!

Why This Exercise Works: This exercise works by opening the individual's mind to other possibilities or alternatives that they could not see or were unwilling to see from their original thought process or stance.

One of the main benefits that come with practicing this exercise is that it helps with building decision-making skills for those who have difficulty with anxiety or overcoming their compulsive behaviors. By practicing their ability to see anything from the opposite or even a more neutral point of view, people who regularly play Devil's Advocate have been proven to be more empathic in their interactions with others, more driven in their professional exploits and as having higher confidence and self-esteem because they are more confident in their thoughts, ideas, behaviors and actions.

Who This Exercise Works Best For: This is a popular exercise for anyone who is looking learn how to think more strategically for work or other activities where they find their thoughts limited or their ideas sluggish. Those who have to deliver sales pitches or present arguments also develop their argument and defense skills with exercises like Devil's Advocate as a way of strengthening any weak points in their pitches or arguments by putting themselves in the same mental status their customer, employer or argument rival.

Eat Right & Exercise: Turn Your Attention to Improving Your Physical Health

One of the steps people can take to feeling better about themselves and feeling more in control of their lives is to take responsibility for their physical health. For some people, this could be as simple as giving up sweets after dinner to get started but for others it may require more intense changes that could mean altering their behaviors and lifestyle. There are a number of factors that can determine what kind of changes a person needs to make in order to improve their physical health to improve their mental, emotional and psychological health for the better:

- When was the last time you went for a physical with your primary care doctor?

  o Going for an annual check-up is something that all adults should make a priority, particularly those getting closer to their middle age years when many people begin to develop health concerns related to their heart, brain and body weight

- How often do you exercise? How regularly?

  o Most doctors recommend a regular exercising routine of 45 minutes to an hour, two to three times a week at minimum to build a healthy habit and maintain a healthy physical form

  o The frequency and time frames for exercising windows should be determined by the intensity of the exercise chosen and how well the individual is able to stay dedicated to the long-term exercise plan and goals they create

- What kind of physical activity are you doing?

  o Is it something that gets your heart pumping and keeps your body temperature higher than normal for a healthy amount of time to burn calories such as running or going for a ride on a bicycle?

o Or is it something like yoga that does not always affect a person's heart rate, but rather focuses on muscle strengthening, emotional control and balance?

Are you already exercising? Maybe it is time to look into changing your diet to improve your physical health by improving the quality or type of food you are putting in your body!

- Do you need to lose weight in order to reach a healthy goal set by you and your doctor for your age, height and personal health status?
  o Look for a diet that encourages calorie burning foods that are high in vitamins, or lower calorie foods that do not have as much fat or processed ingredients
  o Find a diet that is higher in protein and lower in carbohydrates to reduce your calorie intake that way

- Are you unsure of what kind of diet is best for your body type or health conditions?
  o While there is plenty of information available about questions like these, the best bet for those who are worried about their health or have an existing health condition of any kind is to

talk with their primary health care physician or make an appointment with a dietitian or nutritionist

- Give up the fake stuff and try the organic lifestyle!
  - Organic does not have to mean expensive or difficult to find
  - Fake ingredients such as processed foods and those that are packed with chemicals to ensure they can stay fresh until the end of times are not healthy options for those that are wanting to improve their diet to improve their emotional health
  - Chemical byproducts and similar ingredients have been connected to a rise in depression, anxiety, anti-social tendencies and other psychological conditions in men and women of all ages
  - Try basing your meals around what is fresh and in season in your area!

If All Else Fails, Seek Professional Help & Support!

It all goes back to not being afraid to or uncomfortable with asking for help when you need it. If you have tried and tried a variety of different methods, tip and tricks over a respectable amount of time without any forward progress or success, your best bet may be to seek out the help of a counselor or even a medically registered therapist. While some people can get control over their psychological, mental and emotional health by improving certain personality traits or thought processes, there are also a large number of people who do not start to see their largest amount of improvement until they break through their fears and anxieties around going to the doctor and seek out the help of a trained professional.

- A good first place to start (for those who are unfamiliar with medical experts or do not have any standing relationships with any kind of healthcare professionals) is to find a general healthcare practitioner, often known as a primary care or family care doctor, that you can speak to about your questions and concerns

- A primary care doctor can perform a general physical to check your overall health and also answer questions about any emotional or psychological concerns you may be facing
  - o Always remember that the more open and honest you are with your doctors (even if you feel embarrassed at first), the better, more efficiently and more quickly they will be able to help you find answers and solutions

o Never worry about being embarrassed when talking to any kind of medical or healthcare professional! Most likely they already have experience with just about anything you can think, with the exception being the more bizarre or extreme cases. Even then, doctors love hearing about cases they have not yet faced. Like with most professionals, doctors learn best and expand their knowledge most effectively through experience.

• If your primary care doctor does not have the experience or training necessary for your particular needs and questions, they will be able to recommend you to other healthcare professionals in specialized areas such as psychologists to help with emotional issues or specialists in specific parts of the body for those who have physical issues that need the addressing of an expert.

Each person has their own unique struggles and that means that sometimes a technique or plan that works for one person will not work for someone else, even if their issues or concerns are similar. Never be afraid to seek out more answers when you run into trials or challenges throughout your personal journey to self-improvement! Whether that means trying new things or researching new opinions, theories and techniques that are appearing online each day as more and more psychological experts and medical professionals take an interest in habitual psychological compulsions, their dangers and how each kind of personality type or situational stress victim can best learn to overcome those impulses like overthinking and procrastination in order to improve their personal, private and professional lives.

Conclusion

We sincerely hope that with this guide you were able to collect the skills you need in order to overcome your negative and damaging psychological habits like overthinking and procrastination, in favor of positive and beneficial habits that:

- Are emotionally strengthening for better control over emotional reactions

- Are encouraging and motivating during times of great stress or emotional turmoil

- Improve your ability to access and take action with rational thoughts and plans that are based on logical and calm contemplation instead of being impulsive or poorly prepared

- Inspire positive changes, effects and actions like increased physical activity, better psychological understanding and increased emotional intelligence

From this point, the next step for readers is to take what they have learned with this guide and make an action plan that is tailored to their individual needs and built towards their personal goals. Whether you are wanting to overcome overthinking, become more productive or just find a way to be more confident in your own thoughts, words and skills, this guide hopefully delivered to information you needed to get started and provided plenty of options for how to take the information from the thought stage into productive action! Whatever your personal goals may be, we hope that you found the tools you need in order to make a positive change in your life with *Overthinking: The Fast Cure for Women and Men Who Think Too Much and Want to Stop Procrastinating.*

COVERT MANIPULATION

An Introducing Psychology Guide for Beginners – How to Perform Mind Control to Win Friends, to Analyze & Influence People Learning Persuasion Techniques & Reading Body Language

Introduction to Covert Manipulation

Every day, almost everyone engages in the act of manipulation, and downloading this book is a good step into having a clear understanding of the world of manipulation. Usually, it is difficult for you to know if someone is manipulating you since manipulators use various tactics to conceal their evil actions. In this book, you will see multiple examples of manipulation and how manipulators use their tactics to win and confuse their victims. Ultimately, this book takes a step further to analyze languages manipulators use and how you can catch them in their games. To this end, some of the chapters in this book will discuss mind games, mind control, and brainwashing. These are some of the weapons manipulators used to control their victims.

The book shows the manners in which manipulators use them, what everyone needs to watch out for, and also how not to fall into their traps. Reading about these tactics is one thing, but having a glimpse into some practical examples is another. And this is where some of the chapters in this book become quite useful.

You will learn from different models and come away to have a firm grasp as to what to watch out for, so you don't fall a victim. With a clear perception of these tactics out of the way, this book will discuss some ways you can win friends and also influence people with some simple yet powerful practical examples. It will go deeper into the art of winning people to your side and how you can ignite your super senses through the art of reading people.

Chapter 1: What is Manipulation

Manipulation is when you ignore feelings of others, and at the same time, harms their desire to get what you want, similar to applying indirect tactics to control behavior, relationships, and emotions. Manipulators operate by using persuasion, charm, coax, misdirection, and trickery. Fooling people to force them to give them what they want is the underlying idea of every manipulation. Even when caught up in their scheme, manipulators tend to imagine they are doing their victim a favor. When you are not listening to others, disregard their desires, or pretend as if your desires cost nobody else a price, you may find yourself falling into this behavior.

And what about external signs? The presence of a manipulator has a strain, tension, conflicts, and complaints to a situation. Some utilize passive manipulations, employing a 'poor me' scenarios to entice pity and sympathy out of people. For other manipulators, their scheme is laying subtle guilt trips to make others think that what they want is wrong.

For people that engage in periodic manipulation, they tend to tell an acquaintance they feel 'fine' when they are depressed. Technically, this is a form of manipulation since it controls their partner's perceptions of and reactions to them. Particularly in intimate relationships, there is a connection with emotional abuse with some of the insidious consequences of manipulation. When it harms the physical, mental, and emotional health of the victims of manipulation, most people have a negative perception of manipulation. Manipulation is not close to being a healthy behavior, though an impulse that most times stems from profound anxiety and fear, manipulators engage in the act since they desire to control anyone or anything around them. People may find it difficult to bond with their genuine self when they engage in manipulation and others that experience manipulation can go through various poor health.

Why People Manipulate

There are several reasons why people choose to manipulate others. These reasons can vary based on the individual. For some people, they engage in manipulation at times. However, others that primarily interact with manipulation often share some characteristics among themselves. Some of these traits include:

- Fear of being abandoned
- Feelings of hopelessness, helplessness, or worthiness
- Need to raise self-esteem
- Need for control and power over others
- Willingness to put their emotions over the well-being of others

Mental Health Effect of Manipulation

When people overlook it, manipulation can result in weak mental health consequences for the people who encounter manipulation. In an intimate relationship, constant manipulation can also lead to emotional abuse taking place, which in some cases, can have a similar effect to trauma, especially when the victim of manipulation is made to feel ashamed or guilty.

Victims of chronic manipulation may:

- Have depression
- Develop anxiety
- Develop unhealthy coping patterns
- Regularly attempting to please the manipulative partner
- Lie about their feelings
- Put the needs of another person before theirs
- Find it hard to trust others

In some situations, the height of manipulation can be so pervasive that the victim may question their perception of reality. A perfect example is the classic movie *Gaslight*, where the husband of a woman subtly manipulates her until she no longer trusts her opinions.

Manipulation in Relationships

In close relationships such as those between friends, family members, and romantic partners, long-term manipulation can have severe effects. Through manipulation, the health of a relationship can deteriorate, leading to the poor mental health of those in the affair or perhaps the termination of the relationship. In partnership or marriage, manipulation can make a spouse to feel isolated, bullied, or unworthy. Even in healthy relationships, a partner can unconsciously manipulate the other to avoid confrontation or even in an attempt to keep their partner from feeling burdened. Some individuals may even know they are being manipulated in their relationship and choose to downplay or overlook it. In a close relationship, manipulation can take various shapes, including guilt, exaggeration, selectively showing affection or gift-giving, passive aggression, and secret-keeping. For some parents that manipulate their children, they are setting them up for depression, guilt, eating issues, anxiety, and other mental health issues.

In a study, parents who continuously use manipulation tactics on their children may strengthen the possibility of their children using manipulative behavior. Hints of manipulation in the parent-child relationship may consist of downplaying the achievements of a child, lack of accountability from a parent, making the child feel culpable, and a necessity for the parent to involve themselves with various phases of the child's life. Also, others can feel someone manipulates them when they are in a toxic friendship. Manipulative friendship is when an individual uses the other person to achieve their desires without any care of their friend's feelings. Such manipulative friend will use coercion or guilt to extort approvals, including getting loans, or reaching out to that friend during emotional needs and tend to find an excuse when their friend has requests from them.

Examples of Manipulative Behavior

Occasionally, people may manipulate others without having any knowledge of their deed, while some may actively make an effort to fortify their manipulative tactics. Here are some examples of manipulative behaviors:

- Implicit threats
- Withholding information
- Dishonesty
- Gaslighting
- Isolating someone from their close friends and family members
- Passive-aggressive behavior
- Using sex to achieve goals
- Verbal abuse

Also, manipulators use several tactics to control their victims. Most times, however, they target specific characters. Doing so will make it easy for them to manipulate such individual, and particular vulnerability in someone can lead them to manipulation. It may be possible for someone to become an easy mark of manipulator if they are naïve, lack an assertive native, have little confidence, easy to please, and have no confidence in themselves.

Some of the common techniques manipulators use includes:

Not giving the entire account

This scenario is far from being economical with the truth as a manipulator will always hold a crucial part of the narrative to themselves to place their target at a difficult spot.

Lying

On practically anything in their life, manipulators are always lying. They engage in this act to confuse their victim and wrong-foot them. Since they have no qualms about it, lying is one of the techniques manipulators use.

Devaluation and love-bombing

One of the manipulation tactics of the narcissists is love bombing. Manipulators use this technique to operate on a charm offensive, prevail on their victim, and hook them into thinking that the relationship is the best. Then, they will drop them like a pack of dirty cards without reason.

Constant mood swings

One handy tool of the manipulator is when their partner never knows what mood they are going to be when they get home and trying to figure out whether they will be happy or angry. This condition keeps their victim off balance and makes them more malleable.

Denial

Most times, the secure method a manipulator will use to carry out their work on their victim is by denying the offense their target accused them of ever happening.

Punishment

Manipulation can include anything from shouting, nagging, physical violence, silent treatment, and mental abuse.

Minimizing

Most times, manipulators shift the blame on their victim for overreacting by trying to gloss over their deeds as not damaging or critical, thus, turning the guilt of overplaying the issue on their victims.

Targeting the victim

Sometimes, the manipulator puts accusations on their victims for the offense. Manipulators are making their prey defend themselves while they have the upper hand of covering up their manipulation techniques. Consequently, the concentration is not on the accuser, but on the victim.

Diversion

Typical way manipulators take on their victims is to divert the discussion away from their acts and move the dialogue onto a separate matter.

Guilt-tripping

Most times, a manipulator will guilt-trip their partner by telling their victim that they are selfish and doesn't care about them or their life is easy. Doing so will aid confusion and anxiety for their victim.

Flattery

A usual manipulator will use praise, charm, or smooth-talk the partner to gain the trust of that person. Logically, the victim is glad to get such respects. However, by doing so, they unconsciously lower their guard.

Excessive aggression

Most times, manipulators make use of aggression and rage to appall their target to admit defeat.

Also, the anger is a device to extinguish any further discussion on the matter as the victim is nervous, nevertheless concentrated by now on holding back the annoyance instead of the original issue.

Emotional and Psychological Effects of Manipulation

It is most likely for people to see the effects when someone sexually or physically abuses another person. However, this case is not the same when it comes to mental and emotional abuse. The scars are not physical, but they can affect the abused person for the rest of their life, particularly for those that refuse to seek help from a professional. Ultimately, mental manipulation can result in problems with trust, intimacy, security, and respect. There are long and short term effects when it comes to emotional manipulation which we treat below.

Short-Term Effects

1. Confusion and surprise – feeling like whatever is happening cannot possibly right as the victim wonders why the person that has been a friend or loved one is now acting like a stranger.

2. Self-questioning – the victim may wonder if they quite remember things right or if something is wrong with them. This situation is the consequence of the manipulators questioning everything the victim does, or

the manipulators telling them that they have the wrong perspectives, and the manipulative party is right.

3.	Vigilance and anxiety – for the victim to prevent the future case of manipulation, they may become hyper-vigilant toward themselves and perhaps others. They will attempt to avoid behaviors that might rock the boat, or looking for a reaction in other people that point toward an outburst.

4.	Being passive – since taking action may lead to more pain in an emotionally abusive relationship, being passive can become the default. This case is something that can be difficult to do when the victim is in a situation as stressful as they can be.

5.	Guilt and shame – the victim may blame themselves or find themselves feeling guilty of setting off the manipulative presence in their life.

6.	Avoid eye contact – when someone has gone through manipulation, such individual may end up avoiding eye contact and becoming smaller inside of themselves to take up less space and feel less likely to be picked on by the manipulator.

7.   Walking on eggshells – when one doesn't know what will cause a spike in behavior from the other person, the situation can lead to overthinking about every little thing the other person does to ensure one doesn't upset or anger the manipulator.

Long-Term Effects

1.   Numbness and isolation – the victim becomes an observer rather than someone who acts, feeling little to nothing at all, even in cases which should make them joyful. As a result, they feel hopeless and damaged, unable to ever feel emotions again.

2.   In need of approval – this situation manifests in manners like excessive accomplishing, being kind to all and sundry, being a people pleaser, and paying too much attention to appearance. After feeling like they were not enough for an extended period, their instinct is to make themselves appear perfect so others will appreciate them.

3.   Feeling resentful – this case can appear as frustration, impatience, irritability, and blame. Resentment inevitably requires release, but this can be difficult to seek and allow. After a person has experienced forceful

manipulation, it can be hard to see anything but that bad behavior.

4. Excessive judging – the victim of manipulation may find themselves watching for what others are doing and holding people and even themselves, to quite high standards. It is a device of feeling in control after not being in control. Most times, this situation requires time and self-compassion to move past.

5. Anxiety and depressive disorder – following a circumstance of manipulation or other emotional abuse, manipulators have told the victim many lies that they often believe them. However, the good news is that the victims can mend the situation over time.

Common Traits of Victims

Even though a skilled manipulator employs emotional manipulation on almost anyone, they look for some common themes. Common victim types are people that attach their self-worth to meeting the needs of others. This type of individual draws manipulators to them since they are easy to manipulate, blame, and victimize. It will be quite easy for this type of person to succumb to abuse since they need to meet the needs of others to feel loved.

Also, those who have a problematic sense of rejecting something from other people are the usual type for manipulators to prey. By trying to avoid conflict, manipulators may take that advantage to do what they want without worrying about any repercussions.

Individuals who find it hard to express negative emotions will typically avoid confrontation and keep things happy, no matter the situation. With that, manipulators sometimes search for these people since threats may be all that is required to get whatever it is they want.

People with a weak sense of self mostly have it hard to distinguish themselves from the abuser. Such a condition as this makes it difficult to trust their feelings or make decisions that will make them happy. Manipulators appreciate that because they don't need to try as hard to get what they are after.

How to Deal With Manipulation

You have read from the above ways to interact with a manipulative person, but there are things you can do yourself to raise your self-esteem as well. You will be glad to know that when you have higher self-confidence, it will help you fight against a manipulator before they can damage your overall well-being. Follow these guidelines and tips if you are trying to get yourself out of a manipulative relationship or environment.

- Identify and be aware of things that are going on around you. You can go back to read some of the points above, so you know how to catch any manipulator the next time around. Have in-depth knowledge about how manipulation works and where it leads.

- Inculcate a listening habit to yourself and your feelings. In any event of confusion and self-doubting, take serious cognizance of that situation and why you are feeling that way. Pay attention to what the manipulative person is saying or doing and how such actions affect you.

- Give more thought to actions than words. Never assume that when an individual says something, it is the truth or you need to act upon it. Pay more attention to what someone does instead and base your feelings on that.

- Be aware that you are not a problem. In case you have discovered that someone has manipulated you, understand that it is not your fault. Know that you did nothing wrong to cause it and the other person has their problems. Don't allow this situation, however, to lead to sympathy, keep it on an awareness level.

- Be assertive for yourself. You can begin by choosing to stop responding to methods in the manner you did before. Learn to say no and speak out if you want, and their reaction is not your responsibility.

- Ponder over having an affair with someone else. Choose if you wish to speak with friends about how you feel or perhaps confront the person. In any way, consider all the options and do what is comfortable for you.

- By confronting any manipulator, you are taking back your power. However, do this if you do not believe you are in harm's way. In other words, you are not doing anything wrong when you explain how you feel and what is bothering you. Demand that the other person changes their behaviors and never allow them to continue with the same routine. Do what you need to do and take back your power.

Chapter 2: Mind Control and Brainwashing

Distant strangers that have no inch of your best interest at heart may be controlling your mind. If this appears like a paranoid fantasy, brace yourself and read on. The definition of mind control is manipulation, brainwashing, and coercive persuasion, thought reform, coercive control, mental control, and many more. While there are various names for mind control is an indication of a shortage of harmony which leads to distortion and confusion, particularly by people who exploit it in a hidden way for their benefit. Thus, we conclude that mind control comes under the parasol of influence and persuasion – how to transform the behaviors and beliefs of people. Some people may disagree that the whole thing is manipulation. In expressing this, however, we have lost essential peculiarities. Thinking of influence as a continuity will be much more useful. At one side, there are respectful and ethical influences which revere people and their rights. While on the other extreme have devastating impacts which bare people of their independence, identity, and capability to think logically and critically.

Therefore, what is mind control? The best way to define mind control is to look at it as a scheme of influences that considerably disrupts someone of their identity or their very core, which are their beliefs, decisions, preferences, relationships, values, choice, behaviors, and so on, to create a pseudo personality or new pseudo-identity.

In the word of Philip Zimbardo, the psychologist, control is a method whereby agents or agencies distort or modify motivation, perception, or affect an individual or collective freedom of choice and action and as he suggests, everyone is vulnerable to the situation above.

The dynamics of mind control is not some obsolete secrecy that a select few know. Instead, it is a combination of group pressures and words, wrapped up in a manner that it gives a manipulator the power to craft reliance in their cohorts, making their choices for them even as allow them to believe that they are free and can make their decisions themselves. Ultimately, the mind control victim is not conscious of the changes that happen within them, nor the influence procedure.

Brainwashing

It may not be appropriate to imagine that brainwashing is about government representatives becoming reluctant spies against their countries, or head of a group applying mind control to manipulate their cohorts. You can even go further to imagine that brainwashing has a connection with misinformation distributed during the First and Second World Wars to influence large amounts of people.

However, what is brainwashing and whether we must restrict it to the earlier period? In the 1950s, during the Korean War, some people invented the term brainwashing. They used it to give details of the way autocratic administrations had the capability of thoroughly indoctrinating American soldiers using the process of propaganda and torture.

Brainwashing is the premise of replacing the ideas, core beliefs, values, and affiliations of someone so much that such an individual has no independence over their affairs and find it difficult to think independently or critically. So, can anyone brainwash you?

In the movie 'The Manchurian Candidate,' during the war, the Korean soldiers captured a prosperous senator. Then, they use the power of brainwashing on the senator to work for them so they can succeed in eliminating the presidential candidate. The movie depicts that even anyone can brainwash a powerful and intelligent person such as the senator. When you are susceptible to some extent, and you are vulnerable in your ways of thinking, some people can likely brainwash you. This case could include some that have:

- To live on the street through force, particularly young people
- Are suffering from an illness they cannot accept
- Lost their loved one through death or divorce

- They have made redundant and sacked from their job

How People Can Brainwash You

Someone who attempts to brainwash you will take a step further to be familiar with everything about you for them to manipulate your way of life. Their mission will include knowing your strengths and weakness, those you trust or are essential to you, and those that give you advice.

From that point, they will engage you with the course of brainwashing you, and they will naturally take these steps:

1. Us vs. Them
2. Isolation
3. Confrontations on self-esteem
4. Blind obedience
5. Testing

Isolation

This stage is the commencement of the brainwashing process since it is dangerous to them for you to be around your family and friends. A brainwasher dreads a situation where another opinion of someone to theirs is probing what the brainwasher is now asking to accept as real. The process of isolation begins in the process of giving you no access to friends and family or regularly checking where you are and who is with you.

Confrontations on self-esteem

When someone chooses to brainwash another, it can only be possible when the victim has low self-confidence and is in a vulnerable state. A broken individual is much cushier to recreate with the beliefs of a brainwasher.

Therefore, the brainwasher must decompose the self-esteem of the victim. They can achieve this through physical or verbal abuse, sleep deprivation, intimidation, or embarrassment. From there, a brainwasher starts to control all aspects of the victim's life, from food, using the bathroom, and even the time they sleep.

Us vs. Them

For the brainwasher to break down and remold their victim in a distinctive image, they will introduce a free lifestyle which is quite more delightful than their current way of living. The brainwasher achieves this when their target only mix with others that they have already brainwashed and as a result, will worship the latest system. Or the brainwasher could make their victims wear similar dresses, other unbending regulations that support a team dynamic, or have a set diet.

By nature, several pieces of evidence propose that humans are tribal and desire to belong to a group. Therefore, the brainwasher must influence their victim that they are part of an elite group of which is the desire of everyone. Even the brainwashers might give a new name to their victim, as in the case of abducted Patty Hearst, and soon after, her kidnappers named her Tania who eventually, after they have brainwashed her, backed with her captors.

Blind obedience

Blind obedience is the ultimate objective of every brainwasher, where they give orders, and the victim follows them without looking back. The brainwasher achieves this feat when they positively reward their victim when they make them happy, and when the victims do not, they negatively punish the person.

Also, reciting a phrase repeatedly is an excellent technique brainwashers use to control someone. Though the repeated phrase might not be a way of soothing the brain, research reveals that the 'repetitive' and the 'analytical' components of the brain are not identical. What this analysis tells us is that the mind can only perform one or the other, as such, an excellent way to prevent those skeptical thoughts is through chanting.

Testing

It will never occur to the brainwasher that they have ultimately captured their victim since there are certain situations where the person begins to recover from their autonomy and begin to have their own opinions. Not only is testing their victims indicates that they are still under their spells, but it allows the brainwashers to see the extent of the control they still have on their victims. A few aspects of tests could include carrying out a criminal act like burglarizing a home or robbing a store.

Brainwashing is real and present in many forms of today's society, not just the stuff of fantasy or imagination. Here are a few things you can do to prevent yourself not to be a victim of brainwashing:

- Don't believe the hype
- Don't follow the crowd
- Don't accept everything you read
- Look out for subliminal messages
- Don't yield to tactics of scare or fear
- Be wary of the agenda of someone
- Keep to your dreams and visions
- Don't be scared to be different
- Pay attention to your instinct
- Do your research

How Others Use Mind Control Against You

Mind control is a concept by which an external force controls the actions and thoughts of a subject. They achieve this through physical or psychological means, and most times involves breaking down the person so they can gain complete control.

You may be thinking that all this appears entirely implausible and far-fetched, you may want to believe that people engage in mind control in our everyday lives, from media bias in politics to advertising products. Furthermore, you may want to read about these ways someone can use mind control against you:

Isolation

When you discover that someone or a situation is gradually isolating you from your family and friends, then, it is likely an indication that someone is attempting to control your mind. No doubt your loved ones will complain to you about some unusual behaviors with your new friend, but they want to run away from this situation happening. For them to break your spirit, they need you to be vulnerable and alone.

Moody behavior

Be careful in a situation where your partner sulks when they don't get their way. And do you try to routine your behavior to prevent or stop an argument? Such a situation as this may be the beginning of mind control, where you are changing your actions due to the behavior or reaction of someone else. It is a sign of tell-tale that those people are attempting to control your mind and are indeed getting the upper hand.

Metacommunication

Metacommunication is a method whereby someone gives subtle hints and clues with the use of nonverbal cues. An excellent instance is when a woman gets a call from her partner, asking her if she is okay and shrugging her shoulders, she responds by saying yes with a sign. This situation is a clear indication that she is far from being okay, yet her verbal response is affirmative. Some people employ metacommunication to establish subliminal opinions.

Neuro-linguistic programming

NLP or neuro-linguistic programming is a method of layering specific feelings with the use of words into the unconscious mind of someone without the person being aware of their actions. NLP assesses various features of an individual and uses verbal communication to plant ideas.

For example, when someone can adjust to a situation through visual patterns, they will speak to that person with languages that use visual clues like 'can you *see* what I mean?' For someone familiar with auditory cues, they will result in using the hearing language used on them, such as 'Can you *hear* me clearly.'

Uncompromising rules

Does your spouse put irrational rules on your way of living? In case your partner blocks all access to your friends or money, expects you to meet impossible deadlines, regulated bathroom breaks, and mealtimes, then, mind control is happening. This process implies that they deny you of making your own decisions so that you adhere to a precise set of behaviors. Consequently, you stop having your thoughts, and this circumstance makes it easier for them to instill their secret plans.

How to Prevent Mind Control

If you experience any of the above instances and you can recognize them, then it may be time for you to disentangle yourself from that person and their effort to control your mind.

The first step you need to take is staying close in contact with family and friends. Prevent your new friend from getting in the way of your connecting with some of your family members or old friends. Maintain your ground to make contact with them, and you're still getting 'no' for an answer, then walk away. Never accommodate irritable and moody behavior. Deal with it in a disdain manner that it deserves.

Try to inform your partner that their behavior is childish and immature, and you won't put up with it. Also, pay careful attention to nonverbal clues that do not correlate with what someone is saying. Probe them if their responses do not complement their actions or body language. It may be a bit hard to spot NLP since anyone using it will possibly be a professional. However, signs you need to watch are new sensations that you have met your ideal companion, or that the individual you have just found is your perfect match. Be careful of a person who uses blurred expressions that make no sense or keeps mirroring your body language.

Finally, watch out for uncompromising rules. Seek out for advice from family and close friends when someone imposes inflexible regulations on you. Indeed, they would have exhausted you with low self-confidence by the time the situation gets to this point. When you inform your family and friends, their immediate response to your condition should be enough to release you from this dreadful deception.

Gain Control over Any Situation

Don't be like some people whose lifestyle is typical of passengers in an unrestrained and uncontrollable vehicle. Instead of taking charge to control the situation by taking the driver's seat, these people operate the vehicle as commuters. They try to have power over what is out of their influence instead of what is within it. When things appear as if you have no control over them, with these examples below, you can gain control over any situation:

Don't do whatever you feel compelled to do

The more powerfully the circumstance drives you to take instant action, the more likely you shouldn't. When the pull is intense, it may be you have activated your fight-or-flight physiology. That is excellent, especially when you're facing a life-or-death situation and need to react instantly. In most of life's circumstances, it serves you better to reflect before you respond.

Don't let the dynamite explode before you put it out

Sometimes, you may find yourself in dangerous conditions and shrink from facing others, whether family, friends, or colleagues. It can be an enormous blunder you make at the office that can keep the company at a loss, or perhaps you make a poor judgment that hurts a companion. Logically, you will want to avoid these situations since avoiding them will avert any conflict. However, this tactic may unconsciously grind you down, resulting in anxiety and chronic stress. Rather than doing that, face the situation. Instead of dealing with it passively, assume responsibility, and set off the conversation with a high level of confidence. Learn to understand that you have control over how you say what you say and the consequences that might result from it.

Be an action taker

Try to do something instead of feeling helpless and victimized, particularly when it comes to business settings. Most times, employers tend to cheat people when they don't get the bonus they were counting on or perhaps the employer dismisses them. Instead of stewing in frustration, imagine the realistic actions you could take to defend yourself and strive for more substance for yourself. Think of how you can be in charge of your work performance, your rapport with your boss, and whether you are working at upgrading your education out of your occupation to enhance your marketability and skills. In case you are out of a job before now, you can maintain your structure and be in command of your daily schedule. Wake up the usual time every day, clean up, and dress to the nines, and never detach yourself from your routine.

Take a step further to read job placements and submit applications for as many vacancies as possible, exchange ideas with social groups in your field of relevance, or gain new knowledge that will advance you to a more privileged position.

For various situations in life, perception is crucial, and it starts with your mind. As a result, the next time you're in a position where you think you have no power, take a bit of time to adjust your thoughts. It will surprise you to realize how you can transform from feeling powerless to powerful.

Chapter 3: Mind Games and Mind Games Relationships

In a circumstance where there is no coherence in someone's words and actions, and their words do not correlate with their past words, then, mind game is indeed taking place. Mind games force the victim to doubt their thinking or reasoning ability and intuition. The purpose for the person playing mind games is to make you rely on them to make your choices for you since it is hard for you to trust your ability to make the best decisions for yourself. Many motives make people play mind games, just in various ways people live through them. It is crucial to watch out for people that play the mind game and also essential to understand the background in which such individual plays. At length, your reaction to these tactics is vital for you to be familiar with how to tackle those games in the future. In the first place, you must have clear farsightedness that the intention of a co-worker or colleague that plays a mind game is quite not the same with your family member or friend playing a mind game. Discovering the complicated characteristics of mind games will better prepare you to tackle the most illogical reason and extremely complex for such games.

Acquire, safeguard or get control The significant rationale of people playing mind games is to acquire, gain, and preserve control. When they have the power to move you to do what they want or elicit a specific response from you, then they get the powerful feeling that they are in control of how you live and also the entire situation.

In case you experience insignificant and perhaps no control at your job, it may be their method of making up for the loss of domination at the office by taking back that feeling with you. Essentially, on the part of the person playing the mind game, it is a matter of insecurity. At this level, it is your responsibility to look inside and find out whether you are sacrificing control for a particular goal, inclusive of purposely fulfilling the necessity of the person playing the mind game, or someone is unsuspectingly coercing, manipulating, and controlling you. Also, resentment may be the harbinger of feelings of anxiety. When your spouse thinks they have no power over their lives or feels they are a disappointment; then, it is possible they picked you exclusively to relieve them of their frustrations and anger. Sometimes, it may be for the reason that you represent how they want to be. It could be that you display success and confidence that they wished they had, and possibly by engaging in their mind games, they may feel like the winner for a change. In any case, doesn't that make them victorious as well when they beat a confident and successful person?

What Are Mind Games Relationships?

Usually, people engage in mind games as a result of immaturity, insecurity, or possess a controlling behavior. These sets of people are not mature enough to have a lasting association.

Some of the reasons for this begin from lack of confidence and their helplessness to commit and relate with others in a beneficial way. Some of the typical mind games these people engage in relationships include:

Playing hard to get

In this situation, they are trying not to exhibit their affection and interest for someone they are dating. The goal for doing this is to make them appear more critical before their partner. They abhor appearing desperate or easy and take great pleasure in the feeling of someone chasing them.

Projecting

People project when they ascribe their actions and thoughts to another person. For instance, an unfaithful individual might blame their partner for involving in immorality. Accordingly, the person they hold responsible uses their energy protecting themselves rather than controlling their emotions, breathe, and force the concentration on their partner and judging their actions.

Sending varied messages

For a while, someone who sends messages may appear interested and then, disregards you totally, only to later begin to act attracted to you again. So, what point does the person intend to make? In any case, their action can be intentional since the person is not sure of their feelings. However, when this action is deliberate, their goal then is to make you feel insecure, desperate, and have more focus on them.

Guilt-tripping

A person can make use of the guilt-trip method to weaken the personality boundaries of someone else. Most times, when someone feels guilty, they tend to let others outshine them and do awful things they wouldn't allow if self-reproach were not there in the first place.

Withholding affection

Sadly, and most often, this situation happens in relationships. Some people suppress affection if they have no control over relationships. Indeed, don't mix up this case with being mad at your spouse for a reasonable cause.

Playing Mind Games in Relationships

Any communication with someone else has the possibility of involving some mind game. Indeed, many of us are great when it comes to playing mind games in relationships. When someone uses mind games for dubious purposes is when the problems start. Devious people desire to be in power, and several of them have gained knowledge of how to turn the switches of others and get the hang of subtle emotional signals to control the other people. Since mind games include twisting the facts and manipulation, creating doubts to destabilize others becomes so handy for them. When someone has a tumultuous childhood, they are more likely to play mind games. If a child has to deal with unreasonable and unfair parents, such a child will discover habits of manipulating the situation in a smart, passive way to handle emotions. Some of these children take these socially impaired hacking means into their relationships as grownups.

Twisting the facts

For the benefit of the manipulator's account of actions, people engage in mind games to distort the details of an event. A manipulator will perceive the circumstances their way and will usually be short of the compassion to value the opinion of someone else. It is in their custom to disregard feelings and execute their side of events again, effectively avoiding any other outlook of a situation. Such a case as this tends to be provoking for the spouse who feels misunderstood and misheard.

Dismissing and deflecting

Indeed, when someone disregards your feelings, they are playing mind games with you. They will utter something offensive, and when you respond, they will tell you that you are too sensitive. A caring, healthy individual will not enjoy upsetting other person and be careful not to repeat the situation.

As for someone playing mind game, such person will make a mental observation of that weakness and hold it as ammunition they will draw on later to manipulate and control you. Other tactics they use is when you attempt to have a conversation with them about their behavior or a situation you don't like that happen. Rather than communicating or listening, someone exploiting you with mind games will sidetrack the discussion and blame their behavior on another thing you have done.

Subtle erosion of confidence

With time, someone playing mind games with you will lead you to question yourself, and such circumstance undermines confidence. Mind game players may also give comments that you are fortunate to have them as nobody will love you as they do, or you won't find someone else to love you. A player of mind game will talk down at your confidence to keep you feeling degrading rather than bringing the best in you. Consequently, leaving the relationship may never be an option for you.

Is Mind Games Normal in a Relationship?

Have you come across something like this?When you have the feeling that your spouse is undervaluing your relationship with them, tell yourself that it is all right that you are going to make yourself inaccessible this week. True to form, this tactic makes your partner desire you more with a swift turnaround that it is nearly a joke. It's more or less like playing a game, yet it works well.

Many of us adhere to this advice, in some way standardized to accept playing mind game as an active component of relationships. Since the young age, situations taught us about coercion, debasement, charm, retaliation, emotional blackmail, silent treatment, blame, and so many more to get specific reactions from our peers and parents. And our teens saw us pushing the boundaries to distinguish how far it is likely for us to come off with what our desires. By 18 to 25 years of age, many of us outgrow this since we have found better mechanisms to navigate the life of an adult. Sadly, however, many of us don't.

In our teens, for a lot of reasons, something put a break in the development of our emotions. We never got hold of a better tool for navigating the adult life, and to achieve our desires, we result in using the silent treatment, blame, charm, comparison, coercion, and so many more. For us, everyone is doing it, but it doesn't make it acceptable or right for a grown adult to act or think like a teen or adolescent. There must be a distinction involving how a teen attempts to induce interest or love and how a grownup get their wants and needs met. It is possible that, once in a while, some of us relapse to some juvenile behaviors, however, in most cases, as we grow older, our tolerance for infantile behavior decreases that we imagine adults to have outgrown like whining, yelling, self-absorption, finger-pointing, tantrums, and manipulating other people because of what they want.

It may happen that a partner may be taking someone for granted. Rather than calmly asking for what you want, having a matured discussion, and negotiating what meets both of your needs, you result to making yourself less available. Quite predictably, the conversion can be so quick since the insecurities of the other person have taken over; however, only temporary. The moment they feel secure again, they start failing to appreciate you - yet. For most individuals that have immature emotions and who imagine that healthy aspects of relationships are mind games, they apply even more mind games to get the other person to give them the attention, love, respect and so much more that they want. Someone who loves you, devoted to you, and wants their emotions to be in parallel with yours will check out just so that they can bear your childishness for a while longer. Sadly, when the other person emotionally checks out, you engage even further mental games. But by then, the person can't take it anymore.

As for other people, they may not be so tolerant with a grownup who behaves like a child. They move on ahead of endurance any opportunity you may have to play another mind game – also, others who have zero tolerance for unintelligent mind games. To them, teaching you a lesson is the best way to get you to grow up. They allow you to play the player. And since they are fully aware of what they are doing versus you who think it's a normal part of relationships, they can indeed mess you up.

Why People Play Mind Game?

For many people, they experience frustration and confusion in dating relationships. It can be quite tough to figure out the opposite sex or hinder a deep, meaningful connection, especially when such a partner you are interested in plays mind games. There could be several motives why people engage in mind games, and on occasion, they are so ignorant of their own needs, much less you're that they don't even know they are playing games. People play mind games because of the following reasons:

To manipulate

Individuals engage in mind games to selfishly manipulate other people for them to accomplish their wish, such as:

- Always having a company
- Sex
- Having someone to listen to them
- A desire to control another person
- Having someone adore them
- Expecting someone to nurse their deepest wounds back to health

- Enhancing their personality since they have someone to flaunt

It may appear that not all these desires are unhealthy or wrong. It is just the way these people go about achieving their purpose that tends to be hurtful and selfish.

They enjoy the rush

Some people want to get a drift of having another person to like them. It is more or less like a challenge or a game for these people. For them, getting another person fancy them can be quite exciting.

This behavior stems from a low sense of worth and a lack of knowledge of how they upset others. Whereas others are anxious, looking for that excitement of experiencing that someone highly regards them. It is typical of a high.

However, in a short period, they turn off once they realize the person they have been chasing is fond of them. All of a sudden, they have moved on to the next capture, hunting for the subsequent rush. Unfortunately, many are not aware of their actions or the reasons for them.

Test the water

Another reason the mind game players is to discover your feelings for them. Being vulnerable enough to share your deepest needs to wanting to love someone and for that person to embrace you back takes so much courage. How would you feel if you tell a person you are fond of them and they decline you in some way? It may be that you that person lead you on, although perhaps such individual is anxious to initiate the relationship.

For so long, guys have always had the pressure of initiating a relationship. Now, it appears the table has turned as ladies are getting bolder all the time. However, both genders, deliberately or otherwise, count on the guy to make the first move and for the lady to be at the receiving end in any relationship. Remember, so many guys act macho and sturdy, but deep down, they are also nursing so much anxiety of rejection.

How to Deal With Mind Games in Relationships

Those who play mind games can be difficult to change. Meet head-on with any mind game player and let them be aware that you won't tolerate them when you notice their behavior. You should probably move on when you realize that better communication doesn't appear to solve the issue. Some other ways for you to tackle the situation include:

Having strong personal boundaries

We teach others how to behave towards us through the guidelines we establish with our bounders. Learn how to reject mind game players when it's hard to keep up with such behavior and set boundaries for them. When you know what you want and build your confidence, you will achieve firm personal boundaries.

Seek advice from a trusted person

Most times, a third person can examine the situation rationally and more wisely since they are not emotionally involved, and such people can give you unbiased and more practical guidance.

Call your partner on their behavior

A mind game player needs to know that you are conscious of what they are doing. Never make use of the same passive-aggressive techniques in an attempt to take revenge or even prevail over the game. Don't debase your confidence and tell the mind game player that you are aware of their manipulation.

Never attempt to change the player

Trying to change someone can be quite tricky, particularly a manipulative individual. If these people are manipulative and the conversation appears not enough to sort out the issue, chances are it is merely their personality and nothing much you can do about it. If you continue to try, you will be possibly messing around.

Move on from such person

In most cases, people who play mind games may not change for the better, except they are still quite at their young age. A mind game player who manipulates you or tests you is not who you need. Having a relationship with a mature individual with efficient and open communication is all that you need.

Chapter 4: Persuasion, Types of Persuasion, and Power of Persuasion

What comes to your mind when you reflect about persuasion? Do you think about a political candidate who attempts to influence voters to pick their name on the ballot box come to your mind? Or do you see the image of an advertising announcement that incites the audience to purchase a specific item? Since it has a significant influence on society as a whole, persuasion is indeed a dominant force in daily life. The power of persuasion influences legal decisions, politics, news, mass media, and advertising, and it also impacts us in turn.

Also, when you think of persuasion, you may mean something either positive or detrimental to you. An authority, such as peer pressure instructing you to do something, or you won't fit in, could be the perception of others about persuasion. It is so compelling that all of us engage in persuasion, and it is an exciting concept to discuss. At some point in our life, for some of us to accomplish a goal, we have participated in some form of persuasion. Someone has cut down on the price of an item we want to buy, or we have succeeded in getting a job through the art of persuasion. At times, some of us take pleasure in believing that we can resist persuasion. We think that we have the power to comprehend the truth in a situation, possess a natural ability to see through the sales pitch, and with our innate skills, achieve reasonable inferences. While in some scenarios this conviction might be valid, persuasion is not just a commercial on the television tempting you to buy the most fabulous and latest product, or an over-ambitious marketer attempting to convince you to buy a car. Because of the subtlety of persuasion, the degree of our response to such influence will depend on some factors. When we steer our thoughts toward persuasion, what often come to our minds are negative instances. However, people use persuasion as a constructive power. One such great example of persuasion in the public service campaigns geared at people to quit smoking or recycle because they use it to enhance the lives of the people. Some of the crucial features of persuasion are that:

- Persuasion involves a deliberate attempt to influence other people; thus, it can't be accidental

- It is symbolic, applying images, words, sounds, etc

- Techniques of transmitting persuasive messages can happen in various ways such as verbally and nonverbally through radio, television, Internet, or face-to-face communication

- It is vital to have self-persuasion. People using persuasion are not coercing; instead, people can choose without reservation

- People can persuade you in different sorts of ways using different types of media

Persuasion is a symbolic process, and this process makes us try to convince other people to take out attitudes or behavior and change them into something that we want them to do.

How Persuasion Differs Today

Since the time of the Ancient Greeks, the science and art of persuasion have been of interest and how persuasion happens today or the past are the main differences. Five significant ways separate the past form of persuasion and those of the modern:

A tremendous increase in persuasive messages

If you can take a moment and think about how many advertisements you encounter every day, the figure will shock you. As some studies suggest, each day, the number of advertisements advertisers expose an average U.S. adult to ranges from 300 to more than 3,000.

Persuasive communication spreads far more quickly

The Internet, radio, and television all contribute to the rapid travel of persuasive messages.

Persuasion is a big business

Not only are establishments such as public relations companies, marketing firms, advertising agencies, and many others the only companies that rely purely on persuasive purposes, many other companies are dependent on persuasion to promote their services and sell goods.

Subtle form in modern persuasion

Indeed, you may see that the strategies of persuasion in some adverts are noticeable; however, subtle type of adverts is in some modern persuasive approach. A good example is some establishments that entice consumers to get their products or services to accomplish that estimated standard of living through cautiously crafted images.

Complexity of persuasion

Since there are varieties in consumers, they have several choices. As a result, marketers have to be savvier about choosing their persuasive message and medium.

Various Types of Persuasion

The power to convince people in a variety of ways is what several types and principles of persuasion have. While you may have to opt for the appeal-to-reason method in case you have an individual who accepts what they can hear or see since they are exceptional with fact, the technique of appeal-to-emotion will be more suited to those with a bit of belief.

First, let's go through all these methods so it can help you to understand these ranges of persuasion better and also the various impact they have on people:

Appeal-to-reason

A rational line of reasoning is what this technique makes use of with scientific method and logic being the center of the persuasion. Those who find it hard to accept arguments on the ground of faith than fact and require proof of something will be suited for appeal-to-reason. In the event of your conviction that the Earth revolves around the moon, you may need to have several facts to back up your claim if you are to convince a team of scientist to adhere to conviction. If not, persuading them to your argument will be hard.

Appeal-to-emotion

This method is not proof-based; instead, it engages arguments through emotions. Most times, because emotions can govern individuals more than their minds, appeal-to-emotion tends to be a more practical approach for the whole population. All through history, this method is factual, and there are quite a lot of examples that reveal that. For anyone to win people over to an argument, this method appeals to someone through the involvement of their imagination and faith. Also, to get people to concur with you, tradition, seduction, and even pity may come to play. Salespeople utilize the appeal-to-emotion method quite well. Through a test drive of a vehicle for people to imagine themselves in it, salespeople appeal to individuals' imagination. Apart from using seduction to entice you, many use compassion to convince people how sales have been slow, and they may want the deal. Using this form of persuasion are propaganda and advertising. Also, as a technique of getting a person to do your bidding, appealing to emotions uses tradition.

To persuade someone toward your idea and opinion, these four aids, which are:

Body language

Body language takes approximately two-third of our communication. For instance, you need to stand with your hands at your side, have a symbolic gesture of peace with your palm out, if you are looking for someone to consent to your view. It may be a sign of blocking recipient if you have your arm crossed while standing and out of their unconsciousness, they will not wish to listen to you lest dealing with you.

Communication skills

When you are good at writing and speaking skills to spread the message you want to pass out, your message will attract a lot of people. Propose a unique opportunity to them with the right product will see you appealing to them on many sides.

Sales techniques

Over time, people can learn the art of deep-rooted sales method, which is the technique exercises. What works well in sales technique is highlighting only the good points which will appeal to the needs of people and more.

Personality tests

The personality tests devices a strategy is all about the style of the interaction of someone. While some people like to speak with someone present physically, others have a preference for phone calls. Some may purchase an item only when they need it, and as for other people, they even prefer to buy products based on what they see on television. Knowing to sell an idea or a product to people comes from their personality.

The Power of Persuasion

Before reading further, you may wish to know that of all the tools you may have in your arsenal; integrity is the most important persuasion tool.

When we have a clear grasp of motivation, influence, and the theories of persuasion, we will have the control of life's driver's seat. Three simple concepts are the origin of what we desire, or will ever desire in life. You may not even be aware that less than 1 percent of the world's population can indeed apply or have a concise understanding of the twelve rules of persuasion. For that reason, as you have a glimpse into the science of persuasion and the secrets of influence, the accuracy will be complete when you have the potential of persuading and influencing. In an instant, while you accomplish your desire in life all at the same time, you will inspire others to take action as you gain influence over them. As you empower yourself with firm self-reliance, you will be able to prevail over people to your view. As you succeed with increasing your prosperity in sales and marketing, you will also turn into a captivating magnet of success.

Persuasion: The Heartbeat of Economy

In today's world, the influence of persuasion is of critical and extraordinary importance. Persuading or gaining influence of other people to our opinions is what almost all humans encounter. People are always making an effort to persuade one another with no regards to profession, age, philosophical beliefs, or religion. All of us want to have the capability to influence and persuade so other people will follow us, trust us, and listen to us. Some economists discovered in the latest study that the use of persuasion skills in the marketplace directly attributes to a massive 26 percent of gross domestic product. It is thus efficient to say that the gasoline to the economy's engine is persuasion. Since sales professionals are not liabilities to the company, but assets, to trim down on sales forces is almost impossible for any big cooperation. Even in the slowest of economies, there will be employment for first-class persuaders. For doing something positive or negative, the skill to persuade is power. Persuasive individuals prevent wars, keep children off drugs, and enhance lives. Indeed, the influence of persuasive people has also stirred up wars, get children on drugs, and destroy lives. For the advancement and improvement of ourselves, families, friends, and communities, put a premium focus on the power of persuasion. For sure, the arts of influence and persuasion are not gifts majority of us possess since we don't have the natural gift of a persuader. Sure, we have the conventional persuaders who are naturally outgoing, social, and sometimes loud. However, the most excellent persuaders are introverts according to research. The perception of others is that they may seem manipulative, forceful, and pushy with the notion of becoming a polished persuader. But it is dead wrong to have such an assumption. You may not achieve lasting influence from deliberate tactics, calculated maneuvers, or intimidation. Instead, you will be able to influence with the utmost integrity when you have appropriate execution of the latest persuasion strategies. Others will automatically and naturally have confidence in you and want you to persuade them since they trust you. In short, these people will be ready to do anything you tell them to do.

You must be aware that persuasion and negotiation are not the same because an indication of meeting in the middle of backing down is the meaning of negotiation. Contrary to negotiation which compromises, talking the opposite party into embracing your position and abandoning their previous stance is what an effective persuasion is all about.

Can you imagine why is it that some people, as well as some situation, can persuade us so much more than others? Your level of persuasion has a lot to do with the state in which you are. Your power of persuasion may below when you are tired or hungry or lonely or particularly needy in some other way. But understanding the psychology of persuasion is essential, perhaps even vital, for all our sakes.

Boosting Your Power of Persuasion

From podcasts to presentations, from friendly fliers to Facebook ads, from love letters to political speeches, we all have had our fair share of being on the receiving end of a tsunami of persuasive messages. In an attempt to trap our attention, people us thousands of messages to persuade us to do, think, or feel something. Today, persuasion has turned to a household word since what we have is an increase of written opinions on the subject of persuasion. As an entrepreneur, you may be missing out on a powerful influencing tool if you haven't been paying attention to the persuasion principles other people use. With the tips and tricks below, you can improve your influence of persuasion:

Be smart about figures

You may lose the power of persuasion when you use round figures instead of the accurate numbers when putting a value on items for sale, according to research. Never use rounded numbers when you price your services. While you are not cheating anyone with this method, you may need to be smart and prevent potential customers from asking for a discount which will reduce your actual worth.

Leading people to self-discovery

As a psychologist puts it, people usually act for their reasons, not the reasons for someone else. Don't tell people why they must change when you intend to persuade people to do something like convincing a reluctant employee to change negative behavior. Rather, help them discover their reasons for changing.

Repeat, then repeat and then repeat

Among consumers, skepticism is at an all-time high these days. For some people to believe messages about a business, they have to hear it three to five times. As you attempt to present a message that its purpose is to persuade, don't forget to keep this analysis in mind. You may want to use different mediums or intervals to repeat the message. As a result, your power of familiarity will result in approval.

Using Monroe's motivated sequence

There is a time-tested organizing structure, and it is called Monroe's motivated sequence. When you have the intention of persuading with a presentation, you can use it if you want your listeners to do something. Monroe's motivated sequence involves:

Capture the attention

If you want your listeners to pay attention to what you want to say, hook them from the beginning. You have various gambits to accomplish this method, including a brief story, a question or a rhetorical question, a remarkable visual, a startling statistic, and a powerful quote.

Establish the need

Give your listeners the reason to believe that there is a problem that you want to address. Your audience will conclude that they should care when you do this. Your purpose at this point is to make them think that they need to hear this message and perhaps do something about the problem.

Satisfy the need

Your listeners must be aware that you have unique skills or knowledge to fill that need. Let them know that the issue of the problem they may have has a solution which is within your reach.

Visualize the results

Take your listeners through a journey of positive visualization. Help them see the benefits of adopting your proposal or solution.

Make them go through a negative visualization where they will see the consequences of not taking any action. You must know that your main goal here is for your audience to imagine that this is a great idea.

Ask for the action

Then, you must clearly outline the action you want them to take. Here, your goal is for them to decide they want your product or service and desperately by now for you to show them how to get it.

The Difference between Manipulation and Persuasion

Two concepts that are quite related closely are manipulation and persuasion, and occasionally, the thin line connecting the two appears to blur. To have a clear understating of the moment when the crisscrossing to manipulation happens, we have an in-depth look into the meaning of the two words.

With persuasion, we are making people believe or do something. Every day, we engage in persuasion, and there's egotism in the attempt. It is by getting a person to have a rethink about the beliefs that serve them, and change to a perspective that we believe is right.

As one of the various ways of relating to people around us, there's not evil about persuasion. If we have a selfless frame of mind through persuasion means seeing the world becoming a safe place. Even if we want to become wealthy, it is not immoral or evil to make money. You will only have to persuade people they need to spend their money because the people you are trying to convince are looking to keep their money.

Manipulation, on the other hand, use unfair or artful means to serve the purpose of someone. Here, there is no mistake about self-interest since no matter what; you must achieve your desire. Even if there is an advantage to such individual that someone manipulates, that is only an offshoot of the central objective of the person who engages in manipulation. Therefore, three things stand between manipulation and persuasion, and they are:

- The transparency and truthfulness of the method

- The net impact or benefit on the subject

- The purpose that runs desire to persuade a certain person

There is importance to the goal of someone attempting to manipulate or persuasion. With manipulation, the buyer will feel remorse immediately the message is over, while people feel happy to have made contact with you in the case of influence.

The rise of vulnerability

Though trust is perilously low in today's world where the concepts are particularly essential, people need to be mindful of whether they are manipulative or persuasive continually.

Several reasons force us to be susceptible to manipulation. For example, manipulators have become so polished in their system of manipulating people. However, some issues have more connection with the spectators.

As we receive several more messages every day, one significant problem we face is information overload, and consequently, there is a rise of appeal to oversimplification. For more than a decade, politics has taken another dimension. As opposed to the mainstays of news from years ago, sourcing news has moved to social media. As generalization takes on complex issues, we catch memes and slogans.

One can perceive how manipulation penetrates the mix. What's more? Even when several of them may not be what will be most efficient, we have the willingness to snatch at potential solutions since those increased messages have caused us so much anxiety in us.

Chapter 5: Body Language and Nonverbal Communication

People regularly throw off cues to what they are thinking or feeling even when most of them may not articulate their thoughts verbally. The communication of non-verbal messages happens through facial expression, body movements, vocal volume and tone, and other cues people collectively identify as body language. As opposed to spoken language, body language is not always clear.

However, how we interpret it can make a significant difference in how a person interacts with and relates to others. As micro expressions, it is typical of a silent orchestra such as brief displays of emotion that someone attempts to hide, postures, and hand gestures, even though we are not aware of them, we keep details in the brain almost immediately.

No matter how brief, these moments of recognition can have enduring consequences for how someone interprets other people's mood, openness, motivation, as well as how people around them perceive their inner self.

Sadly, some mental health disorders, especially neurodevelopmental; complications such as autism, can make it a bit difficult to react to the body language convey, not to talk of it is more challenging to notice.

Understanding Body Language and Facial Expressions

As nonverbal languages, we use body language to communicate. Experts believe that a massive part of daily communication is the sum of these nonverbal signals. Even when we don't say all these things using facial expression and body language, we pass on plenty of information.

Between 60 to 65 percent of our entire communication uses body language, as some people suggest. While we concentrate on other cues like context, which is also important, it is essential to understand body language. In some cases, rather than paying attention to a single action, you must perceive signals as a group. If you are making an effort to interpret body language, you should look for the following;

Facial expression

If you can pause and reflect a bit, you will know that with a simple facial expression, someone is capable of conveying so many messages. While it can be an indication of happiness and approval when someone smiles, a frown can depict unhappiness or disapproval. In some situations, our sincere feelings about a specific condition come alive with our facial expression. With the look on your face, people may see otherwise when you respond to a question that you are feeling fine. Facial expression can reveal some emotions, such as:

- Anger
- Happiness
- Surprise
- Sadness
- Excitement
- Fear
- Desire
- Confusion
- Disgust
- Disdain

You can even help determine if you believe or trust what someone is saying with the expression on someone's face. According to a study, a slight smile and a slight raise of the eyebrows is the most trustworthy facial expression. As the researchers further suggested, this expression conveys both confidence and friendliness.

Of all the most global mode of body language is a facial expression, and people throughout the world use the expressions to convey anger, fear, happiness, and sadness.

The support for the universality of different facial expressions is what Paul Ekman, a researcher, found, and they have a connection with particular emotions such as anger, joy, surprise, fear, and sadness. Humans make opinions about the intelligence of the people founded on their expressions and faces, according to one study.

The research discovered that some people are more likely to be intelligent when they have more prominent noses and narrower faces. The research also ascertained that individuals with angry expression might not be as smart as those with joyful expression and smiling face.

The eyes

People frequently refer to the eyes as the windows to the soul because they have the power to reveal a lot of thoughts and feelings of someone. As an essential part of the communication process, it is natural for people to pay attention to the movement of the eye when they engage someone in a conversation.

Whether people are averting their gaze or making direct eye contact, if their pupils are dilated, or how much they are blinking, are some of the common things you may notice

Take note of some of these following eye signals if you are attempting to evaluate body language:

Eye gaze:

In a situation when someone is having a conversation with you, and they stare straight into your eyes, it is an indication that they have an interest in what you are saying and are paying attention.

Long-lasting eye contact, however, can have a bit of intimidating in it. Frequently looking away or breaking eye contact, in contrast, might indicate that such person is uncomfortable, attempting to conceal their real feelings, or distracted.

Blinking:

It is natural to blink. However, you must also take notice of whether an individual is blinking too little or too much. Most times, when people are feeling uncomfortable or distressed, they blink more rapidly.

Occasional blinking can be an indication that someone is intentionally attempting to control the movements of their eye. For instance, because a poker player is trying to appear unexcited on purpose about the hand someone is dealing with him, he might blink less frequently.

Pupil size:

A subtle nonverbal communication signal is pupil size. Sometimes, emotions can cause small changes in pupil size even since the levels of light in the surroundings influence the dilation of the pupil.

For example, when someone has an attraction for another person, people may describe the look they give as "bedroom eyes." Another instance is that highly dilated eyes can be a clue that someone is interested or even aroused.

The mouth

To read body language, mouth movements and expressions are also important. For example, when someone chews on the base lip, it may be an indication that the person is experiencing feelings of fear, worry, or insecurity.

When people cover their mouths when they are coughing or yawning, they may be attempting to be polite. However, it also can be an effort to cover up their feeling of displeasure. Perhaps, one of the most excellent signals of body language is smiling, but it is possible to interpret smiles in various ways.

People can use a smile to express happiness, cynicism, or even sarcasm or a smile can be genuine. Take note of some of these lip and mouth signals when you are evaluating body language:

Pursed lips:

When someone tightens their lips, it may indicate disapproval, distrust, or distaste.

Lip biting:

Biting the lips might be an indicator of anxiety, worry, or stress.

Covering the mouth:

To display smirks or smiles, some people may cover their mouth to veil a sensitive response.

Turned up or down:

It may be slight signs of their feelings when people have little changes in the mouth. Someone whose mouth is slightly turned may be an indicator that such a person has optimistic or happy feelings. Meanwhile, a somewhat down-turned mouth can indicate disapproval, an outrage grimace, or even sadness.

Gestures

One of the most understandable and direct signals of body language is gestures. While people use their fingers to give signs of numerical amounts, they also use pointing, waving, and they are all quite easy and basic to understand gestures. However, because people have nationalized some gestures, a peace sign or a thumbs-up in one country might indicate a different meaning when you make the same gesture in another country.

Here are a few possible meanings of some common gestures:

- **A clenched fist** may be an indicator of anger in some cases or solidarity in others.
- **A thumbs down and thumbs up** is a signal people use most times to indicate gestures of disapproval and approval.
- **The "okay" gesture** means "all right" or "okay" and people do it when they have the index finger in a circle, and touch the thumb together while proffering the other three fingers. However, people use the same signal to indicate that you are nothing in certain parts of Europe, while it is indeed a vulgar gesture in a few countries around South America.
- **The V sign** indicates victory or peace in some countries, and people create it when they raise the middle and index finger and separate

the fingers to make a V-shape. In Australia and the United Kingdom, when the back of the hand is facing outward, the same sign takes on an offensive meaning.

The arms and legs

Crucial for the expression of nonverbal information is arms and legs. An indicator of defensiveness is when someone crosses their arms, and there is a sign of discomfort or dislike with someone when, away from such individual, you cross your legs.

Some other forms of subtle signals maybe when you make an effort to appear more commanding or larger is to expand your arms widely while it may indicate an attempt to withdraw from attention or minimize oneself when you keep the arms close to the body.

Watch out for a few of these signals that the arms and legs may communicate as you make an effort to evaluate the body language of someone:

- **Crossed arms** might be an indicator that someone feels self-protective, closed-off, or defensive.
- **Standing with hands placed on the hips** might indicate that someone is in control or is

ready, or the signal may be that of violent behavior.

- **Clasping the hand behind the back** could be an indication of angry, anxious, or even bored feelings.

- **Fidgeting or quickly tapping fingers** might indicate that someone is frustrated, impatient, or tired.

- **Crossing the legs** might be an indicator that someone is lacking privacy or is feeling closed off.

Posture

The way you hold your body can also function as a vital component of body language. In addition to your general physical form, posture is how you hold your body. Posture can express a multiplicity of information about hints about personality traits as well as how someone is feeling, including whether such someone is open, confident, or submissive.

For example, when you sit up straight, it may be a sign that you are paying attention and have your focus at what is happening. On the other hand, when you hunch your body forward while sitting, it may be an indicator that you are indifferent or bored.

Make a careful effort to pay attention to some of the signals that the posture of someone sends when you want to read body language.

- **Open posture** may comprise having the trunk exposed and open. Posture such as this means openness, willingness, and friendliness.

- **Closed posture** is when you hunch forward while you conceal the trunk of the body most times by keeping the arms and legs crossed. When you exhibit this posture, it can indicate unfriendliness, hostility, and anxiety.

Personal space

Have you heard a person talking about their want for personal space? Have you encountered a situation where an individual stands with quite a small space between the two of you, and you begin to feel uncomfortable?

As Edward T. Hall, an anthropologist refers to the term *proxemics* as the distance between people when they interact. The space between people can communicate a great deal of nonverbal information, just like facial expressions and body movements. As Hall described it, there are four levels of social distance that happen on different occasions:

Intimate distance – 6 to 18 inches:

In most cases, the physical distance of this level is an indicator of greater comfort between people or a closer relationship. Usually, this level of distance happens at some point in intimate contact, including whispering, hugging, or touching.

Personal distance – 1.5 to 4 feet

Between people that are close friends or family members, this level of physical distance happens typically. You will notice the degree of their intimacy in their relationship when you see people standing closer and relating to each other with comfort.

Social distance – 4 to 12 feet

In most situations, people who are acquaintances use this level of physical distance. With people you know quite well, you might feel cozier talking at a closer distance like a co-worker you see several times a week. While a distance of 10 to 12 feet may be appropriate in a condition where you don't know each other quite well, like someone you see once in a while.

Public distance – 12 to 25 feet

Mostly in a situation such as public speaking is where people use this level of physical distance. Typical of a teacher who stands and talks before a classroom full of students is an excellent example of giving a presentation at work.

Mainly, you must note the level of personal distance that you need to feel comfortable. From one culture to another, this case can be different. One oft-cited instance is the difference between people from North America and those from Latin cultures. While people from North America tend to feel more comfortable with more personal distance as they interact, those from Latin countries are at ease standing closer to one another.

The Role of Body Language in Communication

Body language function appears to be complicated. In combination with verbal attributes of communication, body language operates to create nuanced and sometimes a blunt message. There is a role for both the sender and receiver to play, and when they have a different perception or interpretation of their communication; the word between them becomes downright conflicting at best and muddled at worst.

While verbal and nonverbal communication goes hand-in-hand, within the communication process, and over the years, researchers have discovered some fundamental purposes of body language. Some of these roles are:

Regulating

To regulate and pace communication is one of the functions of body language. For example, in a gathering, there are several nonverbal cues that people use to indicate it is the turn of someone else when one person is finished speaking.

Substituting

Sometimes, people use body language in place of verbal communication. A good example is when someone is engrossed in a conversation, and they keep talking for so long that the other person finds it hard to speak up and inform such individual that they don't wish to continue with the discussion. As a substitute, you can step away or glance away.

Conflicting

Fundamentally, it is conflicting when your body language indicates different meaning against your verbal communication. For example, if you tell your supervisor that her appearance was beautiful.

However, it is not easy for you to make eye contact while you're making that statement. At this point, there is no correlation between your words and body language. For some people, when the two conflict, they prefer body language over verbal communication.

Accenting/moderating

This aspect of body language enhances verbal communication, or otherwise, it softens, emphasizes, accentuates. It is like putting forth your hand to a child that you are correcting or disciplining or pointing your finger to direct attention to the subject of your words.

Complementing

With some subtle differences, this type of body language is similar to conflicting. You will have a complementing category when you use body language in an attempt to add or support credibility to what you're saying, and people see such body language as genuine.

However, it shifts into the category of conflicting when others identify the body language as misleading or fake.

Repeating

People use this body language to reiterate their verbal messages. For example, as a way of repeating the verbal direction, someone might also point to the door if they tell you to open the door.

It is straightforward to separate some examples of communication and body language in ways that you have a clear expression on one particular component or element. However, it is not always precise or clear cut in the real world.

Do you remember when last you shopped around, or as part of teacher/parent conference, or on a date, or attended a wedding ceremony? Do you notice that body language plays a significant power in these entire real-world scenarios and many different ways?

Indeed, the best way to become more familiar with the function of body language in communication is to take notice of the cues that communicate louder than words and regularly observe your actions and those of others.

Chapter 6: How to Read Body Language and Basic Science to comprehend it

In the last chapter, we have talked a lot about body language and how you can understand the facial expression and body language. This chapter will talk deeply on the basic science of comprehending body language and nonverbal communication. Having a proper understanding of body language is when you can compare nonverbal signals to the verbal messages that someone delivers after you have observed them.

There are three main ingredients you require to succeed in doing this:

1. Nonverbal cues – cues such as body language including intonations and vocal signals.
2. Verbal messages – words, of course.
3. The context – let's look at the circumstances or group or the individual in question. What is their age or culture? What is their social status, and are they female or male? These background factors affect our communication in subtle ways and to pay no attention to them is an amateur's mistake.

When you combine these three ingredients, you will get a perfect depiction of the thoughts and mood of the person that you observe. Nowadays, verbal message, which is number 2 in the list above, is the conscious focus of most people. Though people have subconscious analysis and perception of nonverbal communication, they have not entirely disregarded it.

As a result, does an individual component in our communication has any essence? I urge you to read on:
What is the difference between nonverbal and verbal communication?

Become Observant

You must have cultivated sense to analyze and obtain the nonverbal, subtle signals that some people miss or ignore when people consider you intuitive and perceptive. When you have this sense, it will allow you to analyze people's thoughts and emotions as well as social situations in almost a supernatural way. Reading other people come to you naturally, and doing this doesn't mean you are mindful about it. But what if you are not quite lucky and you can't read body language? Can you guide yourself to become attentive and learn how to read body language? The answer is yes, you can!

However, it is not likely you can do it in a blink of an eye; you must prepare yourself to become conscious and alert of your environment. You will guide yourself to sense thoughts and emotions, typical of Spiderman who can perceive danger. We can analyze the process in three steps to do this:

1. Memorize the meaning of some signs after learning them

2. Pull together various clues after you have watched them in action

3. Achieving the right message after careful analysis of everything

In the beginning, it will appear like a deliberate undertaking. The meaning of various postures becomes clear to you but will do you no good if you don't make an effort to prepare yourself to search for these signs. You need to focus on reading people's body language, after you've taken your time, to set up this in your mind, to make it natural and flowing.

Do you know that, by penetrating a process of mindful meditation, you can achieve one of the best ways to read body language effectively? But, wait, meditation? Well, yes. Even when you need to enter quite a clear attentive, and clear state of mind, it doesn't require you to cross your legs or close your eyes. In this state, you must have your focus on the present moment while you clean your mind from any worries, any random thoughts, or plans. In a short time, you will feel quite peaceful with this fantastic experience and will be familiar with your surroundings. All of a sudden, you will find much more wisdom in the events and people around you, and you will be able to sharpen your sense. Indeed, it is worth the effort even though it takes some attempts to get into it.

Body language in a cluster

Body language is the same as the common verbal language. It is typical of putting single words that you got together to create a sentence that delivers a meaningful message. Nonverbal cues are the ones we substitute for words in body language. Though individually, these "words" may give us the general idea about the personality or mood of whom we observe, it may be quite hard or wrong to assume anything based on that single clue. To finish the puzzle, we need additional clues are the things we need to look for to make the sentence complete.

For example, from a male perspective, when you have an impression that a lady you are observing is interested in you. Why would you have such an opinion as a man? Well, attraction and playfulness is the signal that will come to your mind when you observe her toying with her hair? But can you use that single sign to conclude? The answer is no.

It may not be enough to go all-in even though you might be right with your assumption. Have you studied the person further to consider the gestures she makes and the position of her body? What about sideways glances and whether she is learning forward? Before you decide on the most rational analysis, you must run several questions through your head.

Keep it simple

When you are in a conversation with someone, pay attention to all nonverbal cues, analyze them, and stay focused on the discussion at the same time can be too daunting. The information will not only paralyze you; it will be excessive and burdens you in the end. The key is to let your subconscious mind watch out for the nonverbal communication while you have your conscious focus on the verbal message. To be a forward-thinking individual, keep it simple. Just relax and learn to be more observant rather than attempting to push yourself to analyze and absorb everything. Instead, be mindful of the present moment and expand your awareness without switching your concentration. When you know the signs to look for and their meanings, sensing and evaluating them will be intuitive for you.

When you have nothing in your mind is the natural and best way to start reading body language. For example, do it when waiting in line, you relax in the park or sit alone. Another alternative is to mute your TV as you watch it. And based on the body language of the actors, make an effort to absorb and analyze what you are watching. To confirm if you understand what you are watching, tune up the volume on occasion. The words of the speaker and the harmony between the words of the speaker and body language need to be your foremost goal when you are interacting with people. The person may mean what they say, and they may not, but the most important thing is to trust your gut feelings to help you understand. On a certain level, you will sense it, and signs will surface if the person is not right.

Reading body language in its context

Since you are reading body language, you are dealing with people, and they can be quite unpredictable sometimes. That is one crucial lesson you must understand about reading body language. We may get our result wrong in the end even when we assume something based on the previous knowledge we have.

So, how do we minimize the mistake? The first thing is to be sure you have the right facts. In a country like Bulgaria, we may get into trouble since it is an exact opposite of what we hold that a nod will always mean "yes" nonverbally. The main thing here is to check the manual if you are not sure! As you visit other places with foreign cultures, take time to learn what else this gesture might mean. A foreigner will always be eager to talk about their culture if you ask them. And as they say, there is no shame in asking.

Then, it is time to scrutinize the context after you examined some pointers. Ask some relevant questions; ask about where you are; the situations and the individual you are observing, and other elements present. Different behaviors are as a result of different settings; since there are various social codes are in play, you must know that a board meeting is not the same as a beach party. You may be wrong if you have a presumption that all the lessons you have learned about body language will be applicable the same way in all situations.

Scientific Body Language Secrets That Will Make You More Successful

If you are like some people, your thoughts may stir towards how you sit, move, or stand. But you should, because when we send some nonverbal signals, others impulsively pick them up.

A more critical rationale to reflect on body language is how science identifies that humans learn and understand their nonverbal signals. How we feel, sit, perform, and the gestures we have is as a result of a particularly remarkable effect.

The fortunate part of it all is it is easy. What you are supposed to be doing is not thinking about using body language all day to your advantage. Rather, all you have to do when you feel you need a bit of boost of creativity, confidence, to feel happier, or creative, is to pick the times.

Use the power of touch when you want to be more earnest

Apart from helping you to make a sale, touch can influence behavior, heighten the odds of compliance, make the individual engaging in the touching appear more friendly and attractive. For example, in a study, researchers asked the participants to express 12 different emotions when they touch the forearm of other blindfolded volunteers. Without any spoken word, ranging from 43 to 83 percent rate of accuracy, the participants perceived emotions such as fear, anger, sympathy, gratitude, love, and disgust. Patting someone on the shoulder or upper arm or better still, shaking hands can aid the strengthening of the authenticity of your words when you want to praise someone. When you do this, however small in the life of someone else, you have a difference which will make you feel better and also put the person in high spirit.

Lie down when you want to be more creative and innovative

As Darren Lipnicki, a professor from Australian National University, noted, you can obtain creative breakthroughs when you lie down. He explained that it is when people lie down on their back that their creative thoughts heighten. It is because the chemical noradrenaline could inhibit the creative process, and we release more of it when we are standing. Everyone can now relax, lay back, and try to reflect as an excuse.

Flex muscle if you want to have better determination and willpower

You need blood work at the doctor, and you are nervous when you see the needle. By trying to reduce the pain, it could be that is how your body responds. You need to stay focused, and it will help you when you flex your muscle. Also, you will be able to stand firm from tempting foods intake by flexing. It seems like everyone needs to be flexing now!

Cross your arms if you desire to feel more persistent and determined

We all know, at least we have briefly talked about it before. But do you know that crossing your arms can be a signal to others that you're anxious or closed-minded? That could be a signal of indifferent. If you want to take healthier action on unresolved problems, you may want to cross your arms. Not only will you perform better, but you will also be able to stick around and resolve the issue. As a trait of prosperous entrepreneurs, persistence is what everyone needs in abundance. Also, when you feel stressed and anxious, you can cross your arms to help you calm you down. A bit of warning here; do this in your privacy if you don't want other people to pick up on it. Anytime you are in a puzzling situation, try to cross your arms.

Make your best impression of Superman when you want to have more confident

A professor from Harvard, Amy Cuddy, said that your level of confidence would significantly improve with the power posing for two minutes such as holding your arms towards the sky or holding them out, standing tall, putting your hands on your hips while you stand like Superman, or standing tall, will dramatically increase your level of confidence. Strike a pose if you think you will feel nervous, intimidated, or insecure before you make a presentation. Find a secluded place where no one will see you.

Smile if you want to bring down stress

When the brain receives a signal from your facial expression that you are engaging in a complicated chore, it is as a result of negative facial expression, frowning, and grimacing. By releasing cortisol when your body responds, your stress level rises. In a short while, you will be in a tight spot because stress results in more stress. Here is the cure: smile. Even if the situation is still the same, you will feel less stress when you make yourself smile. Also, there is another cure; there will be little to no stress for people even when you smile, which, as a result, will reduce the level of your stress. So, learn to use one smile to kill two tensions.

Also working out becomes more comfortable when smile. It is natural to grimace when you engage in a heavyweight with reps.

But you will discover that it is easy for you to do more reps when you force yourself to smile. Get ready for odd glances at you from others in the gym if you decide to give it a try.

Tilt your head forward if you want to make people, and even yourself, feel more comfortable

While meeting people, it can help eliminate any seeming disparities in status and shows humility and defense when you tilt your head forward slightly. Smiles, tilt your head forward in a slight way, show the person that it is a privilege to meet them, and make eye contact the next time you meet someone. Naturally, we will reciprocate the gesture when someone showers us with affection. As a result, people will begin to be fond of you if you show them that you are indeed delighted to meet them. Thus, as this gesture will help you to be yourself and help calm your nerves, it will also demonstrate their love for you that they like you.

Mimic their nonverbal expressions if you want to understand better someone else's feelings

Does this sound strange to you? But according to research, you can identify with the emotions other people are experiencing when you imitate their nonverbal expressions. Because of an "afferent feedback mechanism," copying these expressions affect our feelings since we use nonverbal emotions almost all the time. For example, you will better understand the feelings of someone when you mimic their expressions. Therefore, you will be of great use to the person due to those feelings. Also, there is something we do most times without any thought, which is mimicking the facial expressions of someone else. Doing this creates positive effects on your interaction with them.

Stand at an angle if you want to resolve an interpersonal difference

You will induce confrontation when you stand, facing the other person when the tension is high. And it is even more confrontational when standing face to face more closely. Attempt to shift your feet slight once you understand what your posture could challenge the other person. Walk to one side and sit or stand.

And if someone confronts you, don't back away. Create a slight angle by shifting to one side. Make an unpleasant discussion feel less antagonistic by trimming down any seeming confrontation.

Use your hands if you need to enhance information retention

According to a study, children may not have so much impact on improving their learning when the teacher demands that they only speak while learning. However, they will preserve the wisdom they acquire when requiring them to gesture.

This instance can work for adults since this works for children, too. A researcher said that the fundamental function in education is to gesture, and it is a personified way of symbolizing fresh initiatives when you give learners an option.

Chew gum if you want to feel more upbeat and happier

Granted, it may not appear trained to munch on a wad of gum. Still, several studies show that you can be more observant when you chew gum. Also, it can enhance your response times, or sustained and selective attention, as well as your disposition.

Attention here: drop in some gum, cross your arms as you lie down when you want to crack a puzzle. So, go ahead, accomplish your innovation with this fascinating recipe.

Chapter 7: A Comprehensive Look at Covert Emotional Manipulation

Covert emotional manipulation is an exceptional phenomenon that can happen to anybody, even you. Covert emotional manipulation occurs when a person uses dishonest and deceptive schemes to transform your thinking, perceptions, and behavior to gain control and power over you. When you are in a state where you feel less confident, less intelligent, less sane, less reliable, less secure, or less than what you were before, you are covertly emotionally manipulated. Behind the intensity of your mindfulness alertness is where emotional manipulation operates, and restrains you emotionally, while as a victim, you know nothing about what is happening.

Some of what a skillful emotional manipulator will do to you is to influence you to place into their hands all your sensitive safety and senses of self-worth. Manipulators will continually and methodically break off your self-esteem and identity until there is little left the instant you make such a severe miscalculation.

Psychopaths and manipulators manipulate much in the same way as "pick-up artists" and narcissists. As for psychopaths, they have a perception that they are in charge and look down at others as their game to suit their hunting needs. Psychopaths have no compassion, no remorse or guilt, no conscience, and no ability to love. Achieving anything they want, including money, sex, or influence and taking control and power is a game of manipulators. Not only that, but psychopaths also destroy their victims psychologically, emotionally, physically, and spiritually in the course of their actions. They use all tactics to realize their wishes. They will get going to the next conquest after they have won the game, filled with contempt for you and getting bored.

Covert manipulators cannot have a genuine connection even though they are so smart. They have a strategy from the beginning. Apart from that, they are proficient at reading your mind, gaining knowledge of your strengths, weaknesses, dreams, fears, and desires is so easy for them. With an armory of valuable manipulation schemes that they have chosen carefully and personalized only for you, it is not in them to hesitate from using all these against you. They yearn for control and power and will always persist to control you, even if it results in harming you. At a point when you think your life has got the blessing of a tender bond through the magical excitement has made a comfortable and delightful appearance, it might be that something quite sinister and different is behind it. To conceal their exact strategy and personalities is one of the skills of manipulators. The main goal of these psychopaths is to fool you into trusting that they love and ready to do anything for you so you can confide in them in the course of a frenzied process of passionate illusion. They craft this stage of deep attachment not only to pin you but also make you susceptible to the abuse and manipulation that will ensue.

After a while, demeaning will replace loving. From then on, degrading will follow, and manipulators will confuse, exploit, and diminish your self-worth, self-esteem, and self-respect. To keep you eager to do anything to save the relationship and to let you hold yourself responsible for not cherishing a great relationship and vouching to save the affair no matter what, manipulators will make a pleasant appearance as loving individuals that hook you.

To show your devotion to the relationship, you will be eager to acknowledge sheer morsels. You won't have any thought of talking about your emotions, fears, and needs, which is not the concern of the psychopath and consider unacceptable weaknesses. When things go wrong, you will shift the blame on yourself, analyzing every mood and every word, becoming quite confused about what is happening, and recalling the conversations. Not only your life or job will suffer, but also your dealings with other people, and your mental and physical health. Your manipulator will try to have you with them waiting for the time you become a hopeless disaster. At that point, they will let you know with seething contempt and disdain, how they are bored with you and don't want you anymore. Then, they will leave you a sensitive mess who wonders just what happened to your life, speculating your perfect affair crumbled into the gulf of hell from heaven-on-earth.

Struggling with feelings of acute emotional grief and confusion is what comes to all preys of this deceptive and underhanded manipulation. Also, a lot of them experience rage, obsessive thoughts, insomnia, misplaced self-esteem, panic, anxiety, inability to trust, poor health, fear, use of drug or alcohol, and absent of support. Sometimes, extreme and irrational behavior can happen, including withdrawal and isolation from family, friends, and society. Suicidal actions or thoughts are part of what most victims face.

The question is; do these manipulators truthfully want love in the first place? Maybe they never have any desire for love. In a situation such as this, the purpose is that of victimization. The manipulator would have had their plans for their target when they discovered that you are open to their advances.

On the other hand, the occasion might end up badly even if the manipulator has a real attraction for you. The fact is because it is the incentive scheme of the brain, things, and people stimulate and excite these people. Indeed, for those with psychopaths, the system works quite well enough. Indeed, studies have found that far than that of an average individual, the reward system of manipulators is more sensitive.

Consequently, it is with the intensity that they establish a relationship.

A Deeper Look at Manipulation Tactics

Covert manipulative individuals make use of tactics to accomplish two things simultaneously:

1. Conceal their intention
2. Invite you to fear, doubt, and concede

Tactics that are generally the most effective in manipulating other people, especially neurotics, are a few tactics covert manipulative people use more frequently. The key to personal empowerment is to know how to deal with these methods of manipulation when you recognize them. With the use of just about any behavior imaginable to accomplish their aims, it is so amazing how capable the more skilled manipulators can be. Armed with these tactics, manipulators will thoroughly evaluate how they will manipulate the character of their target, when the manipulators know their victim inside out and are familiar with their target's fears, sensitivities, conscientiousness level, core beliefs, and so much more. And in a covert war of dominance, manipulators will have a considerable prospect making way for them to use the traits of that person, especially their most collectively attractive characteristics against them.

It will be appropriate for us to focus our attention of the more conventional approaches they employ and to give in-depth details why the tactics are so efficient because it is not realistic to talk about different feasible behaviors covert manipulators can use to influence another person. Having a good understanding of the fundamentals of the way manipulation works will not only reinforce your insight to the various potential tactics manipulators might apply but also give you superior conscious control of the nature of upsetting encounters with all manipulators.

There is a rationalization tactic which we may call "justifying" or "excuse-making." Originated from the Freudian notion, the word rationalization indicates that, on occasion, against the fear they might have suffered by engaging in dealings that damage their principles, people defend themselves unaware. They will assuage any qualms of conscience when they find reasons that appear to make their achievement more benign, appropriate, understandable, and acceptable. However, the assumption for this situation implies that the person has a highly sensitive conscience. And this type of rationalization is a mostly unconscious process and strictly internal.

Manipulators know what they are doing when they make explanations for their actions in some situations. When this set of people is looking to validate themselves, they certainly have obvious intention in mind. They make use of this approach during the time they know quite well that they plan to do something or have done something most people would regard as wrong. However, manipulators stay determined to do it even when they know it is wrong and how their action negatively represent them. To them, they have permission to do it, such as the situation of the aggressive characters or the case of more self-absorbed individuals, or they may clash against the accepted rules.

One thing most essential to identify is that at the time manipulators are justifying their actions; they are neither unconsciously fending off any anxiety nor defending. Instead, they are actively at war against a set of standard manipulators know society wants them to accept. More importantly, they are also attempting to get your support. As opposed to open defiance, covert manipulative folks have preference for this kind of tactic because it does not only help mask their manipulative goals, and also various revealing parts of their personality, but also concurrently helps them preserve a more positive social image by getting another person to go with the supposed rationality of their actions or have similar perception like them. And when the person accepts their premise with this strategy, the door of wielding the mutual domination and contest of image is opening gradually.

It is not that manipulators don't understand that their actions are wrong or that most people would see them as evil; instead, they hate your negative appraisal of their personality and perhaps end any relationship with them. Also, more importantly, that they should not engage in such behavior again is a notion covert manipulative people don't want to incorporate and allow. Even when at present, they still apply the tactic, they are opposing a standard and holding up the inculcating that standard into their social ethics. It is the visible signal that they are liable to engage in a similar activity in any related situation.

Now, let's us talk about denial, another tactic. Denial is a word that had its origin from the psychology of Freudian. Freud invented it as an unconscious and primitive resistance against intolerable emotional pain. With other tactics such as pretending that they are innocent, manipulators often will use denial. This situation is when someone you have confronted acts as if they know nothing of what you are saying or they pretend in a vain way that they did nothing of which to be guilty or ashamed. At times, they will use faking gullibility and denial with such apparent confidence and intensity that you start to be curious about your sanity and perception. That moment, you start out knowing that you have caught them on the action and one way or another, using this tactic, you begin to wonder if you are making any sense at all. This tactic is quite an efficient one-two manipulation blow!

However, by far the main missiles in the arsenal of any manipulator are the strategy of guilt-tripping and shaming. The fact behind this analysis is that precision defines the high degree of neurotics and cannot stand thinking that their actions are shameful or wrong. As a result, making them believe that what they have done should make them feel ashamed or guilty is the perfect way to control them. Conscientious individuals sometimes attempt to put shame or guilt on their prey with the hope that it will somehow induce modification of their behavior. However, they learn quickly that these strategies prove ineffective on them. For these tactics to function, you will need to acquire a considerable aspiration to be an average person and an equally great sense of wrong and right. In short, since it is a quality lacking in disturbed characters, you need to have intense principles.

Covert Manipulation Victims Mistake Interest for Regard

Most times, victims of covert manipulation marvel how someone they thought love them changed to a wicked person. Things were so different when they meet their other half. To be a part of their life is the desire of the other person. They appeared contented to share their world. They bought them gifts and did quite a lot of activities with them. Their significant others kept telling them they love them with all the things this they did for them. Therefore, why did their relationship change so completely?

The fact is that it doesn't mean someone cares about you when they have their eyes or an exceptional quality in you. Sometimes, it may mean that they hope to possess something of desire to them. It is said that folks who end up exploited often take high regard for great interest. However, that is not true of this case. When someone sees a situation they want to utilize, they can desire you intensely. Maybe you can give them lifestyle and security because you are a stable and financially responsible person. Or perhaps your sheer relationship with them feed their personality because of your physical appeal. It can quite flatter when a person seems to have a strong desire for you. Also, your thought may steer to the fact that they value you more considerably.

Learning the hard way about genuine regard

Everyone would jump into it if loving was that simple? There wouldn't be any necessity to demand it just in the way of every religious head in history. You must know that love is not the same as desire. It takes no effort to desire something because we can see objects of our desire that can please us, and we like it. And sometimes, with great delight, we pursue our desires. Since interest is different from regard, abuse victims learn the hard way.

Sadly, after they have been mistreated and exploited, then they realize what happened. In the long run, they discover that the reflection of capacity for genuine caring is the real character. True love manifests with the combination of genuineness, empathy, free-self-giving, and openness.

Genuine love – unrestricted positive regard

Authentic love does not happen naturally. However, human hearts are made of it. Unfortunately, to grasp it is quite hard for our minds. As we make an entry, a hostile world awaits. We learn to understand ourselves when we see that it is a world where everyone understands, learning along the way to defend and protect.

The Route to Self-Empowerment

The journey to self-empowerment is straightforward when you steer your focus, energy, time, attention, and energy at where you have power. Knowing about the precise means to accomplish will provide you all of the additional required solutions. The answer to personal empowerment is truly simple. But it is not easy to accomplish. Though daunting, the road to personal empowerment tends to uncomplicate. The question is; how do you then do it? The simple answer is you need to break off your attempt at managing situations, people, and things over which you naturally have no power. Instead, you need to focus on activities required of you to advance your interest and protect yourself. You can follow these general rules of empowerment by knowing the personality of an individual with whom you are dealing. What this means is that you have to dig deep, so you unravel any form of disguise in the person and evaluate the patterns of their behavior. To predispose those patterns of behavior, you need to consider the ways and attitudes of contemplating about things. People will talk to you about all kinds of things. It is cheap to talk, and it is most times dishonest. There are tactics people usually bring into play to control and manipulate others; you need to learn how to identify them. To look good that they are doing so, people engage in these tactics to have their way. Don't give in to these tactics to govern your behavior. Instead, you need to allow your actions to be the guide for your integrity. Where you have ultimate power is when you learn to take firm measure on your behalf.

Chapter 8: Secret Codes of Psychological and Emotional Manipulation

Never ignore the warning signs of manipulation. When a person's behavior intends to revise the attitude of someone else through the use of deceptive, devious, or even abuse means is psychological and emotional manipulation. In the event where you discover the behavior of someone to be harmful to you and invariably happen to be the one apologizing to them, such a person might have emotionally manipulated you and the situation. And when a person decides to help you only for them to sigh or whine about it so much that you instantly want to reject the offer, then, someone is controlling you psychologically.

The truth of the matter is, from time to time, every one of us engages in some form of manipulative behavior, however, when it becomes the conventional way in which one interacts with other, then, that person is an emotional manipulator. And like we discussed in the earlier chapter, manipulation differs from persuasion. Having the chance to decide on your reaction to a particular situation is persuasion, while manipulation is all about one's "right" choice; the manipulator's choice. And if you refuse to choose, there will be severe consequences. Individuals that have the highest vulnerability to manipulation are generally conscientious, generous, naïve, or honest people who are unable to make their decision due to self-confidence. A therapist of family and marriage, George James, noted, the possibility that someone is manipulating you is in some clear emotional cues that should draw the attention of anyone.

While it may appear impossible for us to fiddle with the lifestyle of someone else, we have the opportunity of responding to their actions. You can minimize the effects of manipulation by creating stronger boundaries if you discover that there is consistency in some cases whereby someone is manipulating you. Also, your self-confidence will get a boost when you do this. Though, when some people are attempting to use their manipulative tactics on you setting boundaries is manipulative, but it is not! There's a difference in manipulation and establishing a healthy limit since you will set yourself free from your attachment to the outcome when you set the boundaries. Apart from helping you to protect yourself when you set boundaries, it will also give you the confidence to tell directly to your partners when their behaviors are unacceptable to you. Ultimately, you may need to reevaluate your affair with your spouse when you discover that it's impossible to define the relationship you have together, as well as ending any connection with the person altogether. In any case, against the beliefs of manipulators, "no," as a word, is a complete sentence!

Decoding the Emotional and Psychological and Manipulation

When there is an intention of seizing control, power, privileges, and benefits, with the process of undue influence through emotional exploitation and mental distortion is happening, then, psychological and emotional manipulation is taking place. There is a need to distinguish emotional and psychological manipulation from strong social influence. As a mutual part of positive relationships, strong social impact happens between most people. As for psychological and emotional manipulation, someone uses another person for their benefit. Deliberately, the manipulator exploits the victims and crafts an imbalance of power to serve their agenda. It is important to note that not all people whose actions in some of the examples below may have a deliberate attempt to manipulate you. Poor habits are some of the problems of certain people. Nevertheless, it is vital to be familiar with these conducts in some cases where your interest, safety, and rights are in danger.

Advantage of home

A manipulative individual may take a firm decision to interact or meet you at a place where they can implement more control and dominance. In this case, you may lack familiarity and ownership such as home, office, car, or other spaces and whereas, the place may be in favor of the manipulators.

Looking for weakness and confirming your baseline by allowing you to speak first

This is the habit of most salespeople when they prospect you. They will have the capacity of evaluating your weaknesses and strengths when they confirm your basic standard or level of behavior or thinking by asking you general and probing questions. With a hidden agenda, this questioning takes place in personal relationships or at the workplace.

Manipulation of facts

Good examples include excuse-making, lying, or being two-faced. Manipulators make use of this method to blame their target for initiating their victimization. Also, this habit is about vital information withholding or strategic disclosure, deformation of the truth, exaggeration, unfair bias of issue, and understatement.

Overwhelm victims with statistics and facts

By assuming to be most knowledgeable or to be the authority in some areas, most people take great pleasure in intellectual harassment. These people manipulate you by enforcing supposed statistics, the information you do not know, and facts. This can occur in financial and sales situations, in negotiations, and professional discussions, relational arguments, social. The purpose of the manipulator is to impose their agenda more persuasively on you by presuming expert power over you.

Manipulators engage in this technique on their victims when they want to feel an impression of intellectual supremacy.

Overwhelm victims with red tape and procedures

Some individuals use bureaucracy, including procedures, other roadblocks, paperwork, committees, laws, and by-laws to sustain their power and position, as they make things more difficult for you. They also use this technique to delay-truth seeking and facts finding, evade scrutiny, and hide weaknesses and flaws.

Exhibiting negative emotions by raising voice

As a type of aggressive manipulation, it is the habit of some people to raise their voice. They have the assumption that you will give them what they want by projecting their voice so loud or exhibiting negative emotions. Frequently, strong body language like excited gestures or standing to increase impact blends with strong intonation.

Negative surprises

Some individuals gain a psychological advantage over you by putting you off balance with the use of negative surprises. This can range from impulsive job manipulators cannot prevail and dispense in some way, to balling in a compromise situation. In some way, you have no chance to organize and fight their move when the startling negative information comes without warning.

Requesting for an additional concession from you may be one of the tactics of the manipulators to continue working with you.

Giving you little or no time to make decision

This situation is where the manipulators want you to decide before you are ready by putting compelling you. This technique is familiar with sales and negotiation tactics. With the hope that you will 'snap,' when they apply control and tension on you, they have the hope that you will yield to their demands.

Poking at your weakness and disapprove you through the use of cynical humor

Often cloaked as sarcasm or humor, some manipulators enjoy making critical remarks, so you appear less secure and inferior. Some of these cases include many comments ranging from your older model Smartphone, to your appearance, to your credentials and background, to the issue that you were out of breath when you walked in two minutes late. They hope to impose psychological superiority over you when they get you to feel bad by making you look bad.

Criticize and judge you to make you feel incompetent always

This situation is not quite the same as the previous behavior, where they use cynical humor. In this case, they pick on you thoroughly. Through consistent marginalization, dismiss, and ridicule, they keep you unsteady and maintain their superiority. Since no matter how hard you try, you are inadequate and will never be good enough as manipulators deliberately foster the influence that there is always something wrong with you.

Most importantly, they have their focus on the disapproving without providing consequential approaches to assist, or the provision of any constructive and genuine solutions.

The silent treatment

In this situation, manipulators presume control by making you hold your horses and intend to place uncertainty and doubt in you when they deliberately refuse to respond to your logical calls, emails, text messages, or other inquiries.

Pretend ignorance

Playing unintelligent is a classic tactic of manipulation. When manipulators pretend as if they do not know their responsibility to you or your desire, they make you toil by making you take on what is their responsibility. This behavior is popular among the children as they use it to manipulate, delay, and stall adults into taking up the work meant for them. When they have an obligation they wish to avoid or something to hide, some adults engage in this tactic as well.

Guilt-baiting

This situation is for unreasonable blaming when manipulators target your soft spot and hold you responsible for their success and happiness, or failures and unhappiness. They target your emotional vulnerability and weakness and coerce you into accepting irrational demands and requests.

Victimhood

Manipulators use this technique to exploit your guilty conscience, goodwill, sense of obligation and duty, or nurturing and protective instinct, for them to extract unreasonable concessions and benefits. Some of the good examples of this behavior are issues that are imagined personal or exaggerated, purposeful weakness to elicit favor and sympathy, imagined or exaggerated health problems, dependency or co-dependency, martyr, powerless, and playing weak.

Control: The Power behind Psychological and Emotional Manipulation

Has it ever happened to you from a close associate or experienced it from your spouse, colleague, your boss, spouse, a family, or friend? Sometimes, a neighbor can even control you!

Within the human race, as a force so dominant, control is a powerful word. Control symbolizes a capacity to influence, dictate, direct, and maneuver. If you take a moment to search for the word "control," you will see synonyms of intimidating terms like authority, sway, command, jurisdiction, mastery, dominance, supremacy, or sovereignty. These synonyms are quite intimidating, particularly if you think someone is controlling you needlessly. There will be a clash when one person tries to control the other.

The practice takes over our potential of choosing our beliefs, values, and actions without interference, feeling the world as we see it, or acting with the use of free will. On the other side, there would be chaos in the world without control. We will not perform our jobs well enough, we wouldn't find the accustomed stability, and our world would be a mess. And in our daily lives, this type of control is sensible, and we all need it.

However, behaviors that can rob you of every scrap of your personality is the control whereby another person manipulates your emotions and thoughts. The power of this manipulation will be extremely intense that, without your fault, you will begin to experience shame, guilt, lower self-esteem, and pessimistic self-talk. Like we discussed before, you are likely to be in a one-sided and unhealthy relationship if you notice a repeated pattern of this behavior.

The most horrible feelings anyone can have is for someone else to control them. We are people with an intervention toward freedom and self-motivation. In some respects, control cramps our growth and development, learning from decisions we make, and the power to explore the world around us. Whether personal or professional, relationships can tear apart because of control, make other people resentful and defensive toward the person that controls, and destroy trust. Respect, boundaries, compassion, patience, and understanding must balance control.

We can all agree that you would have a better feeling if boundaries, tolerance, and respect would be used by your spouse, boss, or parents to balance control. Control becomes abuse and bondage without these things.

Sometimes, the control appears to be spiritual since it is an influence that rules us far beyond intelligence and logistics. Since that is the reason relationships between employees and even cases of marital violence, the victim has a hard time bending to the will of the person controlling them. In this situation, loss of self-confidence and abandonment panic is most times a crucial reason. Some of the examples of this fear include:

- Loss of camaraderie or friendship
- Loss of employment or opportunity
- Confrontation or argument
- Growth of an inaccuracy complicated social status or reputation

- Loss of basics or essentials for living
- Temporary discomfort or feelings

It is crucial to be able to discover abuse and control. It can sweetly come to you, a bribing way. Below are the patterns of actions that people may exhibit when they want to achieve control of your life:

To keep track of you

Sadly, some people tend to do whatever it takes to keep track of you. Someone who opens the lines of communication by getting in touch with you could do it for their advantage. For example, someone who hooks you up at social media sites or online to check on you and how you're faring, or attempts to email or text you even when they never liked you. Such a person will generally cyber-stalk you.

The effort to get in touch with may not be up to 1 to 3 times a year, and your interactions together the person may be irregular. Using you or manipulating, you may be the objective of the person.

How you deal with this situation is to be cautious of things they know about your life. Having boundaries is quite okay for you, but you can't have 100 percent trusts for someone suddenly wants to bond but who didn't like before. No steps or baby steps is all you need to take.

To make friends with you when it is suitable for them

Do you know someone that regard you quite poorly and doesn't care that they are into you, but suddenly start smiling with you, embrace you, and express amusement with you? You must watch out. Indeed, people may start to like you when they can get familiar with you.

It is possible, though, for some people who have accepted you before and then reject you in another second, only for them to then accept you the next time since it comes to their understanding that they misjudge you. But there some people that do not misinterpret you.

These people don't have any affection for you. But the fault is not necessarily yours! In such a situation as this, never fully trust anyone who jumps from mean to kind and then kind to mean. Don't even look at it that it is a mood swing because it is far from it. You need to be wary of the things they know about you and learn to keep up solid boundaries. Keep a private life and resist from being an open book.

To micromanage you

This case may be a tough one. This situation happens when someone loans you money, or significant possession, or have you in charge of their affair and then keep close tabs on you. It might occur to you when, within the relationship, a base of respect and trust exists. What you must do is to examine the relationship if you realize someone doesn't trust you and is eager to allow you to have access to their possession and pretend they have your interest in mind.

Think about why they behave that way, and if it will help the situation when you talk about how you feel. Some of these people want to control you since they don't trust you. Without being argumentative, bring up the issues and explain that their attempt at controlling you is unacceptable and you are not comfortable with it.

To "mirror" you as if you're a child

For intention that may be proper, it is the habit of some people to "mirror" the people they care about and love. For example, in a tender relationship, when a wife goes out for shopping, a husband may monitor her. Because he is concerned about her, the husband may text or calls the wife to check how her shopping is going.

However, there's a problem that one must not ignore when someone tries to control what you are doing at a point, the extent of your departure, and where you are that you feel demeaned, suffocated, or humiliated. Sit the person down and talk to them is what you must do in this case. Avoid any emotion of anger, frustration, or judgmental when you tell them how and why you are not comfortable with their behavior. Never ignite an accidental fire.

Go about it with a calm expression about your feelings. Then, if the same pattern of behavior continues, you may have to consider if their practice of controlling will increase later on or if the relationship is worth it at all.

How Manipulators Use Language to Dominate

As varied as they are exhausting, as a form of emotional abuse and mental exploitation, the signs of emotional and psychological manipulation in communication and language that require all of us to identify.

Some of the good examples have been discussed earlier in this book including the use of sarcasm, not answering, saying that it is impossible to talk to you, talking down to you, as well as giving threats and ultimatums. The liaison officer between Nazi Germany and the Italian government, Licio Gelli, the Italian financial, was known for his role in the scandal of Banco Ambrosiano and being the Venerable Master of clandestine lodge Propaganda Due that they revealed out in 1981. Many Italian scholars have written about him as neo-fascist specialized in some form of manipulating the people. Gelli once noted that by knowing how to communicate, you could have control over an individual.

His mantra is that to dominate people, language is a weapon anyone can use perversely. And as Goerge Orwell posits, the power of thought can corrupt language, as well as the power of language, can damage human relationships. We all know this fact quite clearly.

There is the almost constant use of manipulation to influence human decisions, control us, and seduce us in the grand universe of mass media, in the circle of politics, and advertising. However, all things become a little more complicated and sibylline when we come to the private sphere. We exchange words with our friends, families, and partners in this aspect. Apparent all around us are the signs of emotional and psychological and manipulation, yet those that use the tactics most times disguise it. Also, out of our consciousness, we use it subconsciously.

Therefore, it is vital to know how to react to those tactics when you detect them. We must have a clear grasp that not only is it essential for us to watch out of our expression but also the manner of the expression. An imbalance in the relationship in question is what happens when we refer to the idea of emotional and psychological manipulation through words. Manipulators use language to benefit themselves.

Also, they have the goal of hurting you while they use it to control you. What creates this covert aggression inside us is our base emotions.

Chapter 9: Emotional Manipulation Tactics Manipulators Use to Win and Confuse You

The superior wisdom of knowing your enemy is a crucial advice everyone must take when dealing with a manipulator. The insight allows you to have a strategic response to issues. For some people, the manner of their reaction escalates abuse, thereby retreating and taking in unacceptable behavior, falling into the trap of the abuser which makes them feel guilty, small, and doubtful of self. When you learn what they are up to, you will be able to empower yourself.

Covert aggression is what appears defensive or passive when someone behaves violently. To what degree manipulators' behavior is unconscious or conscious is controversial. As for the victim, the situation has no significance because the impact is similar. They will be in jeopardy of mistreating them continually when they are overtly-empathic. When a person gives you covert or overt attack, they are aggressive.

As George Simon, a psychologist, argues, covert manipulators do and say things to accomplish their mission, which is to have control and power. As for narcissists, people with borderline personality disorders, and sociopaths, Simon argues tactics of these individuals are not inherent in the pattern that defense mechanisms work usually. The behavior of this set of individuals becomes reflexive that over time, it is so frequent. Without thinking about it, they are nonetheless mindful of it even without thinking about it.

Manipulator's Ambitions

Needless to reiterate this, for achieving their aims, the purpose of all manipulators is to gain influence, but it is for control and power through abusive and deceptive techniques for habitual manipulators. They sustain control through recurring, continuous emotional manipulation, coercive control, and abuse. They are passive-aggressive most of the time. In their attempt to behave unacceptably and deflect any criticism, manipulators may act or lie or surprised by your complaints, or hurt. For manipulators to maintain power and carry out their wishes, they aim;

- To avoid responsibility
- To make you question your perceptions and even yourself
- To prevent any form of confrontation from you
- To continue with their behavior
- To conceal their aggressive intent
- To put you on the defensive

Ultimately, you may not have trust in yourself, your perceptions, and feelings because they have victimized you. Overt aggression may be part of manipulation such as narcissist abuse, subtle forms of emotional abuse, and criticism. Manipulators have preference weapons of violence including bribery, blame, mind games, undermining, assumptions, reversals, evasiveness, emotional blackmail, inattention, forgetting, apologies, fake concern, favors and gifts, and sympathy. Below are some of the tactics manipulators use to confuse their victims:

Lying

Sometimes, habitual liars engage in their act when it is pointless. They are not lying because they are guilty or afraid, but to convince you to obey their orders. Through some manipulative tactics like accusations, many of these people plant you on the criminal side at the same time. Also, through omission of material information and vagueness, lying may be indirect even when their submission is far from being true. For example, a trickster in a relationship would never admit to an adulterous rendezvous, and they might say they are at the gym or working late.

Denial

Because it is unconscious, this type of denial is typical of not realizing that you have an addiction, someone has abused you, are running away from the truths. Rejection knowledge of behaviors, agreements, and promises is what conscious denial all about. Also, it is a form of rationalization, excuses, and minimization. They downsize and justify their actions or act as if you're taking things too far for nothing to win your pity or make you question your actions.

Avoidance

Manipulators will always avoid any situation where you want them to take responsibility for their action when you confront them. Manipulators may refuse to discuss their behavior and evade conversations about it. A situation like this may combine an act of violence, including accusing you of always nagging and you're on the suspicious side which fills you with guilt, blames, or shame.

The state of avoidance can take a discreet and subtle level when a manipulator changes the topic. They may camouflage the subject with compliments, boasting, or remarks that are good to your ears such as asking you to disregard the reason for your annoyance in the first place or telling you about their concern for you. To blur the facts, plant doubts, and confuse you, another tactic they use is the avoidance of vagueness. When you are positive about a relationship, you enter into denial yourself and give someone the benefit of the doubt. Count on them when you have doubts!

Guilt, shame, and blame

A defense where the manipulators accuse you of their behavior, these tactics involve projection. They believe that excellent protection is the best defense. The distressed one is now on the defensive when manipulators swing guilt. While their victims now feel shame and guilt, they perpetrate them freely and remain above suspicion. Manipulators are known to condemn anyone or perhaps their victims.

Typically, they criticize their addiction on others, their 'bitchy' spouse or needy boss. Without any defense, a defendant of crime will show aggression on the police or their technique of gathering facts. Attacking their victim's reputation is one of the habits of rapists. In cases of marital violence, the husband who had beaten his wife blamed her for beating her. Shifting the focus of shaming and guilt-tripping onto you will make the abuse feel greater while it makes you grow weaker. When martyrs express criticism that you are ungrateful and selfish and imply or say after all they have done for you, they are engaging in the use of guilt.

To make you feel that you are not enough, shaming goes beyond guilt. Not just your actions, shaming debases your traits, your role, or you as a person. Manipulators will tell you that if the children had a father who knows how to make a decent living or has specialization in parenting, the children would behave. Their comparison is a strong form of shaming, yet it is subtle. It can be damaging when parents make a comparison of siblings with playmates or even with each other.

To make their mate feel inferior and have the upper hand, some partners make a comparison of their ex to their mate. Blaming the aggrieved person is part of the shaming and guilt. For example, you may discover proof on your spouse's phone that they are flirting. It is likely for your partner to act outrage that you are taking their things behind them. Now, they have succeeded in switching the focus on you. Your spouse avoids the flirting confrontation by playing the victim, which they can lie about, circumvented, or minimized altogether. You don't want to challenge any rationalized rage and feel guilty for your action even as the real casualty, thereby tolerate the flirting, and it continues without dealing with it.

One particular indication of toxicity is when someone applies all tactics to evade any form of responsibility and frequently reluctant to see their inadequacies. Manipulators are making use of projection in this case. By laying them at another person's door, the tactic is a defensive mechanism to displace responsibility of their negative characteristics and behavior. As a detour, the mode of this tactic is to avoid accountability and ownership.

As Dr. Martines-Lewi, a Narcissistic Personality clinical expert once noted, to some degree, everybody use projection; however, most times, it is perceptively abusive for narcissists. In such a way that is excessively cruel and painful, malignant sociopaths and narcissists choose to put their persona on their gullible suspects, instead of acknowledging their imperfections, wrongdoings, and flaws. They have a preference for their victims to feel ashamed of themselves and accountable for their conducts rather than coming clean that it may be to have self-improvement. This way, narcissists succeed in projecting their toxic shame onto someone else.

For instance, someone may indict their spouse of fibbing even when they are lying pathologically; to portray them as the needy ones, a dependent mate may identify their partner clingy; in an attempt to get away from the reality of their efficiency, a discourteous worker may describe their superior inefficient. Playing the blame-shifting game is what narcissistic abusers enjoy playing. Their objective for playing the game is that you lose, they win, and the blame for their behavior is on you or the larger world. While you are plunged into an ocean of self-doubt when this happens, you end up taking care of their weak ego.

As for those narcissists on the other side of the scale, they usually don't care about change or self-insight. For you to validate your identity and concentrate on the actuality of events, it is vital to terminate all relations and cut bonds with toxic people quickly. Another person's cesspool of dysfunction doesn't have to be your burden.

Intimidation

Intimidation can be subtle without being always direct threats. Manipulators achieve intimidation with a tone or look and telling you that no one is irreplaceable, or they always get their way, or the grass is not any greener, or if you have thought of the consequences of your choice.

Narrating a story designed to incite fright is another strategy of intimidation by manipulators by saying that a woman lost everything, including their kids and her husband when she left the husband. Or it could be that one time, they almost killed a guy or boasts that they fight to win.

Playing the victim

Playing the victim tactic is quite not the same as blaming the victim. Instead of blaming you, they will play the victim tactics to arouse your sympathy and guilt so you will give in to their agenda. They will tell you that they are confused if you don't get your support. Most times, if you attempt to discontinue the relationship, more disordered personalities make threats of killing themselves. Also, playing the victim takes place when the manipulator tells you that you have no concern for them, or why you should treat them like that, or no one helps them.

Nonsensical conversations from hell

Don't think you will ever engage in a polite conversation with a manipulator because if you do, you will only get circular conversation, word salad, gaslighting and projection, and ad hominem disagreements to get you off track and disorient you. If you make any attempt to challenge or disagree with them at all, manipulators will do everything to confuse, frustrate, and discredit, thereby putting you at fault for being someone with genuine feelings and thoughts that might be different from theirs and distracting you from the main problem. For them, if you happen to subsist, you are the obstacle. Have you been in a situation where you wonder how the squabble even starts at all when you argue with someone for a few moments? Well, that is a toxic narcissist. When you disagree with them about their ridiculous assertion that the ocean is green, then, prepare to have your family, childhood, friends, lifestyle, and career choices under attack. It results in a manipulative injury for them because your disagreement has grasped their bogus confidence as the omniscient and omnipotent, it results in a manipulative injury for them.

You must watch out for toxic individuals because they may not make a case with you. Essentially, their argument is with themselves while the audience in attendance that witnesses their tiring, lengthy monologues is you. While breathing it, manipulators flourish off the drama. You stock their arsenal anytime your position contradicts their ridiculous assertions. You will have the power to provide yourself with the substantiation that their offensive actions are theirs, not yours when you learn not to feed the manipulators supply.

Use your energy on improving your life and as soon as you figure out your relations with them is growing, break it off.

Generalizations and blanket statements

Many of the malignant manipulators are intellectually lazy and therefore, not always masterminds of intellectual. Instead of being cautious to consider several viewpoints carefully, they generalize everything and anything about your thoughts, making blanket statements that regard the several angles in your submissions and don't recognize the distinctions in your claim. In essence, blanket statements and generalization overthrows skills that have nothing to do with the unsupported schemas, stereotypes, and assumptions of society. Also, to uphold the status quo, manipulators make use of them. The situation where the problem of social justice can turn entirely into obscured is when this form of deviation inflates one perception.

Also, toxic relationships have a bite of these daily micro aggressions. For example, if you make an attempt to mention to a manipulator that you won't tolerate their behavior, instead of dealing with the real problem at hand, most times, they will simplify by telling you that you are easily upset all the time, and you are never satisfied or take to the broad view about your hypersensitivity. At times, you may be oversensitive, but there is a possibility the addict is also cruel and insensitive every time.

The key to taking care of this situation is to stand firm against oversimplifying speeches by comprehending that they are in fact, forms of white and black irrational opinions and hold on to your truth. When manipulators wield blanket statements, they embody the incomplete one of their overinflated sense of self and particular knowledge, and they don't symbolize the entire wealth of experience.

Conscious misrepresenting of feelings and thoughts to the level of absurdity

Your legitimate emotions, life experiences, and differing opinions can get a transformation into the proof of your absurdity and character flaws in the hands of malignant manipulators. To reframe what indeed you are saying, they merge tall tales as a way of making your views appear heinous and absurd. For example, if you attempt to broach your opinions about your feelings with manner a toxic spouse is talking to you, they will use tactics of responding by asking you if they are a bad person or if you are the perfect person, thereby you will see yourself talking. But you haven't done anything than telling them how you feel! This tactic fills you with an impression of shame when you have a go at setting up boundaries and gives them to power to nullify your claim to have emotions and thoughts about their unsuitable manners.

Also, this tactic is a classic form of cognitive alteration and diversion associated with mind reading. Most times, manipulators presume that they have a clear grasp of what you are feeling and thinking. Based on their triggers, instead of stepping back to evaluate the situation mindfully, manipulators regularly presume. Their actions are as a source of their fallacies and delusions, and as a result, no excuse for the harm set off by them. They are notorious in describing you as someone with intents, making you take out of your consciousness, or outlandish viewpoint unconnected to your persona. Even before you have the opportunity of asking them to make a change, manipulators use different tactics to accuse you of thinking them as toxic, and this is also a manner of preventative resistance.

Should the manipulator go on with their accusations against you for saying or doing what you know nothing about, tell the person that you never said that and walk away. When you do this, you have created a solid border in an interaction such as this. Provided that the manipulator can deviate from their conducts and shift the blame, they have made headway to induce you that, for your realistic feedback to them, you should cover yourself in indignity. Also, never give in to derail. Manipulators can pull a switcheroo on you, and you have to exercise the broken record technique of continuing stating the facts without giving in to their distractions. Redirect them by telling them to let the conversation be focused on the real issue. Cut the tie and use your energy on something more positive when you are aware that they are not interested. The tactics manipulators use to confuse you are exhaustible. They are destructive, and over time, they can traumatize you and your self-worth can be severely damaged. The first step is awareness. If you feel you may need help to see things clearly, learn to write out your conversation and try to identify abuse and all the tactics used. When you learn how not to take the words of the manipulator, you will know how to respond to them.

Chapter 10: How to Tell if You Are Being Emotionally Manipulated

If only you ever figure out what is happening, emotional manipulation can be hidden and delicate. For a while, its influence can be so powerful. Many manipulators are vastly proficient. They are puppet master, according to some experts, and if you can understand the signs, you might turn to a mysterious puppet. As the puppet masters pull your strings here and there, you have to obey their commands. It is possible for you to know something is amiss as a manipulation victim, but it's hard to point to the cause of it. You may want to find out when you suspect someone is manipulating you. Your case may be that, in the past, someone has manipulated you, and nothing will make you face the same situation again.

Sometimes, it can be quite tricky to spot emotional manipulation. We believe that, in the relationship framework, our partner has extreme concern for us. As a result, it is possible for us to ignore some cautious signals. However, there are things you must look out for if your partner's behavior is mischievous. When a person is manipulating you emotionally, they will criticize and judge your actions in subtle ways. For example, making a mean comment about your choice of friends is typical for manipulators. When someone tells you that they cannot believe you would say that it may also be an emotional manipulation sign. They may be attempting to generate feelings of guilt and embarrassment, pointing out your weaknesses and faults with the use of humor to undermine or shape their confidence. Also, they will strive to chip away at your perception to cause you to feel confused or doubt yourself, the same impact with gaslighting.

On the other hand, you may want to know that it is not difficult for you to tell if someone is manipulating. Indeed, there may be no need to be familiar with the tactics and methods to realize someone is pulling your strings even though it is smart to learn the techniques of covert emotional manipulation. If you want to know whether someone is manipulating you or not, you only need to observe your persona. And it is quite possible someone is manipulating you if you notice some of these signs;

- Your anxiety of losing your love has departed from the delight you have at finding it. Your relationship kicks off with big dreams, and then, things suddenly change, and you are in a state of confusion as to how things changed as sadness, anxiety, and still, extreme stress replaces your feelings of happiness.

- The condition of your relationship is dependent on your mood.

- Though you are not sure, it is as if you are damaging the relationship.

- A lot of time you are not contented in your affair. However, you don't want to lose it because you are blissful all the time.

- While you are not sure about the reason, the connection with the other person feels quite cumbersome. You likely find yourself telling your friends while talking to them about it that it is just quite complicated or that it is hard to explain.

- The relationship is your obsession. Almost regularly, you are analyzing all aspects of your relationship and at the same time making so much effort to understand it. Every time, you express the state of this situation in your relation to anyone that cares to listen, yet all these attempts are fruitless.

- You ask your spouse all the time if something is wrong. Though it doesn't as if something is wrong, but you are not sure.

- It never occurs to you your position with your spouse, and that makes you continuously nervous and indecisive.

- Most times, you are on the cynical side of your relationship. You discover that your partner misunderstands you, and as a result, you are forced to defend and also explain yourself.

- Conveying negative emotions and thoughts is forbidden and even feels restricted. Consequently, you make an effort to conceal those things. Frustration sets in for you since it's hard to express essential elements.

• It's hard for you to figure out what to do to make your spouse happy. You make several efforts, but you fail at everything.

• You have a sense of lack. Against your feelings before the relationship, you have no joy about yourself. It seems you're less sane, intelligent, less self-assured, less safe, less trusting, and against your past traits, there are so many "less than" in you.

• There's a constantly feeling in you that you are not sufficient enough for your spouse.

• You discover you are always apologizing.

• Most times, there's a sense of guilt in you. There's a persistent feeling for you to patch up the grievance that you believe you've caused. When your partner keeps some distance, you feel you are the cause of it and then blame yourself, and in your confusion, you continue to blame yourself.

• So they don't pull away from you again, you are cautious of your actions, emotions, and word with your partner. Since you keep feelings to build inside you, typical of a volcano, you explode sometimes. This action has never happened to you before. It only worsens your relationship, and you have no power over it.

- You are doing things that violate your limits, values, or boundaries, or you are not comfortable with and want to keep things intact and delight your spouse.

In any relationship, emotional manipulation is deadly, in particular, a loving relationship. Emotional manipulation creates entirely a biased connection, which can cause you to be frantic about clutching any rationale you get from your manipulating partner.

Because manipulators want to keep up full power, fights often happen in this kind of scenario when they try to exercise self-control and individuality. Also, it is sometimes so harsh for the victim of emotional manipulation. You may suffer low self-confidence due to the behavior if you discover your spouse has manipulative practices, thereby begin to doubt your worth.

You will end up losing your power to reason for yourself if you stay in a situation where your partner continually applies control over you. Not only that, in your effort at evading depression, you will always take cues from your partner. The stunting of your emotional growth will eliminate prospects of essential corroboration, and reduce any form of achievement on your part. In return, you will start looking at yourself as being not worthy, consequential, or lovable.

What Do Manipulative People Do Best?

The straightforward and simple answer to that is to cart off your power. Period! You will have fewer resources and tools to rebuild and develop when you have less power to grow. One of the skills manipulators have is to fragment the foundation of your emotion to make you think you need to bad feelings about initiating the end of the relationship and that you are not as much of a person.

When a person who is meant to support and love you makes you feel guilty or wrong, such a person is most possibly attempting to satisfy their selfish needs. Since their manipulative partners convince them that they always do things wrong, victims of manipulation get extremely tired of this behavior to the extent that they start considering that they are inferior, unintelligent, and even harmful. The worst part is when these manipulative partners go on much longer; it becomes harder for the victims to have a different conviction. Also, to dish out food in the right way is complicated for these victims since their manipulators will criticize them on their technique. Manipulators will micromanage and judge their behaviors to the level where they are miserable.

How and why the manipulators do what they do is the main setback for the victim of emotional manipulation since they don't know exactly. Not only are manipulators exceptionally proficient at word-craft, but also know the exact language to inculcate shame, guilt, and anxiety in their partner. Manipulators know how to cut down the confidence of their victims so they can have a bright and energetic personality and for the victim to call on for answers all the time. So they can appear "perfect" to them, the goal of a manipulative partner is to transform their victim behave the right way. You may be blond, and they have a preference for a redhead. Eventually, you may become redhead with the prospect of getting their love and attention. Usually, because they don't even identify someone is manipulating them, many victims don't understand their awful feelings. Above all, manipulators often appear as generous and kind to the people outside their relationship.

Apart from looking sincerely polite, manipulators behave toward everyone else with respect. As a result, when the victims talk to their acquaintances about the behavior of their partner, their friends may appear shocked, telling the victims that they don't observe anything like that at all and they may even tell the victims that they don't believe them.

Eventually, when all your friends see your spouse as someone who has to contend with your madness and think you are ridiculous, then the manipulators have gotten their victory. Since your family and friends are not living with your manipulators, they are not spectators of the clever bad behaviors manipulators do when you are alone together. It may be unclear to you the conducts of the manipulators because, after all, discussions with them, you know that most times you are upset or guilty. So, what is the reason for this? Why is this situation happening?

The answer is because when manipulators talk, you "give them your ears" to them. Indeed, you believe every single thing they say since you trust your love with them and that you're precious to them. Thinking you are precious with the hope for proof and praise, manipulators have put a dirty dig on you to the extent that their words are your breath. Because you are sure your partner will soon shower you with sweet words while they embrace you, you hold on to the manipulative relationship longer than it is healthy. Sadly, after the kindness, love, and understanding, manipulators will often follow up with observation about what you're doing wrong or bad. Later or sooner, it will happen.

The simple fact is manipulators are quite adept at dishing your pleasant compliments. They are geniuses who emotionally engage you by blending kindness, caring, and feeling concerned about you with blame and criticism. For example, manipulators might even inform you they want a solution to a problem they have to induce your empathy and validating your concerns, however, the plan behind this is to make you feel worthless and invalidated. They use this complicated and smart method to reel you in, chew you up, spit you out, and then with the hope, you'll be valuable, they keep you on your heels back to them.

Chapter 11: Winning Friends and Influencing Others with These Tactics to Enhance Self-Esteem

You have made conscious efforts to work out ways to find contentment by evaluating your choices every day and not worrying about the disapproval of other people to have positive thoughts. Ideally, the people close to you would do the same. Though you may not have the capability to transform the way they think and act, you can be an inspiration of positive influence to inspire them to make changes that would result in a more rewarding soul.

Setting a stimulating pattern

Albert Schweitzer, the theologian Noel Peace Prize once said that example is the only thing even if it may not be the main thing to influence people. Rather than listening to what you say, people tend to pay attention to your action. If you have the intention of influencing people positively, you have to engage in your daily life the way you'd expect them to do.

You will succeed in inspiring people, at least enough to make changes to improve their experience, when they notice your business success, happy relationships, and additional upbeat life's component.

Value people

People tend to pay attention to your positive actions and word the instant they have a feeling of a queen or king. As Andrew Carnegie notes in "How to Win Friends and Influence People," his classic book; influencing someone is the most effective way to make them feel worthy or essential. Focus on the upright aspect of every person and make efforts to give honest good wishes. People will have the ability to make the best of themselves when you learn to do this.

Project confidence

When you are a confident person, people will want to follow you. Strive not to be a coach of a basketball team who tells his team that he doesn't know whether the odds will be against them or they will take the victory. The team will have no bearing if he tells them this and as a result, they need direction, and maybe a confident player among them will assure them they can win the game no matter what.

When you convey a thorough self-assurance statement, you will have the power of setting yourself up like an expert. And as an authority figure, you will have a better stimulus ahead of most people. You will realize how much you can be influential when you tap into the authoritative side of you.

A touch of drama isn't bad

You don't have to turn to a drama king or king, but the wonders of blending theatrical can go a long way in your effort to persuade other people positively. They will always remember when you engage them when something you do is conspicuous. For example, you can add the theatrics to your message when you wear a sou'wester with a T-shirt that has an inscription "love others" and give those at the parks cold soda; it will be hard for people to forget it.

The Art of Winning People

Why you like someone may be hard to say. It could be their razor-sharp wit, their goofy smile, or they are fun to be around. You like them. However, people tend to be a pain in the butt at times. You may have a tough time handling them, and eventually, most of us get angry. But yelling and shouting do no good as it is like exploiting our energies in vain. You can force people to do the job by shouting and yelling, but that will generate a feeling of resentment. So, is it possible to win people and influence them to do some things without stirring up resentment?

Below are some simple yet effective rules you can apply in your daily lives. When you do, you will realize how much you influence changes in them without any form of offense.

Sincere appreciation

It is ideal to start with sincere appreciation before you criticize people. When you begin with admiration, it is typical of giving a Novocain before operating. It is important not to offer flattery as sincere appreciation is all that is important. At least everyone has one or two qualities. You have to be the rare individual who can see the good in other people. You need to make the person feel important before you point out the negative parts. This is what the idea of starting with sincere appreciation is all about.

Indirect call of attention to mistakes

It is a great idea to start with sincere appreciation and praise. However, some people add the word 'but' along with it. For example, they may tell someone that they have tried quite hard, *but* the performance is still not satisfactory. You can make a difference by altering the word 'but' with 'and.' For example, you can tell the person that they have tried quite hard, and you hope the unsatisfactory performance will go away soon. Can you see the difference between the two?

Talk about your mistakes as well

Sometimes, we make some mistakes as well. So, why not let the other person know about them before pointing out their mistakes? All you have to do is tell the person that you understand what happened, that you had faced similar mistakes before you were able to work hard to get the result. Tell the person that you want them to know that you expect better results from them.

Never give orders

You need to know that no one likes to take orders. A good leader understands this and makes the team do things, not by giving orders, but by asking questions. An excellent example for that is rather than telling someone to come here and do this thing, as a good leader, all you have to say is – 'Hey there, would it be possible for you to do this thing?' When you ask questions, the other person feels special. The person feels that you care about them and as a result, sincerely complete the work.

Let the other person save face

Rather than putting people down, you need to allow them to save face. So, next time you want to remove someone from a position, avoid telling this; 'We are sorry, but we don't need your services anymore. We hope you have a great future.' Instead, replace it with this; 'You know how useful you have been to the firm. Your services have helped us achieve many deals. We wish to work with you in the future again.'

Praise every little improvement

Do you have any employee who is having difficulties in their work? It may be time you start commending the small details as well. When you do this, it will make them feel special. Great leaders are well aware of the power of sincere appreciation. So, learn to be hearty in your criticism and lavish in your commendation.

Give people an excellent reputation

This idea works on a 9-year-old kid as well. If there is a mess creating, naughty boy in a classroom, the teacher may find it difficult to control his behavior after doing everything. What the teacher can do for the boy is to make him the monitor of the class. The teacher can tell him, 'Boy, you have great leadership skills.' The teacher praises on every minute detail. Guess what will happen? The boy's behavior will improve drastically!

Use encouragement

Using encouragement is quite critical. Rather than criticizing, if you start using encouragement, you will have much better results. Several autistic children have become entirely normal with the use of encouragement. Encouragement gives someone hope. And with hope, the person will move ahead and performs wonderful things. So, next time you see someone performing unsatisfactorily, instead of criticism, use encouragement.

Make others happy about your suggestions

The idea is that someone should feel good about your suggestions. Great leaders understand the rule quite well. They instruct in such a manner that the other person feels responsible for completing the task. The person takes pride in doing the job and sincerely executes it.

Ignite the Art of Reading People through Your Super Senses

If you want to read people, you have to don the garment of a psychiatrist who has the power to interpret cues which are verbal and nonverbal. You need to observe beyond people's masks into their real self. You may not get the entire picture about anybody through logic alone.

You have to surrender to their critical forms of information to interpret the essential nonverbal perceptive cues that individuals exude. For you to achieve this feat, you need to be eager to surrender emotional baggage like ego clashes or old resentments and also any preconceptions which can prevent you from making out the person. It is crucial, as well, for you to obtain information without bias and continue to be impartial without twisting it.

In the process of reading a colleague, your boss, or partner for you to understand them accurately, some walls need to come down, and you need to surrender biases. You need to be ready to let go of limiting, old ideas as far as intellect is concerned. Those who read other people well are taught to comprehend the hidden. They have discovered how they will draw on what is called 'super-sense' so they can take a profound observation beyond where you usually steer your focus when you attempt to hack into transformative awareness.

Examine cues of body language

When you are reading the cues of body language, you have to surrender the focus by releasing your struggle to understand the hidden signals of body language. Never get analytical or overtly intense. Stay fluid and relaxed. Observe by sitting back comfortably.

Focus on appearance

When you are reading other people, take note of what they are wearing. Are they putting on well-shined shoes and power suit? The indication for success is when someone deck out decently. For someone wearing a T-shirt and jeans may be an indicator of that person being comfortable with casual. It may be a signal of a seductive choice when someone wears a tight top with cleavage. A pendant like Buddha or cross may indicate spiritual values.

Notice posture

Postures are an essential aspect of reading people. It's a sign of confident when people's head is held high. Or you can get an indication of low self-esteem when they cower, or they walk irresolutely. You can also get a sign of a big ego when they have puffed-out chest and swagger.

Pay attention to physical movements

When you read others, look out for their distance and learning. In general, people bend forward at those they like and keep a distance from others they don't. Also, when people cross their arms and legs, you can see signs of anger, self-protection, or defensiveness. It is an indication that people are hiding something when they hide their hands by placing them in their pockets, laps, or place them behind them. With cuticle picking or lip biting, you will get a sign of people attempting to calm themselves in a difficult circumstance or under pressure.

Read facial expression

Our faces provide the outline for our emotions. Profound frown lines indicate over-thinking or worry. The smile lines of delight are crow's feet; pursed lips is a signal of contempt, anger, or bitterness. While teeth grinding and clenched jaw are indicators of tension.

Take note to your intuition

It is possible to tune into someone ahead of their words and body language. Though not what your head says, what your gut feels is intuition. Instead of logic, intuition is your perception of nonverbal information through images. If you are in the process of understanding a person, their outer trappings are insignificant, and it is only who the person is what counts. To reveal a richer story, intuition gives the power to distinguish beyond the obvious to tell a richer story. You need to watch out for these checklists cues of intuition:

Respect your gut feelings

Pay attention to voices of your gut, in particular when connecting with someone for the first time, an automatic rejoinder that happens out of impulse. Gut feelings are as a result of if you are tensed up or at ease. As a cardinal response, gut feelings occur in an instant. They are meters of your inner truth that relay to you if you should trust someone.

Goosebumps feelings

Pleasant, intuitive shivers are goosebumps, and they happen when something strikes a chord in us in connection with our resonance to individuals that inspire or move us. Also, goosebumps occur in the course of going through déjà-vu and when you have never met someone before but still recognize them.

Listen to sparkles of insight

During a conversation with people, you may be impressed by those who come quickly. Watch out and stay alert. Or else, you might fail to spot it. For most of us, this crucial awareness is lost because of the inclination to move onto the next idea.

Look for insightful empathy

This cue happens when you have a passionate type of empathy through the feelings of someone's real emotions and symptoms within your body. So, while reading people, take note whether you had pain on your back when it wasn't there before, or if you are upset or depressed following a mind-numbing conference. To determine if empathy is at play, get feedback.

Discern emotional power

The vibe we radiate and the remarkable demonstration of our energy are emotions. It is with an intuition that we procure these emotions. For some people, you will be happy to be around them because they enhance your vitality and mood. Others tend to be draining; get away from them is what you want. Though it is undetectable, you can feel this 'subtle energy' feet or inches from the body. It's called *chi* in Chinese medicine, an essential healthy vitality.

Be aware of the presence of people

Though not substantially similar to our behavior or words, the accustomed energy we discharge is when we sense the presence of the people. It is typical of a rain cloud or the sun that borders around our emotional atmosphere. In the process of reading people, take note of if you get attraction with their presence or retreating due to the willies you are getting.

Watch people's eyes

Humans' eyes convey compelling forces. As the eyes cast off an electromagnetic signal, according to studies, the brain does the same. When you watch people's eyes, you will know if they are tranquil, sexy, mean, angry, or caring. Also, you will have the ability to determine if a person wants intimacy in their eyes or their eyes can give signs that they are comfortable. Even in their eyes, you will know whether they appear to be hiding or guarded.

Observe the feel of a hug, handshake, or touch

Most of us shake emotional energy, similar to an electrical flow during physical contact. You can ask yourself if a hug or handshake feel comfortable, warm, or confident. Or if it is repulsive so much that you wish to withdraw. You can know the sign of anxiety with someone's hand clammy or limp to suggest being timid or non-committal.

Listen to the tone of laugh and voice

Our voice's volume and tone are capable of telling a lot about our emotions. Vibration is as a result of sound frequencies. Notice how people's pitch of voice affects you in the course of reading them. Envisage if the tone is snippy, abrasive, and whiny or if their tone feels soothing.

To read people can be hard sometimes. It takes practice and courage. However, once you are past that, you will gain a significant advantage. Not only will you survive, but you will also thrive in all your relationships with others. People will approach you. Opportunities will come to you. And some people will want to be like you.

Conclusion

Thank you for making it through to the end of *Covert Manipulation: An Introducing Psychology Guide for Beginners* let's hope it was informative and able to provide you with all of the tools you need to achieve your goals whatever they may be.

Chances are if you have made it to this point, it's because you want to make a change. You desire a turning point in your life where not only can you be independent in making a decision about your life, but you will be on top of any tactics manipulators can use on people. Imagine how things would be for you if you have in your hand all the tactics manipulators use on their victim, especially with all the practical examples in this book. You will certainly be able to make constructive decisions that will have a positive impact on your life.

Imagine what your life would be if you have a clear understanding of mind control or brainwashing, or how people influence each other. Imagine the power you will wield if you can distinguish between body language and facial expression. And what would it be when you know all about mind game relationships. You will be able to gain control over any situation you face using some practical examples discussed in this book, like being an action taker and how perception is vital in various situations in life.

You have read about control and understand how powerful it is to denote a power to influence. There are examples of behaviors people display when they want to control you. Also, you have had a fair understanding of how manipulators use language to dominate. Life is all about making conscious decisions every day to have positive thoughts. And you can be an inspiration of positive influence when you know the tactics to enhance self-esteem.

DARK PSYCHOLOGY

How to Use the NLP Secret Methods of Manipulation for Social Influence, Emotional Persuasion, Deception and Mind Control - A Guide Based on Hypnosis and Brainwashing Techniques

Introduction to Dark Psychology

The following chapters will discuss manipulation techniques involving neuro-linguistic programming, mind control, hypnosis, and brainwashing, as well as the concepts and principles that make them up, including the personality traits of the Dark Triad, persuasion, and deception. The final chapter will also include three detailed case studies in order to better understand the concepts covered in the book. Chapters will also contain specific methods of manipulation that can be used in any situation and can even be combined with each other to become even more powerful. Every technique introduced in this book will build on information that has been previously discussed so that learning each new concept will feel like a natural progression and will not be confusing or difficult to understand. By the time you have reached the end of this book, you will have gained a solid understanding of the concepts and techniques that make up dark psychology and manipulation, and you will be ready to try out these techniques in the real world on any target that you choose.

If this book is your first introduction to dark psychology and manipulation, then welcome! The information presented in the following chapters might seem overwhelming at times, but stick with it, and you will find that you have gained valuable skills that can help change your life for the better. Dark psychology is a well-kept secret, and by purchasing this book, you are joining a group of elite and highly skilled people from all around the world. Learning how to manipulate the people around you is an extremely valuable skill to have, and it can help you to improve your relationships with other people, advance further in your career, get more of what you want out of your life, and even feel better about yourself as a person. Soon enough, you will be an expert in the art of manipulation, and you will be able to take your destiny into your own hands like an expert manipulator.

If you have already read other books about dark psychology or have any prior knowledge about manipulation, then this book should serve nicely to supplement and improve upon what you already know. You are also likely to find out something that you did not know before somewhere within the chapters of this book, whether in the form of a manipulation technique that you were previously unaware of, an event in a case study that you had never heard of before, or something entirely different. Keep in mind that knowledge is power, and this book will help you to become an even more powerful manipulator than you already are. No matter who you are or what your background on dark psychology and manipulation is, you will find something useful in this book. If you are more interested in the concepts that make up neuro-linguistic programming, mind control, hypnosis, and brainwashing, or you are completely new to the field of dark psychology, then I would recommend starting at the beginning and working your way through the book from there. On the other hand, if you already have knowledge of the principles of dark psychology and manipulation, or if you cannot bear the thought of theories and concepts, then the latter half of this book will be more interesting for you to read (Of course, I would still recommend going over the concepts discussed in the first few chapters before continuing on. Practice makes perfect!). If you ever feel that you are becoming frustrated with or overwhelmed by the information contained within this book, do not be afraid to put it down and come back to it later.

The following chapters contain plenty of detailed, technical information that can be difficult to absorb all at once. Frequent breaks can be incredibly useful when learning a new skill, as long as you stay determined and do not give up entirely. Remember that manipulation techniques take time to perfect and that with enough practice; you will soon become a master of manipulation.

Chapter 1: Neuro-Linguistic Programming

Have you ever procrastinated by spending time online or bingeing television shows before completing an important project and ended up rushing to finish it in time? Or have you ever had trouble talking to people without feeling anxiety or awkwardness? Maybe you have any number of bad habits that you have been hoping to break, like biting your nails, smoking, or stress eating, but no matter how much progress you might have made in breaking them, you have never found a solution to rid yourself of these feelings or habits permanently. In that case, trying Neuro-Linguistic Programming, also referred to as NLP might work for you. NLP is made up of three components: *neuro*, which refers to the nervous system, especially in the way our brains absorb and process new information; *linguistic*, which is about analyzing language to better understand the information being conveyed in it; and *programming*, which relates back to habits, how they're formed, and how we can harness the power of the good habits and turn down the effects of the bad ones. You might be beginning to see how NLP can help you improve your life, but believe it or not, it gets even better: you can also use it to exert your influence over other people in an inconspicuous and unnoticeable way. Read on to find out more about how NLP was developed as a practice, the concepts and approaches behind NLP specialized NLP techniques, and examples of how to use NLP in the most effective, efficient way possible to improve your own life and to influence the lives of other people around you.

The History of Neuro-Linguistic Programming

The very first instance of Neuro-Linguistic Programming emerged in the United States in the 1970s as an advanced method of psychotherapy and communication, with its reported effects ranging from being able to help an average individual develop the same attributes and personality traits as successful and accomplished people to mitigating the effects of certain mental illnesses, including anxiety, depression, learning disorders, and overly intrusive phobias, as well as physical ailments such as common cold symptoms and problems with vision. NLP was developed by two men, Richard Bandler, and John Grinder, both talented self-help authors, trainers, and speakers who built the practice of NLP on the work of other professionals, including authors, psychiatrists, psychologists, anthropologists, linguists, philosophers, scholars, and psychotherapists. In 1975, Bandler and Grinder published a book called *The Structure of Magic I: A Book about Language and Therapy*, which contained the earliest concepts and abilities of the structure, uses, and effects of NLP. While neither Bandler nor Grinder was themselves trained psychiatrists, psychologists, or psychotherapists, an outside perspective may have offered them an advantage in developing NLP; Grinder stated that "My memories about what we thought at the time of discovery (with respect to the classic code we developed – that is, the years 1973 through 1978) are that we were quite explicit that we were out to overthrow a paradigm…[therefore] I believe it was very useful that neither one of us were qualified in the field we first went after – psychology and in particular, its therapeutic application." In other words, Bandler and Grinder were seeking to start a scientific revolution, and because they weren't bogged down with establishment beliefs and brought a new perspective to the discipline of psychology, they were able to accomplish precisely that.

In the late 1970s, the first workshop on NLP was held by Bandler and Grinder. It was a ten-day session attended by 150 students and covered NLP concepts and techniques to be more successful in both personal matters and business dealings. Later, Bandler and Grinder published transcripts from seminars from the workshop into a series of self-help books. Meanwhile, NLP was gaining a broader following, and a number of scientists, psychotherapists, and other professionals began to expand on and improve Bandler and Grinder's work on the practice. NLP teachings were expanded into other disciplines beyond self-improvement and business and came to be used as valuable tools in a number of different fields, such as education, leadership training, marketing, sales, parenting, therapy, and psychology. Today, over 40 years after NLP was first developed and written about, NLP has spread and blossomed into an international phenomenon, with people learning how to use its specialized techniques all over the globe. Every year, thousands of seminars train tens of thousands of people in the practice of NLP, and countless more people are exposed to the teachings of NLP through the thousands of books and guides that are currently available. And now, it's your turn to learn more about the major concepts of NLP and how to use them to your advantage.

The Key Concepts of Neuro-Linguistic Programming

As mentioned earlier, NLP can be divided into three major components, making up its name: neuro, linguistic, and programming. Of course, these are not the only concepts that govern the use and practice of NLP. In addition to neuro, linguistic, and programming, concepts such as subjectivity, consciousness, and learning (also known as modeling) are essential to the art of NLP. Having a good understanding of these concepts is the key to mastering advanced NLP techniques and procedures to be used in everyday life, as they provide a solid foundation to build and develop your NLP skills on. While the basics will be touched on in this section, more detailed techniques will be explained in the following section.

Neuro refers to the body's nervous system, in particular, the most important part of the nervous system, the brain. While human beings receive information from the outside world by using the five senses, the brain is responsible for sorting through and organizing all of the information that is received and plays a vital role in how you decide to act based on that information. Everyone's brain has a slightly different method of filtering through information: some are faster, more efficient, and more observant, while other people have to take their time in sorting information, and are not able to maximize the value they receive from it, while still others are somewhere in between the two extremes. Of course, ideally, your brain would have a filtering process that is as quick and effective as possible. By utilizing NLP techniques, you can train your brain to handle the intake of information at a faster and more productive pace, and can better determine how to use that information to gain an edge over other people in the same environment.

In NLP, your process for mentally filtering and sorting external information is crucial. After all, neuro is only the first step in the NLP process. Your first impression of the information gained from the filtering process is known as "First Access," and is comprised mainly of feelings, sounds, and images, all embedded within your subconsciousness. By being more attentive to the world around us, we can increase the strength of our First Access, and therefore have a better quality of information to feed our subconsciousness, which plays into how we make conscious decisions. Having a stronger First Access also impacts the ability to communicate with others, both on a conscious and subconscious level; if you have better access to information than another person, then you can better use that information to steer them in the direction that you want them to go.

If neuro is all about taking in outside stimuli and processing that into useable information, then *linguistic* is about what we do with that information once it has been fully sorted and processed. Once information has been gathered by the brain and has gone through First Access, we then put that information into words, both for us to be able to better understand and categorize the information as well as for us to be able to better communicate our understanding of that information in the way that best suits us and our situation. In NLP practice, the linguistic stage is known as the Linguistic Map, as well as sometimes being referred to as Linguistic Representation. While First Access is limited to the subconsciousness, the Linguistic Map is dominated by the conscious mind, which focuses on decision-making and communication skills. Therefore, having a stronger Linguistic Map will ultimately help you in developing superior decision-making and communication methods. Just like with First Access, paying more attention is the key to improving the Linguistic Map. Having a solid understanding of language and how it is used is extremely important to having a strong Linguistic Map, and by paying more attention to details such as sentence structure, speaking style, tone of voice, speaking speed, and the words being used, you can enhance the quality of information being utilized in your Linguistic Map. Having a stronger Linguistic Map also directly affects your ability to communicate with others, and if you have a better understanding of how to use language than they do, then influencing them will be much easier.

Finally, *programming* is the third step in the process and occurs after you have gathered and processed information through First Access and have conceptualized and made decisions about that information by using your Linguistic Map. Programming is critical in forming a behavioral response to information received and processed. This is where the habit-forming process comes into play: habits are built on repeating behaviors, and by having better information to build those behaviors on through a strong First Access and Linguistic Map, you can form more productive habits through stronger behavioral responses. Having a stronger sense of programming also helps you to weed out bad habits. By having a better First Access and Linguistic Map, you will no longer fuel your bad habits with poor quality information, and they will fall by the wayside as a result. Programming is also essential in manipulating the actions of other people; by having a stronger sense of behavioral responses in general, you will be able to better understand what kind of response other people will have to certain stimuli, and you can choose what information to give them in order to facilitate the reaction that you want to happen.

Of course, the concepts of neuro, linguistic, and processing are bolstered by three additional concepts: subjectivity, consciousness and learning/modeling. *Subjectivity* refers to how people perceive the world around them and the information contained within it. Rather than experiencing the world in an objective way, or based strictly on facts, human beings have a tendency to view the world from a subjective, or mainly opinionated, point of view. Because of this tendency, the information gathered from our surroundings in First Access is recorded and sorted in an inherently subjective manner. To better illustrate this point, think about the way your memory works: how often do you remember a certain event in exactly the way that it happened, with every detail preserved perfectly? You likely remember some particular parts of memory better than other parts, and even then, those parts may not even necessarily be completely correct. The way that your brain processes external information in First Access directly affects the way that you remember things, and what is memory is worthy of more importance than other parts. Fortunately, there is always a pattern in the way that subjectivity affects First Access, your Linguistic Map, and your programming and behavioral responses. By becoming more familiar with the pattern and intently studying the structure of how exactly subjectivity affects you, you can learn how to have better control over the information you take in, and from there, you can modify your behavior accordingly. Once you have a mastery over subjectivity, you can begin to directly control how subjectivity affects other people around you, allowing you to be able to shape their access to information and their behavioral responses in turn. In addition to subjectivity, it is important to understand the concept of *consciousness*, which is divided into two separate parts: the conscious segment and the unconscious segment. The conscious segment encompasses all mental processes and behavioral responses that you have awareness and control over. On the other hand, the subconscious segment involves all actions, thoughts, and reactions that you do not have any control over. Your subconsciousness is typically associated with First Access, while your consciousness is generally correlated with the Linguistic Map; however, it is important to keep in mind that neither the subconsciousness nor the consciousness is limited solely to First Access or the Linguistic Map. All three processes contain elements of both the subconsciousness and the consciousness. For example, breathing is a subconscious behavioral response, as you do not have to actively think about breathing in order to perform the action, and it occurs largely outside of your awareness. At the same time, an example of a conscious behavioral response would be speaking, as you have to think about forming words into spoken language, and you are completely aware that you are involved in the action of speaking. In NLP, any subjective information that you gain is considered to be part of what is known as the "unconscious mind." By manipulating how subjectivity affects another person, you can influence their unconscious mind, meaning that you can program them to have specific behavioral responses to stimuli that you give them, without them ever realizing that you are actively shaping their response. Finally, the last core concept of NLP to have a solid understanding of is *learning*, which is also commonly referred to as *modeling*. For simplicity's sake, *learning* is the term that will be used throughout the rest of this book, although you may encounter the term *modeling* elsewhere when researching NLP. Learning is widely considered to be the most difficult concept in NLP training to master, but it is also the most indispensable and necessary skill to know in order to best perform acts of manipulation and exert outside influence on the people around you. Essentially, learning is all about being able to recognize patterns in behavior and is most often used in order for ordinary people to copy the behaviors and attributes of people who are extremely talented specialists in their field, regardless of the behavior displayed by the specialists. However, once you learn how to properly utilize learning, you can also reverse engineer the concept for purposes involving manipulation. Once you understand how to analyze and imitate patterns in speech, behavior, and thought, you can better lead people to copy your own actions, and can send them down whatever path you decide on. I know that these concepts can be difficult to comprehend at first, but by reviewing them on a regular basis, as well as seeing how they are put into practice in specific NLP techniques, you will soon come to understand them on an intimate level, and your ability to perform NLP procedures on both yourself and other people will soon become impeccable. Before we continue to the next section that will cover NLP techniques in detail, it is a good idea to take time to recap the core concepts of NLP. *Neuro* refers to the nervous system, the brain, and how the brain processes and sorts of information collected from the outside world.

Neuro is covered by the NLP stage that is known as First Access. *Linguistic* refers to the way in which people use language, how the information gathered in First Access is translated into particular words and phrases, and the specific patterns and structures of communication which are used by both yourself and by everyone else around you. The NLP stage that focuses on the intricacies of linguistic is known as the Linguistic Map, or sometimes referred to as Linguistic Representation. The final NLP stage is *programming*, which refers to the behavioral response you produce to the information processed in First Access and labeled in your Linguistic Map. Tied to the three NLP stages are the concepts of subjectivity, consciousness, and learning. *Subjectivity* is the idea that information gathered from external sources is collected and sorted in a way that is based on opinion rather than fact, which then has an influence on how that information is utilized in the future. *Consciousness* refers to your awareness of thoughts, actions, and behavioral responses that occur as a result of the process of gathering and sorting information. Consciousness is divided into two different components: the subconsciousness, which has to do with all responses that you are unaware of, and the consciousness, which refers to all responses and behaviors that you have control over and actively think about. Finally, *learning*, which is also referred to as *modeling*, refers to recognizing particular patterns and specific structures in behavior and modifying your own behavior to reproduce those same behavioral patterns and structures. Read on to find out more about how the concepts of neuro, linguistic, programming, subjectivity, consciousness, and learning are combined into specific NLP techniques that can be used on anybody.

Manipulation Technique #1: In-Depth Learning Strategies

As mentioned earlier, learning is the most important component of any NLP strategy, so it is important to learn how to use it to its fullest potential in order to have a complete mastery of NLP techniques in general. Learning is essential to being able to influence others, as it allows you to get a sense of the other person and how they think, which gives you a road map that shows you the easiest way to steer them in the direction you want them to go. In order to perfect your learning methods, there are two components to learn: observation and questioning. Observation is vital to understanding other people, especially in picking up the habits and routines of their subconsciousness. Because they are not aware of processes in their subconsciousness, they have no control over how they communicate those processes. Therefore, only by paying close attention to their movements, speaking patterns, and actions can you discern what drives their subconsciousness and how you can best influence it. Watch for physical indicators such as what they're looking at, what they're doing with their hands, how their feet are pointed, as well as linguistic elements such as word choice, sentence structure, and tone of voice. All of these subtle factors can clue you in as to how a person is thinking and feeling. In addition to observation, questioning is essential to the learning experience.

Questioning appeals more to the consciousness, although it can be useful in understanding the subconsciousness as well. Ask a person directly about themselves, and try to keep the conversation going: the longer they talk the more that you know about them, and the more time you have to observe their behavioral and linguistic habits. Be sure to ask questions asking for more detail, such as "How do you know?" and "What does that mean?" Don't be afraid to ask your target to tell you more about what they're talking about.

Once you have completed both the observation and questioning phases of learning, you can review the information you have gained by entering into a state known as "deep trance identification." First, make sure that you are sitting comfortably in a safe, secure place. Next, think about what characteristics of your target you want to most closely understand, and imagine them showing off those traits. The more time you have spent with a person, the easier this process will be. As you imagine them, let your consciousness enter their body, so that you are experiencing what they experience through sight, sound, touch, taste, and smell. This process should be a sort of meditation, and you should not by physically performing any actions; allow the target work for you. Once you feel that you have a decent understanding of the target, exit their body and return to your own. You should have retained any important information, which you can now perform yourself. Repeat the process several times, and then exit the trance. Congratulations! You now know the target's thought, speech, and behavioral patterns, which you can now reverse engineer in order to better manipulate them.

Manipulation Technique #2: Manipulating Beliefs

In many ways, beliefs are a self-fulfilling prophecy. Believing that you can do something is the first step in accomplishing it, while not believing that you can do something makes you far less likely to pursue it. By changing another person's beliefs, you can directly influence what actions they take next, or you can prevent them from taking action at all. In order to manipulate beliefs, it is crucial to understand what a belief actually is. Beliefs are made up of two parts: the body of the belief, and the significance of the belief. The body of the belief is generally a broad, sweeping statement about a certain person or thing. An example of the body of the belief is a statement such as, "My boss is not interested in what I have to say." Meanwhile, the significance of the belief encompasses the impact of the belief on your behavior. For example, the significance of the previous statement about your boss means that you likely feel resentment towards your boss, and do not work as diligently as you could as a result. By planting the body of a belief into someone's mind, including either their subconsciousness or their consciousness, the significance of the belief will take hold, and direct their future actions. The main way to plant the body of a belief into your target's mind is through communication, which is where learning comes into play.

The easiest way to initiate and follow through on successful communication strategies is to know how your target thinks and communicates themselves. They are more likely to believe something that is already familiar to them, so having some idea of what their background is or what their personality is like can pay dividends. Of course, if you do not have access to this information, then another method of achieving familiarity is to imitate their speaking patterns. While you are planting beliefs, be sure to keep subjectivity in mind as well: because new information is processed based on opinions rather than facts, you may interpret a belief in a different way than your target. Make sure that your wording is precise, and that there is little to no chance that your statements can be misinterpreted. The more carefully you phrase a statement, the more likely that your target will internalize the body of the belief that you are attempting to implant in them. Ideally, your wording will be exact, but also subtle; after all, if the target thinks that they developed a belief themselves, not only will they be more likely to buy into it, but it will also be virtually impossible to trace back to you. If your method of communication is not proving to be effective, do not be afraid to try a different strategy, or try again at a later time after you have completed more learning. Patience is key, and if you are not successful on your first try, do not become discouraged; with more practice and more time, you are sure to succeed. Once you have successfully implanted the body of a belief, the significance of the belief will naturally take hold in due time, and all you will have to do is simply waiting for the effects to occur.

Takeaways

As you continue on through the rest of this book, be sure to keep in mind the concepts of neuro, linguistic, programming, subjectivity, consciousness, and learning. These concepts will continue to be relevant and are critical to comprehending other topics discussed in the following chapters. In addition, more NLP techniques will be discussed in chapters that are relevant to them. This way, these techniques can be better understood within the context of more advanced theories of dark psychology and NLP. Be sure to revisit techniques that you have already learned, and practice them often. Techniques often build on other techniques, and through frequent practice, you will be sure to hone your skills and be well on your way to becoming a master of the many uses of NLP.

Chapter 2: The Dark Triad

In order to best be able to manipulate others to the fullest extent possible, there is a commonly used and researched concept in psychology that is absolutely necessary to learn about: the Dark Triad. While the name certainly sounds sinister, it is a completely legitimate field of study within psychology, and can often be used to characterize people and behaviors in real life, even if those using it are not even aware that it exists. The Dark Triad is made up of three personality traits, which are known as narcissism, Machiavellianism, and psychopathy, all of which characterize negative social qualities in human behavior. While they all definitely sound malicious in their own way, there is nothing inherently wrong with any of the three of them. In fact, there is much that can be learned from the principles and characteristics of narcissism, Machiavellianism, and psychopathy, and by using your knowledge of the Dark Triad, you can use those principles to better influence the people around you, and you can also more easily recognize when other people are trying to use the concepts of the Dark Triad to manipulate you. While reading about the three components of the Dark Triad, be sure to keep in mind the six concepts of NLP (neuro, linguistic, programming, subjectivity, consciousness, and learning) that were discussed in the previous chapter, and try to see how they could be combined with the Dark Triad to create powerful methods of manipulation.

Concepts of the Dark Triad: Narcissism

The term narcissist is derived from an ancient Greek myth, in which a young, handsome man named Narcissus is tricked into looking at his own reflection in a river, which he falls so deeply in love with that he refuses to move and spends the rest of his life staring at himself. When you think of a narcissist, you might think of someone who displays similar behavior: someone who is obsessed about every detail of their appearance, or someone who goes out of their way to take too many selfies, or someone who generally spends far too much time being focused on themselves. But within the context of the Dark Triad, being a narcissist takes on a slightly different meaning. Narcissism is a personality trait which is characterized by a combination of pride, arrogance, pretentiousness, and most importantly, a noticeable lack of empathy. People who are narcissists are more likely to be extraverted, and they are also more likely to display signs of psychopathy as well. Men are more likely to show signs of narcissism, but a variety of studies show that the number of women who display narcissistic tendencies is generally increasing. But what is the easiest way to recognize a narcissist? There are several telltale signs to look out for. First of all, people who are narcissists tend to have a flair for the dramatic, and view themselves as not only more important than the people around them, but also one of the most important people in the course of history overall. They tend to view themselves as better than other people, and will not treat people who they view as below their standards with empathy or consideration. In general, while most people are usually satisfied with only receiving praise as a result of a specific action or accomplishment, people who have narcissistic traits see praise as something that they are owed simply for existing. On the other hand, narcissists have a hard time dealing with even the smallest amount of criticism and are likely to be angry if ever rejected or chastised. An example of a narcissist might be a coworker who constantly complains about not being recognized for their work when they do not work as hard as they could and refuses to listen to criticism that they could be working harder. When making a determination about whether someone is a narcissist or not, you can keep the concepts of NLP in mind. For example, a narcissist's sense of subjectivity will revolve almost entirely around themselves, and they will likely either not be interested or even unable to process any information that is presented to them that does not have anything to do with themselves or their lives in general. When attempting to manipulate someone who displays narcissistic personality traits, be sure to use plenty of praise and flattery in order to make them like you more. Do not say anything that they might think is criticism or rejection, as they will be alienated by you and will likely not be open to having any future conversations with you. (Of course, if your goal is to drive away a narcissist, then be sure to stick to topics that they are not interested in, including ways that they could improve in their own lives.) Once again, using learning to its full extent will help you to influence people who are narcissists, as you will know more about them and be able to target them with more specific praise or criticisms. The more specific you are in dealing with a narcissist, the greater the chance of success you will have in achieving the outcome that you want to happen.

Concepts of the Dark Triad: Machiavellianism

Have you ever heard the phrase, "It is much safer to be feared than loved"? Or maybe the phrase, "Never attempt to win by force what can be won by deception"? Or perhaps, "Everyone sees what you appear to be; few experiences what you really are"? All of these quotes come from a book called *The Prince*, which was written by a political philosopher and strategist named Niccolo Machiavelli. Machiavelli's writings and *The Prince*, in particular, are known for advocating for ruthless, manipulative, and cynical behavior in order to get ahead in life. Similarly, people who display the trait of Machiavellianism are often extremely skilled at exploiting other people in order to influence events to go in the direction of their own self-interest. Machiavellianism goes beyond simply influencing people from time to time; people who show hallmarks of Machiavellianism are constantly thinking in a strictly strategically manner in order to fully maximize their own advantage over other people. Machiavellianism is often the most difficult attribute of the Dark Triad to recognize in others, as people who display

Machiavellianism are generally secretive and are good at hiding the ways in which they manipulate other people. Of course, there are specific signs to watch for in order to recognize whether or not Machiavellianism is present in somebody else. Most importantly, people with Machiavellian tendencies place a high priority on keeping up a public persona, which is different from who they really are. They know the value of having their peers view them in a positive light, and are careful to have their public image be as positive and harmless as possible, as that way they can better manipulate and exploit other people while avoiding the blame for any consequences that may occur as a result. For example, think of any major celebrity. They have an interest in keeping up a specific, positive public persona, so as not to drive away their fans and the fame and income that those fans provide. Some celebrities are better than this at others, and those who are involved in scandals often lose their reputation as a result, which can lead to the end of their careers. This is not to say that all celebrities have Machiavellianism as a personality trait, but by understanding the importance of having a clean public image, you can learn how to spot someone with Machiavellian tendencies much more easily. Learning is incredibly important in dealing with a person who has Machiavellian traits; by knowing as much about your target as possible, you can begin to recognize their public image, and you will know when they are using their persona and when they are exposing their true personality. Of course, maintaining a public image is not the only trait displayed by people with

Machiavellianism. By paying attention to how your target treats and speaks to other people, you can determine whether or not they display Machiavellian tendencies. For instance, if your target is genuinely friendly with other people and is willing to offer their help to others, then they most likely do not possess Machiavellianism as a personality trait. However, if they take other people help more often than offer their own and treat people as tools to accomplish their own goals rather than friends, and then the target most likely has Machiavellian tendencies. These differences can be difficult to pick up on, but if you pay enough attention, eventually you will notice a pattern in your target's behavior. When attempting to manipulate a person with Machiavellian tendencies by using NLP techniques, you must be sure to be extremely careful. After all, they are incredibly skilled manipulators themselves, and will not have a difficult time picking up on what you are attempting to do if you are not precise. The best way to try to influence people who display Machiavellianism is to appeal to their sense of self-interest. If you put them in a situation that directly benefits them, then even if they know that you are trying to manipulate them, they will still go along with you, as they know that they will ultimately gain something. Of course, if what you are trying to influence them to do might be harmful to them, then appealing to their sense of self-interest will not work. Instead, you can threaten to expose their private life and reveal the truth about their public image. Privacy is incredibly important to people who display Machiavellianism, so if you can manage to threaten their privacy, they will go to extreme measures to protect it. When dealing with a person with Machiavellian tendencies, you have to be sure to be subtle. Hide your intentions in carefully precise language, and never explicitly reveal anything about your plans for what you want them to do. After all, if you tell them anything directly, not only will they know that you are attempting to influence them, but they will also try to manipulate you in response. It is extremely difficult to out-manipulate someone who displays Machiavellianism, so it is best to avoid those battles completely if you are able to.

Concepts of the Dark Triad: Psychopathy

When you think of a psychopath, you most likely think of someone who is a cold, unfeeling, violent criminal, or someone who gets enjoyment out of doing horrible things to other people. While psychopathy is largely considered to be the most dangerous trait out of the Dark Triad, its actual characteristics are a little bit different from those displayed by popular stereotypes of psychopaths. In real life, psychopaths tend to seek out thrills, show poor levels of impulse control and have a distinct lack of empathy for other people. They also tend to display antisocial behavior, and studies have shown that there is a link between psychopathy and antisocial personality disorder. Of course, this does not mean that most psychopaths simply shut themselves away from the rest of the world; instead, they have lots of difficulty with forming lasting, healthy relationships with other people, and have no problem with ruining another person's life on a whim. In general, try not to think of psychopaths as terrifying, emotionless serial killers, and think of them more as an attractive, charismatic wolf in sheep's clothing who are skilled at charming people into relationships that turn out to be disastrous for the victim. People with psychopathic tendencies are more common than you might think and include a high proportion of CEOs, major executives, billionaires, and other extremely successful people. This is because their remorselessness and their nearly complete lack of empathy allow them to make difficult, ruthless decisions that other people might morally struggle with, and so they are able to gain an advantage in their field and achieve massive levels of success. Because psychopaths are so dangerous to form relationships with, it can be very difficult to be able to identify someone as a psychopath while still remaining safe. Psychopaths do fit better into certain groups of people than others; for example, men are far more likely to display psychopathic traits than women, and certain research has indicated that blacks, Native Americans, and Hispanics are more likely to have psychopathic tendencies than whites and Asians. Of course, keep in mind that these patterns are not in any way definitive proof that someone is or is not a psychopath, and that anybody can have psychopathic personality traits. One other way to more easily determine whether or not someone is a psychopath is by first identifying them as either a narcissist or as someone with Machiavellian tendencies. Research has shown that both narcissism and

Machiavellianism have a positive correlation with psychopathy, meaning that if someone is a narcissist or has Machiavellian personality traits, then there is a greater chance that they might also be a psychopath. This works both ways: if you identify someone as a psychopath, then there are also significantly likely to show signs of narcissism, Machiavellianism, or both. This is in part why psychopaths are such dangerous individuals; by having a combination of more than one component of the Dark Triad, they show high skill levels of manipulative behavior and lack any ethical concerns about how they use those skills on the people around them.

Everything that they do is done to exclusively benefit themselves or to directly harm other people. Therefore, it is very important that you do not fall for a psychopath's charms because if you do, your life will likely be ruined by the psychopath in a matter of time. Because of the danger that psychopaths pose to your safety, attempting to use learning techniques to fully understand them is not always a good option. When you observe a person with psychopathic tendencies from a distance, however, you will have a better chance of identifying them while keeping any risk to your own safety at an absolute minimum. With this in mind, in addition to the common physical characteristics that many psychopaths have and the overlapping personality traits of the Dark Triad that they might possess, there are also certain patterns in behavior and methods of speaking to look out for. One of the most major traits that psychopaths commonly possess is certain attractiveness to other people. While psychopaths can certainly be physically attractive, and many of them are, this attractiveness is more in line with a general charisma. Psychopaths excel at luring in other people by using an engaging personality, and their victims are drawn to them like magnets. Of course, there is a difference between someone having the charisma that is natural and someone that is charming because they have manufactured a charming personality. Psychopaths do not actually care about the people who are drawn to them and the charm that a psychopath display is never deeper than surface level. People with psychopathic tendencies will never use more charisma than is absolutely necessary to lure in their victims.

When trying to determine whether or not someone is a psychopath, trust your gut instinct; if something does not feel genuine, then it most likely is not, and you are probably being manipulated. Another recurring trait to look out for when attempting to identify psychopathic traits is dishonesty. Psychopaths are notorious, habitual liars, and will display dishonesty about anything from even the smallest details to the largest, most consequential pieces of information. If you manage to catch someone in multiple lies, regardless of whether or not they are told to you or to another person, then there is a good chance that that person displays psychopathic tendencies. If you think that someone might be a psychopath, be sure to be a skeptic of anything that that person tells you, and use your best judgment. Of course, not all liars have psychopathic tendencies, and accusing someone of being a psychopath is a good way to drive them away permanently. Because of this, if you catch your target in a series of multiple lies, do not immediately assume that they are a psychopath and do not accuse them of anything. Instead, either confront them about their lies or wait for someone else to do so, and take note of their reaction: do they regret having to lie, or do they seem unworried about it? Remember that people with psychopathic tendencies generally to not feel guilt or remorse for their actions, so a person who sincerely regrets lying is probably not a psychopath. It is important to keep in mind that having a good excuse for lying is not the same thing as expressing guilt, so even if your target has a legitimate excuse for telling lies, if they do not hold any regrets about the incident, then they still could very well be a psychopath.

Manipulating a person who displays psychopathic tendencies may seem impossible, but if you are sure to hone your skills to the level of an expert and exercise the utmost caution, it can be done. Once you learn how to recognize their methods of using charm and charisma to lure in their victims, you will also know how to avoid these same methods. That way, you can get close to someone that you suspect is a psychopath and begin to use learning to model their personality traits without being at risk of danger or harm to yourself. By recognizing a psychopath's attempts at using a fabricated, charismatic personality, you can pretend to be drawn in, but you will not be tempted to make any decisions that might end up presenting very serious harm to your health. In fact, if you are good enough at playing along with a psychopath, then you are at an advantage. If you do not allow them to realize that you are simply pretending to be drawn to their personality, then they are far more likely to underestimate you and not see you as a threat to themselves. Once you have fooled the psychopath, you can use NLP techniques as you would any other person. Because psychopaths are often more impulsive than the average person and actively seek out thrills, they might also follow your suggestions more readily than other people, especially if you make your suggestions sound exciting and interesting. When attempting to influence anyone with psychopathic tendencies, of course, caution is the most important thing to remember. If at any point you do not feel safe while using NLP techniques on a psychopath be sure to walk away and choose a new target before you end up in real trouble. After all, once you have practiced your skills more, you can always come back to your target at a later time.

Why Should You Care About The Dark Triad?

At this point in the chapter, you may be wondering why the Dark Triad is covered at all in the book. After all, people who display narcissistic, Machiavellianism, psychopathy, or a combination of all three are generally rare. However, there are important lessons to be learned from the three concepts that form the Dark Triad. Now that you know what the hallmarks of the Dark Triad are and how to recognize them in other people, you can use those same hallmarks to your advantage. You see, none of the three traits in the Dark Triad are explicitly harmful unless used to an extreme degree. People do not have to be narcissists, Machiavellian, or psychopaths in order to display behavior that is commonly associated with those traits. The average person uses many of the tactics belonging to the Dark Triad every day, often without even realizing that they are doing it. At some point in your life, you have also used these same tactics to get ahead and achieve success. Therefore, there is no harm in integrating the features of narcissism, Machiavellianism, and psychopathy in with your NLP techniques. Using the principles of the Dark Triad can help you be more flexible in using NLP techniques and can help you find more success in influencing people to do what you want them to do. You might have noticed already that all three components of the Dark Triad involve the skilled use of manipulation, and you can see how imitating narcissism, Machiavellianism, and psychopathy might be useful to you in pursuing the art of manipulation.

Narcissism, for example, teaches you that other people tend to prefer praise over criticism, and by appealing to their sense of self-worth, you will have a much easier time in convincing your target to go along with what you want for them to do. In a similar vein of thought, Machiavellianism teaches you that by thinking about other people in purely strategic terms and by valuing your own needs above the needs of other people, you will maximize the benefit that other people give you and you will better be able to position them in places that you want them to be in. While extremely dangerous, psychopathy teaches you to use your personality to its full extent as a resource in manipulating other people and to not be afraid to cut off relationships with others when the timing best suits you. While you should not practice any of the values of narcissism, Machiavellianism, and psychopathy to a harmful extent, do not be afraid to integrate them into your NLP techniques, as they will make you better and more effective at influencing the people around you.

The Dark Triad: Recap

I know that this chapter covered a lot of information, so it's important to take a moment to review everything. These concepts of the Dark Triad will continue to be relevant throughout the rest of this book, so it is vital to know them well. First of all, the Dark Triad is a well-studied and researched topic in contemporary psychology, and is made up of three distinct components, which are known as narcissism, Machiavellianism, and psychopathy. Narcissism is named after Narcissus, the character from ancient Greek mythology, and is characterized by self-obsession, a need for praise, an overbearing sense of superiority to other people, and a lack of empathy for other people. The second component of the Dark Triad is Machiavellianism, which is named for the political philosopher Niccolo Machiavelli, and encompasses personality traits such as valuing one's own self-interest at the expense of other people, being ruthless and uncompromising, having a separate public persona from one's own self, and a desire for privacy at all times. Psychopathy is the most dangerous concept in the Dark Triad and is characterized by being impulsive and seeking thrills, displaying antisocial behavior, and using charisma and charm to reel in potential victims before ruining their lives. When attempting to manipulate anyone with explicit personality traits belonging to the Dark Triad, in particular when dealing with people who might be psychopaths, be sure to be careful, and never put yourself in a situation that might be harmful or dangerous.

Being able to recognize narcissism, Machiavellianism, and psychopathy in other people is a useful skill, although it can be more difficult to manipulate people who possess one or more of the traits contained within the Dark Triad. Of course, once you know enough about narcissism, Machiavellianism, and psychopathy, you can begin to integrate them into your own NLP techniques to become even more skilled at influencing the people around you, just as long as you are sure to be cautious and not take the three traits to the extreme. As Machiavelli stated in *The Prince,* "He who seeks to deceive will always find someone who will allow himself to be deceived." As you continue to make your way through the rest of this book, be sure to keep the concepts of narcissism, Machiavellianism, and psychopathy in mind. You should try to apply them to future concepts and techniques that will be discussed, as the concepts contained within the Dark Triad will often enrich NLP tactics and make them even more effective to use.

Chapter 3: Persuasion and Deception

So far in this book, the term "manipulation" has been brought up over and over again. But what does manipulation really mean, and how does it actually work? While both the six core concepts of NLP and the three traits that make up the Dark Triad certainly make up a part of the puzzle of manipulation, there are two other concepts that are also incredibly important to know about: persuasion and deception. While these two concepts may seem like the same thing, they are actually two separate entities, and should not be confused with each other.

Think of that difference like this: persuasion is all about trying to get another person to believe in what you are saying, while deception is more about trying to get another person to believe that *you* believe in what you are saying. While they are similar, they both have different strategies in order to use them effectively, and they both relate back to the concepts of NLP and the Dark Triad in different ways.

A master of manipulation should know the difference between persuasion and deception, and how to use both of these concepts by utilizing their respective strategies and tactics to their full effect. Once you are familiar with persuasion and deception, the principles of most NLP techniques, as well as more advanced manipulation procedures such as mind control, hypnosis, and brainwashing, should come much more easily to you and feel more natural to use.

Psychology, Robert Cialdini, and the Six Principles of Persuasion

Persuasion is well-studied in the world of psychology, and there are many guides, books, and websites dedicated to the subject. One of the most famous and respected books are called *Influence: The Psychology of Persuasion*, written by a man named Robert Cialdini. Cialdini is an accomplished psychologist, college professor, author, and public speaker, and is known as the "guru of social influence."

In his book, he outlined six separate principles that make up the art of persuasion, which he discovered from his time spent studying car dealerships, telemarketing phone banks, and organizations that work to raise massive amounts of money and the training programs that they use to prepare new employees for their jobs. The six principles of persuasion that Cialdini identified are as follows: authority, reciprocity, likeability, commitment and consistency, social proof, and scarcity. In 2016, he discovered another principle of persuasion, which he referred to as the unity principle. For simplicity's sake, this chapter will only be covering the original six principles of persuasion, and will not include the unity principle, as it shares many characteristics with the other six principles. By learning more about authority, reciprocity, likeability, commitment and consistency, social proof, and scarcity, and by combining these principles with the six concepts of NLP and the three components of the Dark Triad, you will have a very thorough background in the art of influencing and manipulating other people, and you will be ready to move on to the more advanced and more difficult concepts of mind control, hypnosis, and brainwashing, and you will be well-prepared to use these concepts in the real world rather than just in theory.

The Six Principles of Persuasion: Authority

You are probably familiar with the commonly used cliché that in commercials that advertise toothpaste, something similar to the phrase "Four out of five dentists recommend this brand" at some point in the advertisement.

This is because the marketing team behind these commercials has a good understanding of the principle of authority, which simply states that human beings are more likely to believe other people who appear as if they know what they are doing. I have already used the principle of authority in this very chapter when I mentioned Robert Cialdini and his many accomplishments and credentials. Of course, while having and talking about accomplishments and credentials is certainly useful when attempting to establish your authority, it is not necessarily a requirement to have those things. Go back and read the definition of the principle of authority one more time. The keyword to keep in mind is "appear." You do not have to actually know what you are talking about or be an established expert in your field so long as you can convince people that you know what you are talking about.

As long as you do some research ahead of time or manage to come up with terms and phrases that seem to be legitimate, then you can easily fool another person into believing that you know more about that field than they do and that they should listen to what you are saying. Confidence is key, and if you can convince yourself that you are correct in what you are saying, it will be far easier to convince other people as well. It is also useful to keep in mind that in general, people are more likely to believe people who claim to be experts in fields that they are not already familiar with. This makes sense: it would be much more difficult, if not impossible, to convince someone who is already an expert in their chosen field of something in that field that they have not heard of before. Therefore, when selecting a target to use the principle of authority on, be sure to find out whether they already have some background knowledge of a topic or not before you try to convince them of something.

In addition to these baseline rules in the principle of authority, there are also other tricks that you can use if you really want to convince someone that you know what you are talking about. In addition to simply being confident and talking about a subject as if you know all about it already, there are other visual cues that people pick up on in order to determine whether somebody is an expert or not. The first visual cue that you can use is wearing a uniform. Costumes are handy for more than just Halloween; by wearing a uniform, you have become visually associated with the topic that you are pretending to be an expert in, which will add to your overall believability.

Think about it like this: would you be more open to believing that someone is a pilot if they were wearing an old t-shirt and ratty jeans, or would you believe them more if they were in their full uniform? Of course, uniforms are not completely fool-proof, and they can be expensive and time-consuming to obtain or create. Fortunately, there are other cues that you can use in order to better convince people of your authority.

The uses of specific titles that are associated with a particular field are also highly useful when you are using the principle of authority. For example, a title such as "Dr." lets you know that the person in question has earned a doctorate degree, and has a huge amount of knowledge about a specific topic. Titles can also include specific jobs. For instance, if someone tells you that they are an attorney, then you would be more inclined to believe that they know about the law and legal processes more than someone who is not an attorney. Linking a job title to a specific company and being able to explain what the job involves is also helpful when you are attempting to establish authority.

The Six Principles of Persuasion: Reciprocity

The principle of reciprocity is, at its core, very simple: people are going to be more likely to follow your lead if they feel that they owe you something. If you can make someone feel indebted to you, then they will be motivated to pay back that debt in whatever way they can, including by being convinced to do something that they would not normally do.

Of course, there are a few tricks to getting reciprocity to work for you in the right way. Just because you give somebody else something random does not mean that they will feel that they owe you anything. Reciprocity works best when it is used in a selective, strategic way, so you have to think it through in a thorough way in order to have it be as effective as possible for you. There are three components that you can use in order to make the principle of reciprocity work well: be the first one to offer something, make your offer unique, and make sure that your offer can only come from you. By following these three steps, the person who receives your offer will understand that you have taken the time to consider all of their needs, and will, therefore, have a greater likelihood of feeling like they need to pay you back for your gift.

The first component in performing the principle of reciprocity is perhaps the most important out of all of them. When you make sure that you are the first one to offer your target something, you are laying the foundation for their feelings of gratitude and obligation to you. Do not allow them to offer something to you first, as in that case, you are the one who much pay them back, which do not benefit you. In a similar vein, do not stand by and let another person offer your target something before you can do so. You will be giving up your relationship with your target to another person, and they will become indebted to that person, not to you. This first component requires patience from you; you have to make your offer at the right time, in order to maximize the other person's feelings of obligation towards you. If you make your offer at the wrong time, then the other two components in the principle of reciprocity will no longer be of any use to you, and you will have to try another tactic or technique on your target.

Along with being the first person to make an offer to your target, you have to also make sure that your offer is unique to them. If you offer your target something that you could have offered to anybody, then your offer will not be as effective. By specifically personalizing your offer to your target's own personality, you will make them feel special, and because of that the level of gratitude they will fell towards you will be much higher than normal, and they will be more likely to do what you want them to do. The more you make your offer unique to your target, the more likely that person will be willing to do things that they would normally be uncomfortable with doing. If being the first one to offer your target something will first make them feel that they owe you something, then making your offer unique to them will make them less likely to say no to whatever it is you want for them to do, no matter what it is.

The third concept in the principle of reciprocity, being sure that your offer can only come from you, is very similar to the second concept. If anybody can offer what you are offering, after all, why should your target feel particularly indebted to you? You need to work hard to set yourself apart from the rest of the pack, or else your target will not be willing to follow your lead. You can see how this concept ties in neatly with the other two: by being the first person to make an offer, making sure that that offer is personalized to the person that you are trying to manipulate, and being careful to make sure that your offer can only come from you, you offer will be very compelling to your target, and it is incredibly unlikely that they will turn it down.

Once they have accepted your offer, let their feelings of gratitude sink in for a couple of days, and then make a suggestion of what you want your target to do for you. Instead of being demanding, try to use a friendly tone, and only remind them that they owe you if they explicitly refuse to do what you want them to. The more aggressive you are, the less they will want to work with you any longer, and their feelings of obligation to you will not be enough to keep them involved with you if you drive them away.

The Six Principles of Persuasion: Likeability

Likeability is perhaps the easiest of the six principles to understand and to perfect, as you likely already deal with likeability on a regular basis in your own life. The principle of likeability simply states that human beings are more likely to go along with suggestions from people who they like. This means that someone who is your friend is going to be easier for you to influence, but the principle of likeability is not limited only to friends. For example, if your favorite celebrity endorses a certain product, then you will likely view that product in a more favorable light and will be more likely to buy it, even though you do not personally know the celebrity.

Therefore, you will be more successful in using the principle of likeability if you are able to form a relationship with your target, whether genuine or not. There are a couple of tricks that can help you be more successful with likeability. First of all, people who you do not already know will be more likely to want to be your friend if you are more physically attractive, so taking care of your appearance is important when attempting to use likeability. Of course, being physically attractive is not a requirement for likeability to work; in fact, since what each individual finds attractive is different from person to person, physical attractiveness is highly subjective, and may only help you out in certain situations. Another tip that you can keep in mind is to use compliments to your advantage. When you first meet somebody else, try to pick something out from their appearance to compliment; it can be something that they are wearing, such as a shirt or jewelry, or a physical attribute, like their eyes or their hair.

Everyone likes to feel good about themselves, and compliments can be an easy way to fulfill that need. After you have started to get to know your target a little bit better, there are additional strategies in the principle of likeability that you can use. For example, be sure to keep in touch with your target. Modern technology has made it easier than ever to stay in contact with people, and while you should not harass your target or try to talk to them too much, you should not let them forget that you are there, either. If you can, try to see them in person on a regular basis. If they invite you to go somewhere, do not turn them down. The more you stay in contact with your target, especially when you are consistently meeting them face-to-face, the closer they will feel to you, and the more open they will be to doing whatever you suggest. Even if you cannot form a close friendship with whoever your target it, try to make contact with them before you attempt to influence them so they have at least a little bit of familiarity with who you are.

The Six Principles of Persuasion: Commitment and Consistency

To best understand the principle of commitment and consistency, take a moment to think about a river. Rivers flow in one, singular path, and it is often very difficult to force a river to follow a different path. In many ways, human beings behave in a similar manner. Once a person has committed to a specific plan of action or a certain set of beliefs, they will be consistent in following through on that plan or those beliefs, and it can be difficult to try to make somebody else change their mind. While this might seem like it would make it hard to manipulate someone into doing something they do not want to do, you can easily make the principle of commitment and consistency work for you.

Using commitment and consistency is all about establishing a pattern with your target. If you know enough about them that you can piggyback off of an existing set of beliefs, then doing so will make manipulating them much easier. However, if what you are trying to influence your target to do go against their established set of beliefs, then you can still work around that. In that case, you should try to create a new pattern for your target to follow. Start with small things and work your way up to larger tasks, as this will allow for them to become ingrained in a new set of habits, and will make them more open to doing whatever you suggest.

When trying to influence a target while using commitment and consistency, be sure to reward your target for following your lead. When you give them positive reinforcement, their idea of commitment to you and your influences will be more positive overall, and they will be more likely to go along with whatever you want in the future. The principle of commitment and consistency works best when it is combined with one of the other six principles of persuasion; for example, it works well with the principle of likeability. With likeability, if you have a strong relationship with your target already, then you have created a path for them to follow, and by force of habit, they will be more likely to do whatever it is that you want for them to do. Remember, with commitment and consistency, your first attempt at influencing your target will always be the hardest. So long as you implant a pattern of behavior into your target's mind, they will be easier to influence in your future attempts.

The Six Principles of Persuasion: Social Proof

Social proof is very similar to the principles of authority and likeability but occupies a slightly different set of ideas. Essentially, the principle of social proof holds that people tend to go along with whatever is already popular or whatever has already been recommended by people who are popular. The second part of the principle of social proof includes a wide range of people, including professionals or experts in a given field, famous people, and groups of people, which is also referred to as the "wisdom of crowds." This is why the vast majority of online stores have space where reviews can be left on a particular product; even though other customers on the website are anonymous to you, when you see a large group of positive reviews, you are more likely to consider buying that product. But how do you apply the principle of social proof to manipulate other people? There are a couple of different methods that you can try to use. First of all, you can do some research before beginning to try to influence your target. If you can find quotes, books, or other works from a well-known person or from a large group of other people, your own reasoning behind your influences will seem to be much more solid, and your target will have a harder time in seeing any flaws or leaps of logic in your arguments.

The more sources that you have to back you up, the more credible you seem, and the less your target will be able to rationalize away why they might not want to be influenced by you. The other method that you can use to get used out of the principle of social proof is to team up with another person or even a group of several people in order to influence your target. You on your own are not a crowd, but if you can find people with similar goals and desires to your own, you can create your own crowd. Once your target finds themselves surrounded by people with the same mindset as you, they will have little choice but to go along with you. Of course, you have to be careful when creating your own group, as you do not want to frighten your target away or make them feel intimidated. Keep your group small, and try to prevent them from getting aggressive. It is also important to be sure that all members of your group are loyal to you and that you retain control of the group, as you do not want to worry about anyone in the group telling your target what you are attempting to do to them.

The Six Principles of Persuasion: Scarcity

The principle of scarcity is a bit different from the other six principles. Scarcity is the idea that if something is rare, limited in quantity, or hard to come by, people will be more drawn to it and want to have it more than something that is commonly available. To better illustrate the concept of scarcity, imagine yourself in a room with eight other people, and all of you are hungry. Now imagine that a pizza is delivered, and there is just enough of it for everybody to be able to have a slice.

All eight people in the room are now satisfied because they each got a slice of pizza. Now, imagine the same situation, but instead of there being eight slices available, there is only one slice. The singular slice in the second situation has a far greater value than the eight slices in the first situation since not everybody will be able to be fed. This is the principle of scarcity in action. Scarcity can be valuable to keep in mind when attempting to manipulate another person because of the effect it has on a person's decision-making habits. For example, when a company advertises a product as a limited edition version, they are creating scarcity in order to encourage its customers to buy it, a strategy that works most of the time. If people are afraid that they might miss out on something, they will be more likely to try to obtain it while not taking into consideration any negative consequences. Limited edition versions of a product are more expensive for a reason; the product's scarcity is more important to consumers than its price is. You can use the principle of scarcity in your own attempts to manipulate the people around you.

If a person feels that they could do whatever you want them to do at any time, then they will not feel as urgent about listening to you. However, if you frame whatever you want your target to do as a limited-time opportunity that they could potentially miss out on, then your target will feel more motivated to do what you want them to do. When you are attempting to use the principle of scarcity, remember that it is more important to be a salesperson than a manipulator. The more you sell what you want your target to do, the more likely your target is to be invested in that action, and the more that they will feel that they would be missing out on something if they do not follow your instructions.

Deception

Remember, deception is a slightly different concept than persuasion, and while it has not been studied to the same extent as persuasion, it can be just as useful in your manipulation attempts. Deception can range between a wide variety of uses, from small lies to enormous scams. While deception is generally considered to be more malevolent than persuasion, there is nothing inherently wrong with either of them and in fact, people use tactics that are associated with both of them on a regular basis. In fact, the six principles of persuasion can easily be blended with tactics used in deception to make you an even better manipulator.

But what are some deceptive tactics? The first and most important tactic is the art of lying. Lying is the most commonly used tool of manipulation, and is used all the time by people all around the world. Everyone has lied at some point in their lives, but of course, some people are better at it than others. The most skilled liars know that lying is most effective when it is used along with the truth. Not only does mixing the truth and lies together help you remember what you said, but it also makes it easier for your target to believe what you are saying. Lies are also more convincing when your target is not familiar with the thing that you are lying about. A person is not likely to question information when they do not know about any alternatives, but when they have some idea of what the truth actually is, then you will need to work hard to convince them that their information is faulty. Another tactic of deception that is easy to use is the act of omission. Omission simply means that you are telling the truth, but not all of it. The omission is easier to use than lying is, but it cannot always be used as a tactic in any situation. Oftentimes, it is best to use omission in addition to lying, or as an excuse to fall back on if you are ever caught in a lie. If your target believes that you are lying about a certain subject, then your best strategy is to abandon the subject entirely and move on to a new one. For example, when speaking about a particular topic, you can always change the flow of the conversation by saying that you forgot the rest of whatever story you were telling, and move on to a new topic of discussion. You can also say that you were traumatized by a certain event, which gives you a good excuse not to talk about it any further and move on to a new topic.

Takeaways

Along with the six concepts of NLP and the three personality traits that make up the Dark Triad, the principles of persuasion and deception are the final pieces of the puzzle that makes up mind control, hypnosis, and brainwashing techniques. By having a good understanding of all of these concepts, you should be able to easily pick up and eventually master everything presented to you in the following chapters. However, you should return to these first three chapters frequently and review what you have learned so far. After all, without being able to sufficiently understand the basics, you will have a more difficult time being able to perfect anything that is more advanced. Also, keep in mind the old mantra that practice makes perfect, and the more time that you spend practicing these basic concepts, the more naturally that mind control, hypnosis, and brainwashing will come to you. Above all else, never feel discouraged, and remember that setbacks are a part of the learning experience. If you ever feel stuck, just return to these earlier chapters and try to gain a new perspective on the concepts covered within them.

Chapter 4: Mind Control

Now that you know all about the concepts of NLP, the three components that make up the Dark Triad, and the principles of persuasion and deception, you are finally ready to move on to the concepts and techniques that make up mind control, hypnosis, and brainwashing. But of course, you may be wondering what the difference between mind control, hypnosis, and brainwashing are and what separates those three concepts from simple manipulation and influencing. This chapter will cover those differences in detail, as well as debunking popular myths about how mind control actually works and teaching you techniques that are proven to be effective.

This chapter will also work to relate all new concepts back to the foundation that has already been laid by the concepts of NLP, the Dark Triad, and the principles of persuasion and deception. Keep reading to master the techniques of mind control so that you can become an even better manipulator!

What Is The Difference Between Mind Control, Hypnosis, And Brainwashing?

Mind control, hypnosis, and brainwashing are all closely linked together as concepts, but it is important to keep in mind their differences so that you know which one is the best technique to use in whatever situation you might find yourself in.

Keep in mind that hypnosis and brainwashing will be discussed in detail in the next two chapters, and this section is not meant to explain them to their fullest potential. This section is only meant to distinguish hypnosis and brainwashing from the concept of mind control. While all three terms have to do with extreme, powerful manipulation techniques, they all work in slightly different ways, and you might find that one works better for you than the other two. They all have both pros and cons in their use, and if you want to become a master of manipulation, you should have a good understanding of all three concepts.

Mind control is perhaps the most subtle out of the three concepts, but it is also easily the broadest as well. Mind control refers to any series of words, actions, or behaviors that you can speak or perform in order to take command of another person's mental processes and dominate them. Ideally, when you perform mind control techniques, your target should not be aware of what you are doing, both before they have been mind-controlled and afterward. Your target should not be able to trace mind control back to you. Instead, you should be able to use mind control techniques without being detected, which is made easier when you model your mind control techniques on concepts from NLP, the Dark Triad, and the principles of persuasion and deception. In addition, mind control is not a permanent procedure. While you can certainly perform mind control techniques on a particular target more than once, they will not remain mind-controlled by you for a very long time.

There are ways to extend the amount of time that your target is mind-controlled, but they will never remain mind-controlled for incredibly long periods of time. Out of the three concepts, mind control is the easiest to pull off successfully and requires the fewest amounts of resources for you to use.

Hypnosis is easiest to think of as the middle ground between mind control and brainwashing. You can perform hypnosis in either a subtle or a more involved way, which is why hypnosis is the most flexible of the three concepts. You see, hypnotic suggestions can be made in one of two different ways: verbal or nonverbal. Verbal hypnotic techniques are just what they sound like: they involve using language in a very specific way in order to hypnotize your target. On the other hand, nonverbal hypnotic techniques are performed through specialized behaviors and actions. (Both verbal and nonverbal hypnotic techniques will be discussed in more detail in Chapter 5.) Just like with mind control, hypnosis is very difficult for a target to successfully detect, and should not be traceable back to you. However, unlike mind control, hypnosis cannot be performed on just anybody, so you must be careful to choose your targets with care.

Overall, hypnosis is the concept that relates the most easily back to the concepts of NLP and is more powerful and has an effect that lasts longer than mind control, but it requires more knowledge, more skill, and more precise target selection to pull off than mind control does, so it cannot be used in as many situations as mind control can be. However, if you have enough practice with it, then hypnosis can be invaluable in manipulating people to do what you want without them ever knowing about it.

Out of all three concepts, brainwashing takes the longest amount of time to pull off, but it is also by far the longest-lasting and most effective method of them all. Brainwashing requires more skill, patience, and discipline to use than mind control and hypnosis, but it will also more deeply affect your targets for a longer duration of time than the other two concepts. Like hypnosis, brainwashing is most effective only on certain people, and may not work on everybody that you try it on, so you have to be sure to choose your targets carefully and strategically. Similarly to both mind control and hypnosis, if performed correctly, brainwashing should be undetectable by your target, and they should not be able to trace it back to you once the process has been completed.

However, brainwashing has an additional component that both mind control and hypnosis lack: even if it was possible for your target to be able to trace brainwashing techniques back to you if you are precise in how you perform brainwashing techniques, then they would not even want to attempt to trace it back to you. (Brainwashing techniques will be discussed in more detail in Chapter 6.) While brainwashing is by far the most powerful of the three concepts, it is also extremely time-consuming and difficult to pull off correctly, so it is not always the most ideal method to use unless you have unlimited time and plenty of skill to dedicate to your target.

Mind Control: Myths vs. Reality

Take a moment to think about how mind control is portrayed in movies, books, and the media. What popular stereotypes and commonly used tropes come to mind? You might have thought of someone with superpowers, taking complete control of another person just by touching their fingers to the side of their head. Or you might have thought of a situation in which someone's entire reality is all part of a giant, elaborate simulation, which causes them to think and act in very specific ways. Of course, no matter what example you thought of, chances are very good that it did not show what mind control is or how it works in a completely correct manner. But there is a reason why so many stories involving the use of mind control are so compelling; as the author Terry O'Brian stated, "Mind control is such a powerful image that if hypnotism did not exist, then something similar would have to have been invented: the plot device is too useful for any writer to ignore. The fear of mind control is equally as powerful an image." While he mistakenly uses the word "hypnotism" in place of mind control, his statement has plenty of truth and wisdom to follow, especially the last part. To most people, their mind is a sacred place and something that only they ever have access to, and having their control over their mind is taken away by something or somebody else is a terrifying thought to have. In fact, it is such a terrifying thought that it is also seen as an outlandish or even impossible task to pull off, and is portrayed in movies, books, and other media in a ridiculous and over-the-top way. What these stories do not confront, however, is that mind control is a subtle, gentle process, and is not nearly as powerful as it is portrayed to be.

While it can be fun to look at the ways in which mind control is presented to an everyday audience and point out all of its flaws and the ways in which it is completely wrong, there is also a valuable lesson to be learned from these stories. Most crucially, these portrayals give newcomers a good idea of what mind control specifically is not, which is important in order for you to temper your expectations. If you are expecting mind control to work in the same way that it does in movies when you are first beginning to practice it, you will become disappointed and may lose interest in pursuing mind control and manipulation, in general, any further. By having more realistic expectations of what mind control is and what it is capable of, however, you can avoid being disappointed and you can be more confident in your abilities, which is critical if you ever want to become a master of manipulation. In addition, the way that mind control is portrayed in popular media can also be useful to you as an excuse to fall back on. The fact that the power and use of mind control are so ludicrous in stories actually provides you an advantage, as most people do not believe that mind control really works or exists at all. This is good for you for a number of reasons. First of all, because your target is not aware that the mind control methods that you are using actually exist, they will be much less likely to notice that you are doing anything to them at all. Secondly, if you are ever accused of using mind control techniques on another person, whether by your target or by a different person, then you have an excuse to fall back on.

You can easily claim that because you are not performing any actions that might be shown in a movie as valid mind control techniques, then you cannot possibly be mind-controlling your target. In fact, you can also say that you think that mind control is ridiculous and you do not believe that it is actually real, which is a reasonable thing to say within the context of how mind control is portrayed in books and movies. You can even use a particular book or movie as an example, which is likely to make your accuser feel embarrassed and not want to press the issue any further. As long as you are willing to be creative and do not mind employing some of the principles of deception, you can easily turn around the way in which mind control is portrayed to work in popular stories and make it work for you in ways that might not be expected.

Manipulation Technique #3: Mind Control, Storytelling, and Controlling the Narrative

At its very core, mind control is all about the flow of information. The better you control how information is used and what information is given to your target, the more control you will ultimately have over their mind and their actions. This is why the way that you choose to present information to your target is extremely important. In order to best control the way in which you introduce new information to your target, it is vital to understand the technique of how to control the narrative. Think of controlling the narrative like telling a story: the more relatable, engaging, and well-told your story is, the more likely your target is to feel a connection with it and believe in it. Controlling the narrative is a useful tool because it allows for you to easily implant new beliefs in another person's mind, and if those beliefs are expressed in a compelling way, then they are much more likely to stick around for a much longer, extended period of time. But what are the best ways to tell stories and control the narrative? First of all, take a moment to think of what stories are generally used for and how they play a part in people's everyday lives. While we may not always realize it, stories are essential to teaching us how to behave and what morals we should be following, and play just as big a role in the lives of adults as they do in the lives of children. The better told and more relatable a certain story is, the more firmly the lessons taught by that story will take hold in an individual's mind, and they will be more likely to adjust their behavior in response to the lessons learned from that story. The ultimate goal of telling a story should always be that the reader or listener will be motivated to change the way that they act after hearing the story. With this in mind, you can better learn how to tell stories that will benefit you and will help you exert influence over another person's mind. The most important aspect of whatever story you choose to tell should always be moral. The moral of the story is the lesson that the story is trying to teach its audience, and should always relate back to a certain behavior that you want your target to change or perform. Of course, there are a couple of reasons why you should hide the moral within a story rather than directly stating it to your target. The first reason is that morals are far more effective when they are used in a subtle way.

Think of it like trying to make a dog take a pill: when you simply give the dog a plain pill, the dog wills most likely spit the pill back out. However, if you coat the pill in peanut butter, then the dog will happily eat the pill, many times without even realizing that there was ever a pill at all. When you simply tell someone that they are wrong about something and that you think that they should change their behavior, the other person is not going to take your opinion well, and will likely think that you are bossy and that you should mind your own business. When you hide your moral within a story, however, the message will not be absorbed as strongly within your target's consciousness, but rather it will stick in their subconsciousness, which will allow them to think about and internalize the moral of your story without realizing that you are telling them to do something, and they may not even realize that their behavior has changed as a result. Of course, simply using a story to express a moral is not enough to successfully implant your message within your target's mind without them realizing it. You have to be subtle when you are controlling the narrative, and you have to demonstrate your skill as a storyteller. If you make your stories too ridiculous or too hard for your target to follow, for example, then they will likely lose interest in your story and stop listening to it. In addition, if you make your moral too obvious, then the rest of the story no longer matters, and you will come off as preachy and smug, and your story will seem artificial. If you focus your time and skill on making your story simple, realistic, and above all else, subtle, then you will be much more effective at controlling the narrative.

Of course, when you are attempting to control the narrative, the stories you tell are not like stories as you might typically think of them. Stories used in controlling the narrative would not make good books or movies, for instance, and they generally work the best when they are short, sweet, and to the point. In their simplest form, stories are just slightly more complex lies. When you are controlling the narrative, you can make your story about yourself, or you can make your story about another person, who can either be real or completely made up. The only people you should generally avoid telling stories about are your target or people who your target has close relationships with, as stories about these people can easily be revealed to be false, and your target will likely end up being offended by them. When structuring your story, make sure that it follows two important rules: first that it relates back to whatever topic you and your target are talking about; and second, that your story makes logical sense. Stories are the most effective when they are used to add to and enhance a point that you are already in the process of making. When you bring up a story seemingly out of nowhere, the story is not compelling to your audience, and they have no reason to become invested in it. When you weave in a story with a related topic of conversation, however, the story adds to your authority and adds an element of social proof to your argument that is difficult to ignore. The other thing to keep in mind when attempting to control the narrative is that the story that you are telling has to make logical sense. If your story does not make sense, then your target will not be able to relate to it, and will therefore not be affected by any moral that you choose to put in it.

Of course, your story having to make sense is not the same thing as it having to be true, and as long as you keep all events in your story consistent, then you can have it be about anything that you want. Making your story short and precise will also help with making sure that it makes sense, as a shorter story will have fewer details that you have to keep track of. Creating a structure for your story to follow will also help you make sure that it makes logical sense. Good stories should have a beginning, middle, and an ending. The beginning is the part where you introduce your story to your target, the middle is where you lay out the events that occur during your story, and the ending should explain what happened as a result of those events. The ending should also be where you present the moral of your story. When your story follows a set beginning, middle, and ending, your target has a timeline of events to follow along with, which will help them relate more to the story. Having the moral be at the ending of the story also helps your target to remember the moral, as the ending will be the part of the story that they have most recently heard and the part that is the freshest in their mind.

Putting together all of these concepts can be tricky at first, but once you have learned how to construct a narrative and are comfortable with the process, you will find that you will be able to construct narratives on the fly without any prior planning at all. Of course, I know that this is a lot of information to keep in mind when you are first starting out, so I have created an example for you to refer to. For instance, if you are talking to a target and your goal is to get them to stop talking to somebody else, you can construct a narrative to accomplish your goal. You can say something along the lines of, "You know, I knew somebody that was good friends with that guy. They were close for a while, but it turns out he's kind of a jerk. Apparently, he gossips about other people all the time and says really horrible things about them behind their backs. My friend heard him talking about him, and it was bad enough that they don't talk anymore. I don't know everything about what happened, but I know that I would stay away from that guy." In order to understand what this story is getting at, let's break it down piece by piece. First is the beginning, which takes up the first two sentences. It introduces the person that you know and also sets up that the other guy is not a good person. The middle takes up the next two sentences and brings up exactly what the other guy did that makes him a bad person.

The last sentence is the ending and contains the moral: stay away from that other guy. The use of the phrases "apparently" and "I don't know everything about what happened" also give you an excuse to fall back on in case your target confronts the other person about what you have said. Through this example, you have planted seeds of doubt about this other person in your target's mind, warned them to stay away from the other person, and given yourself plausible deniability about the entire situation, all in just five sentences. In the context of a conversation, you can see where controlling the narrative is an invaluable strategy in controlling someone else's mind without them ever knowing. When you are constructing a narrative, there are certain themes that you can use in your morals that are more powerful than other themes. Mind control is especially powerful when you are working towards a couple of different goals, most importantly isolation, criticism, and identity formation. While each of these concepts will be given an introduction here, they also share lots of overlap with hypnosis and brainwashing and will be discussed in greater detail in the following two chapters. Isolation is the act of keeping your target away from other people and any information that they might provide to your target. It can be carried out by physically keeping your target alone, but when used to achieve mind control, using nonphysical methods is far more effective and safer for you.

The easiest way to bring about isolation through only the words that you use is by utilizing criticism. Criticism refers to when you associate any outside influences to your target with negative imagery, and can be even more effective when you both describe other people as negatively as possible while also referring to yourself in more positive terms. This will make your target prefer you and the information that you provide to them over anything from the outside and will draw them closer to you. Finally, the last concept that benefits from constructing a narrative are the formation of a new identity in your target. Forming a new identity is the most permanent concept that can occur using mind control, and will also make your target much easier for you to control. Controlling the narrative can help you shape your target's new identity to be what you want it to be, and once their new identity takes hold, they will become almost inseparable from you and what you want them to do.

Takeaways

While mind control, hypnosis, and brainwashing have similarities between them, mind control is the easiest for a beginner to manipulation to pull off consistently and successfully. By practicing controlling the narrative in addition to the other manipulation techniques that have already been discussed, you will be able to manipulate other people in a wide variety of situations and scenarios. For more powerful and longer-lasting techniques, however, you will have to learn more about hypnosis and brainwashing strategies. Be sure that you have a good understanding of all of the concepts and techniques that have been discussed up to this point before you move on, and as always, remember to keep up with practicing these techniques in order to improve.

Mind control maybe the easiest concept to learn initially, but it is by no means easy to completely perfect, so do not be discouraged if you fail and be sure to keep on trying. As long as you remember to control the narrative in a smart, precise, and effective way, you will find at least some level of success.

Chapter 5: Hypnosis

If mind control is the best set of manipulation strategies for beginners to pick up and be able to learn quickly, then hypnosis is the next natural step in the process towards becoming a master of manipulation. In general, hypnosis lasts longer and is far more powerful than mind control is, although it also requires more skill to successfully pull off. While hypnosis has some concepts that overlap with mind control and brainwashing, it also has completely unique components, which can make it more challenging to learn. Hypnosis has a long a rich history, and today it is used in a wide variety of fields and industries, including in medicine, sports, psychotherapy, self-improvement, meditation and relaxation, forensics and criminal justice, art and literature, and the military. Of course, all instances of hypnosis share common characteristics no matter what context it is used in, and these same characteristics can come in handy when attempting to manipulate someone else. Having a good understanding of the principles and concepts of hypnosis can turn you from a mediocre manipulator into a highly skilled one.

The History of Hypnosis

Believe it or not, hypnotic techniques have been used for thousands of years, originating in India within the Hindu religion. The Hindus practiced a type of hypnosis called temple sleep, which they used to cure the sick and disabled who came to their temples. From there, hypnotic techniques were also discovered to have been used in Persia (modern-day Iran), Switzerland, Austria, Ireland, and Bavaria (now a part of Germany). However, hypnosis was not formally organized into science until the mid-1770s, when a scientist named Franz Anton Mesmer developed the theory of mesmerism, which stated that one person could exert control over another person through a magnetic force held within the body. While mesmerism was later proven to be largely untrue, parts of it were still found to be valid. Those parts were built upon by other scientists, the most notable of which was James Braid, a Scottish surgeon who first used the term "hypnosis" in his 1842 work, *Practical Essay on the Curative Agency of Neuro-Hypnotism*. Braid described hypnotism as "a peculiar condition of the nervous system, into which it may be thrown by artificial contrivance, and which differs, in several respects, from common sleep or the waking condition," which essentially means that rather than believing that hypnosis occurred as a result of a magnetic force, Braid believed that you could put someone in a hypnotic trance by manipulating their attention in specific ways.

In 1843, he published the first book ever written on hypnosis, which he titled *Neurypnology*. After Braid's book was published, hypnotism began to be studied and used all over the world, especially in France, the United States, and decades later, Russia. As theories about hypnosis spread and began to grow, entire schools studying the subject began to pop up all over the world, the most famous of which was called the Nancy School, which was located in France and directed by two different men, Ambroise-Auguste Liébeault and Hippolyte Bernheim. Liébeault and Bernheim were both physicians that had been trained in France, and contrary to popular opinion at the time, believed that anybody could be hypnotized under the right conditions. Many prominent scientists and psychologists in the 20th century, including Sigmund Freud, Clark L. Hull, and Milton Erickson, used the work done at the Nancy School to further develop their own theories. Erickson became extremely skilled in the use of hypnotic techniques, and later in his career founded the American Society of Clinical Hypnosis, which still operates today and offers courses and workshops for improving your own hypnotic expertise, as well as publishing the American Journal of Clinical Hypnosis. Through the end of the 20th century, hypnosis remained a popular topic to discuss, study, and research, and are still an important part of psychology and the study of behavioral responses today.

But why is knowing the history of hypnosis and its many forms helpful for actually learning the techniques associated with it? There are a couple of reasons. First of all, because the term "hypnosis" has gone through so many stages and forms meaning slightly different things, being more familiar with the history of hypnosis will help you know exactly what type of hypnosis you are dealing with. If, for example, you read about hypnosis being associated with magnetic, supernatural forces coming from within the body, you will know that you are reading about Franz Mesmer's work and that there are far more accurate theories of hypnosis that you could be reading about instead. Knowing even a little bit about the history of hypnosis can help you to avoid bad or even completely false information, which means that you can spend more time absorbing information that is actually useful and putting it into practice. Secondly, by knowing all about the way that hypnosis has evolved from definition to definition over the course of its lifetime, you will better understand that hypnosis is not necessarily a singular, fixed topic, and that there are many methods out there that you might find to be helpful if a certain concept is giving you too much trouble. The more theories of hypnosis that you learn about, the abler you are to find the one that works best for you. After spending a suitable amount of time practicing and studying hypnosis, you might even come up with your own theories!

Manipulation Technique #4: The Hypnotic Trance

At its core, hypnosis is all about planting ideas into somebody else's subconsciousness in order to influence their consciousness. If you manage to infiltrate a person's subconsciousness with enough skill, they will not be aware of what you are doing, and will never know that you ever influenced them at all. The best way to access someone's subconsciousness is to coax them into a relaxed, meditative state known as a hypnotic trance. Getting your target into a trance is the most difficult part of the process of hypnosis, but once you finally manage to pull it off, you will have a much easier time successfully manipulating them. Putting your target into a trance allows for you to have direct access to their subconsciousness, as their consciousness will no longer be an active part of their mind for the duration of the trance. The trace is what separates hypnosis from mind control, and the ability to induce it in somebody else is what separates a beginner of manipulation from a budding expert.

The best way to think of a hypnotic trance is a form of deep relaxation. You are likely already familiar with the overall concept of the trace, due to portrayals of hypnosis in book, movies, and popular culture in general. Of course, in real life, you cannot put somebody else into a hypnotic trance simply by waving a watch in front of their face or by using a magical code phrase that will put them to sleep. Instead, putting someone into a hypnotic trance takes lots of time and skill, and it may not always work on every single person that you try it out on, especially when you are first starting to attempt to use it. In fact, for the best introduction to the hypnotic trance, you may want to find a friend who is willing to allow you to put them into a trance in order to practice doing it, or if you cannot find someone who is a willing participant, you can always put yourself into a hypnotic trance using this same method. If you fail at putting somebody into a trance, you are likely to face a negative reaction from that person, as they are likely to recognize suspicious behavior when they see it if they still have full awareness of their surroundings. This is why it is important that you practice this technique several times before attempting it on any outsiders, as you are far more likely to succeed in putting somebody into a hypnotic trance if you have some familiarity with how it already works.

The first step in putting your target into a hypnotic trance is to make sure that they are in a sitting position, or even better, lying down. After all, once your target is in the trance and their consciousness has temporarily faded away, they will no longer physically be able to stand up or support the weight of their own body. An action as forceful and abrupt as falling on the floor will be enough to wake them up from the hypnotic trance, and once they have regained their awareness, they will likely want an explanation as to what happened. Obviously, this is not a situation that you want to be caught in, so it is important to make sure that your target's body is in a secure position that will not fall over or cause them to wake up once you have put them in the trance.

This also means that you should not attempt to hypnotize anybody unless there is a couch, chairs, a bed, or another piece of comfortable furniture for your target to use. Convincing your target to sit or lay down sounds more difficult than it actually is.

Remember that your target will be more likely to sit or lay down if a piece of furniture is offered to them to do so on and that you should be prepared to sit or lay down first, as your target will be more likely to do the same if they are following your lead. If all else fails, you can always mind control them and influence them to sit or lay down where you want them to. Do not worry too much about *how* you make your target get into the best position and instead focus your attention on what comes after you have already convinced them to do so.

The next step in the process of putting someone into a hypnotic trance is to get your target to listen to the sound of your voice. In hypnotic techniques, your voice can be a powerful tool as long as you know how to use it correctly. Take special note of the fact that this step does not instruct you to start a conversation with your target, but rather to get them to listen to you. This is because when attempting to put another person into a hypnotic trance, your voice is not being used to express any meaning or to describe any information, but rather as a way to create a sort of white noise, which will allow your target to slip further and further into a deeply relaxed state. If your target is engaged by what you are saying and tries to respond, then they are not letting go of their awareness, and their consciousness is still very much active. When attempting to put your target in a hypnotic trance, when you are first beginning to speak to them, the content of what you are saying matters a tremendous amount. You need to choose a topic that is interesting enough for them to want to stick around and listen to, but not so interesting that they are completely engrossed in what you are saying and are trying to speak back to you. The topic that you choose is likely to vary from target to target, as everyone has different tastes as to what kind of subject they are willing to pay attention to or not. This is where skills learned under controlling the narrative can come in handy; if you are able to tell a long, meandering story instead of a short and sweet one, especially about something that your target does not particularly care about, then they should begin falling into a hypnotic trance relatively easily. When you are speaking, be sure to use a calm, soothing voice, and choose words and phrases to use that are generally simple and easy to understand.

This allows your target to focus on the overall sound of your voice, rather than what exactly you are saying. However, if you make your voice sound too calm and soothing, your target may think that something is wrong with you or may grow suspicious of your intentions. Therefore, try not to sound too much like a guided meditation instructor and instead attempt to model your voice in the style of the narrator of a nature documentary. Keep in mind that your goal is to relax your target, but not to put them to sleep. If you make yourself sound too soothing, you will run the risk of having your target be too relaxed. If your target is asleep, after all, they will not be open to any suggestions that you make, as they will be unconscious. Once you see that your target has fallen into a more and more relaxed state, the content of what you are saying to them will not matter as much, and as long as you keep your voice in a steady, soothing tone, you will not have to worry about what topic you are speaking about any longer.

In addition to using your voice as white noise, there are some other techniques that you can use in order to lull your target into a hypnotic trance. One trick is to have your target eat or drink something before you attempt to put them in a trance. Whatever they consume will be more effective if it is easy to digest and is warmer rather than colder. Eating or drinking something will cause your target's body to allocate resources and energy to digest what they have consumed, which will take resources away from their overall energy levels and will cause them to feel more tired and sleepy as a result. Be sure that they do not eat or drink too much of a substance, since feeling too full will cause them to focus on that feeling rather than on you. Another trick that you can use to better put someone into a hypnotic trance is to turn on relaxing music. Music is another excellent source of white noise, so long as the music is itself relaxing and easy to listen to. In general, the more simple the music is, the better the white noise that it makes. For example, you should consider using solo piano tracks with a relatively simple melody over tracks that feature many different instruments and voices with loud, energetic melodies. Music that you may use should follow the same principles as your voice: it should be soothing and easy to listen to, but not so simple that your target will grow bored of it. You should also keep in mind that not everyone is relaxed by too much noise and some people may even be distracted by any music that you decide to play, so music is not always an effective tool in hypnosis. Finally, another easy trick to use is making sure that the temperature is comfortable for your target. While you do not always have control over what the temperature feels like, if you can ensure that the temperature is always at a normal level and would be comfortable to fall asleep in, you will have a much easier time with putting your target in a hypnotic trance. If the temperature is too hot or too cold, your target will be unable to sufficiently relax, and their awareness will always be affected too much by their surroundings for it to ever fade away.

You can tell if you have successfully put your target in a trance or not based on what they look like. If they appear to be in a deep sleep, taking deep breaths and are completely unaware of what is going on around them, then they are most likely in a trance. Once you believe that your target is in a hypnotic trance, you can begin to ask them questions and influence their subconsciousness. The first questions you ask should be to determine whether or not your target is in a trance. For instance, good questions would include things such as, "Do you know where you are?" and "Do you feel relaxed?" Asking yes-or-no questions is a good way to let your target ease into their trance while still providing you with answers. If your target says that they feel relaxed and that they do not know where they are, then they are in a hypnotic trance, and you can begin to influence them in whatever direction that you like. Remember that while your target is in a trance, suggestions are powerful, and while you should never state outright what it is you want your target to do, you can strongly hint at your goal, which they will pick up on in their subconsciousness.

There are two methods of changing the speech patterns that you can use in order for your suggestions to be more effective while your target is in a trance. First of all, you should phrase your statements in the form of a question, which allows your target's subconsciousness to form an answer, therefore planting the statement and the answer in your target's mind. This works best if you can phrase your question in such a way that would be ridiculous or even impossible to say no to. As long as you know your target's personality and individual preferences, tailoring questions to their own judgment should not be difficult to accomplish. Secondly, when speaking, you should try to integrate storytelling techniques along with your suggestions. Using vivid imagery in your speech will help your target's subconsciousness better visualize what you are talking about, and it will be more likely to latch onto your suggestions as a result. The easier you make your suggestions for your target to understand, the more successful you will be in influencing them.

When you are ready to wake your target from their trance, simply talk them back to a state of awareness. For example, you could say something along the lines of, "I know you are feeling very sleepy now, but as I talk to you, you will begin to feel more and more awake. I am going to count to three, and by the time I am finished, your eyes will be open, and you will be awake. One...two...three." When your target is awake, they will likely be confused about what has happened. They will not remember anything that you told them while they were in the trance, and they will not be aware that they were in a trance at all. You can tell them that they simply fell asleep, and you can even joke with them about the occasion. In the days after the trance, they will begin to perform behaviors that are in line with what you instructed them to do during the trance. During this time, keep in contact with them, and influence them further with mind control and NLP techniques as needed. If they are not making as much progress as you would like them to, you can always put them in another trance and make more suggestions. Try to avoid putting somebody in a trance too many times, however, as they will eventually catch on to the fact that they have not been simply falling asleep. Of course, a singular trance is generally enough to manipulate a target and see successful results come out of it.

Manipulation Technique #5: Choose Your Targets Wisely

As I mentioned earlier, not everyone is as vulnerable to being hypnotized as other people, and a small percentage of people are not able to be hypnotized successfully at all. On the other hand, some people can become hypnotized quite easily, and the effects of hypnosis are far more powerful on them. With so much variety within the human population, how are you supposed to choose targets? There are many different factors to keep an eye out for, and over the course of time, you will find people with certain characteristics that personally work better with the habits and techniques that you find to be most useful. Of course, when you are just starting out at manipulation and hypnosis, choosing a target to influence can be incredibly overwhelming. Fortunately, there are three common factors that you should look out for no matter what level your hypnosis skills are at: the target's (1) personal life, (2) personality, and (3) relationship to you.

In general, a target's personal life cannot be influenced by you and should be considered baggage that comes with a potential target. If the target has a stable personal life with several strong relationships with other people, they are not going to be a strong candidate for hypnosis. The more support a person has in their life, the more influences they are going to encounter outside of you, meaning that your input is competing with many other inputs and does not matter that much. If, on the other hand, a target is largely isolated from other people and frequently comes into contact with stress and conflict, they will be much more vulnerable to hypnosis. Instability in another person's life gives you the opportunity to be a shoulder for them to lean on, and they will form a much stronger, more trusting bond with you than if they had other outlets in life.

Just like with their personal life, a target's personality cannot be changed by you, unless you dedicate enormous amounts of time to doing so, and even then only small changes will be achieved. There are certain personality traits that determine whether or not a person is a good target for being hypnotized. Some people, for instance, are more open and trusting than other people, which makes them better targets for manipulation. People who are superstitious and believe in a supernatural activity such as ghosts and aliens are also more able to be hypnotized than people who are more skeptics. In general, you should avoid trying to hypnotize anyone who is extremely intelligent or possesses any of the traits in the Dark Triad, as these people are not only less able to be manipulated, but the consequences for attempting to manipulate them can be dire.

A potential target's relationship with you is unique in that it is entirely influenced by you. The stronger your relationship to a potential target is, the more effective any hypnosis or manipulation techniques will be on them. Think of a relationship as an exchange of information. The more information you have about a target, the better you will understand how their mind works, which is an invaluable part of the hypnosis process. In addition, people that you have a strong relationship with are less likely to be suspicious of you, meaning that you can try riskier, more advanced manipulation techniques on these people without them necessarily believing that you are doing anything at all. If you cultivate a relationship for long periods of time, you can also manipulate your target for that much longer, as you will have routine contact with them and can reinforce any and all of your influences on them on a regular basis.

Takeaways

Hypnosis can certainly be both difficult to learn and difficult to master, but at the same time, it is generally the most powerful option of manipulation available to you with the lowest amount of risk. While brainwashing is more effective and it lasts longer, it can be incredibly risky to attempt, which makes hypnosis an extremely valuable technique for experienced manipulators. As with all other techniques discussed in this book, the key to truly mastering hypnotism is to practice well and practice often. The more experience you gain with hypnosis, the more effectively you will be able to use it. As long as you know the history and the techniques of hypnosis, you should be able to find success when putting it all into practice. Be sure that you have a solid understanding of the ins and outs of hypnotism before continuing on to the next chapter, which will discuss brainwashing and its techniques in detail.

Chapter 6: Brainwashing

Brainwashing as a manipulation technique is far more powerful than both mind control and hypnosis, but it also requires far more training and expertise in order to be used in the most effective way. While many of the concepts used in hypnosis and mind control overlap with those of brainwashing, there are also new techniques made available to you when you learn about brainwashing. Just like hypnosis, brainwashing is a popular topic and plot device in many books, movies, and other media.

Of course, as well as being the most powerful technique, brainwashing is also more high-profile than both hypnosis and mind control, and has been used extensively in certain large-scale scenarios, including by certain governments, cults, corporations, and in other instances. While brainwashing has been known throughout history by many different names, including thought reform, thought control, coercive persuasion, re-education, and menticide, for the sake of simplicity, this chapter will only refer to it as brainwashing. By learning more about what brainwashing is and how it actually works, you will not only have gained a valuable technique for manipulating other people, but you will also be able to more easily recognize when you are being brainwashed by another person or by an organization.

The History of Brainwashing

One of the most well-known portrayals of brainwashing on a massive scale in fiction is found in the book *1984*, which was written by George Orwell in 1949. In the book, a massive government entity maintains complete control over its citizens by creating propaganda, using surveillance to spy on people, rationing food, and even training people to use a different language. There is no magical technology that allows the government to directly control the thoughts and actions of its citizens, but through the laws it creates and the way that it enforces those laws, it can make its citizens think and act in only the ways that it wants them to. Even though *1984* is a work of fiction, governments like the one described in the book have certainly existed in real life, and still, continue to do so today. Of course, brainwashing has been used by other organizations than governments in its history, and different groups have used brainwashing successfully in different ways in order to further their goals.

While certain forms of brainwashing techniques have been in use for thousands of years, the public did not become aware of brainwashing on a large scale until the 1940s and the 1950s. At that time, brainwashing was a major part of society in China under Mao Zedong, the Chairman of the Communist Party of China and the leader of China overall. In fact, the term "brainwashing" comes from the Chinese phrase *xǐnǎo*, which literally translates to "wash brain" in English. Americans were not made aware of brainwashing as a phenomenon until after the Korean War had begun. During the war, American soldiers were captured as prisoners of war (POWs), and during their time spent in Chinese prison facilities, they were brainwashed by the Chinese government. The POWs that had been brainwashed were more likely to give over classified information to the Chinese and give false confessions, more willing to do what their captors wanted them to, and even defended the actions of the Chinese government. The United Nations commander at the time stated that "too familiar are the mind-annihilating methods of these Communists in extorting whatever words they want...The men themselves are not to blame, and they have my deepest sympathy for having been used in this abominable way."

In other words, the Chinese were extremely skilled at brainwashing their victims, who would feel the effects of being brainwashed for years after it had been done to them. After American POWs were found to have been brainwashed, the United States Central Intelligence Agency (CIA) ran a series of experiments over the span of twenty years that tested mind control and brainwashing capabilities, the most famous of these experiments being called Project MKUltra. In addition, to testing general brainwashing techniques, the CIA also experimented with drugs as a tool for manipulation and attempted to create a so-called truth serum that would be used for interrogation purposes. Both the Chinese brainwashing institutions and the CIA experiments will be discussed in greater detail in the following chapter, but as they are an essential part of the history of brainwashing, it is important that they are mentioned here as well. From there, brainwashing took hold in the minds of the public and began to play a large part in popular culture. Stories involving brainwashing were received by large audiences, and movies such as *The Fearmakers*, *Toward the Unknown*, *The Bamboo Prison*, *The Rack*, and most famously, *The Manchurian Candidate* were all inspired in some part by the experience of American POWs during the war or brainwashing in general. Beginning in the late 1960s and extending through the mid-1970s, brainwashing as a concept was so deeply rooted in the public consciousness that it even seeped into the criminal justice system. Perhaps the most famous example is that of Patty Hearst, an heiress who was kidnapped and brainwashed by a terrorist group known as the Symbionese Liberation Army (SLA). She later joined the group as a member and was arrested during an attempted bank robbery. Her trial was the first widely publicized instance of using brainwashing as a legal defense in court, and while she was ultimately found guilty, the defense caused a renewal of interest in and concern over brainwashing.

Since the 1960s, brainwashing has also been widely used in recruiting members to cults. The most well-known instance of brainwashing being used in cults is probably that of the Manson

Family, founded in 1967 by Charles Manson. Manson was an extremely skilled manipulator, and successfully recruited nearly 100 people, mostly women, into his own cult following. He had such a strong influence over them that he was able to convince them to commit a number of different crimes, from assault and robbery all the way to mass murder. Nearly all cults use some form of brainwashing to indoctrinate potential recruits and convince them to join, from the most infamous to cults you have never heard of before. Some cults, such as Heaven's Gate and The People's Temple, used brainwashing to such a powerful effect that their followers were convinced to commit suicide.

Cults are especially important to study in regard to brainwashing because they demonstrate how far the power of brainwashing techniques can really take people and are a good indicator of when things have gone too far. Obviously, if you are thinking of using brainwashing or any other type of manipulation on a person in order to make them inflict harm on themselves or anyone else, you should refrain from doing so and seek professional help for yourself. But why is the history of brainwashing so important to learn about? After all, you are not a government entity such as the Communist Party of China, and you are hopefully not planning on dabbling in becoming a cult leader of any kind. Of course, there are valuable lessons to be learned from the history of brainwashing that you can apply to how you approach and implement brainwashing techniques in your own life. First of all, having a good understanding of the history of brainwashing should mean that you also have a good understanding of just how powerful brainwashing can be, even on the most unwilling targets. If American soldiers can be brainwashed into defending their captors, enemies of the country that they vowed to serve, then imagine what brainwashing can do for you if used correctly. Secondly, the history of brainwashing teaches the important lesson that unlike mind control and hypnosis, anybody and everybody are susceptible to brainwashing techniques. If you focus on honing your talents and become a skilled enough manipulator, you can brainwash not just one person, but multiple people at a time into doing whatever it is that you want for them to do. The most talented manipulators can exert their influence over hundreds of people all at once, and each and every single one of their targets will be as thoroughly indoctrinated as the last one. This leads me into the final reason why the history of brainwashing is important to have at least some knowledge of because brainwashing is such a powerful and effective tool that can be used on so many people, it can be easy to take brainwashing too far, and force your targets into criminal or even life-threatening situations.

By studying the history of brainwashing, you will know how horrible the effects of brainwashing can be for the target, the manipulator, and for anybody else who gets caught in between. While brainwashing as a tactic is not in and of itself harmful, when used with reckless abandon, things can quickly spiral out of control. As the manipulator, it is your responsibility to know when to stop before something terrible has occurred. Above all else, the history of brainwashing demonstrates the need to be safe, sensible, and responsible when using brainwashing techniques, as the consequences can be dire if brainwashing is used irresponsibly.

Manipulation Technique #6: Isolation, Criticism, and Identity Formation

Isolation, criticism, and identity formation are essential concepts for any aspiring manipulator to be very familiar with. These three topics are extremely important not only in brainwashing but in the art of manipulation overall. While these three topics were already mentioned briefly in Chapter 5, they will be expanded upon here, so that you have a full and complete understanding of them before attempting any brainwashing techniques or strategies.

Isolation refers to the act of separating your target from any external information or stimuli that they might receive, particularly when that information comes from people other than yourself. The ultimate objective of isolation is to make yourself the main provider of information in your target's life, as that way you can expressly choose which particular types of information that they might have access to in order to better control them. Of course, you cannot ever control each and every single piece of information that your target has access to, but isolation will help you to not only control as much of that information as possible but also to control the narrative about any information that you do not control in order to downplay its importance to and impact on your target. There are two different ways that isolation can be accomplished. The first method of isolation is physical. This method is fairly straightforward: placing physical barriers between your target and information that you do not want them to have access to is relatively simple and theoretically easy to accomplish.

An example of physical isolation would be locking your target in a room, which would contain only information that you would want to share with them. Of course, with this example, you can also easily see the downside of physical isolation, which is that it is often illegal and will almost certainly backfire on you at some point. Therefore, physical isolation should be used sparingly, and only in situations that do not violate any laws or the rights of your target. The other method of isolation, nonphysical isolation, is more subtle and difficult to successfully pull off but will be the more useful option available to you a majority of the time. Nonphysical isolation is accomplished through mind control methods such as manipulating beliefs, controlling the narrative, and through the use of criticism, as well as through the principles of persuasion and deception. At its core, nonphysical isolation is not about actually placing restrictions upon a person and the information that they have access to, but rather making them believe that there are restrictions in place. Planting that belief in your target is crucial, since if they believe that a certain type of information is not legitimate or that certain people are not good friends to them, then they will begin to monitor their own behavior, rather than you having to do it for them. This is especially useful at times when you cannot be around your target for whatever reason, as you can still be certain that they are not receiving information from sources that may undermine your goals.

One of the most useful tools to achieve isolation is called criticism. Used in the context of dark psychology, criticism refers to something slightly different than what you might be used to. Criticism is best used when you criticize the world around you and your target, rather than criticizing the target themselves. When you point out everything that is harmful and untrustworthy in the world around you, by default you will make yourself seem more trustworthy to your target. After all, if you are both smart enough to be able to see everything wrong with the outside world and also do not point out anything that is wrong with yourself, then your target will assume that there is nothing that is wrong with you and decide to trust you. Of course, you do not have to be entirely honest when you are using criticism, and you may find it effective to criticize certain things that might actually not have anything wrong with them. The principles of persuasion and deception can be very useful when using criticism, as they will make your claims be even more convincing to your target. As long as you can make the world around you seem unsafe and untrustworthy while making yourself seem to be a positive influence, your target will naturally gravitate towards you rather than gathering information from the outside world, and you will have achieved nonphysical isolation on your target. When you are performing any kind of manipulation strategy, whether that would be NLP techniques, mind control, hypnosis, brainwashing, or some combination of several strategies, your ultimate goal should always be to form a new identity within your target. Identity formation is the most permanent type of manipulation that you can pull off, as it ensures that your target will be deeply connected with you for the foreseeable future, as long as you do not make any mistakes or allow any other new identities to take hold within them. Identity formation is the most effective when you use frequent repetition on your target.

When you are attempting to form a new identity within your target, you should follow three steps: (1) isolate your target, (2) seek verbal confirmation from your target, and (3) test your target's new identity. The first step, isolates your target, should be fairly straightforward to you now and involves everything that was discussed in the previous two paragraphs. Isolating your target is critical to forming a new identity within your target, as it allows for you and you alone to shape whatever you want their new identity to become. Remember that isolation takes time, and if you rush the process, you may risk your target catching on to what you are attempting to do and losing any connection you might have already established with them.

The second step is to seek verbal confirmation from your target. It can be difficult to tell when a target has been sufficiently isolated, and the best way to tell if a new identity has begun to take hold within them is to simply ask them. Of course, you should not ask them about any changes in their identity directly. Rather, you should ask them how they feel about you, and specifically whether they think you are a good person or not. Controlling the narrative can come in handy here, as you can craft a story where you might have been having doubts about your own self-worth or morality, and your target will rush in to reassure you about your own worth. Having your target state that they believe that you are a good person might seem like a small thing, but it is actually a major milestone for two reasons. First of all, having your target say the words themselves is far more powerful than them listening to you say them and proves that the belief is rooted deep within their subconsciousness. Secondly, by admitting that you are a good person, they will be more likely to go along with whatever you want in the future, as they will not want to have their statement proven to be wrong. Accepting this first statement will lead to them accepting more and more in the future. This leads to the final step, which is to test your target's new identity. This step sounds complicated, but it can actually be quite simple. All you have to do is ask your target to carry out some action related to their new identity. While the second step is all about a verbal commitment, the final step requires a change in behavior, which is much more serious. It is one thing to talk about new beliefs; it is another thing entirely to act upon those new beliefs. By choosing a relatively small and unimportant task for your target to carry out, you can make it easier on them to change their behavior. Just like with the second step, your target will be more likely to move on to bigger and more involved actions after they have first committed to something small, as they will not want to be proven wrong about you. Once they have performed some kind of task for you, you can be assured that even if their new identity has not been entirely formed yet, then it is well on its way, and your work as a manipulator will be almost finished.

Manipulation Technique #7: Managing Your Target's Expectations

Contrary to many popular depictions of the brainwashing process, brainwashing is, at its core, actually very simple. Above all else, brainwashing is about managing your target's expectations. Exactly how you manage your target's expectations is up to you, but there are certain factors that you should keep in mind when attempting to brainwash a target. The process of brainwashing can be divided up into three steps, with managing your target's expectations being essential in each one. The first step is known as the introduction and refers to how you present yourself to your target upon first meeting them. If your target is somebody that you already have a prior relationship with, do not worry; while the introduction will not necessarily apply to you, you can still manage your target's expectations and follow the other two steps. The introduction serves as the chance for you to make a first impression on your target, and present yourself as somebody that your target will want to get to know more closely. If your introduction is the first time that you have met your target, then managing your target's expectations will be easy, as they will likely not know what to expect from you, meaning that you will be free to present as whoever and whatever you choose to be.

However, if you have a prior relationship with your target, then you will have to take a far more active role in managing their expectations. If your relationship is positive and they already trust you, of course, then you will not have to put in the work of an introduction. However, if your prior relationship is negative, not very close, or a combination of the two, then you will have to work to change that relationship for the better. For example, if you have offended your target in the past in any way, be sure to apologize, and show them that you are no longer that same person. Similarly, if your target is only familiar with you through unflattering rumors or gossip about you, then it is up to you to prove to them that those rumors are false. Whatever you have to do in order to fix your relationship with your target, do so. Remember that other mind control techniques can help you in this respect. The second step in the brainwashing process is to build trust between your target and you. This step is where your role in managing your target's expectations should expand. In addition to managing your target's expectations about yourself, you must also begin to manage their expectations about the world around them. This step is the most time-consuming in the brainwashing process, but it is also the most crucial.

A bad introduction can always be repaired, but if there is no trust between your target and you, then you will not be able to manipulate them. The easiest way to build trust is through the use of isolation. If you can convince your target not only that you are a good influence on them, but that the rest of the world is potentially dangerous and harmful to them, then your power over your target will be greatly increased. Not only will you have built trust between your target and yourself, but you will have also created a situation in which they depend on you as their main source of information, which will pave the way for you to manipulate them however you want in the future.

Another good way of building trust is through controlling the flow of information that your target receives in a very precise, particular way. You should always start off by feeding your target small and uncontroversial pieces of information that are easy to understand, then work your way up to bigger pieces of information that might be harder for your target to accept. By starting small, you are conditioning your target to accept whatever it is you say, which will make it easier for them to follow your lead when you move on to ideas or beliefs that your target would previously have been more likely to have an issue with. Whatever method you choose to use, remember that the more time you spend building trust between your target and you, the easier it will be to successfully manipulate them, and the more likely they will end up forming a new identity that revolves around you and your influence. The final step in the brainwashing process is to test your target.

Testing your target allows for you to see if you have managed your target's expectations to a sufficient degree or if there are still things left that you need to tweak. This step works in a similar way to testing a target's new identity formation, and if you are skilled enough, you can use the same test to check on both a target's identity and if they are brainwashed or not. The test that you choose should not ask too much of your target, but should also be something that they would not normally do if they were not brainwashed. For example, if you know that your target does not like the taste of a certain food, ask them to eat that food in front of you. If they follow your instructions, then the process is complete, while if they refuse, then you will have to further manage your target's expectations. If your target fails the test, do not become angry with them; instead, focus on what things you need to change before they will listen to you. On the other hand, if your target passes the test, remember that your work is not over; brainwashing is strong, but it does not last forever, and you will have to continue to monitor your target and manage their expectations according to what you want to occur.

Takeaways

Now that you have read all about mind control, hypnosis, and brainwashing, you are well on your way to becoming a master manipulator. Do not feel the need to treat these methods as absolute laws, and if you find something different that works better for you, do not be afraid to use that instead. Most importantly, keep in mind that with great power comes great responsibility, and never put your target in a situation where they pose a danger to themselves or to others. Read on to find out more about how manipulation techniques have been used for both the good and the bad.

Chapter 7: Case Studies

After reading this far, you are now familiar with the techniques associated with the principles of NLP, mind control, hypnosis, and brainwashing, and you might have even begun to put these techniques into action. Of course, having a few examples to see how these techniques are used in the real world can be hugely beneficial in understanding how to use and improve your skills of manipulation even more. This chapter will be taking an in-depth look at three ways that manipulation techniques have either been used in the past or are being used today: the use of NLP techniques in modern medicine, how thought reform was used by the communist Chinese government, and the experiments the CIA carried out in order to study brainwashing. These case studies are meant to help bolster your understanding of manipulation techniques as a whole, and while they might not line up exactly with what you are attempting to do with these techniques, they should allow to you see the possibilities offered by these techniques in an entirely new way. These examples can also help to illustrate the dangers of manipulation techniques when they are taken too far. While it is not necessary to know every detail of the case studies discussed in this chapter, if you want to improve your abilities and become a master manipulator, you should at least be familiar with these examples.

Case Study #1: NLP Techniques in Modern Medicine

You might remember that way back in a section from Chapter 1, the history of how NLP was developed and first used was discussed. You might also remember from that section that one of the ways NLP techniques were first advertised was as a way to cure various mental illnesses, including anxiety, depression, certain learning disorders, and overwhelming, unreasonable phobias. While NLP techniques later became more well-known in fields such as business and education, a dedicated group of therapists, psychologists, and other medical professionals continued to develop and perfect NLP techniques for use in medicine and therapy.

Today, NLP techniques are used in a specialized setting in order to treat mental illnesses and have grown increasingly popular with people seeking treatment all over the world. But how do NLP techniques actually work in treating mental illnesses, and how is it relevant at all to develop your skills of manipulation? After all, it probably seems like NLP techniques used in a medicinal setting are completely different from techniques used in order to influence somebody else. However, these two fields have more in common than you might expect, and understanding the uses of NLP techniques in medicine might give you some new ideas to use when you are attempting to manipulate someone else. When NLP techniques are used in a medicinal setting, they take place between a medical professional (usually a therapist, psychologist, or psychiatrist) and their patient. In this setting, the professional's use of NLP techniques on the patient is always consensual, as the patient is expressly seeking treatment in the form of NLP, so manipulation methods such as isolation are not necessary for the professional to use. Instead, they use NLP in medicine relies more on techniques that are similar to manipulating beliefs and controlling the narrative, but are just different enough to make them unique. The key difference is the patient's willingness to submit to NLP techniques, which allows for the medical professional and their patent to work together to come up with personalized strategies for the professional to use on the patient.

This gives the medical professional an edge over someone in the role of the manipulator, as the manipulator cannot speak openly to their target about what strategies might work best for them. This advantage also allows for the NLP strategies used by the medical professional to be used on the patient much more quickly than a manipulator could use the same strategies on a target, as the manipulator has to spend far more time gathering information about the target in the form of learning than the medical professional does. The NLP techniques that are used by a medical professional are also different from those used by a manipulator in their content. As you are already familiar with, techniques used by a manipulator depend heavily on information, in particular controlling what information a target does and does not have access to in order to accomplish a goal such as manipulating a target's beliefs. As a manipulator, if you cannot adequately and skillfully use the information to your advantage, then successfully manipulating a chosen target will almost certainly be impossible to do. On the other hand, when NLP techniques are used by a medical professional, then the concept of visualization is more important than the use of information. The term "visualization" refers to the images that a target (or in a medical setting, patient) sees in their mind when they are processing information. In other words, the precise use of information is most important in the use of NLP for manipulation, while the way in which information is processed is most important in a medical context.

In a medicinal setting, visualization is extremely important for two reasons. First of all, because the medical professional and the patent are working together in order to change something about the patient's mental illness, the patient already has access to most, if not all, of the information being used in the procedure, so controlling that information in a precise way is not possible. Therefore, the medical professional has to work harder to change the patient's prior thoughts and feelings about that information, which is where visualization comes in. Secondly, visualization allows for the patient to make better comparisons of information that they already have. When treating mental illness with NLP techniques, a medical professional will generally want a patient to compare a bad part of their life, such as how their mental illness makes them feel, with a good part of their life, such as any achievements or accomplishments the patient might have earned. Visualization allows the patient to better understand what separates the good from the bad, as well as what they can work on changing in order to turn the bad parts into something more positive. You might already be beginning to see how you can use the principles of NLP techniques used in a medicinal setting to improve your own manipulation skills. There are a couple of different lessons to be learned from the use of NLP by medical professionals.

The first lesson is that you should always work to have the strongest relationship with your target possible before you attempt any serious manipulation strategies on them. One of the main reasons why NLP techniques are so effective in treating mental illnesses is because the medical profession and the patient have a high level of trust between them, and while you cannot necessarily be as honest with your target as a medical professional can be with their patient, you should still certainly focus on building a good relationship between yourself and your target. The second lesson is that while information is extremely important to the process of manipulation, the way the target processes that information can be just as valuable to you. Even if you do not necessarily use visualization as part of your manipulation techniques, the fact that NLP techniques used for medicinal purposes are so effective should impress upon you the importance of doing more than simply controlling the flow of information. Finally, the third lesson you should take away from this example is how critical it is to have an end goal in mind when you are using manipulation techniques on another person. I know that this seems like it should be obvious, but you would be surprised at how often people are so focused on the process of manipulation that they forget about what they actually want to accomplish. When NLP techniques are used for medicinal purposes, the end goal is always to treat the patent's mental illness, and every single action that the medical professional takes is done in order to fulfill that end goal. You should keep a similar philosophy in mind when using NLP techniques and other methods of manipulation on your target: do not rush the process, but remember that every step you take should lead you closer to a final goal.

Case Study #2: Thought Reform in Communist China

As mentioned in Chapter 6, thought reform, which is also known as brainwashing, was used in China under the rule of Mao Zedong and the Communist Party in order to make both citizens and American POWs accept the government's control and its ideology. The thought reform campaign was so successful that when POWs had been returned safely home, they still defended their Chinese captors and thought that they had been doing the right thing all along. The government started the thought reform campaign by targeting Chinese scholars, professors, and teachers, urging them to accept Marxism-Leninism over more traditionally European-American schools of thought. From there, the teachers taught Marxism-Leninism to students, and the government's chosen ideology spread throughout the educated populace and eventually through Chinese businesses, peasant organizations, and even prisons until nearly the entire population was brainwashed into accepting the government's ideology.

The government's goal was to create a population made up of what was called the "New Socialist Man," which referred to embracing a communist revolution and an entirely new way of life, as well as being loyal to the Communist Party, participating in labor activities, showing no signs of selfishness, and having a heightened awareness of the class system in China. American POWs were brainwashed to accept and conform to the model of the New Socialist Man, as well as being brainwashed into giving the Chinese critical intelligence about the Korean War. A psychiatrist named Dr. Robert J. Lifton worked closely with brainwashed POWs that returned from the war and learned about how the Chinese used thought reform so successfully in the process. He identified eight distinct criteria for thought reform.

The first criteria for thought reform are known as "milieu control." Milieu control refers to controlling a person's environment in order to achieve isolation. Controlling a target's environment ultimately limits what information that they receive, which leads them to become overly dependent on whoever is controlling the environment (in this case, the Chinese government). It also pushes the target away from society as a whole, resulting in a population that is highly isolated from one another and therefore easily controllable.

Lifton called the second criteria for thought reform "mystical manipulation." Despite how it sounds, mystical manipulation does not refer to any real supernatural event. Instead, it simply refers to the act of faking such events in order to prove that you have some kind of special talent or ability, which results in you obtaining a status of authority. You can then use that authority to create more planned "supernatural" events or to take a more active role in religious life. Mystical manipulation was most often used to claim that a person or group had been chosen by God to lead everybody else, which gave that person or group the authority to do nearly anything that they wanted.

The third criteria for thought reform are known as a "demand for purity." Demand for purity refers to the need for targets to view the world in uncomplicated, black and white terms. There is no room for doubt or vagueness in the target's mind; everything must either be right or wrong. Demand for purity is most useful when it is used to control a group rather than an individual, as the group will enforce the rules and punish anyone who does not conform to the terms outlined in the demand for purity.

The fourth criteria identified by Lifton are known as "confession." Just like a demand for purity, confession is also most useful when used within the context of a group of people rather than an individual. Confession is best understood in terms of "sins," meaning a person's innermost thoughts, feelings, and attitudes. Sins are confessed openly to the group, and no secrets can be safe for long. The group's leaders use this information to their advantage and use the dynamics of the group to exploit members who might cause trouble.

The fifth criteria for thought reform are known as "sacred science." Once again, sacred science works best when it is used to control the behavior of a group of people rather than an individual. Sacred science refers to the principle that within a group there is a dominant ideology, and that any other competing ideology is completely wrong and invalid. Outside groups are also completely invalid simply because they do not belong within the "correct" group. In a similar vein, the leader of the group cannot be criticized or disagreed with, and their word is taken as law.

The sixth criteria for thought reform are known as "loading the language," which involves using new words and phrases in a specific way in order to confuse outsiders. This way, certain groups can remain separate from other groups while also manipulating the terms in which their members think about and process information, which grants the leaders of the group a large degree of control over everybody else. Loading the language also makes it very difficult for current members of a certain group to leave and join a different group, particularly if they have been a member of the group for a long period of time and/or through formative years, as they will have a hard time understanding the way the outside world communicates and struggle to adapt accordingly. Lifton's seventh criteria for thought reform are known as "doctrine over person." Doctrine over a person is relatively easy to understand, as it mostly supplements the other criteria rather than being its own distinct idea. Doctrine over person refers to the idea that an individual's own, personal experiences mean nothing unless they fit within the ideology of the group. In other words, experiences must fit into the sacred science in order to be considered valid, and if they do not fit, then the experiences are considered not to have happened at all.

The eighth and final criteria for thought reform are known as "dispensing of existence." Dispensing of existence is the most powerful criteria out of all of them and should not be taken lightly. Dispensing of existence simply means that a group (or more specifically, a group's leaders) is in charge of determining what is allowed to exist and what is not. This does not mean that the group terminates or kills anything that it decides does not exist; rather, dispensing of existence takes on a more advanced form of shunning, in which the group ignores the presence of anything that it has determined does not exist. Anybody who leaves the group is also removed from existence in the minds of the remaining group members. Dispensing of existence applies to oppose ideas, groups, and even individuals, which makes it difficult to rescue anybody from a group that has been influenced by thought reform, as members will ignore anything that opposes their sacred science. So what lessons can be learned from the use of thought reform in communist China? First of all, this example shows the extreme power that brainwashing can have if used in a skillful and methodical manner.

The Communist Party of China managed to not only brainwash their entire population through the use of thought reform, but they were also able to influence people who came from entirely different culture using the same process as well. Although a singular manipulator lacks the power of a government, you can certainly see how thought reform could be used to influence multiple people at once. This leads into the second lesson learned from this case study: brainwashing is more effective when it is used on a group of people all at the same time rather on individuals. While you can absolutely brainwash singular targets, certain tactics are far more effective within a group, as you can shape the group dynamics to become self-enforcing. This can pressure members of the group to follow the group's ideology, which you can determine as the leader of the group. The third lesson is, of course, the eight new techniques described as Lifton's criteria for thought reform. While you may not be able to use all of these during the brainwashing process, and indeed not all of them are always necessary to use, you will likely find the eight criteria for thought reform very useful to keep in mind when using manipulation techniques, especially when you are working within a group setting.

Case Study #3: The CIA Brainwashing Experiments

After American POWs came home from the Korean War, people were shocked to witness how effectively the Chinese government had altered their personalities and their loyalties, and many wanted answers as to how such a thing could have happened. American government officials sought answers just like everybody else, but they also wanted to learn how to harness and improve brainwashing techniques for themselves so that the United States could gain an edge in the developing Cold War. Both the CIA and the Department of Defense created a series of experiments in order to determine the manipulation techniques used by the Chinese and went on to involve different settings and elements, most notoriously the use of mind-altering drugs. The CIA went on to develop Project MKUltra, which was created in order to produce a "truth serum" that could be used on people who were suspected of being Soviet or Chinese spies. Brainwashing experiments took place on both American and Canadian citizens, and the CIA's ultimate goal was to gain control over foreign leaders and manipulate them into instituting policies that were far friendlier to the United States' own agenda. In 1973, a majority of the documents relating to brainwashing experiments and Project MKUltra were destroyed, and although 20,000 documents happened to survive, countless more were lost, and even today not much is known about what exactly the CIA learned about brainwashing and how they used that knowledge in the field. However, enough information has survived to make a useful case study out of, and while we will never know how much the CIA accomplished in their experiments, the information that is available should help you further your understanding of manipulation techniques in general.

One of the more interesting pieces of information about the CIA brainwashing experiments is that there was a wide variety of people who were experimented on. Certain people were more likely to be experimented on than others, and prostitutes, the homeless, current and former drug addicts, and incarcerated criminals were all chosen to be in the experiments. In addition, a number of CIA agents were experimented on by their own employer, and the experiments were not limited to only those of American nationality: Canadians were also targeted. In a majority of cases, the people who acted as test subjects in the experiments were unwilling participants and were never compensated for their part. Due to the extreme nature of the experiments, it made sense that the CIA would tend to choose people in society who would generally not be missed by the general public, or in the case of their own agents, people who the public was not even aware existed. More surprising, of course, is the fact that the Canadian government allowed for the CIA to experiment on their citizens, especially when most of them did not give their consent to participate.

Even more interesting than the CIA's wide selection of targets is the variety of experiments that they performed. CIA documents recovered in 1977 state that "chemical, biological, and radiological" procedures were carried out as part of MKUltra specifically, and an even greater variety of methods were used in other experiments, including electroshock procedures, various hypnosis techniques, psychological abuse, and severe isolation, sleep deprivation, and sensory deprivation processes. Most of these procedures were carried out at hospitals, universities, and prisons, and in many cases, not even the researchers knew what the experiments were really being used for. The CIA also experimented with a shockingly wide variety of drugs, including LSD, psilocybin, MDMA (more commonly known as ecstasy), salvia, a mixture of barbiturates and amphetamines, morphine, heroin, marijuana, alcohol, and other hallucinogens. The CIA had 17 goals that it wanted to achieve through the use of drugs, including attempting to speed up or slow down the aging process, causing nonreversible brain damage in targets, and even causing a target to lose control of all bodily functions and become completely paralyzed. Most of the drugs were administered to unwilling participants, many of whom were unaware that they had been put under the influence of any kind of substance.

CIA agents would even go so far as to spike their coworkers' food and drinks with LSD to see what would happen, which resulted in the death of at least one agent. Even though the results of these experiments remain largely unknown to the public, the range of the types of experiments shows the CIA's determination to see progress made.

Unlike the previous two case studies, the lessons that can be learned from the CIA brainwashing experiments might be a little bit harder for you to determine. One of the more obvious lessons to be learned from this case study is the importance of target selection. When target selection has been discussed previously within this book, the purpose has mainly been to describe which types of people are more susceptible to methods of manipulation than others. However, the CIA brainwashing experiments present another important component of target selection: the fewer connections a potential target has already, the easier they will be to manipulate. Many of the targets chosen by the CIA were people who already had a high degree of isolation from the rest of society, including prostitutes, prisoners, and drug addicts. These people certainly had fewer meaningful connections with other people than, for example, a man with a steady job or a woman with a family to take care of.

Of course, this is not saying that you should only try to manipulate prostitutes and criminals — in fact, you should try to keep your distance from those people most of the time. Instead, you should seek out people who are generally isolated from a society already, whether that is because they are unemployed or have few friends, to begin with. Another lesson to be learned from the CIA brainwashing experiments is the importance of using a number of different techniques in order to successfully manipulate your target. While the use of drugs or physical measures such as electroshocks is unacceptable techniques to use, you should never be afraid to diversify your techniques in the manipulation process. Remember that every target is slightly different and will react in different ways to different manipulation techniques, so be sure to experiment often.

Takeaways

You are ready to go out into the world and begin practicing the art of manipulation if you have not begun to do so already. Remember that these case studies are not meant as strict examples of what to do, but rather are here to help add to your preexisting knowledge of NLP, mind control, hypnosis, and brainwashing, as well as the concepts of the Dark Triad, persuasion, and deception. Keep in mind that these case studies, in particular, case studies #2 and #3, are also meant to illustrate the dangers associated with manipulation and dark psychology as a whole. Be sure to practice the techniques found in this book on a regular basis, and above all else, always be sure to act responsibly.

Conclusion

Thank you for making it through to the end of *Dark Psychology: How to Use the NLP Secret Methods of Manipulation for Social Influence, Emotional Persuasion, Deception, and Mind Control*, let's hope it was informative and able to provide you with all of the tools you need to achieve your goals whatever they may be.

The next step is to put the techniques that you have learned into practice out in the real world. Find a target that you want to manipulate and try some of your favorite techniques out, whether that means trying to control the narrative, attempting to manage your target's expectations, or making an effort to manipulate your target's beliefs.

Do not expect to get everything right the first time, and do not be afraid of failure; if something goes wrong, simply learn what you can from the experience and move on to the next target. Learning a new skill is always a process, and that includes learning how to manipulate people in the world around you. If you feel that you have to, take a break from manipulation and come back to it at a later time. Frustration is never good for the learning process, and will only serve to make you want to give up altogether. As long as you keep trying, you will get there eventually. I know that I have repeated myself over and over, but remember that practice makes perfect. Once you practice long enough, you will find that you have mastered the techniques of manipulation and influence, and you will have very little difficulty in making targets bend to your will. You should also take the time to come back to this book every so often and review the topics covered within, from the most basic concepts to the more advanced material. Even if you are practicing what you have learned on a regular basis, it is always a good idea to review in order to make sure that you are using the techniques correctly.

The practice is a great thing, but only when you are not enforcing bad habits instead of developing good ones. The best way to tell good from bad is to go back and read about whatever concept you might be struggling with, instead of letting bad habits take hold for the foreseeable future. If you have any further questions about dark psychology, the art of manipulation, or any of the concepts or techniques discussed in this book, do not be afraid to research topics yourself. You might find new information that can help you to become an even better manipulator, or you might find old information presented in such a way that you understand it better. Do not assume that this book holds all of the answers, and feel free to look up any topics that you still have an interest in or concerns about.

Keep in mind that if you have made it all the way through this book to this point, then you already have far more knowledge about dark psychology and manipulation than most of the world's population is even aware exists. By getting to this point, you are already far ahead of the vast majority of people who you might try to manipulate. Feel free to try to discover the exact method of manipulation that you prefer, and do not be afraid to combine different techniques and concepts to create incredibly effective combinations. If you find the techniques that work best for you, then you will be more comfortable with manipulation as a whole, and you can work your way up to taking bigger risks and facing greater challenges. As long as you take the time to develop your newfound abilities and use them as responsibly as you can, then you will be guaranteed at least some level of success in your life.

You are already a powerful and skilled manipulator, and frequent practice and occasional review sessions will help you develop into a master of dark psychology, manipulation, and influence.